The Transfer of Scholarly, Scientific and Technical Information Between North and South America

Proceedings of a Conference

edited by

VICTOR ROSENBERG

and

GRETCHEN WHITNEY

The Scarecrow Press, Inc.

Metuchen, N.J., & London

1986

Library of Congress Cataloging-in-Publication Data

The Transfer of scholarly, scientific and technical
    information between North and South America.

    Includes index.
    1. Communication in science--Congresses.
2. Communication of technical information--Congresses.
3. Science--Information services--Congresses.
4. Technology--Information services--Congresses.
I. Rosenberg, Victor, 1942-   . II. Whitney,
Gretchen, 1948-   .
Q223.2.T73 1986   338.9'26'091812   86-15625
ISBN 0-8108-1935-X

TABLE OF CONTENTS

The Wider Context

Problem Areas

Dependency

Internationalism and Nationalism

Toward Resolution

Country Situations

The Discussions of the Conference

The Discussions of the Conference

FOREWORD AND ACKNOWLEDGMENTS

In April of 1983, a Conference of North and South American librarians and information specialists was convened at the University of Michigan to deal with the issues arising from the challenges posed by the new technologies and their affects on the way scientific and technical information is acquired and distributed. These developments are changing not only the way scholars and libraries work but also how nations govern the flow of information crossing their borders.

The objectives of the Conference included (1) the identification of factors that inhibit the flow of information between countries, (2) an assessment of the special information needs of various countries and research communities, and (3) the development of alternative proposals for improving the exchange of information.

The last decades have witnessed dramatic changes in the production and transfer of information, and the changes show no sign of abating. A number of scholars have likened the current developments in communication technology to the invention of printing over 500 years ago. Individuals and nations are anxious to understand the technology and formulate creative and appropriate policies to deal with it.

Although in its broadest sense information technology covers everything from mass media to private telephone conversations, the Conference concentrated on scholarly, scientific and technical information. In the past, such a

restricted topic would have included the means of transport-
ing the materials (mail), the creation of the materials
(publishing), and the storage and circulation of the items
(libraries). Now, in addition to these topics we must consider online computer systems, electronic publishing,
transborder data flow, library networks, and fee-for-service
information services.

As the Conference unfolded, it became clear that the
most fundamental problems of national infrastructures, of
still unsettled definitions of terms such as *information*, of the
status of professionals in the field, and of dependency of
Latin American countries upon North America, remain to
hinder the smooth and equitable flow of information. Even
the role of information in national development could not be
clearly identified—but its significance must be taken as a
professional belief. Further, the generation, circulation, and
use of scientific and technical information could hardly be
separated from mass media in many cases. Most of these
problems are not resolvable by individual librarians. They
will require cooperative efforts between librarians and
national policy makers, between librarians and those in related disciplines such as computer science, and among
librarians themselves. Most important, they will require, as
they have in the past, the continued cooperative efforts of
librarians and others within and among the various
countries of the Americas. We believe that this Conference
has marked another step in increased understanding of the
problems confronted and progress that has been made.

Acknowledgments

The Tinker Foundation (New York, NY) provided
funds for the Conference, and we are most grateful for this
assistance.

University Microfilms International (Ann Arbor, MI) also provided funds, hosted a reception for participants, and contributed resources in staff such as Tony Bowman, Manager, Latin America and the Caribbean. All of this was most appreciated, as their efforts contributed greatly to the success of the Conference and these Proceedings.

The Organization of American States was also a sponsor of the Conference, and we are grateful for the assistance of Oscar Harasic.

The Conference was held under the auspices of the University of Michigan School of Library Science, and this aid was indispensable to the implementation and success of the Conference.

The Conference itself was coordinated by Gretchen Whitney, doctoral student at the University of Michigan School of Library Science, ably assisted by Mary Minow, a recent graduate of the School's Master's (AMLS) program. Arthur Duncan provided artwork, culinary expertise, and assisted in the smooth running of the discussions. A cadre of School of Library Science students and recent graduates provided the variety of support necessary for such an event. These included Annette Anderson, Elba Barcelatto, Peggy Benson, Debbie Cantor, Dick Doolen, Joan Fiscella, Ann Frantilla, Guy Gattis, Dee Mater, Carolyn McCormick, Patricia O'Donovan, Cecelia Paas, Caroline Panzer, Heleni Pedersoli, Reynaldo Ruiz, Deane Troyer, Jeanette Valentin, Malaika Wangara (Ph.D. student), and Julie Yates. A most gracious Pre-Conference welcome to all guests was offered by the Michigan Chapter of the American Society of Information Science. To all of these individuals and groups, we express our thanks.

These Proceedings also are a joint effort by many. Gretchen Whitney coordinated the assembly of the manuscript, transcribed and edited the discussions, compiled the Conference Conclusions, and prepared the index and

Introduction. Laurence Hallewell, Latin American Bibliographer at Ohio State University, edited the background papers, compiled the list of abbreviations and acronyms, edited Spanish portions of the discussions, and coordinated author comments on revised manuscripts. Nancy Becker Johnson, post-Masters School of Library Science student, prepared final draft copies of the background papers, and assisted in the final preparation of the manuscript. Adolpho Carvalho, University of Michigan student, transcribed Spanish portions of the discussions. Elaine Kinney contributed to the compilation of the lists of abbreviations and acronyms. Peter D. Ward of the University of Michigan Statistical Laboratory served as consultant in the final typesetting of the manuscript. The participants' contributions are presented herein in the form of discussions and papers, and they also contributed by responding rapidly to requests for comments on their papers and the Conference Conclusions. To all of these individuals, we are most grateful.

INTRODUCTION

While the countries of Latin America and the Caribbean are each culturally and politically unique and thereby unique in their positions regarding scientific and technical information, the countries share several important characteristics. These characteristics set the region apart from other developing areas such as Asia, Africa and Oceania.

First is the region's geographic proximity to the United States. While the United States certainly has influence in other areas of the world, it is its closeness to Latin America and the Caribbean which heightens awareness of the country to the North. Tourism and broadcast media help to maintain a constant presence in many areas.

Second is language. Asia must cope with multiple languages and dialects. Africa primarily relies on English, French, Arabic, and regional languages. Latin America works in Spanish and English, and in Portuguese in Brazil. At least on the surface this suggests a unity and commonality in communication of all types of information.

Third, there are historical relationships,and regional organizations such as the Organization of American States, through which the two continents have communicated and worked together as a body for years.

These characteristics formed one set of themes which permeated the Conference. Geographic proximity was reflected in concerns about postage rates, about travel of scientists, consultants, technicians, and the like, and access to major collections located outside of borders. Linguistic concerns brought out the need for translations of primary sources and secondary services, and for demands on language training. Historical relationships have promoted cooperative efforts and provided a forum for discussion.

At the outset, the Conference focused on six major areas of concern. These were:

1. Access through Bibliographic Systems

What is the impact of the large international bibliographic databases in giving Latin American countries access to the world's literature? How can countries gain access to these databases? What policies will enhance a country's ability to garner needed information from these systems? What is the responsibility of system providers to those wishing access? Can the developing countries of Latin America create their own bibliographic systems individually or cooperatively?

2. Dependence

How can the imbalance between information exporting countries and net importers be reduced? Can dependency on foreign information be reduced? Can the cost of information be lessened? Should the creation and dissemination of scholarly and scientific information be a for-profit or not-for-profit activity?

3. Electronic Publishing

Does electronic publishing, where books, reports, and journals are printed on demand, offer new opportunities for authors in smaller countries where the market for books and journals is small?

4. National Information Policies and Scholarly Information

To what extent do national policies governing data transmission and telecommunications affect the flow of scholarly information? When do the interests of scholarly activity and the vital interests of a country or government conflict?

5. Needs for Information Policy

When is an information policy needed? Under what circumstances is no policy and the free activity of the private sector an appropriate response?

6. North/South Relationships

What, in the area of policy development and in the exchange of scholarly or scientific information, can or should, the "North" offer the "South"? What should the "South" offer the "North"?

THE SUBJECT OF INFORMATION

A major initial concern for the Conference was the concept of scientific and technical information, as reflected in the early discussions.

From one perspective participants sought to define the concept in terms of the ultimate recipient. Is scientific and technical information for the scientist? The government official? Any decision maker? Anyone at any level? Can we even define scientific information by its ultimate user?

From another perspective, the subject scope of scientific and technical information was debated. Does it include the humanities? Social science information? Mass communication? Certainly, national news blackouts are indeed dramatic and highly visible instances of government control over information, as Freudenthal suggests. In his paper he points out the difficulties of separating "humanistic" from "scientific" areas, as does Dosa. The proposals for the New World Information Order do contain references to libraries.

From yet another perspective, the form in which scientific and technical information is issued and distributed plays a role in its "definition." As McCarthy notes in the discussions, Brazil taxed all film at the same rates and did not distinguish between entertainment movies and microfilms of journals. McGinn notes the importance of indexing services to newspapers as a way of accessing scientific information. Hallewell and Carvalho both discuss nontraditional means of getting science information to rural users.

Dosa points out that we must not limit the discussion to just printed literature, either. Raw data, especially in machine-readable form, as well as all other types of media, must also be considered resources.

While defining information and its related fields is an intellectual exercise for some, it is a matter of near survival for others. In the United States, library schools are grappling with these and similar issues as they attempt to meet challenges of new technologies, policies, and relationships between producers, controllers, disseminators, and users of information. And Alma Jordan's paper points out that policies may well be unformulated and communication with government officials may be impeded because of a lack of a workable definition. What is information to the government may not be information to the librarian, and so forth.

CONFERENCE THEMES

The themes that underlay the Conference discussions and papers reflect the complex issues and the various actors involved. Tensions between differing values, goals, and positions necessarily remain as they have for years. If broad themes had to be described up in a few thoughts, they would include the need for the recognition of the importance of all types of information at the highest levels of government, the need for continuing improvement in the general communications infrastructure, and the need for continued development of the profession. These are not new, nor are they unique to the region. Factors leading up to them, however, are unique, and it will be at the specific local or national level that progress will be made.

The arena is fraught with paradoxes, such as a lack of resources and an overabundance of resources, the need for standardization and the need to account for individual institutional and national needs, dependency and a desire for independence, a desire for improved local science and for participation in international science. The profession cannot by itself resolve these paradoxes. Rather, they remain descriptive of the environment in which the profession must operate.

The major themes include:

Development

The concern of development is people, not industry, agriculture, or any other specialized area. Scientific and technical information is needed not just by the professional scientist, but by all people in a society. How to provide what information to whom is a major challenge to be met.

Further, development takes place within a cultural context. Technologies cannot be introduced without accompanying cultural values, and without confronting cultural values where introduced. Libraries and other information resources/services are also culture-bound institutions, with national and local values. They have served to both help and hinder projects in the past.

Wiltshire suggests that underdevelopment is not a state but a process, suggesting that continuing programs are needed rather than one-shot actions to turn the process around.

It is difficult to think about libraries and information resources when faced with pressing problems of education, housing, food, and even national security. It is even more difficult in the face of no demonstrated causal relationship between improved information services and resources and improved progress in development. In spite of this, the value of and need for information is taken as "a belief."

Dependency

The theme of dependency is perhaps the one most fraught with tensions arising from economic realities and expectations. Northern information and related products and services have been developed largely for Northern markets, yet in order to carry out many areas of science and commerce, access to this information and these technologies is necessary. At the same time, many Northern firms perceive the South as a potentially lucrative market, yet find some resistance because the products and services they have to offer are often culturally inappropriate.

Fundamental discrepancies are described by Smith: strong Northern information resources (especially in the commercial sector) and pressures to expand, against weaker information infrastructures in the South to control, access, or counterbalance the flow. One of her suggestions is that technology transfers would include a carefully defined information component, presumably to tailor and control both the technology and the information.

Dependency has its cultural facets as well. Freudenthal notes the problem of English: undue "reverence" for it promotes neither independent science nor independent information resources.

In publishing, for example, many areas of research information are being drained out of countries for publication by Northern journals, yet how can a scientist be blamed for wanting international recognition through publication in these journals? In the same context, libraries and others are often then in the position of importing secondary services to gain access to this literature.

Infrastructure

A country's infrastructure includes the basic means of conveying goods, people, money and information within and outside of the country. Without roads, telephone service, postal service, educational institutions and the like, it becomes very difficult for any sector of the country to move. Libraries, publishing, information technologies, and related industries form a part of this infrastructure and rely on it to exist.

Planning for the infrastructure and the economy itself can be an area for information systems, as Feliú's paper describes. This system must deal with issues of standardization, with definitions, with multidisciplinary approaches, and differing perceptions of the nature of society and the role of government.

Wiltshire describes specific components of the information infrastructure, including physical resources such as libraries human resources, telecommunications, and policies.

Libraries and Librarians

While technological advances suggest and make possible new information products and services, the library remains one of the fundamental units for the collection, storage, organization, and dissemination of information. While progress has been made, much work remains to be done in the development of basic collections, programs, and human resources to staff them. In many areas, major collections on countries are located outside of those countries. The familiar litany of the lack of money, staff, status, appreciation, resources, and facilities still plague the institutions.

Libraries, publishers, and governments form but one triangle attempting to formulate and implement policies. McGinn notes government decrees reserving 25% of government publications to the national library for distribution, and another prohibiting public sector libraries from purchasing from publishers ignoring copyright law.

The profession itself in Southern countries continues to need improvements in its skills and education, for fundamental as well as advanced areas. It seeks allies with other professions for advancement. It seeks interaction with national governments. It recognizes that these interconnections are essential, yet difficult to establish. However without the human resources, and without the strong leadership Sandoval emphasizes as critical, prospects for progress are not good.

Of particular concern is the intellectual development of the librarians, beyond the development of basic skills. Part of this is the division of intellectual labor − McGinn's paper notes that indexing in Venezuela is done customarily by computer scientists, and not librarians. McCarthy's paper notes problems of training librarians for indexing and abstracting activities.

Technology

New communication, computer, and storage technologies have exacerbated existing gaps between the North and South, as Rosenberg suggests, but also offer promise for rapid advancements or even leapfrogging as in McGinn's discussion of optical disk technologies. The new technologies blur the distinction between types of information being disseminated.

The new technologies have exploded the availability of large files of bibliographic references and other secondary services, both as local online catalogs and as files to be accessed at home and abroad. This raises a variety of logistical and policy questions. Cunha, Shepard and McCarthy's papers reflect the diversity of undertakings in this area, and the challenges of determining an appropriate role for them within the country. Countries strive to control these developments in part to preserve their own economies and to assure continuing access. The dilemma of dependency and independence is clearly outlined by Cunha and McCarthy.

There remains also the problem of evaluating technologies offered by the North, and this applies to all types of technologies, not only those related to information. It is of particular importance when the technologies come heavily laden with cultural content. This evaluation in itself is an information problem.

At the same time, there is the continuing need to gain access to, and exploit, traditional means such as the printed book. As McCarthy notes, it is all well and good to develop a machine-readable database, but then smaller libraries in rural areas may well not be able to have access to the information at all. Chen and Sandoval describe the lure and fascination with the newer technologies which influence people to prefer them, when in fact the question may be better answered with the printed page.

Print remains the democratic medium, but for the literate society. Technologies must also be brought to bear upon problems of education and illiteracy. As Sandoval notes, many in Mexico receive much of their information from the television.

Users

With all the attention given to the glamour of new technologies and international policies, it is can be easy to omit consideration of the recipients of information, the users. As the discussions indicate, definitions are elusive, collection policies are not well formulated, and services disintegrate, without an understanding of the user and his or needs and situation. As Oyarzun de Ferriera suggests, we may have unsatisfactory interactions with adult users now because of their insufficient exposure to resources in the lower educational grades.

Sandoval argues that the less developed have a greater need for information than the developed, but at the same time an equally greater inability to express this need. This must be taken into account on the national as well as individual level. Many papers, including his, stress the need for information services and resources in the elementary grades. Resources and services for children must be a part of Jordan's broad definition of what information services are all about.

Information Policy

Information policy was the focus of the last morning session, but its problems and issues were raised throughout the Conference. Because information policies concern so many areas of a country's culture, and yet are an intricate part of the politics and economics of a country, they cannot be separated from these sectors. Cunha's paper speaks of this political and economic mix, for example of improved relations with China improving the availability of materials, of the possibility of using information (or the withdrawal of information) as a weapon, and of the United States economic preference for profit-making approaches (as opposed to non-profit schemes like many of the cooperative international ventures). As Rosenberg's paper points out, they can be part and parcel of trade policies.

International aspects also cannot be ignored. Oyarzun de Ferriera points out that the benefits from international cooperative projects, of increased flow of information, training, standardization and professional contacts make all of the work well worth while.

The participants of the Conference generally agreed that policies are needed, that government at the highest level must be involved, and that virtually all possible actors must be brought into its development.

Papers by Batres, Jordan and others list specific areas requiring government attention, such as copyright, promotion of research, credit policies and the like.

Much of the policy discussion centered on measures to affect the control and dissemination of information. Wiltshire and Freudenthal suggest that measures must also be taken to turn policy attention to the generation or creation of information, that is, science itself. Increased funding and other means of promoting scientific research and developing its resources are equally necessary.

Underlying the discussions seemed to be first economic, and then political issues. Ideals of providing the "right" information to all the "right" people at the "right" time in the "right" form are not to be abandoned. But it is under economic and political constraints that these ideals will be pursued.

Gretchen Whitney
School of Library Science
University of Michigan

CONCLUSIONS OF THE CONFERENCE

Scholarly, scientific and technical information, as a national resource, includes primary numeric data, bibliographic data, textual information in print and non-print, audiovisual sources and oral communication (such as oral history or broadcast programs). While mass communication information is often transmitted through channels similar to those used for scientific and technical information, the latter is to be distinguished from that information intended to entertain or to persuade (e.g. advertising and propaganda).

The Conference accepts as a basic tenet that scientific and technical information is an essential input in the development process. While no direct causal relationship can be put forward at this time, its role is believed to be significant.

I. INFORMATION POLICY

Scientific and technical information, as a national resource, should be planned, managed and used according to an integrated set of national policies. As it is significant in all sectors of the economy, and indeed in the fundamental planning process itself, programs promoting its generation, control, dissemination and use should be coordinated to assure equitable access and use as appropriate within each country's governmental structure.

The Conference favors national policies which permit the free (i.e. unrestricted) flow of information across national borders. Imported information of any kind should be given preferential tariffs (when such is necessary) compared to other commercial rates.

Policy Development

In accord with each individual country's national structure, national information policies should be established at the highest possible governmental level. This is to promote policy acceptance and, as appropriate, consensus at all levels, and to acknowledge the importance of scientific and technical information in national development.

Relationships should be established between communities of professionals at the highest levels, including those of library and information science, and those of science and technology.

Users of information and high-level representatives from sectoral and planning ministries should be involved in policy development and subsequent activities. Their input regarding sectoral needs, patterns of information use, and the like, are essential components in the planning process as well as the content of the policy itself.

Links should be explored between and among government and private sector science and technology transfer centers, centers producing social science numeric and bibliographic databases, university research efforts in the sciences and humanities, and libraries of all types (including academic, public and special). In this context, changes in the role of the traditional library in relation to these non-library institutions will need to be explored. The role of the library certainly is not expected to be diminished, rather it is expected to be enhanced by its operation in a wider context.

The work of each type of institution will—and must—complement that of the others.

A national acquisitions program should be developed as a part of the national information policy.

Need for Policies

Coordination of information resources at various policy levels, and awareness of them at the operational level, would insure their more effective and economical use through formal and informal cooperation.

Information policies are needed to:

(1) Create incentives for the production of and access to information and knowledge applicable to national development goals. Necessarily, this includes fiscal policies favoring these developments, and the encouragement of indexing and abstracting services to facilitate access to literatures.

(2) Provide national plans to protect cultural heritage, national sovereignty, and the individual's right to equitable access to information.

(3) Establish accepted standards for the development of and use of information technology in the service of individual human and social goals, science, and scholarship.

(4) Establish a legal framework to support the national information structure, and relationships between libraries, information centers, data banks, archives, and other agencies generating, storing, and disseminating scientific and technical information

(5) Promote the development of information and telecommunication networks and assure equitable access to them.

(6) Provide resources for research in all sciences, including library and information science, and for the dissemination of results.

(7) Provide resources for education and training programs for information professionals and users.

(8) Promote cooperation between information systems internationally on the basis of equal partnership.

(9) Promote movement toward a total environment which will allow access to information by specialists as well as the urban and rural masses.

II. ACCESS TO INFORMATION

Despite international agreements to enhance the free flow of information, many economic, social, legal, political or socio-cultural barriers do exist. Some are merely a nuisance. Some are imposed by governments in the interest of national security. Some are imposed by the private sector to restrict access to commercial information. These must be recognized at the policy level, and where appropriate, removed or coped with at the operational level.

Because of the vast amount of information that is available, the selection and acquisition of information relevant to South American needs is of far greater concern to the Conference than the problem of access to restricted information (whether such restrictions are on the basis of national security or corporate proprietary interests).

Databases

The present database environment is made up of a few major commercial vendors, such as Lockheed and SDC, a few international participative systems such as AGRIS and INIS, and numerous small local systems.

Local systems offer the greatest potential benefit for South American users because they are under local control and sovereignty, are more responsive to local needs, can more easily include local documentation, and can provide South American with direct experience in database construction and maintenance.

International participative systems are also of great value for South America because they operate on the basis of the free exchange of information; they place local information in an international context, on an equal footing with that of other countries; they give South Americans the experience of collaboration in world-wide networks; and they encourage the development of national information and bibliographic resources.

National and cooperative regional databases should be encouraged in South America in order to improve the bibliographic control of information generated in the region.

It is recognized that the major commercial database vendors will have a significant role to play as backup to local and participative systems, but the Conference has reservations about their un-restricted use because many are concentrated in a single country, and they are commercial in nature. Further, South American countries do not participate in their control, and there is a lack of regional content and relevance.

Database producers in industrialized countries should stimulate an increase in coverage of Latin American materials. For example, making HAPI available through one of the online services such as Dialog would start this process. This would provide a worldwide dissemination of the documentation generated in the region.

Libraries and documentation centers should enter into agreements to exchange data internationally and /or link databases within the region, ultimately developing a South American database. The merging of bibliographic data from national databases into a potential regional database can be made possible by assuring that the MARC format is used in national databases. Those now being produced in Venezuela, Mexico and Brazil can be merged, because they are all in the MARC format and use AACR2. An IFLA Intermarc Committee project at the National Library of Canada may produce a means of converting ISIS data to MARC format, which would permit merging of that data as well.

Creation of new databases should be coordinated by a regional organization, such as the Organization of American States or CLADES, so that they can be developed in the context of existing services. This conclusion does not intend to suggest a restrictive and controlling function, rather, one of awareness of what exists already, for users and for prospective database developers.

The South American content of major databases should be evaluated. Reasons for their slow coverage of Latin American materials should be identified. Where appropriate, steps should be taken to remedy problems.

Recent developments in Brazil in the creation of the Interdata system have extended enormously the access of Brazilian users to foreign databases, even though the present telecommunications costs are high. The lowering of Telex costs by 30 percent in the early 1980's points toward further decreases. In countries such as in Brazil, this may reduce national programs for acquiring databases themselves and offering searching services in-country.

Bibliographic Control

We reiterate the importance of bibliographic control of the intellectual output of each country. This control should include not only monographs and serials, but also conference proceedings, AV materials, maps, dissertations, theses, mimeographed materials, scientific reports, various editions of newspapers, printed music scores and government publications. The final products, especially union catalogs, should be widely distributed because of their importance for current awareness and acquisition of new materials.

In support of this, efforts should be continued to identify those agencies which generate information, and make this information available through the publication of directories of agencies and research in progress.

Collection and Resource Development

Greater attention should be given to the techniques of the selection of materials, and to the creation of realistic development policies. The problems of inadequate bibliographic control, the lack of national bibliographies, indexing and abstracting services for all types of materials, seriously hinder the development of adequate selection policies. Accurate and appropriate selection policies, based on the realistic needs and expectations of identified user groups, need to be developed and implemented to tailor collections and services to these groups, and to screen incoming materials, whatever their source, to the best advantage of users.

Central repositories of periodicals are needed in many situations, especially of scientific and technical periodicals, and they should be created where appropriate. Such centers should give greater attention to user profiles to accurately determine user needs at all levels. These should form part of improved and realistic collection development policies for central repositories and for individual libraries.

Systems should be developed to facilitate shared acquisitions programs and interlibrary loan. Coupons may be a mechanism for payment for loans and copies, as the COMUT program in Brazil.

The translation of English-language journal articles published outside of South America into Spanish and Portuguese should be promoted and increased.

Older materials need to be adequately preserved, through such mechanisms as cooperative preservation schemes, regional deposits for older materials, and the like.

Further, an inventory and assessment of existing information stores and document collections and related resources should be conducted.

Indexing Services

The indexing of South American periodicals is still inadequate, and the improvement of indexing coverage is an urgent priority. Without such access mechanisms, literatures increased through funded research, development projects or translations will be used at a less than optimal level. Some steps to improve this situation are noted below.

Indexes in applied science should be translated into Spanish and Portuguese, even though the full text of the article may be in English.

Indexing terms should be standardized. This is necessary to insure compatibility for database development, to insure that indexing reflects South American needs and to promote regional independence.

Cost studies should be carried out to evaluate the feasibility of more local indexing of journals imported into Latin America.

III. THE PROFESSION

As other professions have arrived at an integration of their various specialties, information professionals should work toward similar goals. Professional organizations, educational programs, and joint meetings may serve as mechanisms for this integration. This activity will support a society-wide and systematic approach to the management of information for the benefit of all.

Creative leadership is needed for the profession to participate at the level of decision making, in the formulation of national information policies and the development of an infrastructure which will support the effective collection and dissemination of scientific and technical information.

There is also an need for active recruitment of new professionals who can develop strong knowledge bases, technical skills, and service attitudes toward their work.

IV. PLANNING AND COORDINATION

A multinational body should be created with the responsibility and authority to coordinate the development of an Interamerican network and to develop clearinghouse services.

Developments in information technology should be monitored, so that compatible systems which promote information sharing can be developed.

A directory of South American information agencies, specialists, and services should be prepared by the OAS, to outline the information infrastructure that is already in place.

V. INFORMATION FOR DECISION MAKERS

Information professionals in the region need to develop more information specifically for decision-making, and insure that it is distributed to decision makers.

It is essential that there be increased interaction between information professionals and their users, and that studies of user needs be actively undertaken. An in-depth analysis of user needs of various groups will support the development of user profiles which are essential to the development of collection development policies noted above. Further, they can serve as the basis for the repackaging of information from various sources to suit those identified needs, and the needs of decision-makers in particular.

VI. EDUCATION AND TRAINING OF IN-FORMATION PROFESSIONALS

Generally throughout South America, expertise needs to be increased in the development and management of information services.

The Conference considers of great importance the budgeting of information services at a level which encourages students to study library and information science for a career in the field.

Although no one library or information center can encompass all of the different types of information carriers mentioned above, information professionals should be made aware of them and their interrelationships during their education for work in the field.

For information professionals, attitudes and communication skills are deemed as important as theoretical or technical skills so that professionals can participate effectively in decision-making.

Library schools should train students in practical indexing and subject content analysis. The establishment and improvement of information services in South America will depend to a large degree on the availability of trained indexers.

Library school students should also be trained to critically evaluate information resources and materials, for the collection and for individual users.

Aspects of library and information science should be incorporated into the general education curriculum. This will promote the development of an educated user population, and a general increased awareness of the integration of information into research, planning, and daily life at all levels.

VII. CONSULTANTS

While in many circumstances consultants from international agencies are welcomed and have essential roles to play in the local development of information resources, it is important that they receive feedback from and give feedback for whom they work. This will insure that the local institution receives assistance properly targeted to the problem of concern, and that the consultant understands the problem within its social, legal, political, and scientific context. It is worthwhile to reiterate here that the problems of development are not isolated cultural events. Each country and area within a country functions as a system, and each situation has cultural ramifications beyond the situation itself, which must be taken into account by the consultant. Beyond insuring local agency participation for continuation of the work, acceptance of and working within cultural factors will support proper identification and resolution of the problem.

VIII. SCHOLARLY RESEARCH AND PUBLICATION

Latin American scholars in the social sciences and humanities prefer to publish in their own countries' publications. Medical and scientific scholars, on the other hand, prefer to publish outside their countries, principally in U.S. publications.

The English language is already a "lingua franca" for medicine and the sciences on a global scale, and this is reflected by the relative ease with which English-language documents in these fields are accepted in Latin America. There will, however, be a constant and continuing need for translations.

Pre-publication information is needed to help eliminate duplication of research. This can be accomplished through registers of research in progress, from which written reports may be generated, as well as through cooperative efforts with major science and technical publishers. While replication of research efforts is an important technique in confirming scientific findings, it is most appropriate that this be deliberate and not unintentional. Libraries and information centers make an important contribution to science by gathering and disseminating this information.

Due to the conditions of academic life in South America, when low-paid researchers may have little motivation to publish, it may well be appropriate to offer incentive payments for authors publishing locally. When South American researchers publish in a North American or European journal, they should be encouraged to publish translations of their papers in South American journals, or present them at South American conferences. This will require a change in South American attitudes, because translations of papers published overseas are not always considered original works, and therefore are not always acceptable locally.

IX. FINAL REMARKS

The Conference concluded that scientific and technical information is essential to the continued progress of South America and the region as a whole, and as such requires attention at the highest national level. Access to information can be improved and increased through the further development of resources, the improvement of the profession, and creation of links to scientists, to government, and to users. Improvements are needed in all aspects of information generation, control, and dissemination in the countries of Latin American and the Caribbean. While there have been many improvements in recent years, there is still much to do to insure equitable access throughout the region.

CONFERENCE PAPERS

KEYNOTE ADDRESS:

PROFESSIONAL ORGANIZATIONS' ROLE IN INFORMATION FLOW

by Ching-Chih Chen
Graduate School of Library and Information Science
Simmons College, Boston, Massachusetts, USA

RESUMEN

Papel de las Organizaciones Profesionales
en el Flujo de la Información

Las organizaciones profesionales pueden ayudar a alcanzar las metas de cooperación y conocimiento de asunto internacional. La ciencia por definición es una actividad internacional que supera las fronteras nacionales y con asociaciones profesionales los científicos en el campo de información pueden hablar libremente de tópicos tales como de los derechos humanos en laciencia. Recientes acciones politicamente motivadas que impidieron la asistencia de algunos científicos a reuniones en Hong Kong y Egypto, son ejemplos de las violaciones de los derechos humanos dentro de la comunidad científica, las cuales no pueden ser toleradas.

Aunque debemos reconocer el derecho de un gobierno de restringir informacion por razones de seguridad y reserva nacional, tales acciones a no ser por absoluta necesidad son deplorables como obstáculos a la libre investigacion. Con la voz collectiva de una asociación, los profesionales en el campo de la información en los paises de desarrollo, de otra manera, enfoca mas en eventos de soeranía y economía nacional. Las asociaciones pueden servir de un foro para debate de las perspectives, apoyo y mutuo reconocimiento de objetivos y valores de los paises desarrollados o en desarrollo. Las asociaciones además pueden sintetizar la literatura en asuntos mayores, proveer oportunidades para contacto informal, trabajar con otras organizaciones regionales e intragubernamentales para alcanzar objetivos mutuos.

As a proud graduate of the University of Michigan, it is always a great personal pleasure to come back to Ann Arbor. I not only feel like I have "come home," but I also have the opportunity to renew friendships and to make new friends with colleagues from the United States and other numerous countries of the North and South.

While world communications have become such a central topic for discussions, debates, and writings in recent years, this "Conference on the Transfer of Scholarly, Scientific and Technical Information between North and South America" is truly vital for us as information professionals, particularly at a time when the United Nations General Assembly has cited 1983 as "World Communications Year." This pre-conference function, co-sponsored by both the Conference and the Michigan Chapter of the American Society for Information Science, further signifies the kind of cooperation and common understanding desperately needed for any kind of free flow of communication and information. By professionals gathering together in conferences and professional organizations, the free flow of communication and information can be promoted.

While I came here primarily to learn from my esteemed colleagues from the North and South, I shall also risk displaying my ignorance and share with you some of my personal observations on the role of professional organizations in information flow.

A quick perusal of the recent literature on the topics of "information flow" and related subjects such as "information policy," "transborder data flow," and the like show how vast and diverse the terrain is. Discussions on these topics have always foundered on the fact that the concept of information flow means several different things to as many different groups. There is no consensus on either the definition of the term or the terms, or on the problems and issues related to the subject. Different countries and groups select different areas for focus, exploration and debate. The complex political, economic, social and technical issues involved in international information flow have just begun to be recognized. We are in a state of "helplessness," like Toffler's metaphor of a third wave. Thus, at best, we can only select a few areas where opportunity and importance converge. We must continue to search for alternatives, solutions and compromises.

To reach any of these goals, we shall need to promote a much more common understanding of the problems and issues at hand. We must initiate new attitudes toward the problems. We must create cooperation among groups and countries, an awareness and acceptance of differences among people, and compassion in dealing with each situation as it arises. Needless to say, professional organizations have had, and should continue to have, strong responsibilities as well as promises toward these concerns.

Allow me to elaborate on the following areas, even though the definition of "information flow" may be quite different from one to the other:

- Human rights and international politics
- Transborder information flow
- Implications of new technologies to information flow

HUMAN RIGHTS AND INTERNATIONAL POLITICS

When related to issues of human rights and international politics, "information flow" means quite a different thing. In this respect, it generally refers more to free "access" to information and communication in the context of a government's or group's attempt to deprive individuals of an opportunity to participate in, contribute to, and learn from the information flow and exchange process. Citizens of many countries, specifically those of the Western world, generally view such acts as infringements on one's ability to perform as a free citizen of the world and as a violation of basic fundamental human rights. Fundamental as it is to us, this strong view is not shared by governments or even citizens of some other countries.

Human Rights

American democratic tradition cannot tolerate any restraint of information and will thus advocate the free flow of information. The United States government is oriented toward the individual and his or her individual freedom. However, we should realize that this strong belief of the United States government is not subscribed to by all nations.

Many nations are oriented toward the group and its welfare. Thus, for various political and other complex reasons, they do not accept the "free" flow of information at its face value.

Professional organizations are set up to serve a given professional community and to permit the free and open exchange of knowledge. Knowledge is international and national boundaries should have no impact on the universality of knowledge.

Science is a prime example of the universality of knowledge. Scientific communication is traditionally worldwide and international in character. Science transcends geographical boundaries and belongs to all mankind. For technology to grow, science must be open, discussed, critiqued and created in an environment where questioning fundamental assumptions is the rule rather than the exception.

In my view, professionals and professional organizations have an obligation to speak out in defense of the human rights of other professionals. The reactions to this issue were very clear in the Scharansky case of the period of 1977–79 and several more recent cases. Many professional organizations, including ASIS, went on record in public to oppose the arbitrary curtailment of any activity as an infringement upon one's basic human rights. Thus, it is important to remember that we need to concern ourselves, not only as professionals, but equally as citizens. We need to speak up on issues such as these, yet by speaking collectively through our professional organizations we will have a greater influence on society.

International Politics

It is a cliché to say that knowledge knows no political boundaries and the free flow of information should not be impeded because of political considerations. On the surface, it would be difficult to find an individual authority, group or nation that would go on record as disagreeing with these concepts. Yet, life is not so simple. Reality tells us again and again that international politics, or for that matter any politics, has and will continue to intrude into the domain of knowledge. We, as information professionals, have a special responsibility to help insure the free flow of information among all people and all nations.

Because of this responsibility, it was particularly disturbing and embarrassing when the arbitrary restriction on the free dissemination and exchange of information was made by information professionals. I am particularly referring to two recent and most unfortunate events. The first was when our Russian colleagues were denied visas by the Hong Kong authorities to attend the most recent Annual Meeting of the International Federation of Documentation held in Hong Kong in September 1982. The second was when our Israeli colleagues were prevented from attending and participating in the first International Information Conference co-sponsored (supposedly) by the Egyptian Society for Information Technology (ESIT) and ASIS.

Both situations were clearly politically motivated. Yet the implications and reasons for annoyance to us as information professionals are not quite the same. The restriction on FID participants was placed by the Hong Kong government. FID, being the professional organization in this case, deplored the Hong Kong government's actions and protested explicitly. In the case of the Egyptians, the tense political situation in the Middle East took its toll and the Egyptian Society for Information Technology made a unilateral decision to place the restrictions on their Israeli informational colleagues in December 1982. The Egyptian scenario is quite clear, and it is not difficult for all of us to imagine the tremendous pressure ESIT officials were facing with their government and their countrymen. However, the fact was that they went on record in selecting the worst possible alternative available to them.

I know that I am speaking to many concerned ASIS members here. As a member of the ASIS Board, the Executive Committee, and the chair of the task force, I want to personally convey to you that the decision was made by ESIT unilaterally without any discussion of the situation with ASIS until only a few days prior to the meeting, when many of the ASIS delegates and members were already on their way to Egypt. This matter was taken up very seriously and carefully by ASIS, which reaffirmed its official position on the free flow of information and launched a strong protest to our ESIT colleagues.

This kind of political intervention, which prevents the free movement of people among nations, cannot be tolerated. Professional organizations should speak up in strong protest and should develop measures to prevent any similar events from happening.

TRANSBORDER INFORMATION FLOW

Let us now focus on a major area of information flow which relates to an international transferability of information, the flow of data and the processing of information across national boundaries. The issues involved here are much more complex. Between the right and wrong, and the white and black areas, there is a vast gray area where no one knows who is right and who is wrong. Each side can present their reasons and views convincingly, and each will continue to develop their own so-called "information policy" based upon their own national prior convictions and perceptions. Let me expand on this topic by discussing:

- Barriers to or the control of information flow and national information policy;

- International information policy

Barriers to or the Control of Information Flow and National Information Policy

It is generally accepted that the control of information flow can be justified on the basis of national security, privacy, economics or nationalism. In each of these sub-areas, the views of developed and developing countries (commonly referred to as the North and South) differ greatly.

The Developed Countries

In developed countries such as the United States, national security and privacy seem to have been viewed as the primary reasons for restricting information flow to other countries. Governmental agencies have regulations and legislation supposedly to insure that national security will not be jeopardized. There is also a keen concern that protection of privacy be appropriately afforded, which has become an even greater issue in light of the electronic age. The United States government has put a high priority on privacy.

Recognizing the government's right to restrict information flow for the reasons mentioned above, professionals tend to view regulations as detrimental to free inquiry and scholars deplore this restriction. They are generally disturbed by the government's attempt to restrict the dissemination and exchange of scientific and technical information.

In the United States, for example, the National Academy of Science has formed a panel to study this matter. They have expressed the idea that the national welfare, including national security, is best served by allowing the free flow of all that scientific and technical information which is not directly and significantly connected to technologies critical to national security. The panel thus concludes that the government has the responsibility of defending, in concrete terms, the technical areas in which controls on information flow are warranted.

Regarding economic factors, developed countries also base their information policies on nationalism. Generally, their policies promote a free flow. Rather than control the international flow of information, which has been viewed as a form of trade, there is a greater economic benefit to multinational corporations not to do so. When the prospect of profit ceases to be the motivation for information export, the policy on the flow of information will often be adjusted quickly.

Professional organizations, such as the American Association for the Advancement of Science and the American Chemical Society, are quick to go on the record to endorse the findings of the National Academy of Science panel and oppose government restrictions on the dissemination, exchange, or availability of unclassified knowledge. Many professional scientific and technical organizations, such as the American Chemical Society, are constantly monitoring developments in the legislative and executive branches of the United States government in the areas of scientific communication, technology transfer, and national security. Thus, the organizations have played an important role in the process of developing national information policies. As non-profit organizations, they want to ensure that national information policies can provide a balance in a way that is sensitive to changing times, responsive to changing technology and fair to all concerned.

The Developing Countries

Regarding barriers and the control of information flow in the developing countries, the issues will relate much more to economic factors and national sovereignty. These are very sensitive factors in these regions. Information policies of developing countries, similar to those of the developed ones, are also created to protect the vital interests of the individual countries.

Information in the modern world is characterized by a basic imbalance which reflects the general imbalance of the international community. The flow of information has always moved in a single direction from North to South. As the South grows more and more dependent upon the North for information, specifically in specialized, scientific and technical areas, the cost for such information provision will sky-rocket. The developed world is evolving toward an information society and already the main inputs to economic growth and the creation of wealth are based upon the growth of information and knowledge.

The developing nations live in the same economic world as the developed when trading exists between them. But as yet, they find growth elusive and are rarely competing with one another. Thus, the threat to political and economic independence and to cultural identity by the expanding transborder data flows have become top-priority concerns of the governments of the developing and third-world countries. In the last several years, the poorer nations, in a variety of forums and varying levels of stridency, have stated their demands for the renovation of international economic relations. They claim a greater voice in the decisions that affect them and a more just share of the global prosperity. Many have advocated and demanded a "New World Information Order" and a "New World Economic Order."

It would be wrong to pretend that some of the criticisms of information flow have no basis in fact. We should try to understand and recognize the legitimate aspirations of governments to protect the economic and cultural well-being of their citizens, and their overriding responsibility to insure the safety and security of their countries. Unpleasant and frustrating as they may be, the developed countries, with tremendous opportunities to export information goods and services, should expect to have a constant struggle against closed markets and trade barriers abroad as the developing countries try to protect their home-grown industries.

Unless efforts are made, and made quickly, to recognize the valid differences and needs of the developing countries, we will never be able to acquire international agreements. Professional organizations can play a significant role in promoting the kind of mutual respect and understanding which seeks to achieve an "information detente." Last year ASIS formed a Special Interest Group on International Information Issues precisely for these purposes. As the co-chair of the group, I am happy to report that the membership of this special interest group has grown from zero to over two hundred members since last year.

International Information Policy

Issues related to international information policies can be grouped into four broad areas: economic; social; political; and cultural. We have dealt with the economic and political aspects in the earlier discussion of barriers to information flow. Therefore it is now necessary to point out the significant social and cultural differences between the North and the South.

An information society presupposes a generally high level of literacy, critical faculty and skill in turning information into knowledge. In short, the nation must build a first-world social model. In the rural parts of the developing countries, where much of the world's population lives, other problems of information exist. There is a great educational problem in that many people are illiterate and literacy is generally confined to native languages. These is a lack of social desire to solve problems and to change the state of affairs. There is also a lack of interest in communication both horizontally and vertically, causing the information infrastructure to be weak. There is little intellectual stimulus for professionals to broaden their knowledge and to change the status quo. There is a greater dependency on human-to-human relationships and communications. Developing country views and philosophy, in short, are very inconsistent with those of the Western world. They want to be philosophical, humanistic, and speculative, while they mistrust the action-oriented, problem-oriented and scientific approach to social problems. It is no wonder that Universal Access to Publications (UAP) promoted by UNESCO has been received, to the great amazement of the Western information professionals, with less than enthusiastic response from Third World countries.

In this kind of social and cultural environment, even if the technology could somehow make all information accessible to the inhabitants of developing countries, we are faced with several other questions. Who is going to use it? To what extent is it going to be used? How would they benefit from it? What would they be using it for? And where would they apply their newly-gained knowledge? The fundamental questions are: "Do they really need this vast amount of information at all levels of sophistication? Can they consume the information given to them in foreign languages? And do they really need the high technology now?" However unappealing this may be, we will find that there is a serious mismatch between what is being offered to them and what is really needed by them.

Thus, meaningful international exchange of information can be successful only if we are aware of the specific constraints faced by the less developed countries. We must attempt to nurture a true spirit of cooperation which begins with mutual respect for differences in perspectives and for the economic and cultural differences which produce them. Professional organizations, especially the transnational ones, are ideal agencies to provide a mechanism whereby professionals from nations, regardless of their social relations, can work together. They must form a structure to achieve cooperation; to expand the intellectual horizon of those who may have influence in their own countries; to strive for agreements between nations; to share the wealth of the profession as it is developed in local areas; and to open contacts between groups and individuals across political boundaries in order to raise the intellectual content of various cultures.

The Institute of Electrical and Electronic Engineers (IEEE), for example, as a transnational organization of more than 220,000 members in more than 110 countries, also has an active relationship with its more than 5,000 members in Central and South America. A duly elected director for the region sits on the IEEE Board of Directors to ensure the fostering of international understanding between regions. In our own information field, the International Federation of Library Associations (IFLA) is an association of about 140 library associations from every part of the world, and the

International Federation for Documentation (FID) has sixty-nine national members. Both IFLA and FID fulfill responsibilities similar to those of IEEE.

NEW TECHNOLOGIES AND INFORMATION FLOW

Though time does not permit me to elaborate, I cannot leave my discussion on information flow without touching on the topic of technology. For those of us living in the developed countries, we know that an "information age" has descended upon us.

This information age involves the convergence of computer and telecommunications technologies, the extensive use of other technologies such as the laser, and the penetration of all of these deeply into the home, the office, and the school.

We will soon see new departures in scientific and technical communication because the orientation is changing. We are seeing a shift away from bibliographic systems toward development of information systems which are more directly available to individuals. On the other hand, we do not know if we should expect to see all these changes happen in the developing countries. Many of these countries are far from achieving a level of sophistication to be able to integrate this kind of high technology into their own cultures and systems. Unless the socio-economic environment is ready for the appropriate application of new technology, backed with trained personnel, a minimum level of technical know-how, and the basic facility requirements of electricity and the like, technology will be a kind of luxury for which they will pay dearly but which will accomplish little. This will not reflect very much in the overall improvement of the quality of life in their countries. This must be clearly understood by all parties concerned. Professional organizations, specifically those scientific and technical ones, have their obligations to promote further constructive communication on the imbalance and differences between the North and the South.

IMPLICATIONS FOR INFORMATION PROFESSIONALS

Information is our business. Its control, use or misuse, and availability are critical. However, we must also consider views different from our own. While we may not always agree, we do need to understand. We need to seek ways of recognizing differences while working together to promote progress for all, though we may define progress differently. Efforts by government and individuals to promote international understanding place upon us, as information professionals, the obligation to inform ourselves about international issues to further intensify our efforts in promoting the understanding of international affairs. Yet, it is difficult to keep up with international developments and issues on information flow. This is another aspect in which our professional organizations can assist us by providing:

(1) conferences, meetings and forums for open discussions and interchanges of problems and issues of mutual and critical concern;

(2) literature synthesizing the major and new developments on key issues; and above all,

(3) opportunities for informal contact with our colleagues from all over the world.

International information work bears all of the burdens of varying national political influences. Though it is difficult and frustrating, patience is the key to our success.

The fast-changing information and communication environment has drawn the attention of national governments. Most countries are in the early stages of grappling with the political, legal, economic and social ramifications of the "information society" for their own economies. Nevertheless, because of the movement of information and knowledge, which is not restricted by territorial boundaries, many of these issues are now under deliberation by regional, international, and intergovernmental organizations as well. Our professional organizations can play a major role on information flow by working closely with these organizations to attain our goals.

CONCLUSIONS

I stand before you boldly sharing my personal observations on international information flow. I have no all-encompassing and sophisticated theory. But I understand the differences among people and countries, for I have been on both sides of the fence.

As I traveled around the world, whether standing on the top post of China's Great Wall, which artificially divides the endless mountain ranges beyond the end of the horizon; or climbing up laboriously through the inner narrow path to the inside top of the Great Pyramid; or standing at the Wailing Wall where the Jews and Hassidics pray religiously; or marveling at all the marbles, rubies, emeralds and sapphires of the beautiful Taj Mahal and the glorious eternal golds of King Tut's collection at the Cairo Museum; or wandering about the Roman ruins or standing at the Acropolis; or being at the Aztec temples and the Machu Pichu ancient cities, I have come to realize in my own way how people and their cultures are different. And they are all treasures.

I have come to appreciate even more what "America, the land of opportunity" means to me. It is a place where no one culture prevails and there is no long tradition to slow down progress and prevent innovation and changes. It is a melting pot where compromises have been reached and people from all backgrounds and cultures are working together to learn to communicate and work in harmony with each other. This is what we should strive for as far as international information flow is concerned.

Recently, a local elementary school in Somerville, Massachusetts experienced a newfound celebrity overnight when President Reagan read a segment of the letter sent by twenty-one second graders of the school after his Easter message. The letter stated in part:

We studied about countries and found out that we need each other to share our goods with...

We want no wars. We want to keep our buildings from being destroyed. We want to be able to talk to one another. And we want to be able to travel around the world without fear...

Do you think we can have these things some day?

President Reagan responded:

Well I do. I really do. Nearly 2000 years after the coming of the Prince of Peace, such simple wishes may still seem far from fulfillment. But we can achieve them. We must never stop trying.

Surprisingly enough, these simple wishes also apply to us in local, national, and international information work. Through our professional organizations, we can work for these goals collectively. I leave you with this thought: "We must never stop trying."

CHILE, LATIN AMERICA AND THE TRANSFER OF KNOWLEDGE: BETWEEN INFORMATION FREEDOM AND INFORMATION DEPENDENCY

by Juan R. Freudenthal
Graduate School of Library and Information Science
Simmons College
Boston, Massachusetts, USA

RESUMEN

Chile, America Latina y la Transferencia de Conocimiento: Entre la Libertad de la Información y la Dependencia de la Información

El contexto de información científica en Chile, incluye una comunidad universitaria la cual recientemente fué puesta bajo control gubernamental reenforzado, varias juntas para apoyar la ciencia y la investigación y una dependencia intelectual en otros paises quienes tiende a promover un virtual estancamiento intelectual. Los obstáculos contra el progreso para aleviar la situacion para quella ciencia pueda seguir adelante incluye una falta de entendimiento de parte de los que hacen las reglas del papel de la ciencia en desarrollo. La educación Latino Americana tiende a enfatizar tópicos humanisticos en lugar de tópicos cientificos lo cual instala un cimiento de desconfianza en el avance de la tecnología. Además, el monopolio de los Estados Unidos en la información produce desconfianza en el uso de dichas tecnologías en America Latina. La información debe ser considerada como un asunto político. A través de conecciones entre profesionales del norte y los del sud en el campo informático, una concentración en información que es genuinamente necesitada y una misión claramente definida y establecida, mejores alianzas políticas pueden ser formadas. Una imperativa geográfica une a los Estados Unidos y America Latina y las dos regiones deben aprender a trabajar juntas. A pesar de los recursos sobreabundantes del norte, la transferencia de información entre los dos paises debe ocurrir en el contenido de co-desarrollo del potential humano.

THE CONTEMPORARY INFORMATION
ENVIRONMENT IN CHILE

Higher Education and Chilean Universities

Before January 3, 1981 all eight Chilean universities were academically and administratively autonomous. Two, the Universidad de Chile (founded November 19, 1942) and the Universidad Téchnica del Estado (newly renamed the Universidad de Santiago, established July 6, 1947) were state universities. The others, founded between 1888 and 1956 were considered private or semi-autonomous, although heavily dependent on state funds. The Government, however, felt they had all become centers of social unrest, placing politics above learning, and a new law introduced sweeping reforms, decentralizing higher education provision by the creation of new universities and giving government greater control through *juntas directivas*, made up of one-third presidential nominees and two-thirds appointees of the faculty and the rector (himself chosen by the President). Allocation of government funds would depend in part on the standard of students admitted, as measured by a national aptitude test.

The wide and controversial reorganization has raised questions on the impact it may have on future training of scholars and scientists. Chile's most venerable newspaper, *El Mercurio*, fears a proliferation of masterships and doctorates from institutions lacking adequate faculty and research facilities (including libraries): "in general, we support research in inaugural speeches and verbal declarations more than in practice" (Orrego Vicuña 1982)—a commentary applicable to Chile's whole cultural history and a reason for failure to create first-rate academic libraries and information centers capable of supporting major research.

Recently there has been a movement to create a National Scholarship Plan to support graduate studies (Plan de becas... 1982) but this will apply to a few disciplines only and most higher degrees must be sought abroad. Thanks to its democratic traditions, Chile has never suffered a major "brain-drain" syndrome. Through most of its history it has been a haven to Latin American intellectuals in exile, who have infused the country's cultural life with a reservoir of great teachers and new ideas. The early 1970s saw this tradition disrupted, many Chilean professionals being lost to foreign institutions. The situation, however, is already being redressed, particularly by the scientific community which is striving assiduously towards an effective national science policy.

Science and the Scientific Community: Problems and Prospects

In the 1950s Chile's scientists proposed to government the creation of a commission to assess national scientific and technological needs and to obtain new revenues for these beyond what was allocated by the universities and by national or foreign government-sponsored projects. A foremost concern was Chile's dependence on foreign resources for basic and applied research, the bulk of which was provided by the United States. Information resources available within the country were desperately needed. Many universities had fair holdings and gave adequate service but had not received the attention they deserved. In 1954, the government established a national fund for university construction and research and created the Council of Rectors of Chilean Universities to review and coordinate the universities' educational and scientific activities. Following advice from the United States, the Council established in 1963 the National Center for Information and Documentation (CENID), a referral center emphasizing the coordination of special information and the analysis of scientific knowledge at the national level. In 1968, the government created the National Commission on Scientific and Technological Research (CONICYT), a consultant body administered through the Education Ministry, but reporting directly to the President. In 1969, CENID began operating within the framework of CONICYT. In July 1977, CONICYT, with OAS support, sponsored the First National Seminar on Scientific and Technological Information. During January 1981, the Chilean-North American Institute in Santiago sponsored a seminar on "Computer Applications in the Field of Information, the Chilean Experience."

Finally, awareness of the need for national and worldwide standardization of cataloging practice and faster access to all types of information (due in part to UNISIST) has led to library automation (cataloging, acquisitions, circulation and retrieval) and the use of MARC tapes at the Universidad Católogica. The National Library also is considering MARC for catalog automation. Chilean scientists and information professionals have striven hard to make government officials realize the need to formulate a realistic national science policy.

The latest and potentially most far reaching achievement has been the creation of the National Endowment for Scientific and Technological Development (FNDCT) (decree of October 17, 1981). FNDCT, administered by the Education Ministry through CONICYT, consists of three councils: Consejo Nacional, headed by the Education, Finance and Planning Ministers; Consejo Superior de Ciencias, administered by seven scientists; and the Consejo Superior de Desarrollo Tecnológico (Higher Council for Technological Development) with five scientists. The Consejo Nacional's major responsibility will be obtaining funds, through the national budget and international economic assistance. In 1982, FNDCT received $1,600,000US from the government to support several programs; this met with a mixed reaction from Chile's intellectuals (Gran paso 1982).

In his 1979 essays, *Ciencia y universidad*, Igor Saavedra, theoretical physicist, teacher and 1981 recipient of the National Science Prize, pointed out that 1,862 papers of a scientific nature had been published in Chile from 1967 to 1973, but output had since declined: political and cultural developments had brought such publishing almost to a standstill. Scientists' pay had improved since 1973 but more important had been the lack of the mechanisms that would have allowed more open and effective participation in the universities and CONICYT.

Saavedra is particularly critical of Chile's academic libraries. Research is hampered by incomplete periodical runs. The few instances of a complete and current journal run have been achieved at the expense of book acquisitions. The high cost of imports means that most university library books are donations from international agencies.

Saavedra's most consistent criticism is of Chile's intellectual dependency, in which he echoes many other educational philosophers, such as Ivan Illich, who preach the need for radical changes in Latin American education. Such writers believe that the most dangerous underdevelopment of all is the result of a state of mind.

> If a visitor comes from abroad, and particularly if he speaks English, we hear him with reverence. This is a clear symptom of mental underdevelopment. We should of course hear what he has to say, but to believe everything he utters, particularly when he is only just beginning to know us, is something else. I am not so critical of what visitors say about us, but worried about our own attitude of dependence ...

> In 1967, we were publishing about the same amount of scientific publications as Brazil, Argentina, Mexico and Venezuela. Ten years later, Venezuela and Chile had become stagnant... A country that does not think is not a country but just another colony (Saavedra 1979).

In 1981, the Chilean Institute's Academy of Sciences published a series of studies and analyses of scientific activities in Chile: mathematics, physics, chemistry, biology, agriculture, earth sciences, engineering, medicine, health sciences and oceanography. Commenting on these papers, with their wide spectrum of experimental data, Saavedra felt they would serve as a springboard to stimulate further scientific activities in Chile. Nevertheless, despite some progress in all these areas, severe obstacles remained: lack of adequate budgets, of human resources and of a younger generation of scientists capable of providing continuity and further stimulus (Analysis... 1982).

There has never been a holistic understanding of Chile's cultural and scientific needs. There has been a lack of integration between government policies and institutional changes and a failure to understand the vital role science and technology could play in a largely humanistic-oriented society. Research cannot be isolated from the country's needs and so, despite the government's best intentions, most Chilean scientists will have to look abroad at present for wider collaboration and recognition.

Towards a National Information System

Contemporary developments have led to the establishment of several information subsystems in Chile (Burgos 1982, Fuentes July 1982). Although automated storage and retrieval is recent, its effects are already being felt in the commercial, banking, industrial, educational and private sectors. A viable national network may emerge in the near future. Meanwhile, new databases, online services, attempts at resource sharing and the adoption of MARC tapes for information storage and retrieval remain the first and most important steps towards this.

According to a 1981 CLADES report, Chile's profile is as follows. Major information sectors, private, non-profit, state or semi-public, are mostly located in Santiago and serve researchers, university students and teaching staff. Most requests are in education, economics, general culture or scientific research. Interlibrary loan services are better organized than selective dissemination of information; most budgets are below minimum standards, and although manpower is sufficient, little of it is professionally trained. Collections are inadequate, due to low budgets and lack of effective acquisition guidelines, and there are only a few union catalogs of periodicals. Salaries for even the best qualified information experts and librarians are below the averages of many other South American nations and chances for promotion and continuing education are poor (CLADES 1982).

LATIN AMERICA AND THE TRANSFER OF KNOWLEDGE: BETWEEN INFORMATION FREEDOM AND INFORMATION DEPENDENCY

One Culture and the Information Professional

In 1959, C.P. Snow's *The Two Cultures* claimed that scientists were not sufficiently appreciated by society and that there was a dangerous split (particularly in England) between the literary/humanistic and the scientific communities: a thesis raising questions on the nature and implications of such divisiveness in modern Western societies.

Educational systems in Latin America continue to give priority to humanistic subjects, creating an artificial separation between those nurtured in the world of pure imagination—the subjective expressions of man—and those trained to think systematically—the more objective, logical methods of scientific inquiry. No matter how artificial or unfounded this division, it creates a schism cutting across all disciplines, reflecting differences in the way educational and informational purposes are perceived; differences in the way the world is understood, and, above all, differences in the way individuals (including information professionals) view their obligation to society.

In the United States, a greater emphasis on the inter-disciplinary nature of knowledge (spearheaded most recently by memory storage and the synthesizing capabilities of new information technologies and some important adjustments between specialization and broader liberal arts offerings), has resulted not only in a greater dialogue between the two intellectual worlds but in a language with the potential of defining common purposes. The humanistic-derived societies of Latin America distrust technological advances as imper-sonal and unrelated to existing human conditions. But to es-cape economic and cultural dependency they must adapt and respond to these advances. Their educational leaders must seek a new humanistic paradigm. International political and cultural cooperation and the sharing of insights among various disciplines offer the information professional a holis-tic, "one culture" approach to knowledge, and the challenge to become a new cornerstone in information transfer, a "comprehensivist in an age of specialists."

The Role of Modern Innovations: Towards a More Positive View of Technological Progress

> The machine itself makes no demands and holds no promises: it is the human spirit that makes demands and keeps promises.
>
> Lewis Mumford

Humans resist change; strong resentment against the ascendance of technology is not new. It is seen as having become a significant political factor in its own right and and alienating force run amok rather than an act of will. Its consequences may be unforseen, even adverse; automobiles bring parking problems, traffic jams, pollution, accidents.

The computer age has created the "information over-load syndrome," not to mention frustrations of "down time" or "noise," tasteless "menus" and the intrigues of electronic espionage, theft and infringements on individual privacy by power elites. But solutions to misuse evolve. From the invention of the wheel to space flight, man has been capable of expanding his choices, even when such changes have meant dislocations in time. People have always had the gift of transcending their limitations to cope with change and the tyranny of progress.

Socrates dissociated himself from the scientific interests of his predecessors by emphasizing the primacy of human issues. Questions about society, ethics and human relationships preoccupied Erasmus, Montaigne, Harvey, and Galileo. At a time of far reaching scientific discovery, Jonathan Swift wrote savage caricatures of the Royal Society and what he considered irrelevant research subjects. The Faust legend characterizes the present dilemma: Goethe develops his character as an old scholar who yearns to comprehend not so much all knowledge as all *experience*. Faust embodies what most people wish to hear from the angels: "He who exerts himself in constant striving, him we can save."

Scientific and technological striving, so peculiar to United States society, has influenced the world. Economic, strategic and cultural forces such as the English language have transformed whole regions into clusters of its satellites. Effects on Latin America include the transfer of scholarly, scientific and technical information. A technological monopoly flows north-south, causing social disruption, professional insecurity and constant bitterness among the under-privileged whom progress barely touches. Many Latin American information professionals view the situation with distrust, doubtful whether technological advances accepted in the United States should be adopted or even adapted in their own countries.

Contemporary counter-cultures see technology as deterministic. Jacques Ellul (1964), Lewis Mumford (1970), René Dubois (1968), Charles Reich (1970), Theodore Roszak (1972) and others have been eloquent about the demonology of technical progress, creating new dogmas as dangerous as those they condemn. Their argument that technical innovations tend to pursue their own course independent of man, dehumanizing his environment, have propagated an anti-technological atmosphere: a typical humanistic distrust of anything highly efficient, sophisticated and controlling.

If there has been some dehumanization, there have also been many instances to the contrary. The choice is ours. If we face today the problem of too many people wanting too many things, the cause is not technology, but the type of creature man is. The demand by the masses for greater dignity, comfort, choice of lifestyle and access to information seems overwhelming, but already in most advanced countries we find the average citizen with more freedom than was possible in earlier ages. Exploitation of the masses *decreases* with technological advance.

Information Professionals and Politicians: Precise versus Imprecise Language

> Political language has to consist largely of euphemism, question begging, and sheer cloudy vagueness ... political speech and writing are largely the defense of the indefensible.

George Orwell, 1946

Historically, politics and information flow share an uneasy relationship. This springs largely from the use of language itself, particularly in the international ambiguity of political rhetoric. While politics relies on the imprecise use of words, the information professional seeks to convey exact meanings through the elaboration of precise vocabularies.

Ambiguous language is used to disconcert; specific meanings to resolve. Politicians use generalities to talk about specific events, information professionals use specific data to enlighten a broader need or request. This issue of ambiguity versus precision illuminates the entire problem of information transfer. Language has to adapt to the pragmatic nature of political decisions and the fluidity and interdisciplinary nature of knowledge. Honesty of language is the ideal but history has repeatedly shown that while people wish their politicians to be honest, they seem not to expect them to be so: politics so often depends on the ability to deceive. Communication of information and ideas, nationally and internationally, has to take place within this cleavage of values.

Information, Politics and Some Moral Imperatives

> Leadership of social trends is not a common or natural characteristics of [our] profession.
>
> Maurice Line

Information and politics are inextricably tied by historical imperatives: neither can exist without the other. Information illuminates the political process from every angle, whilst politics is a force directed toward problem-solving, exploiting information in a narrower, self-serving context. Information can help us make moral judgements, but something in the nature of government makes its leaders resistant to moral values. With better access to information perhaps they could make better decisions. For this the information professional's responsibility is one of support: to organize, retrieve and preserve information for politicians to use for good or ill.

It is hard to determine accurately how the transmission of ideas affects man's actions. The impact of paper and printing as democratic media is well documented, but that of the new electronic inventions is still being explored; they persuade, and shape attitudes, in their own subtle ways, contributing to the acquisition of knowledge that will direct man toward, not the "pursuit" but the "attainment," of happiness. For the Latin American masses, unfortunately, this promised life remains the fragment of a broken dream.

If Latin America's destiny is for Latin Americans to decide, then moral questions about human misery, fragmentation of learning and lack of freedom must be addresses and resolved; information professionals cannot escape the political process to which they belong and which nurtures them: their social responsibility is to facilitate access to information to those who need it most.

Government decision-makers, in the turmoil of *Realpolitik*, view power as the dominant factor and equate information with power: they need it to function and govern. Most information environments are secondary support systems for the functioning of government, education or research. Information professionals, with limited access to the power elite, approach the political world uneasily. Lack of aggressiveness, timidity of social concern and a failure to define our mission has given us a negative image and relegated us to the periphery of the managerial and financial fringes of power. Naming major political or literary figures to important library positions in Latin America has had its advantages: they can interact more effectively with those who govern.

Information professionals, north and south, should link forces, become more visible and involved in the political process, making our voices stronger and our expertise recognized and used. But more political lobbying is not enough. Ortega y Gasset admonished librarians as early as 1934 to become a "filter interposed between man and the torrent of books" (Ortega y Gasset 1935). Even the greatest research facilities are not used to half their potential, demonstrating the inefficacy of too much information gathering. The "information overload" syndrome threatens the very foundations of our communication system by interfering with efforts to maximize the utility of recorded knowledge, and information professionals are best suited to understand and handle it, acting as intelligent gatekeepers between the information needed and the surfeit.

The politics of information is a vital ingredient of the management of human affairs. Latin American information professionals need to concentrate on minimal and essential information, avoiding the information wasteland of post-industrial societies. Less is more. Forcing too much information on nations that can make no effective use of it has led to misunderstanding the nature and future application of large volumes of information. Reducing technological gaps would not necessarily improve social conditions. Lack of synchronization between the pace of technological advance and the adaptability of people to it has created social and psychological dislocations.

Let us understand the nuances, subtleties and pressures of our social and political processes and adopt a professional ethic that will assure our citizens access to information at the right time, displaying sensitivity of the many ways this information can be provided. To do less would be to relinquish our mission and to play into the hands of the information multipliers who obstruct the access to essential educational and research activities.

Finally come the questions of who controls information and how. Given a propitious combination of trained personnel and technological know-how, would the application of new library automation techniques suffice to develop appropriate national information systems? I fear that, while print and paper remain the democratic medium *par excellence*, electronic communication (as recent news blackouts in Argentina and Poland suggest) will be used by power elites, undermining the transfer of all types of information. Might not universal bibliographic control through the standardization of information carriers lead to electronically stored databases used for totalitarian purposes? The basis of democracy is the transfer of information; the basis of totalitarianism is control.

The library profession has always been more preoccupied with the recording of physical entities than with intellectual content. The vision of Otlet and LaFontaine at the turn of the century, taken up by UNESCO and the Library of Congress after World War II, led on to the 1961 international Paris conference on cataloging principles, AACR of 1967 and to the International Standard Bibliographic Description of 1971. The cumulation now appears to be a worldwide exchange and standardization of scientific information sponsored by UNESCO'S UNISIST and the distribution of MARC tapes. Standardization is crucial but we should be cautious in its application. Cultural differences, for instance, need to be taken into account.

The cybernetic revolution has ushered in a new phase of human progress, but the problems created by rapid transmission of knowledge without personal contact have to be confronted. Face to face communication and the rich texture of the Spanish and Portuguese languages remain a vital aspect of human interchange in Latin America.

Information must not become the domain of a few "experts." The responsibility of information professionals is forcefully to extricate information from political influence, creating a market for information systems and services that will guarantee the free flow of knowledge in all directions, and across all disciplines and national boundaries.

The Flow of Information across National Boundaries: Between Information Freedom and Information Dependency

> The uniformization of cultures and their times would mean a perpetuation, even an exacerbation, of the factors that have contributed to the difficulty of life in our age...
>
> Carlos Fuentes

Latin America and the United States are opposites, brought together by geographic imperative into rather uncomfortable alliance. Despite cultural and political differences, they need to work toward common goals. Political and social changes will have constant and unforseen impacts on the transfer of scholarly, scientific and technical information between them. Carlos Fuentes, with keen intuition, suggests the core of the dilemma:

> ...the re-emergence of cultures as an expression of dissatisfaction with the synthetic quality of ... ideologies ..., the sacrifices imposed by the indiscriminate rush toward the dogmatic values of the future and progress..., the internal tension with the cultures themselves between the technocratic, multinational demands of the so-called global village (in reality a very tiny, if far-flung, village, containing a small minority of mankind) and the assertion of local differences, regionalisms, decentralizations and subcultures... (Fuentes 1982)

The question of the legitimacy of information transfer is related to real versus perceived information needs: vast pools of information (international databases) forced on limited information systems, creating the illusion that mere possession of it can bring progress and prosperity. *The transfer of knowledge needs to happen within an exchange that speaks not of development and underdevelopment but of co-*

development, of human potential, of the subtle relation between human records and learning, within an infrastructure that still speaks of libraries as social systems rather than information systems *per se*. Information transfer, the sharing of knowledge, should be used, not to control man, but to liberate the mind and improve the human condition.

Latin America still has to cope with the basic information needs of the masses regarding family life, health and education, to permit them more active and creative roles in society. Suddenly a spectre of interconnection has emerged, where no one is left alone or left out.

We cannot have a fair exchange of information between Latin America and the United States. With its shift toward knowledge-producing occupations and the systematic expansion of research, the latter has created a conglomerate of repositories, aptly described by George Steiner as "the archives of Eden," that give it global control over the organization, transmission and preservation of knowledge. Many Latin American archives are now in United States collections, forcing scholars there to pursue their investigations.

Besides scientific and scholarly underdevelopment and dependence, Latin America suffers a "brain drain" due to low salaries, lack of suitable job opportunities, insufficient intellectual stimulus and political instability. Such factors have weakened research creativity and will continue to produce professional dissatisfaction and misunderstandings about the functions of a need for scholarly productivity.

All these issues are variations on the theme of national information policies. International exchange of knowledge depends on the commitment of each nation to implementing viable national information programs, which, taken together, can govern, with some degree of success, the international flow of information.

The Industrial Revolution introduced radical changes in work patterns, modes of transportation, habitats, leisure time, individual expression and politics. This experience shows us how mankind takes the best of an experience and directs it toward a future that, in due time, becomes our own. The Information Age has its own hosts of angels and demons. But we can still look forward toward an improved future in our continent—one in which the transfer of knowledge beyond national boundaries will play an important if not central role—without seeking the uniformization or control of our diverse cultures.

REFERENCES

1) Academia de Ciencias. Corporación de Promoción Universitaria. *Una visión de la comunidad científica nacional: las actividades de investigación y desarrollo en Chile.* Santiago: CPU; 1982. [2 v.].

2) Analysis de la realidad. *El Mercurio*; March 18, 1982:C-3.

3) Asheim, Lester. Ortega revisited. *Library quarterly*; July 1982; 52(3):216–226.

4) Burgos M., Alejandro; Gomez F., Héctor. Bases de dados bibliográficos en Chile: un alternativa para la búsquada de información. *Trilogía-Ciencia-Técnica-Espiritu*; 2:3037. [Instituto Professional de Santiago, 1982]. [ISSN 0716–0356].

5) Canas C., Raul; Gasman, Marilyn. La investigación cientifica chilena en el contexto internacional. *Cuadernos del Consejo de Rectores de las Universidades Chilenas*; May/August 1982; 17:1–28. [ISSN 0716–0577].

6) Ciencia nacional no es poca ni nula. *Últimas noticias*; June 26, 1982:30.

7) CLADES. *La infraestructura de información para el desarrollo de América Latina y el Caribe.* Santiago: CEPAL; 1981.

8) Dessarrollo cientifico es un problema de seguridad nacional. *La Tercera*; May 12, 1982:37.

9) Desarollo científico. *El Mercurio*; November 12, 1982:A-3.

10) Dubois, René Jules. *So human an animal.* New York: Scribners; 1968.

11) Ellul, Jacques. *The technological society.* New York: Knopf; 1964.

12) Freudenthal, Juan; Gomez F., Héctor. *Toward a national information network in Chile.* [Paper contributed at SALALM, 27th, Washington, March 1982.] [To be published as a monography by SALALM.]

13) Fuentes, Carlos. Writing in time. *Democracy*; January 1982; 2(1):61-72.

14) Fuentes, Carlos. Mending U.S.-Latin relations. *Boston Globe*; July 18, 1982:69,72.

15) Gran paso para la ciencia en la actual situación. *El Mercurio*; June 13, 1982:C-5.

16) Igor Saavedra: premio nacional de ciencias 1981. *CRECES*; 1982; 2(10):29-34.

17) *El Mercurio*; June 1, 1980:D-5, D-6.

18) Mumford, Lewis. *Myth of the machine. 1: Technics and human development.* New York: Harcourt, Brace and World; 1967.

19) Mumford, Lewis. *Myth of the machine. 2: The pentagon of power.* New York: Harcourt, Brace Jovanovich; 1970.

20) Negme, Amador. Literatura científica. In: *Curso: literatura científica en el area bio-médica.* Santiago: Vicerrectoria de Extensión y comunicación de la Universidad de Chile; 1980.

21) Orrego Vicuña, Fernando. Universidades: entre la libertad y el miedo. *El Mercurio*; October 19, 1982:A-2.

22) Ortega y Gasset, José. Misión del bibliotecario. *Revista del occidente* 47/48 (1935), translated by James Lewis and Ray Carpenter as The mission of the librarian. *Antioch Review*; Summer 1961; 2(2):33–54. [Reprinted: Boston: Hall; 1961].

23) Plan de becas para doctorados en Chile. *El Mercurio*; April 25, 1982:C-3.

24) Reich, Charles Alan. *The greening of America: how the youth revolution is trying to make America viable.* New York: Random House; 1970.

25) Roszak, Theodore. *Where the wasteland ends.* Garden City, New Jersey: Doubleday; 1972.

26) Saavedra, Igor. *Ciencia y universidad: corporación de estudios contemporáneos.* Santiago: Edimpress; 1979.

27) Saavedra, Igor. La investigación cientifica en Chile. *Cuadernos del Consejo de Rectores de las Universidades de Chile*; May/August 1982; 17:44–55.

UNITED STATES INFORMATION POLICY AND ITS RELATION TO LATIN AMERICA AND THE CARIBBEAN

by
Victor Rosenberg
School of Library Science
University of Michigan
Ann Arbor, MI

RESUMEN

La Política de Información de los Estados Unidos y su
Relación con America Latina y el Caribe

Las políticas de informacion de los Estados Unidos pueden
ser caracterizadas como "fragmentadas y no bien coor-
dinadas." El intercambio libre de información e ideas es
promovido, pero restricciones están siendo desarrolladas.
Estas restricciones están dirigidas hacia la circulacion de información y tecnología a realisticos y potenciales adversarios
para otros paises que son o pueden ser competidores
economicos en información y servicio que puede tener valor
comercial.

Generalmente, las políticas de Estados Unidos son
manejadas por concernimientos economicos y siguen una
política de comercio extraterritorial. No se han hecho distin-

ciones de política entre paises en desarrollo y paises desarrollados. Mientras que America Latina no está aislada para
tratamiento especial está sujecta a los effectos de la politíca
de Estados Unidos. Estos effectos incluyen el enlargamiento
del vacio entre los que tienen acceso a la información, tecnologías y servicios y aquellos que no lo tienen. Esto impide
el flujo o circulación de informaciones cientificas y tecnológicas entre los investigadores. La tecnología del
microcomputador mas barato y los precios que rebajan en
los sistemas de telecomunicaciones pueden poner productos
al alcanze de los investigadoes, particularmente en los paises
de desarrollo y pueden ayudar a sobrellevar las numerosas
barreras en la circulacion de informacion científica y tecnológica.

The policies of the United States with regard to information flows are fragmented and not well coordinated. Some may well argue that the United States has no policy at all. As in most countries information policies are made to coincide with national self interest. Until recently the rhetoric of free trade has been backed up by policy. The United States continues to advocate the free exchange of information and ideas, but is slowly moving toward some restriction on such policy.

The United States remains the largest net exporter of information products and services and so it is in the interest of the United States to have the flow of information between nations as unrestricted as possible. There are increasing pressures for the Government to change this position and to impose more restrictions on information flow. In the past it did not matter much whether information was allowed to flow unimpeded to all corners of the world. With the exception of military or governmental secrets, most information was not useable against the interest of the United States. Even if the entire blueprints of a factory became available to a foreign competitor, the information was relatively useless because no country had the industrial infrastructure to make use of the information effectively. Now, however, it is becoming widely recognized that industrial information is extremely valuable and that other countries can not only make use of the information, but they can set up competing enterprises that can operate at a competitive advantage. Against this backdrop there are increasing pressures upon the government to halt the free flow of information that many see as a onesided flow that threatens the economic position of the United States.

In the debate on information policy, little or no attention is paid to the nature of the information that is being disseminated. When the director of the United States National Security Agency, Admiral B. Inman identified the outflow of scientific and technical information as a hemorrhage, it stirred a furor in American academic circles. Since this time the rhetoric has subsided somewhat, but the concerns are stronger than ever.

AREAS OF CONTROL

Essentially, there are three areas where controls on information are sought. The first is the restriction of information flow to real and potential adversaries. This is usually seen as the restriction of information and high technology equipment from going to the Soviet Union or its allies. The second area of restriction is the flow of information to countries that might use the information to compete with the United States. The Third area is the restrictions on the flow of information products and services that have commercial value. It is the second and third areas that have the most impact on the flows of information between North and South America.

The area of information policy that has seen the greatest activity is that of defense related technological information. The government is making an effort to restrict what it sees as information potentially valuable to an enemy. Computer software is one area where this activity has focused. The Defense Department has been trying to put greater and greater restrictions on the flow of computer software abroad. Currently all exports of software must be registered with the government. This policy is directly at odds with the government's avowed policy of encouraging exports to provide a favorable balance of payments. The result is one branch of government working to increase high technology exports and another branch working to restrict such exports.

TRADE POLICIES

For the most part, American policy makers are more concerned with the restrictions that are put in place by other nations. Increasingly, barriers on information flow are seen as restrictions on United States trade and are thus opposed by the Government. As such, information policy has followed the general outlines of trade policy. The Reagan Administration has been slow to react to the demands for increased restrictions on trade in the form of import duties and quotas. It has been similarly slow to react to the calls for increased restrictions on information flows coming into the United States. Part of the inaction has been due to this deliberate policy and part has been due to the confusion over jurisdictions in the area of information. Within the government the locus of information policy responsibility has been hard to determine. Several departments of the government have been claiming information as an area of responsibility.

Although it may be assumed that the American Government has no particular reason to deny technology to Latin America and the Caribbean, the region must necessarily suffer in the process. Controls on export of information technology have not distinguished between the developing and the developed world.

The developing nations of Latin America and the Caribbean for their part are making every effort to become independent of their northern neighbors. Brazil in particular has been firm in restricting the import of computers of the type that are manufactured in Brazil. Unlike any other industry, Brazilian computer firms must be 100% owned by Brazilians. The result so far has been a proliferation of companies that copy the designs of popular microcomputers. Eventually, it is hoped that these companies will have enough experience to develop superior designs locally. Although many experts inside and outside of Brazil predict that this restrictive policy will result in less rather than more technological development, the leaders of the industry and government are adamant about retaining the policies. Those who oppose the policy argue that it is the application of computer technology not the technology itself that is most important.

POLICY EFFECTS

The end result of the policies on both sides is a widening gap in the areas of information technology. Rather than bringing the countries closer in scientific and technological achievement, the polices are pushing them farther apart. It is sad to see the United States begin to put a computer in every classroom, while even the most sophisticated sectors of other economies do without. It suggests depressing prospects. This information technology gap makes it increasingly difficult for scholars to exchange information in the same way they do with their domestic colleagues.

At the same time there is some cause for hope. The cost of computer technology is coming down rapidly and the power of the smaller inexpensive computers is rising with equal rapidity. This means that in many areas the absolute cost of information technology is falling and coming within the reach of more and more people in the less developed world. The telecommunications technologies are also coming down in price and these offer greater opportunities for access to world wide systems.

Although there are many barriers to the flow of scholarly information between North and South America, the most significant barriers appear to be economic. Without the resources to purchase the acquired technology and the information itself, the countries of Latin America and the Caribbean will continue to have difficulty in fully participating in the information interchange of scholars.

THE DEVELOPMENT OF INTEGRATED INFORMATION POLICIES WITH SPECIAL REFERENCE TO THE ENGLISH-SPEAKING CARIBBEAN

by Alma Jordan
University of the West Indies
St. Augustine, Trinidad

RESUMEN

El Desarrollo de Políticas de Información
con Referencia Especial al Caribe de Habla Inglesa

El artículo tiene cuatro partes; en las dos primeras se presenta información de índole introductoria y de trasfondo. Se considera primero la situación del mundo y la importacia de la información, especialmente para el desarrollo socio-económico de los países en desarrollo. Se presentan las posibilidades de la transferencia informática en el contexto de sistemas de información regionales e internacionales y con respeto a su dependencia de sistemas nacionales e infraestructuras.

La segunda parte se enfoca en el clima informático en el Caribe con respeto a la información científica e técnica, la cooperación regional en la informática, y los patrones actuales de la transferencia de información con utilización mínima de las tecnologícas nuevas.

En la tercera parte se considera el asunto complejo de la política de la información. Se presentan doce áreas de la política informática que hay que tomar en cuenta, y se considera las necesidades nacionales y regionales del Caribe con respeto a las políticas internacionales pertinentes.

La cuarta parte desarrolla el tesis de que la diversidad de conceptos, terminología, programas mundiales y áun de la profesión, han servido para oscurecer los asuntos, confundir a los que crean políticas, y detener el crecimiento de una política informática integrada mundial. Para controlar el futuro, hay que crear nuevas iniciativas regionales e internacionales armónicas. Incluye bibliografía.

SCOPE AND LIMITATIONS OF THE PAPER

This paper focuses on the requisites for, and obstacles to, the formulation of national information policy in the Caribbean, and the harmonization and possible integration of this with regional and international policies. It is largely limited to a review of the existing literature, although it also speculates about the future.

INTRODUCTION

The Information Era

Even outside the widening circle of those directly involved as professionals in the "information revolution," few have failed to hear its "rumbling" or to remain untouched by the "avalanche" that has slowly followed, threatening to engulf us all in its cataclysmic dimensions. Superlatives abound and a whole new vocabulary is in the making as we grapple with this unmanageable, yet not wholly unwelcome harbinger of change. English parallels to the French "informatique" and "télématique" have yet to be widely accepted, but there is no doubt that the computer and telecommunications have ushered in an increased awareness of "the new information era", "the information society" and "the information economy" (Viken 1982).

Information for Development and the Developing Countries

It is difficult to reach a single satisfactory definition of the concept of information (Parker 1982, Rowley 1978, Viken 1982) but its dramatic social and economic impact is widely recognized. It is an industry in which Marc Porat's classic study found nearly half the American workforce already engaged (Neustadt 1979). Its essential role in government, decision making and development leads to the view that its effect on the developing countries may be "more acute than the usual North-South situation" (Viken 1982). The Third World has clamored for strategies to correct the resulting imbalance (Sardar 1980). Information systems for technology transfer (Page 1978), patterns in transborder information flow and international coordination of information services (Page 1980) have all been studied in this and wider contexts.

World Information Systems: UNISIST and NATIS

Although scientific and technical information has been especially favored (as promoting development), efforts have been made to cope with information availability for users at all levels of society, notably through Unesco's initiatives to develop information organization and use in all forms. Its UNISIST, or World Science Information System, concentrated on an ideal global system for access to scientific and technical information, while the broader NATIS program included the social sciences, focusing on a total approach to information sources and users in information for development as a whole.

Concurrent use of both concepts has detracted from the all-embracing PGI idea. Preference for UNISIST— UNISIST II Conference occurred in 1979, while plans for a second NATIS Conference were quietly abandoned—has caused confusion at government levels and within the profession itself.

Role of National Systems and Infrastructure

International cooperation depends on an adequate national infrastructure (Intergovernmental Conference... 1979, Unesco. UNISIST... 1971). A 1972 report to United States AID recommended that it "give primary attention to developing and strengthening appropriate information infrastructures of these countries" (Unesco. UNISIST... 1971).

Definitions

Caribbean region

The paper relates to the Commonwealth Caribbean (Antigua and Barbuda, Barbados, Belize, Dominica, Grenada, Guyana, Jamaica, Montserrat, St. Christopher-Nevis, St. Lucia, St. Vincent and the Grenadines, and Trinidad and Tobago), countries sharing a common socio-economic heritage which have continuously struggled towards unity and a shared regional identity. The West Indies Federation lasted only four years but CARICOM provides links in trade, health, education, and the like, and since 1981 all but Barbados, Belize, Guyana, and Trinidad and Tobago have participated in OECS. Information is one of the areas where formulation of joint regional policies is under way.

Information

Scholarly information includes scientific and technical information, while the latter has broadened in scope to embrace all information pertinent to social and economic development, the sense in which scientific and technical information still be used in this paper.

INFORMATION CLIMATE OF THE CARIBBEAN

Historical Review

Pre- and post-1960

The limited early literature on information services in the Caribbean is descriptive surveys (Bateson 1945, Savage 1934) with similar recommendations: enlarged units, better buildings and increased support. A 1960 survey (Jordan 1970) found services still poor in all but the three largest MDCs. The LDCs had virtually no libraries except public libraries, and these had only just begun free service, boosted by an externally-funded regional agency which became defunct. Special libraries were seldom properly organized:

> With the exception of the six most developed special libraries in Trinidad, four in Jamaica and a scattered few ambitious ventures, the typical small collection ... accumulated haphazardly, is indifferently housed and is tended periodically by a clerk (or higher ranking employee on the general staff) or is completely neglected and disorganized (Jordan 1970).

The 1970s: impact of NATIS and information service concepts

Although UNISIST I of 1971 had minimal impact, a flurry of activity followed the 1974 NATIS Conference and a resultant NATIS workshop for the Caribbean was sponsored by Unesco and JLS. The logical NATIS concept of pooling all a country's archival, library and documentation centers suggested an economy of operation that governments could appreciate. Two 1977 conferences are notable for their concern to identify user needs and plan services accordingly.

Although few of their papers reported results of formal research, their discussions of the information needs of specific user groups, of marketing strategies and of the conscious development of outreach services were a breakthrough (Armstrong 1978, Collins 1978, Nunes 1977). Also in 1977, the IDRC-sponsored Inventory of Information and Documentation for Development was done by CLADES in several countries "to carry out a diagnosis at the national and regional level to stimulate activities for the strengthening and integration of these services, which are indispensable in the handling of information for development (Information and documentation... 1978).

The 1980s

Scientific and technical information in the region: national level

The background paper prepared for the 1980 Unesco Consultation on the Coordinated Development of National Information Systems in the region outlines the information infrastructure (Consultation on the Coordinated... The present... 1980). The LDCs have shown improvement in public and school libraries but in sectoral information have hardly advanced from the 1960s: "science and technology information is virtually non-existent in any organized setting except for Geological Survey Department libraries" (Consultation on the Coordinated... The present... 1980). Scientific and technical information is better in the MDCs: both Cuba and the Dominican Republic (included in this survey) have noteworthy agencies; Jamaica and Trinidad have networking plans. Since then particular progress has been made in Barbados and Grenada.

Barbados

Michael Chandler observed that "...Barbados where neither agriculture nor science boasts an organized library (except for scientific fields covered in the UWI main library) ... is probably typical of the Caribbean" (Chandler 1979–80). Two years later, Carl Keren, finding "no information services in the modern sense," held that "little is known about the potential users ... [nor] about what types of information are needed urgently and which can wait ..." (Keren 1982) but within a year of his report BLAIN was established and planning the use of modern information retrieval systems (Bretney 1983). The existence of a National Council for Science and Technology and the newer NACOLADS should facilitate scientific and technical information provision.

Grenada

A comprehensive national information system development plan in 1981 (Collins 1981) followed a government-requested Unesco mission. Lack of personnel and funds has so far precluded more than an embryonic documentation center, but the networking concept has been adopted with participation in the regional system mounted by ECLA's Caribbean office.

Guyana

Knee (1976) has described the information activities of Guyana's NSRC (established 1972). A scientific and technical information network has been proposed, based on existing informal cooperation. An ad hoc committee of the Guyana Library Association has proposed a National Commission on Information Services and a Unesco consultant has reported on developing an agricultural information network (Arboleda-Sepúlveda 1981).

Jamaica

Despite the 1960 creation of Jamaica's SRC, the scientific and technical information picture in NACOLADS' 1978 survey was of patchy collections and services inadequately staffed (Jamaica 1978) but its development plan has resulted in the STIN, whose range of activities is already impressive. Further development can be confidently expected.

Trinidad and Tobago

Trinidad's NCTD began in 1968 as the National Scientific Advisory Council. A 1979 White Paper (Trinidad and Tobago. White paper... 1977) on a National Institute of Higher Education (Research, Science and Technology) identified information as among the scientific and technical services given scant attention in the past. A scientific and technical information survey has just been completed but its results are not yet available.

Less Developed Countries

The small LDCs with agriculture-based economies have usually had no scientific and technical policy bodies and have lacked the access to scientific and technical information needed for development.

Regional Cooperation for Information

Caribbean Community Secretariat

CARICOM has taken a lively interest in regional information services, sponsoring a 1979 survey of the LDCs

(CARICOM. Survey... 1979) and, more recently, a study of regional information flows (Wiltshire 1982). Their librarian has also served as a Unesco consultant for many of the LDC plans prepared.

Economic Commission for Latin America

ECLA's CDCC is the region's most significant agency for both science and technology and information. Governments have supported its programs enthusiastically and shown clear perception of the importance of information. CDCC/ECLA is the secretariat of the very effective Caribbean Council for Science and Technology. *CARISPLAN Abstracts* based on input from all planning ministries appears regularly and a machine database now exists. CDCC's Caribbean Documentation Centre coordinates the information system, offers training programs and advisory services and has actively promoted national information systems in the LDCs.

Association of Caribbean Universities and Research Institutes

Besides organizing a Commission on Science and Technology, UNICA has contributed by sponsoring the first conference of Caribbean librarians in 1969. This created ACURIL, a pioneer of regional cooperation with a membership including libraries of all types and extending to Florida. Among the results of the professional contacts fostered by ACURIL and SALALM was the erstwhile linking of the UWI Trinidad with the George Mason University for database searching.

University of the West Indies

The three campus libraries of the University of the West Indies have provided outreach information services to

the wider Caribbean. The one in Trinidad has been particularly involved in agricultural information, being proposed
as the CDCC's Caribbean Information System's subregional
focal point for this sector.

Caribbean Agricultural Research and Development Institute

The Trinidad-based CARDI (1975) also provides outreach services in agricultural information, including a literature service (CARDLIS) aided with IDRC funding.

Caribbean Development Bank

The CDB works closely with regional organizations to
promote integration. Its TIS has established close links with
NTIS whose publications it makes available (CDB. Annual
Report... 1982), and its Technology and Energy Unit has
also been active in information dissemination.

Current Information Transfer Patterns

The recent CARICOM study of information and communication flow had three main objectives:

(1) "to identify the major problems being encountered with
respect to scientific and technological information ... in
priority areas of science and technology";

(2) "to determine the degree of interaction among agencies
and personnel in CARICOM countries involved with
science and technology";

(3) to identify "gaps in the information infrastructure"
(Wiltshire 1982).

The report showed that lack of information on existing resources hampers information transfer within the region and from outside; it suggests that existing services publicize their capabilities in a concerted program.

Hardcopy Acquisition Problems

A 1977 study on interlibrary lending corroborates some of these findings. There is little interaction between library and information service units at the regional level. Lacking union lists, research libraries rely almost wholly on foreign sources. ACURIL conferences have concerned themselves with the difficulties of acquiring locally published material, but not material from the developed countries. One all-pervading problem is slow mail delivery.

Awareness of the importance for development of adequate information infrastructures has grown in the 1980s but "critical shortcomings" still exist, particularly "the absence of national policy which places information as a vital resource in the development process." But "failure to define a policy might be due in part to the difficulty in defining information—even among its specialists—in a way that allows it to be conceptualized by government planners" (Consultation on the... The Present... 1980)—a diagnosis that strikes at the root of the problem.

TOWARDS INTEGRATED NATIONAL, REGIONAL AND INTERNATIONAL INFORMATION POLICIES

Information Policy

The need for "national information policies" is the cornerstone of Unesco programs and recurs in regional consultations and meetings and elsewhere in the literature (Anthony 1982, Bushkin 1979).

Alma Jordan — 61

There seem unfortunately to be no single or simple
definitions or concise but all-embracing enunciations of the
specific areas to be covered in formulating an information
policy, partly because the subject has many ramifications
(Brown 1982), and definitions in this area are subject to
variations and ambiguities.

Guidelines

Two Unesco information policy guidelines, UNISIST's
Information Policy Objectives (1974) (Unesco. UNISIST...
1974) and NATIS's *Information Policy* (1976) (Unesco.
NATIS... 1976) demonstrate the problem. The first focuses
on information "as a resource and an instrument for shaping
of government policies, scientific and technical development..."; it seems to be aimed at the professional and stresses the need for a national agency or focal point "to guide,
stimulate and coordinate the development of information
resources and services in the perspective of national,
regional and mondial cooperation" (Unesco. UNISIST...
1974). It goes on to enumerate these responsibilities:
developing scientific library resources, assessing user needs,
and information transfer through networking. The latter
document, however, framed in the broader NATIS context,
is clearly addressed to decision makers outside the profession. Recognizing that the "scientific information problem is
only part of the total information problem" (Unesco.
NATIS... 1976), it takes a much more general and user-
oriented view. Yet both purport to guide the formulation of
"information policy."

Information for national development

Despite such inconsistencies, there is wide acceptance
of the relation between access to information and the

process of national development planning and progress. "The aim of a national information policy can be stated briefly as to identify the information requirements of the country and to ensure that they are satisfied as fully, promptly, cheaply and conveniently as scarce resources allow" (Gray 1979).

Policy development and needs: planning and research

Information planning is an essential part of development and requires

(1) Identifying and setting up the appropriate planning and coordinating bodies, centers and/or mechanisms.

> "Ideally the coordinating body should be executive but in view of the wide ramifications of the information system it will usually be impossible to make it executive with regard to all information activities. However, to the extent that it is advisory, the coordinating body should not be subservient to any minister or government department either as regards the subjects it considers or the dissemination of the results of its deliberations" (Unesco. UNISIST... 1971).

> Size and composition are all-important and John Gray (1979) stresses the need for providing it with sufficient resources.

(2) Identification of potential users in different sectors and at all levels of society and detailed assessment of their information needs. Distinction between needs, wants and demands (1978) and due regard for potential users are critical.

(3) Surveying available library and information resources and services, assessing their capabilities to match user

needs and evaluating actual information flow and flow failure, *analytically*: not mere description.

(4) Developing phased and detailed plans of action, and an implementation program to establish/perfect the infrastructure to service all information needs defined in a coordinated system, with appropriate regional and international links.

CARIBBEAN PATTERNS AND NEEDS

The pace of Caribbean development, especially in Jamaica and Barbados, has quickened since 1980, but no detailed analytical studies of user needs appear to have been done, although the CARICOM report (Wiltshire 1982), the CDCC 1977 conference papers (Regional Cooperation... 1978) and some recent LDC consultation reports provide some description of such needs.

Trinidad is an interesting case for closer study. Despite early development and its large number of special libraries, it has lagged behind Jamaica and Barbados in creating a coordinating mechanism.

Promoting Primary Source Publishing

The new technology has created machine readable and other new publication forms, while the region's oral traditions give nonprint materials special importance, hence the National Library of Jamaica's current promotion of local history programs and, on a smaller scale, that of the University of West Indies Library, St. Augustine.

Local book publishing could be promoted more. Few of the recommendations of Trinidad's International Book Year Seminar report (Stockham 1975) have borne fruit. A subcenter of Unesco's CERLAL for the English-speaking Caribbean is a possibility to explore. Local music publishing, printed and recorded, is another area with special problems.

Thanks largely to Unesco's UBC program of the 1970s, the region has four regularly published national bibliographies, but legal deposit, especially of non-book materials, needs improving. CARICOM is producing a regional bibliography, including some LDC imprints.

Developing and Managing Material Resources

National policy must include the identification of national resource centers responsible for extensive collecting of local and foreign literature in a field and for developing relationships with similar centers abroad for interlibrary loan purposes. Each such center must plan to fill gaps in its own resources and seek to rationalize acquisitions nationally for efficient resource management. Special attention must be paid to the grey area of unpublished reports, speeches, conferences papers and the like.

Jamaica is implementing sectoral network plans and ACURIL has adopted resolutions on regional resource planning but there is need to coordinate national, regional and international plans and to make UAP the logical counterpart to UBC.

Ensuring Effective Retrieval Through Secondary Services and Systems

Abstracting and indexing services

Indexing and abstracting services, hard copy or online, tend unfortunately to limit their coverage by format, usually to periodical literature. Caribbean research libraries often maintain partial in-house indexes, but published services are incomplete, even for journals. The ACURIL-sponsored CARINDEX (CARINDEX... 1977) is a manually produced service now extending to 125 journals and newspapers in the humanities and social sciences. AIRS, (AIRS... 1975) a computerized index to Jamaica's *Daily Gleaner*, has appeared intermittently since 1975 despite production problems. These two are the only indexes for sale, but in May 1983 the CDB began a computerized *Index to periodical articles in the Caribbean region* (AIRS... 1975), designed for in-house use and covering only twenty-one journals, but a possible first step towards a saleable Caribbean database.

Two regional non-commercial services are *CAGRINDEX* (CAGRINDEX... 1980/81) and *CARISPLAN Abstracts* (CARISPLAN... 1980). The former, from the University of the West Indies, St. Augustine, the library responsible for Trinidadian input to AGRIS, abstracts the English-speaking Caribbean's agricultural literature following the AGRINDEX format. The latter is linked with ECLA's INFOPLAN and has a subsidiary *SECIN index* covering Jamaica's socio-economic network input to CARISPLAN.

The region's need is for logical planning of such secondary services in relation to user needs and their coordination internationally. The IDRC-funded DOERS project at the University of West Indies (Jamaica) Institute of Social and Economic Research was for a mission-oriented social science index conceptually linked with DEVSIS; this would have been such a service but it has yet to publish a formal index.

Several suggestions have been made for cooperative solutions (Gray 1975). If, for example, authors would submit abstracts and select keywords from a thesaurus for computerized indexing (United States... 1973), Utopia may be nearer than we realize.

Translation services

Despite its advantage of having English as its main language, the area needs access to translations: affinity with the French-, Dutch- and Spanish-speaking Caribbean is growing and the literature of several non-English speaking countries is relevant. The need is for: (a) information on existing local expertise and the development of translation services; (b) local short courses in foreign language reading; and (c) coordination of translation information and facilities.

Promoting Networking and Providing Technological Facilities

Networking is library cooperation automated with modern computer and telecommunication technologies. Proposals for a worldwide General Information Network (GIN) have been countered by suggestions that a Third World one (TWIN) (Sardar 1980) would be a more effective way to information sharing. The obstacles are manpower, materials and money, particularly the cost of South-North telecommunication links—despite statements (such as that by Dr. Thomas J. Galvin, then ALA president, to the White House Conference on Library and Information Services, November 17, 1979) and resolutions (Consultation on the Coordinated... Final... 1980) that libraries be given special rates.

Interest in OCLC has survived delays in introducing dedicated lines to reduce telecommunication rates. Barbados now has such a networking facility (Bretney 1983) and Trinidad expects to have one in the near future. The University of the West Indies is experimenting with a dedicated line linking its three campuses with other stations in the Eastern Caribbean for a distance teaching project and possible library use, including "facsimile transmission."

Promoting International Standards

Local information personnel are well aware of international standards and adopt them wherever applicable, e.g. in cataloging and classification for national bibliographies. The problem is lack of international agreement in the technological field. A 1982 Unesco-sponsored study of standards in indexing and abstracting was timely.

Developing and Managing Human Resources

Manpower planning is pivotal (Hope 1983) and will determine future development. The University of the West Indies has provided formal training since 1971 but long-proposed manpower surveys have yet to be implemented by governments. The Unesco Consultation Meeting (Consultation on the Coordinated... Final... 1980) recommended extending the University of the West Indies' Department of Library Studies to provide:

(1) a wider range of specialized courses in the curriculum;

(2) regular programs of continuing education; and

(3) special courses for both professional and other information personnel at the Mona Campus and at training institutions in other territories, to meet the manpower requirements in the region.

It also urged a manpower survey, the first phase of which is complete (Moore 1982), although its data are inadequate for Trinidad and Tobago. Not articulated, however, is the need for management training.

There is also a dire need for retraining created by the new technologies. Many short courses available in North America and the United Kingdom could usefully be mounted in the English-speaking Caribbean, by the same experienced personnel.

It is also important to secure appropriate status for all trained information professionals.

Ensuring Adequate Financial Support

For the region's unstable one-crop economies, financial support has always been one of the weakest links in the chain of information services. The smallest LDCs may always need outside aid, and even the MDCs have problems caused by past years of neglect. The bureau appointed by the Unesco 1980 Consultation Meeting to monitor progress has ad success in coordinating project plans and priority funding.

Copyright

Restrictions arising from copyright law have been tackled at the international level, and machinery exists through WIPO and Unesco for continuing study and input with the developing world receiving due attention. CARICOM has been active and its Harmonization of Copyright Laws recommendations have affected a new Barbados law and draft legislation in Jamaica and Trinidad.

Classified Material and Pricing Practices

Lack of clear policies on declassifying sensitive materials is a much discussed subject (Collins 1981) for which CARICOM might suggest guidelines.

National and regional policies might also be evolved regarding subsidization of services, pricing practices and access to industrially produced information, and the recent establishment of a patents documentation center within the CDCC's documentation center is welcomed.

Promoting the Effective Use of Information and Information Services

Three main reasons account for under-use of information. Firstly, users lack understanding of information systems; even graduate students receive little pertinent instruction (Gray 1975). The University of the West Indies, St. Augustine Library has successfully introduced appropriate courses since the 1970s, although these are still outside the formal curriculum. The University of Guyana has incorporated such courses in its curriculum for science and technology students.

Secondly, researchers prefer informal personal contact: "the gatekeeper" and "invisible college" channels (Gray 1975). This tendency hinders use of the services provided. The CARICOM study (Wiltshire 1982) already cited shows how existing local sources of needed information were unknown and untapped.

Lastly, complex services and cross-disciplinary networks pose difficulties for users who need information specialists trained both in information and in specific disciplines to act as intermediaries. Such specialists have yet to be provided in the region and their functions understood by the profession.

A major aspect of policy must be the development of curiosity of mind throughout the education system, supported by suitable library resources and programs. An "information culture" starts by fostering from early childhood the habit of seeking information and using it as a problem solving resource (Unesco. General... Transfer... 1981).

Research on Information Science

Although countries the size of those in the Caribbean cannot be expected to lead major research programs, "some is necessary in each country simply for purposes of good management" (Unesco. General... Transfer... 1981). User studies, for example, and adaptation of library automation systems to suit local circumstances are needed, as is a better understanding of the information field itself to surmount the confusion now existing in terminology. The role of graduate schools of information science in regional research should become a point of focus in the area as the present University of the West Indies Department of Library Studies enters its second decade.

Regional and International Cooperation

The scope and size of the information problem extend well beyond what a single nation can do. Effective cooperation, regional and international, is an essential part of national policy, both in short-term projects and in long-term continuing programs to keep abreast of developments. North-South cooperation for information transfer should be planned in this framework. Various recommendations have already emerged in national (Gunter 1979, United States... 1972) and international forums for such links.

The effectiveness of international aid depends on adequate national planning and due thought to needs and priorities. International organizations can greatly help in the formulation of national plans and policies, although there is need to coordinate the efforts of the many bodies involved. While Jamaica, with Unesco help, and Barbados, with IDRC help, have rapidly progressed from planning into implementation, Guyana and Trinidad and Tobago, which have not used consultants (except for their agricultural networks) or outside financial aid, are lagging behind.

THE TERMINOLOGY AND DIVERSITY DILEMMAS

The powerful, persuasive logic of the concept of integrated national, regional and international information policies is belied by the incoherent reality of current overlapping and individualistic, diffuse and uncoordinated activities, even within the developed countries. Although some of the reasons—economic conditions and financial and human resources—are in part outside the profession's control, other, imaginary and unnecessary barriers have developed, some of them almost unwittingly. One such is the diversity in approaches, concepts and terminology used: "it is a matter of concern that, because of historical accidents, a profession dedicated to easing the flow of information suffers itself from imprecise terminology in describing its own activities" (Gray 1975). Six main areas of difficulty may be identified.

Information—the Commodity

Information is difficult to define: being used to identify many different concepts it means different things to different people. Information is facts, data, knowledge about something. It is said to be data of value for decision making, but many recipients do not use all the information reaching them, nor receive all the information channeled to them, so communication media are relevant. It may be produced, stored, communicated, processed and used in many forms. It may be printed or recorded in other forms, published, transmitted orally or communicated through signals and other channels devised for the purpose. Since it has no simply definable characteristics, attempts to define it invariably turn on definitions of various needs for information of different types and of users or uses of information. Information is said to make it possible for us to use all other resources effectively and efficiently (Gray 1975).

With such imprecision, it is little wonder that it is not consistently recognized officially in any single or standard form. A government setting up a Ministry of Information to channel the flow of essential information its citizens need, will embrace or not libraries and other information services, depending on the prevailing concept of information. Traditionally libraries have been seen as cultural agencies or extensions of the educational system: parts of the education minister's portfolio. Suggestions that they are part of the business of providing information of all kinds are not necessarily grasped in their full import.

Talk of "libraries and information services" is still ambiguous: introducing the undefinable "information" hinders rather than helps. There is an urgent need to crystallize the modern information concept and have a wider understanding and acceptance of its incorporation in the NATIS idea.

The New Information Science

The new technology has inevitably led to a wealth of new terminology. The complex inter-disciplinary skills involved in information transfer have created the concept of information science. Although several professionals have major input in the new science, it is far to travel for the old-fashioned layman who views libraries as storehouses for books. Unity of concept between the old and new cannot be readily apparent to outsiders and misunderstandings arise.

The Service Entity

There is even greater diversity in the terms applied to the service entities that provide or handle information. Libraries were too slow in moving to active user-oriented service; their failure to keep pace with user needs for subject information in depth led to the emergence of documentation centers as a new, improved concept of special library service. Coblans (1974) stresses the harm done by two warring groups who failed to see themselves as related parts of the same profession. While the consequent ambiguous discussions are now taken in stride by practitioners, they are a real dilemma to the uninitiated, thwarting national policy formation and hindering the advancement of information service as a whole.

Several offshoots of the documentation concept have added to the plethora of names: technical information services, information bureaus, information centers, information units in government and industry, and so on.

The Professionals and the Profession

Such changes have led the professionals themselves to become known by titles more descriptive of their information function than "librarian". Apart from the all-embracing "information professional" (yet to gain currency), information specialists, documentalists, information managers, and information scientists have all emerged. That laymen users and decision-making officials often fail to understand them, and the shades of difference we may or may not intend, is to the detriment of the cause we seek to promote.

The profession's training programs and qualifications are themselves a hodge-podge. Non-graduate, undergraduate and graduate programs of varying length award associateships, licenses, first degrees, diplomas, certificates and graduate degrees for vastly different requirements and with such varied content that attempts to identify a common and basic core become necessary to ensure some uniformity in standards. Inevitable mechanization created changes from the 1960s and a whole new vocabulary entered the glossary of librarianship (Saunders 1966), but, despite some forward-looking programs (Saunders 1966) that managed to integrate old and basic courses with newer needs, the confusing split between librarians and their information counterparts has extended into requirements for posts, training and certification programs and to the societies and associations in which the professionals congregate and which provide the essential framework for the split itself. Unity of purpose is barely recognized, even nationally. Internationally the two sides, IFLA and FID, must come together, and soon.

In the developing world such diversity can spell disaster for national development for library and information services. Bombarding the non-information-initiated with jargon requests and dazzling them with our changing concepts and terminology is bad strategy. As Kenneth Stockam once put it: "It is high time that we in the library and information business try to tell each other and even more important, try to tell governments, what is needed in simpler and more straightforward language... If only we could try to say what we want in plain words" (Stockham 1975).

Priority Users and Programs

The UNISIST program emphasized scientists and technologists as the priority users for whom the World Science Information System was to be devised. But the reality of wider needs soon prevailed, leading to the NATIS program which took all needs into account. Several systems have also been devised for planners and decision-makers, and the trend towards worldwide information systems, whether discipline-oriented like AGRIS, or mission-oriented like DEVSIS, is the most promising approach.

International Programs and Goals

Against this background of incoherent diversity it naturally behooves international organizations to pull the strands together. It is a source of grave concern that Unesco's change from UNISIST to NATIS and now to the General Information Program has added to the confusion rather than dispelling it. In countries where national policy is still to be formulated, and where international programs are the pegs upon which national aspirations are hung, continually shifting targets can be destabilizing.

A follow-up NATIS intergovernmental conference is needed; it might well adopt an "Information For All" target through interconnecting NATIS systems.

CONCLUSIONS

The pace of development nowadays suggest that, once goals are agreed upon and well defined, their attainability in some degree is fairly assured. Perhaps the increasing diversity of recent times—the cacophony of tuning up—has been a necessary prelude to the emergence of a more systematically constructed and well orchestrated work with all performers worldwide playing their parts in due rhythm and harmony. But this symphony of information systems is possible only if the performers are willing and able to play their individual parts with suitable instruments and continuous practice.

Information professionals must be prepared to work in harmony and see their many solo performances as parts of the whole.

> We must look to our own profession and our professional bodies in particular. We stand at the moment as a house divided by what I believe to be artificial boundaries. We must take steps to eliminate these boundaries, we must utilize the strengths of each section for the total overall benefit, and we must avoid energy-expensive overlaps of interests. ...[W]e must

present a much more united front whether we are presenting a case to the government, confronting information and equipment suppliers or organizing education and training (Cliffe 1980).

REFERENCES

1) *AIRS: index to the "Daily Gleaner."* Kingston, Jamaica: West India Reference Library; October/ December, 1975- .

2) Anthony, Laurence James. National information policy. *Aslib proceedings*; June/July 1982; 34(6-7):310-316.

3) Arboleda-Sepúlveda, Orlando. *Sharing agricultural documentation and information resources in Guyana.* Georgetown, Guyana: Unesco; 1981.

4) Armstrong, Eric. Information needs of national policy makers. In: *Regional Cooperation for Access to Information in the Caribbean.* Papers presented at the meeting of librarians and documentalists, November 29 — December 2, 1977. Port of Spain: ECLA; 1978: 16-27.

5) Bateson, Nora. *Library plan for Jamaica.* Kingston, Jamaica: Government Printer; 1945.

6) Borko, Harold; Menou, Michel. *Index of information utilization potential (IUP) Phase II: Interim report.* [Prepared under contract for Unesco]. Los Angeles, California: Graduate School of Library and Information Science, UCLA; 1981.

7) Bretney, Nel. Dailog information retrieval service in a Third World country: a case study. *Bulletin of Eastern Caribbean affairs*; January/February 1983; 8(6):1-9.

8) Brown, Royston. Towards a national information policy. *Aslib proceedings*; June/July 1982; 34(6-7):318.

9) Bushkin, Arthur; Yurow, Jane H. Developing national information policies. *Library journal*; September 15, 1979:1752-1756.

10) CDB. *Annual report 1981*. Barbados: CDB; 1982: 53.

11) CDB. *An index to periodical articles on the Caribbean region: a current awareness bulletin*. January/March, 1983— .

12) *CAGRINDEX: abstract of the agricultural literature of the English-speaking Caribbean*. St. Augustine, Trinidad: UWI Library; 1980/1981— .

13) CARICOM. *Survey of public library services in the less developed of the Caribbean Community countries*, by Carol Collins. Georgetown, Guyana: Caribbean Community Secretariat; 1979.

14) CARICOM. Unit for harmonization of laws. *Copyright and neighbouring rights: a report and model legislation*. Georgetown, Guyana: Caribbean Community Secretariat; 1978.

15) *CARINDEX: social sciences*. St. Augustine, Trinidad: ACURIL Indexing Committee (English-speaking area); 1977,1(1)— .

16) *CARISPLAN abstracts*. Port of Spain: ECLA Office for the Caribbean; 1980— .

17) Chandler, M.J. *Agriculture science and technology: resources of information in Barbados; a survey*. Barbados: National Council for Science and Technology; 1979-1980: iii.

18) Cliffe, G.R. Can we face the information explosion? *Aslib proceedings*; February 1980; 32(2):106.

19) Coblans, Herbert. *Librarianship and documentation: an international perspective.* London: Deutsch; 1974: 36.

20) Collins, Carol. Existing facilities for meeting the information needs of planners and policy makers — CARICOM member countries. In: *Regional Cooperation for Access to Information in the Caribbean.* Papers presented at the meeting of librarians and documentalists November 29 — December 2, 1977. Port of Spain: ECLA; 1978: 69–86.

21) Collins, Carol. *Grenada: plan for the development of a national information system.* Paris: Unesco; 1981.

22) Collins, Carol. The sharing and dissemination of information. In: Green, J.E.; Collins, Carol, eds. *Research and documentation: report of a workshop on research and documentation in the development sciences in the English speaking Caribbean, Kingston, Jamaica.* Kingston, Jamaica: Institute of Social and Economic Research, UWI; 1977: 127.

23) Consultation on the Coordinated Development of National Information Systems in the Caribbean Region, Kingston, May 19–23, 1980. *Final report and recommendations.* Paris: Unesco; 1980.

24) Consultation on the Coordinated Development of National Information Systems in the Caribbean Region, Kingston, May 19–23, 1980. *The present state of information infrastructures in the Caribbean libraries, archives and documentation centres.* Paris: Unesco; 1980.

25) Dierickx, Harold. *Caribbean region: a proposed common format for existing and projected computerized*

bibliographic information systems. Paris: Unesco; 1982.

26) Gray, John G. *Information policy and planning for economic and social development: a dynamic approach.* [Working document prepared for ... the first UNISIST Meeting on Regional Cooperation in Information Policy and Planning for Development in Latin America and the Caribbean, Lima, Peru, October 1–5, 1979]. Paris: Unesco; 1979.

27) Gray, John G.; Perry, Brian. *Scientific information.* London: Oxford University Press; 1975.

28) *Guyana: report on activity towards the creation of a national information policy.* [Country report ... for the first UNISIST Meeting on Regional Cooperation in Information Policy and Planning...]. Georgetown, Guyana:. Ministry of Information; 1979: 2.

29) Gunter, Jonathan F. *Library and information services for increasing international understanding and cooperation: a discussion guide prepared for the White House Conference on Library and Information Services.* Washington, D.C.: National Commission on Libraries and Information Science; 1979: 23–28.

30) Hope, Kempe R. *The administration of development in emergent nations: the problems of the Caribbean.* Public administration and development; 1983; 3:49–59.

31) Information and documentation for development: analysis and presentation of an inventory for a Latin American country. In: *Regional Cooperation for Access to Information in the Caribbean.* Papers presented at the meeting of librarians and

documentalists, November 29 — December 2, 1977. Port of Spain: ECLA; 1978: 127.

32) Inter-Governmental Conference on Scientific and Technological Information for Development. *UNISIST II, main working document.* Paris: Unesco; 1979: 85–86.

33) Jamaica. NACOLADS. *Plan for a national documentation, information and library system for Jamaica.* Kingston, Jamaica: NACOLADS; 1978.

34) Jordan, Alma. *The development of library science in the West Indies through interlibrary cooperation.* Metuchen, New Jersey: Scarecrow Press; 1970.

35) Jordan, Alma. Sharing library resources in the English-speaking Caribbean. *Interlending review*; January 1978; 6(1):10–17.

36) Keren, Carl. *A national library and information service system in Barbados: report of a consultancy mission.* Ottawa: IDRC; 1982. [IDRC manuscript reports].

37) Knee, Christopher. The role of the National Science Research Council of Guyana in the dissemination of scientific information. *Guyana Library Association bulletin*; 1976; 5(4):1019.

38) Moore, Nick. *Survey of library and information manpower needs in the Caribbean. Preliminary version.* Paris: General Information Programme and UNISIST, Unesco; 1982.

39) Neustadt, Richard M. Information policy: progress and prospectus. *Library journal*; September 15,1979:1743.

40) Nunes, Freddie. Research and documentation: what, for whom, at what price? Some basic considerations. In: Green, J.E.; Collins, Carol, eds. *Research and documentation: report of a workshop on research and documentation in the development sciences in the English-speaking Caribbean, Kingston, Jamaica.* Kingston, Jamaica: Institute of Social and Economic Research, UWI; 1977: 409–422.

41) Oettinger, Anthony G. Information resources: old questions, new choices. *Bulletin of the American Society for Information Science*; October 1979; 6(1):16.

42) Page, John. Cooperating for economy: international coordination of information services. *Aslib proceedings*; February 1980; 32(2):45–52.

43) Page, John. *Information systems and networks for technology transfer: final report.* Paris: Unesco; 1978.

44) Parker, Yakup. Information technology in polytechnics. *Aslib proceedings*; October 1982; 34(10):430.

45) *Regional Cooperation for Access to Information in the Caribbean.* Papers presented at the meeting of librarians and documentalists, November 29 – December 2, 1977. Port of Spain: ECLA; 1978. [See also items 4, 20, 31].

46) Rowley, J.E.; Turner, Christopher Mark Durham. *The dissemination of information.* London: Deutsch; 1978: 13,54.

47) Sardar, Ziauddin. Between GIN and TWIN: meeting the information needs of the Third World. *Aslib proceedings*; February 1980; 33(2):53–54.

48) Saunders, Wilfred Leonard. Education for librarianship. In: Collison, Robert L., ed. *Progress in library science 1966*. London: Butterworths; 1966: 125,126.

49) Savage, Ernest Albert. *The libraries of Bermuda, the Bahamas, the British West Indies, British Guiana, British Honduras, Puerto Rico and the American Virgin Islands: a report to the Carnegie Corporation of New York*. London: The Library Association; 1934.

50) Stockham, Kenneth. *The planning of national information systems*. [Paper presented at the Unesco/JLS workshop on the planning of NATIS Library and Documentation Networks for the Caribbean area, November 10-14, 1975, Kingston, 1975]. 1.

51) Trinidad and Tobago. *White paper on National Institute of Higher Education (Research, science and technology)*. Port of Spain: Government Printery; 1977.

52) Trinidad and Tobago. National Commission for Unesco. *From imitation to innovation; report of the seminar on regional problems of book production and distribution organized ... to mark International Book Year*, UWI, St. Augustine..., April 13-15, 1972. St. Augustine: 1972.

53) Unesco. *NATIS: National Information Systems; national information policy*. Paris: Unesco; 1976: 3,26.

54) Unesco. *UNISIST: information policy objectives (UNISIST proposals)*. Paris: Unesco; 1974: 1,26.

55) Unesco. *UNISIST: synopsis of the feasibility study on a World Science Information System*. Paris: Unesco; 1971: 66-68.

56) Unesco. General Information Programme. *Transfer and utilization of information for development in the 1980s: main problems and strategies for their solution.* [Issues discussed at a consultation meeting held in Toledo, Spain, May 11–15, 1981]. Paris: Unesco; 1981: 3.

57) Unesco. General Information Programme. *First meeting of the Bureau of the Pilot Project for the Coordinated Development of National Information Systems in the Caribbean Region, Caracas, November 1–2, 1982: Final report.* Caracas?; 1982: 1.

58) United States of America. National Academy of Sciences. Office of the Foreign Secretary. *Scientific and technical information for the developing countries: a report of an ad hoc advisory panel of the Board on Science and Technology for International Development.* Washington, D.C.: National Academy of Sciences; 1972: 3,4.

59) United States of America. President's Science Advisory Committee. Science, government and information. In: Sherwood, John; Hodine, Alfred, eds. *Reader in science information.* Washington, D.C.: Micro-card Editors; 1973: 302.

60) Vinken, Pierre. Information economy, government and society. *Aslib proceedings*; August 1982; 34(8):330–337.

61) Wiltshire, Winthrop W. et al. *Information and communication flows in priority areas of science and technology within the CARICOM region — 1982.* [Study done for CARICOM Secretariat under the aegis of the United Nations Interim Fund for Science and Technology].

SOME ISSUES IN THE TRANSFER
OF SCIENTIFIC AND
TECHNOLOGICAL INFORMATION IN CHILE

by María Oyarzun de Ferreira
Centro Nacional de Informac'ón y Documentación
Santiago, Chile

RESUMEN

Algunos Asuntos Sobre la Transferencia
de Información Científica y Tecnologica en Chile

La información en Chile está principalmente centralizada en las universidades, donde principalmente se utiliza, y en donde los sistemas de información son en general de tipo tradicional. Las dificultades en desarrollar sistemas modernos tienen que ver con la dependencia informática, la falta de recursos económicos, expertos profesionales, aparatos, y en la posición geográfica de Chile. Chile toma parte en algunos sistemas internacionales, especialmente el AGRINTER. Chile tiene una necesidad de reducir su dependencia informática de los Estados Unidos; el movimiento de información entre los dos países se encuentra con serios problemas de costo y del control bibliográfico inadecuado. Incluye bibliografía.

INFORMATION AND DEVELOPMENT

Development is concerned with the people's welfare and their material, cultural and spiritual well-being. The importance of scientific and technical information at all levels in improving and expanding productive capacity is widely acknowledged and international gatherings such as UNCSTD and UNISIST II have recognized its crucial role in social, economic and cultural development. It is a major concern of UNESCO's general information program.

Although better information systems could reduce the North-South gap, developing them is difficult for Third World countries where other problems (food, clothing, shelter, education, communications) have higher priority. Yet these other problems are difficult to solve, in part, precisely because of inadequate access to information.

Planning development implies efficient management of resources of all kinds so as to create the knowledge and skill needed to produce the necessary goods, services, industrialized world. facilities and opportunities. But national development should emphasize each country's culture and traditions: it is not necessary to reach the same state as the industrialized world.

CHARACTERISTICS OF INFORMA-
TION FOR DEVELOPMENT

Development information is information involved in, contributing to, or generated by, the development process. It is of potential interest and benefit worldwide, regardless of where it is generated, and so should have the widest possible dissemination.

Socio-economic development requires information from many sources: scientific and technical information, although fundamental, must be complemented by information in all the rich variety necessary for a truly national development. The important influence of the economic, social, political, technological and cultural environment means it must be collected at the national level: the objectives, selection criteria and method of analysis of foreign sources mean that this foreign information does not always correspond to the needs of the developing countries.

THE TRANSFER OF SCIENTIFIC AND TECHNOLOGICAL INFORMATION IN CHILE

Developing a national scientific and technical information system is the responsibility of CONICYT through its Centro Nacional de Información y Documentación (CENID) whose main purpose is to carry out studies and organize programs to promote better utilization of national resources and to improve access to foreign sources.

The national system is made up of sectoral subsystems corresponding to the main fields of national development. Progress has been made in coordination, training and standardization, and in national bibliographic control.

FACTORS AFFECTING INFORMATION TRANSFER IN CHILE

The chief factors affecting information transfer in Chile are the infrastructure, human resources, the users, access, technology and geography. Their characteristics are similar to those of other developing countries.

The Infrastructure

Chile, with 237,200 professional people and technicians (of whom 4,823 are engaged in scientific and technical research) and 117,500 students in 24 institutions of higher education, has 407 information centers and special libraries, in the government, private and university sectors—mostly the last. They are concentrated in Santiago and their services are the traditional ones, catering to the faculty, researchers and students of their own organizations.

Chile's national bibliography has been compiled by the National Library since 1866. Various organizations have attempted to produce national subject bibliographies, but these only cover short time periods and few are regularly updated. The Instituto de Recursos Naturales maintains a graphic database on natural resources. Information on current scientific and technical research is gathered by CONICYT which has has developed a database on research in progress. The Instituto Nacional de Estadísticas is responsible for national statistics, including the population and housing censuses. The Dirección de Promoción de Exportaciones is developing a database on national and international commercial data, and the Oficina de Planificación Agrícola one on agriculture, fishing and forestry. The Empresa Nacional de Computación maintains a public network for data transmission, nationally and internationally.

Human Resources

The country's capability of collecting, evaluating, selecting, processing and disseminating information is determined by the human resources available.

The University of Chile's Escuela de Bibliotecología was established in Santiago in 1947 and officially accredited in 1959. The new university law of 1980 has made it part of the Instituto Professional de Santiago. The professional degree of librarian is awarded on completion of an eight semester program. A similar program established at the University's Valparaíso campus is now at the Academia Superior de Ciencias Pedagógicas.

Efforts to secure continuing education for information professionals include an intensive training program in new techniques in handling information run by CONICYT from 1969 to 1980, and courses by the Escuela de Bibliotecología and the Colegio de Bibliotecarios de Chile AG. The library schools have modernized their curricula and Chilean librarians have been granted scholarships abroad, both for short courses and for graduate study. These efforts must be intensified if the profession is to keep up with today's developing information needs.

Users and Their Use of Information

We may group users of development information into four categories, representing a wide variety of needs, according to the use they make of information: decision makers, scientists (and technologists), agents of change, and the general public.

Although the study of users needs should precede the creation of information services, few serious studies have been carried out in Chile, and problems arise because services are not attuned to real needs. When modern services are introduced, they usually derive from the traditional ones. Once established, there is little attempt at marketing them, or at evaluating their efficiency or productivity, or the use made of the information they provide.

Lack of emphasis on information in secondary and higher education means that few users have been systematically trained in its use. Scientific and technical information, despite being largely in foreign languages, is used more widely than development information, which, being mostly generated inside the country, is unrecorded. Attention must be paid to the needs of all user (and potential user) groups, and information services developed that are suited to their manifold requirements.

Access

Document availability is essential in information work. In developing countries like Chile it is often easier to learn of information from foreign sources than to obtain that produced locally. But access to information from the North is limited by high cost (and the need for hard currency), and the language barrier. Cooperative efforts have been made to complete periodical sets and increase library stocks, but much remains to be done.

Most information originating in Chile goes unrecorded, making it difficult to locate and obtain. Most reports, from government, research institutions or university departments, are never published, so that potential users do not know of their existence and valuable information remains untapped. And much information from other Latin American countries is similarly unrecorded or unpublished.

CONICYT is endeavoring to improve document access, by developing the National Union Serials Catalog and translation and photocopy services. Other institutions have made arrangements with foreign and international organizations for their libraries to become depositories of their publications. Even so, many documents, both Chilean and foreign, remain inaccessible and efforts should be concentrated on remedying this.

Technology

Technological advances in information and communication promise to improve both access to foreign information and control of what is produced in Chile. Two services offer online access to North American databases. Some information units have access to the computer facilities of their parent organizations. Much has been done to develop local databases and a public network was inaugurated in 1981. But Chile is still far from solving its information transfer problems: it lacks enough financial resources, trained manpower and appropriate equipment to take full advantage of recent developments, and the top decision makers responsible for resource allocation are not fully familiar with the pros and cons of the new devices.

Geographical Situation

Chile's geographical position is another factor to be considered in information transfer. The great distance from the developed world increases both cost and access time. Contact with foreign specialists and attendance at professional meetings abroad are limited by the high cost of travel.

PARTICIPATION IN INTERNATIONAL SYSTEMS

International and regional information systems are important, not only in facilitating information flow, but because they increase national capability of making optimal use of local and international information resources. Chile participates in AGRINTER, AGRIS, INIS, INFOTERRA, ISDS and REPIDISCA. Besides its impact on the management of nationally produced information within the respective subject fields, this participation has promoted: (a) personnel training, (b) use of common rules, manuals and documentary languages; (c) photocopying agreements (coupons, common prices); (d) participation in the network coordination activities; and (e) contact with foreign colleagues.

The effects of this international participation may be gaged by Chile's participation in AGRINTER, which has become quite widespread since 1974. It has done more to increase information transfer within the country than to increase information flow from abroad. A recent survey found that sixty-five of Chilean researchers knew of the *Índice agrícola de América Latina y el Caribe* but only twenty-five used it. They were unfamiliar with both the publications from elsewhere in Latin America and with their authors and preferred consulting literature from the developed countries whose scientists are well known in Chile. They also found the information in the *Índice* irrelevant to Chilean conditions for climatic reasons: that from the North was, again, more acceptable. Unfortunately, although this northern information can be found through AGRINTER, it is more difficult to obtain, due to lack of photocopying agreements.

Participation in international systems has imposed an increased work load on the limited staffs of the information units involved. With no compensatory staff increases, job performance has suffered. This is an aspect of the subject that planners of such systems do not always take into account.

THE NORTH-SOUTH FLOW OF INFORMATION

Aware of the economic value of information, the North has used modern technology to develop a commercially-based information industry, marketing it like any other good and ignoring the problems and needs of the South. The incipient information systems of the South, in contrast, generally disseminate documents on a gift or exchange basis. Also, while users in the South, at the highest level, speak English as a second language and so have access to literature from the United States, they are obliged to write in this second language when they wish to publish the results of their research. All this puts the United States in a dominant position and action is needed to mitigate this.

The Flow of Information from the
United States to Chile

A large proportion of Chilean library holdings consists of material from abroad, mainly the United States. United States AID, the University of California-University of Chile Program and other cooperative projects were significant in this. Uncertain library budgets make the updating of collections very difficult, and often periodical subscriptions cannot be renewed.

Using photocopy services in the United States is affected by administrative complications and by difficulties in maintaining deposit accounts. Solutions adopted between developing countries include the use of coupons (e.g. those of AGRINTER) where only an initial investment is needed, and the use of exchange contracts, where participants' accounts are balanced at the end of the year. Such arrangements have not yet proved acceptable to northern countries.

Chile is connected online only with the North American commercial networks. The Instituto de Investigaciones Tecnológicas has offered a connection since 1977. The Empresa Nacional de Computación has just become the second such service and is still at the implementation and promotion stage. Use of foreign databases is low: cost is high and users are not yet familiar with the new resources.

The Flow of Information from Chile
to the United States

Most Chilean documents containing development information, including scientific and technical information, are non-conventional publications, in limited editions and unavailable through traditional channels.

The approximately 600 Chilean scientific and technical serials do not have annual indexes, and are not covered by the international indexing services because of their irregularity, and there are no domestic indexing or abstracting services that would cover them.

Although authors in the basic sciences, seeking worldwide dissemination, publish abroad, those who write on subjects of local interest publish in local journals with limited diffusion. The scientific community has itself studied this problem and published on it.

Information on Chile published abroad or made known to international and regional systems is included in international databases and United Nations agencies have been very important in developing these.

Going to conferences promotes two-way information transfer. Besides presenting their own works, authors meet other specialists, and can have access to their documents and discuss topics of mutual interest. Support for this comes from government and university funds and through international cooperation, but it is felt that more money is needed.

ASSESSMENT OF NATIONAL INFORMATION NEEDS AND THE EXCHANGE OF INFORMATION

Assessing national information needs is of vital importance in organizing information transfer for development. National goals and the economic, cultural and social environment must be taken into account. Better control of local information will help reduce the information imbalance between North and South, allowing the latter to participate as a provider as well as a consumer of information.

CONCLUSIONS

Chile's information infrastructure has a solid basis. Strengthening it would improve both national and international information transfer. This could best be done if national development projects, whether nationally or internationally funded, would include funding to cover the information activities necessary for such projects. To ensure the best use of such funding it should be managed by the information systems themselves.

International and regional information programs have proved useful in developing national capacity, thereby promoting information flow between participating countries. Such programs should promote not only bibliographic control but also document availability and access.

A major obstacle to information transfer from the United States to Latin America is cost. It could be overcome through United States participation in regional programs to secure information interchange and document access at reduced cost. Wider use of coupons for photocopying would be administratively simple and mitigate the lack of funds for acquiring bibliographic materials and services.

Poor bibliographic control of locally produced information is the main problem facing information transfer from Chile to the United States in some areas. It is therefore urgent that current bibliographies and local databases be developed in such areas.

REFERENCES

1) Adams, Scott. *Scientific and technical information services in eight Latin American countries: developments, technical assistance, opportunities for cooperation; a report to the Office of Science Information Service, National Science Foundation.* Louisville, Kentucky: 1975.

2) Crowther, Warren. *La participación latinoamericana en los sistemas, redes e intercambio internacional de información: problemática y surgencias.* [Paper contributed to the Reunión latinoamericana y del Caribe sobre información para el desarrollo, Cali (Colombia), October 23–28, 1977].

3) Elso G., Sonia. *Evaluación de uso en Chile del "Indice agrícola de América Latina y el Caribe."* [Paper contributed to the VI Reunión interamericana de bibliotecarios y documentalistas agrícolas, Santo Domingo RD, June 15–18, 1981].

4) Gray, John G. *Política y planificación de la información para el desarrollo económico y social: un enfoque dinámico.* Paris: UNESCO; 1979.

5) Krauskopf, M.; Pessot, R. *Estudio preliminar sobre publicaciones y productividad científica en Chile.* Archivos de biología y medicina experimental; 1980; 13:195–208.

6) Neelameghan, A. Information systems for national development: the social relevance of information systems. *International forum on information and documentation;* 1980; 5(4):3–8.

7) Salman, Lamia. The information needs of the developing countries: analytical case-studies. *UNESCO*

journal of information science; October 1981; 3(4):241-246.

8) Tocatlian, Jacques. Information for development: the role of UNESCO's General Information Programme. *UNESCO journal of information science;* 1981; 3(3):146-158.

9) Winter, A.A. Information for problem solving in socio-economic development. *International forum on information and documentation;* 1981; 6(4):3-6.

10) Wysocki, A. International cooperation in information transfer. *Journal of documentation;* 1978; 3(4):300-310.

SOME IDEAS ON INFORMATION FLOW BETWEEN THE DEVELOPED AND THE UNDEVELOPED AMERICAS DERIVED FROM THE EXPERIENCE OF A UNIVERSITY IN THE SOUTH

by Armando M. Sandoval
Centro de Información Científica y Humanistica
Ciudad Universitaria
Mexico

RESUMEN

Algunas Ideas Sobre el Movimento de Información entre las
Americas Desarrollada y No Desarrollada a Base de la Experiencia de una Universidad Del Sur

Los países del Sur son dependientes de los del Norte para la
mayoría de su información. Entre las instituciones que
tienen un papel importante en la reducción de esta dependencia es el CICH de la UNAM. El CICH tiene extensos
números de revistas, herramientas bibliográficas, servicios
para índices y abstractos, y muchas revistas. Entre los
aspectos en que el Sur se revela más como dependiente del
Norte para información son la publicación de revistas y
documentos, bases de datos, y sistemas de información
adaptados a las necesidades regionales. Entre las
publicaciones bibliográficas que sirven para hacer más ase-

quible la información de origen regional son *Bibliografía Latinoamericana, Citas Latinoamericanas en Sociología, Economía y Humanidades, y Periódica: Indice de Revistas Latinoamericanas en Ciencia.*

INTRODUCTION

The impact of electronics on the speed of document circulation has made information transfer a fashionable topic. But the developed world is so far ahead of the South in information gathering that this transfer always flows North-South, and across a gap that is growing steadily wider as the southern countries are less and less able to accompany the rapid growth of science and technology.

The very relevance of this transfer and the close relationship of information to decision making is seldom appreciated in countries still battling to provide adequate elementary education. The few instances of effective information services in such countries are isolated responses to rare occurrences of demand, usually from professors in universities.

LIBRARIES

In countries almost without school or public libraries, modern information services may seem out of place. Good specialized libraries exist only at the highest academic levels, and their holdings are limited, and seldom accessible to outside users. Scholarly information is largely transferred through foreign journals. UNAM, by far the most important recipient of this in Mexico, subscribes to some 10,000 journals for its 120 departments. But this number is falling as subscription rates rise and interlibrary loans are difficult: union catalogs are out of date. Despite the time, cost and complications, it is easier to borrow items from abroad. Users of online services are frustrated when they learn promptly of items that take three months to arrive. Loans from abroad cost in Mexico $4.00US at the least: one percent of the monthly salary of the average UNAM professor and almost beyond the reach of a state university professor. CICH's document procurement service has been obtaining 80% of its requests from abroad, which is a drain on university funds and on national hard currency reserves.

To rationalize resources, a central journal repository has to be accepted as top priority by decision makers in government and universities. What could be done is shown by the success of the BLLD, CICH's main source of documents. We should remember that one reason for the creation of BIREME was the volume of interlibrary loan requests received from Latin America by the National Library of Medicine; it is now South America's chief source of biomedical information, medicine being the discipline that receives the most attention in the region by far.

Although journals are the most common format for the North-South information flow, their subscriptions have always been a serious burden for libraries and the first casualty of any financial crisis, hence the discontinuities in most library holdings. Creating a consciousness of the crucial importance of periodicals has been an aim of CICH ever since its creation. Despite drastic cuts in funding, UNAM has now gone ten years without stopping any subscription.

In 1972, CICH was prepared to offer only simple services such as document procurement and manual retrospective bibliographic searching. For the latter it relied on the UNAM library system, but holdings, when existing, were incomplete or not readily available. As a result, eight years ago, even before the advent of online retrieval, CICH organized its own library, one that is unique among the over 100 UNAM libraries. Besides the basic bibliographic tools in library and information science, it has over 200 active indexing and abstracting services, including complete runs of those most frequently used, such as *Biological Abstracts* and *Chemical Abstracts*. These cover almost all disciplines of actual or potential use in a large university and while some duplicate titles held by other UNAM libraries, many are the only copies in all Mexico. The library also has important holdings of Latin American periodicals.

A perusal of CICH's list of journal subscriptions demonstrates the enormous dependence of the South on the North for scholarly information. Of 10,000 plus subscriptions of some 120 university departments, 42 come from the United States, which figure increases to 60 when the subscriptions from the United States and United Kingdom are combined. If Scandinavian, Dutch, Swiss and other European journals written in English are added, we must conclude that our Spanish traditions are fighting a probably hopeless battle against Anglophone science and technology and Anglophone culture.

But the South is not passive in this, for there is a South-North transfer. It is frequently overlooked that our researchers export the best fruit of their work in the form of over 3,000 manuscripts a year sent for publication in some 2,000 foreign (mostly United States) journals. This is an appropriate adaptation to present-day requirements, but it is a contribution that is largely hidden because of the dispersal of the articles and because they are presented in English. It is, unfortunately, a further aspect of dependency as such publication patterns prevent our own journals from reflecting the real quality and quantity of southern reason.

It cannot be overstressed that, in any information concern, the scholarly periodicals library is the basic unit of a proper infrastructure, and should receive top priority. This has to be considered as the beginning of the North-South information transfer.

DOCUMENT PROCUREMENT

No library or information system is self-sufficient, but southern dependency is something else. Although much information flows informally between northern and southern scientists as professional colleagues, the need remains form prompt availability of printed documents. In the South these are almost all northern, whether journal articles, technical reports, patents or theses. The South-North flow is insignificant: as we have just indicated, to learn of southern contributions, both North and South must rely on northern journals.

RETROSPECTIVE BIBLIOGRAPHIC SEARCHES AND SELECTIVE DISSEMINATION OF INFORMATION

Retrospective searching and selective dissemination of information can be done manually or by computer. But we never heard of selective dissemination of information before computers entered information work, and the computer has meant a cosmic jump for retrospective searching.

The computer exemplifies Northern technical superiority. The financially poor South has to make a disproportionate diversion of funds to import this vital resource, to keep up in a race handicapped by (usually) obsolescent equipment and the need to train highly specialized personnel in a context of great educational deficiencies.

Eventually, sometimes years after making the original decision, the Southern experts have their equipment connected to Northern databases, and information flows swiftly through technical channels developed in the North. Since the Southerner's purchasing power is disproportionate to the real cost, the service must be highly subsidized. And for many of the documents it indicates that he must depend on foreign sources—involving foreign currency, long delays and costly administrative complications.

Retrospective searching is in great demand by both faculty and students. Low demand for SDI may reflect failure by faculty to appreciate such a current awareness service, although one can be of little use without the support of a good library infrastructure, notably a depository of northern documents.

PROCESSING REGIONAL PUBLICATIONS AND PREPARING REGIONAL DATABASES

Socially and politically Latin America is very diverse. Communications are poor, distances immense. Neighbor countries mistrust one another and have only one general characteristic: the North as their common pole. But they do not present a common front to this pole. Each relates to it separately, in total economic and technological dependence.

Many first rate journals could be produced in the region were it not for the "literature drain" referred to of articles published abroad in search of worldwide distribution. As it is, much of what does appear locally is of inferior quality. Nevertheless, there remain some 1,500 Latin American journals (out of an estimated 3,000 total) of quality. Their contents in fields like agriculture, biology, earth sciences, food, health, natural history and population are not negligible at all, and many in the social sciences and humanities are original and of good quality, even though mostly local in character. As such journals have small circulations, the work they include is very little known outside narrow academic circles. Various international gatherings, such as those sponsored by UNESCO at San Juan in 1964 and by OAS at Caracas in 1970 (not to mention national and regional meetings) have stressed the need to quantify the "literature drain" and to index what is published in the journals of Latin America.

Bibliografía Latinoamericana

Only UNAM has faced and accepted this double challenge, as part of the activities of its CICH. Since 1974, CICH has·been reporting papers by Latin Americans appearing in foreign journals, in the twice-yearly *Part One* of its *Bibliografía latinoamericana*. This shows Latin American research to be very active (an average of 2,800 items were indexed over the last 5 years) and of high quality, particularly in medicine. Two thirds of the materials indexed comes from universities or similar institutions. Brazil leads with 33%, closely followed by Argentina and then, far behind, by Mexico, Chile and Venezuela, in that order. Together these countries make up 90% of the total. As expected, the "lingua franca" is English. Despite all the political, social and economic problems faced by these countries, their output shows a steady increase: between 1974 and 1980 it rose 38%.

Part Two of the *Bibliografía* indexes articles *on* Latin America in foreign journals by foreigners. These equal about half the amount of *Part One*: an indication of the interest of foreign academic researchers in Latin American society and politics.

Citas latinoamericanas en sociología, economía y humanidades (CLASE)

Latin American humanists write little on themselves in foreign journals, giving local journals an unparalleled information role in this area. But as this was something scarcely covered by the world's leading abstracting and indexing services, *CLASE* was begun by CICH in 1977 as a current awareness service to cover it. *CLASE* appears quarterly, with each issue including a list of abbreviations, material analyzed, tables of contents, keyword index, citation index, author index and institution index. In 1982, 654 issues of 562 journals were analyzed.

Periódica: índice de revistas
latinoamericanas en ciencia

As stated, there remain some areas even in science where material in local journals is important. In 1977, CICH began *Periódica* to index Mexican science journals, extending its coverage to all Latin American science journals the following year. It too is quarterly and arranged similarly to *CLASE* but with an additional keyword index in English. In 1982, it covered 1,229 issues of 611 journals.

Both *Periódica* and *CLASE* and the *Bibliografía* are computer produced and all the periodicals they index are held in CICH's library for photocopying or reading. The four indexes complement each other and together provide a unique, systematic display of the total output of scholarly work in and on Latin America. Nothing like this has been attempted before and the undertaking is a good example of information flow from Latin America to the rest of the world.

CONCLUSIONS

The need for scholarly information is universal, and the less developed a country is, the greater this need will be. Paradoxically, however, the less developed the country, the less it can express its need. At the bottom of this lies a great educational problem, related to perhaps insurmountable socio-economic problems.

Modern information technology is costly and difficult to afford because it all has to be imported. And such dependency seems not only irreversible but to be increasing.

Planetary information flow is North-South. The North Pole is always on top. Far from being free, it has to be paid for and for the southern recipients it is unreasonably expensive. If the North so pleases it can try promoting southern libraries, documentation centers or information systems. But unless such efforts are part of a national plan or otherwise included in the sincere and conscious priorities of the recipient countries or institutions, the results will be disappointing if not totally wasted. Examples are innumerable: discontinuity is a southern characteristic.

In the end, information systems and services flourish where they are really needed. This conference should start by quantifying and qualifying this need, in both the North and the South.

IMBALANCES BETWEEN INFORMATION EXPORTING COUNTRIES AND NET IMPORTERS: CAN DEPENDENCY ON FOREIGN INFORMATION BE REDUCED?

by Merline E. Smith
Scientific Research Council
Kingston, Jamaica

RESUMEN

La Falta de Balance entre los Países que Exportan
la Información y Los que Principalmente la Importan:
Se Puede Reducir la Dependencia en la
Información Extranjera?

Los países en desarrollo, el "Sur," tienen una dependencia informática y hay muchas dificultades en vencer esta situación. La tranferencia de la información tiene lugar principalmente en las grandes corporaciones, y esta información no esta ajustada a las necesidades de las regiones en desarrollo. Los países en desarrollo tienen que crear estructuras nacionales de coordinación de información para sus proprias necesidades. Se ha creado en Jamaica un buen modelo de un servicio informático, la STIN. Los países en desarrollo tienen que mejor utilizar los recursos y fuentes de información que ya tienen, aumentar el personal adiestrado y especializado, y aumentar la publicación de la investigación científica. Incluye bibliografía.

INTRODUCTION

The ultimate goal of science and technology is to serve national development and to improve the well-being of humanity as a whole. Recourse to the products, processes and practices resulting from science and technology is therefore necessary in all sectors of economic and social activity. Information, the communicable form of knowledge, and especially scientific and technological information, is a main prerequisite for the rational use of national resources, the development of human resources, scientific and technical advances, progress in agriculture, industry and services, the blossoming of culture and the enhancement of social well-being. Assimilation of scientific and technological information is therefore an essential precondition for progress, particularly in the developing countries (Unesco VII 1982).

Industrialized countries ("the North") are characterized as information exporters; the developing countries ("the South") are importers. In the North, users have instant access to much current scientific and technological information through data processing and telecommunication technology. Of the approximately 900 bibliographic and numerical databases available online internationally, under one percent is produced in the south, where few countries even have the means to access foreign databases (Unesco VII 1982), being inhibited by the initial equipment costs, lack of skilled manpower and the high cost of telecommunication.

What scientific and technological information is produced in the south is poorly organized and only partially included in international databases. This difficulty of access deprives both North and South of information that is vital for understanding the problems faced by developing countries and for developing strategies to overcome them (Unesco VII 1982).

With 95% of the world's research and development being executed in the North, which has only 30% of the world population, determined national and international measures are needed to redress the balance. Otherwise the North-South gap can only widen.

This will require communication—national, regional and international, which can only occur if the South establishes the necessary infrastructure to support the flow of information.

Imbalances

Fair distribution of the benefits of science and its application is still far off, but even countries with a scientific tradition cannot develop all the technologies they require, and all depend to a greater or lesser extent on the transfer of technology. Such transfer, particularly from North to South, is mostly channeled, however, through multi-national corporations, whose primary concern is profit. They bargain from extremely strong positions, and by skillfully manipulated contracts prevent Third World countries from acquiring the information contained in the technologies they are supposedly transferring. Exorbitant fees are extracted through patents, trademarks, licenses, royalties and other restrictions. Although the importing countries may understand money and commodity systems, they are often ignorant of the technology market and make extremely bad purchases. By playing one country against another the sellers squeeze the maximum return, and the buyers may get locked into costly and marginally economic contracts that inhibit attempts at indigenous scientific and technological development.

Northern countries, aware of the potential of the information being generated, have developed technologies for handling it which have ensured them a dominant position in information transfer. Unlike the South, they have the financial and human resources and the technical capability to create databanks and other information systems on a scale that guarantees them control of the greater part of information generation and transfer in the world today, a situation that seems likely to long endure. As these countries move from the "industrialized" to the "information" era, more information is generated than their societies can absorb: hence the pressure to export.

But the products of this information industry are based on the perceived needs of the North. Little thought is given to the requirements and infrastructure of the South, which has technical problems to overcome in establishing connections with international systems and economic difficulties in paying for the materials and services provided, particularly when this has to be done in hard currency. The language barrier adds to the expense of translation if full benefit is to be derived (Tocatlian 1981).

Most Southern countries suffer from weak information infrastructures, which restrict their technological options. New forms of information handling may present problems of a social or cultural nature. Other hurdles include: (a) obstacles to access to information, obstacles to the availability of publications, and obstacles to the absorption and effective use of information (Tocatlian 1981); (b) lack of incentive for local science and technology workers to publish locally (appropriate vehicles do not exist, or lack the prestige of those in the metropolitan countries where many such workers may have received their training); and (c) limited exchange between countries at the same level of development, and even between those in the same region with similar problems.

SOLUTIONS

The existing North-South imbalance in the circulation and distribution of scientific and technological information stifles the scientific potential of the Third World, contributing to its intellectual isolation and its technological dependence. Fortunately there is an increasing awareness of the important of scientific and technological information for scientific and technical advance and its application to economic, cultural and social development: the need is realized for a wider and better balanced diffusion of information, for its freer circulation, and for a greater reciprocity in the flow of such information.

In the 1960s, development was regarded in the South as synonymous with progress: a striving to reach in two or three decades the stage then attained by the North. This perception has changed. Southern countries now seek endogenous development, one more closely attuned to their own cultures and traditions. There is particular concern for the social and economic consequences of the application of imported technology (Tocatlian 1981).

Accepting the North's perception of development undermined the developing countries' capacity to decide what is most appropriate to their needs, a problem aggravated by lack of adequate information relevant to national needs and objectives, and by the inability of many decision makers to use effectively the information available.

Only by looking at the prevailing conditions in the Southern countries can solutions, and a reduced dependency, ensue. In some of them, information services are lacking. In others the essential infrastructure exists, but there is under-utilization of locally produced information. Thus the local information necessary for preparing and applying sectoral and national development plans is either unavailable or unused. This may prevent any improvement in present

planning practice. It means too that the information services will not get the priority they need to improve: funds
will be too scant, or provided so haphazardly as to preclude
their being developed systematically.

Development of a National Information Infrastructure

It is extremely important that southern countries establish national coordinating infrastructures, i.e. that complex of institutions, organizations, resources, systems and
services that support the flow of information from generator
to user, including its acquisition, processing, repackaging,
transfer and delivery. Such a system will so organize all a
country's available information that potential users will
know what is available, where and under what conditions.
It will be calculated *inter alia*: (a) to encourage the use of locally available information, reducing the number of requests
to foreign sources for information that can be obtained
quicker from local resources; (b) not only to facilitate the
flow of information, but also to increase national capabilities
for innovative development, for creativity and for making
optimum use of local resources; and (c) to allow the country
to identify alternative courses and work out solutions for its
own problems.

To develop a country's technological capacity, special
programs in the information field should be initiated. An
adequate network is needed to ensure a flow of fairly
detailed data and material on production and technical requirements projected both for the economy as a whole and at
the micro-level with specific growth projections and technical
requirements of significant production sectors and
enterprises. Once the nature and magnitude of sectoral
growth projections and technological requirements are
defined, the information systems should also be able to
provide possible technological sources, both local and foreign.
For specific projects and enterprises they should provide: (a)
production capacity in various or selected sectors, production

techniques employed, utilization of capacity and technical problems encountered; and (b) the nature of proposed expansion—the flow of information should also cover the need for new enterprises that may have to be set up to cover critical production gaps.

Some countries have solved some of their problems by establishing national information systems. Jamaica in its "Plan for a National Documentation, Information and Library System for Jamaica," as proposed by NACOLADS and accepted by the government in 1974, has addressed the question of subject networks coordinated by designated focal points (NACOLADS 1978), aiming at centralized listing of holdings of all information units. Each focal point will operate switching and referral services, with national overall coordination by the National Library. This system lends itself to cooperative acquisition, thereby reducing duplication and safeguarding scarce foreign exchange. A vital role is entrusted to the focal points: these are expected to assess needs (expressed or latent), assign priorities, and coordinate, encourage, create or strengthen suitable services and systems, to conduct a continuing evaluation of the capacity of these services to meet requirements and to see that they participate effectively in regional and international information systems.

The focal point for Jamaica's Science and Technology Information Network (STIN) is the Technical Information Service of the Scientific Research Council (SRC). STIN's activities include: (a) a union list of serials held by units of the network; and (b) directories of research and development projects, of science and technology equipment, of STIN resources and of expertise available—its "Skill Bank." Other focal point activities are a survey of scientific and technological activities in Jamaica, a multidisciplinary information service to small and medium sized industries and other methods for the dissemination of scientific and technological information.

A national scientific and technological information policy to give the proper directives in keeping with national development goals now forms an integral part of the science and technology policy being developed by the Jamaican government (Draft national... 1981).

Access

Access to locally produced information is unsatisfactory. Often there is no collection of official reports. Since most of these are unpublished, potential users are unaware of them and a valuable information source is wasted.

Access to information from abroad is limited by its cost, among other factors. Too little world literature is to be found in the developing countries, and where it exists, it is divided between different information units without cooperative agreements to facilitate access.

Remedies are various. Efforts are needed to acquire official reports, national statistics, inventories of current research and of development projects, and translations of foreign publications. There should be national-level review of procedures for acquiring, locating and supplying such material, a coordination of information activity and such inter-library cooperation as has been mentioned earlier. International agreements on technology transfer should include a carefully defined "information" component.

Utilization of Information Services
in Southern Countries

Inhabitants of the Southern countries tend not to use what information facilities they have. These facilities in consequence remain underdeveloped and the societies uninformed; research and development are not stimulated and there is no input into the world pool of scientific and technological information. Some users distrust local information as out of date and unreliable, insisting on information directly from abroad even if it be unsuited to their needs.

Information personnel have to show that such mistrust is unjustified. Services should be evaluated to ensure they meet users' needs effectively and efficiently. Demonstration courses should be organized for the training of users. Marketing should include user participation in the design, operation and evaluation of services. Policies framed as a guide to long term action should concentrate on the factors (social, cultural, educational and other) which motivate users: how they organize their work; how they perceive their needs; and their attitudes towards existing services.

Promotion should be aimed at all user groups, but especially at policymakers, planners and managers, who may not be sufficiently aware of the role of information in their respective fields, or of the benefit that scientific and technological information can provide to the national economy.

Manpower

Lack of skilled manpower is a major obstacle. When inadequately trained staff provide poor service, it is difficult to enlist support for information services. Even when education and training facilities exist, inadequately trained staff are used and recruitment remains difficult for professional staff. Low salaries and status discourage people of the right caliber. All too often training still follows traditional patterns inappropriate to modern needs.

Training cannot be overemphasized, and countries should develop proper local training institutions. Qualified staff are needed, not only to operate information systems, but to keep abreast of rapidly evolving technologies, to promote innovative development and to make optimum use of local and international information sources. There is also need to develop information management capabilities at the national level, educating personnel who can act as "liaison" officers in national policy formulation.

Publication

In the North, "publish or perish" policies result in considerable production and consumption of all kinds of information. In the South, scientific and academic research seldom has this stimulus: the production of information and particularly of systematically organized technical information is not yet a major objective. Incentives are needed to encourage Third World scientists and technologists to contribute to research and development and to make their findings known.

South-South Cooperation

Although less than in the North, countries of the South are working for their own development, creating new philosophies, inventing new techniques, rejecting imposed formulae and providing solutions to some of their problems. In all this, the experience of another developing country is often more relevant than the experience of the North.

Yet South-South channels for sharing such experience barely exist. North-North and North-South communication is constant, but between developing countries it is a mere trickle. Despite the small extent of such inter-communication, there is a growing awareness in the South that: (a) information is the ignition key to the engine of multi-purpose cooperation; (b) with reliable inter-communication, development researchers can coordinate their activities, pool resources and build new and more self-reliant knowledge, applying their cumulative potential towards innovative solutions to development problems, such as alternative technology and energy sources; and (c) greater knowledge of each other's development endeavors will help reduce intellectual dependency on the North and modify the negative images of each other that have constituted immense attitudinal barriers to cooperation.

It was this type of cooperation that was addressed in the United Nations Conference on Technical Cooperation among Developing Countries (TCDC) in Buenos Aires in 1978, where one objective was "communications among developing countries, leading to a greater awareness of available knowledge and experience as well as the creation of new knowledge in tackling problems of development." Such cooperation is envisaged as taking place at national. regional and interregional levels, linking all developing countries (Buenos Aires... 1978).

CONCLUSION

If nothing is done, the North-South development gap will widen as the years pass, making the developing countries increasingly dependent. It is therefore imperative that appropriate steps be taken. Third World countries should aim towards an exchange situation. Rather than always "stretching" out their hands to receive, they should also be "giving" and, in doing so, be contributing to the world pool of scientific and technological knowledge.

REFERENCES

1. *The Buenos Aires Plan of Action: the United Nations Conference on Technical Cooperation among Developing Countries.* Buenos Aires: 1978.

2) *Draft national science and technology policy for Jamaica.* Kingston: 1981.

3) *NACOLADS. Plan for a national documentation, information and library system for Jamaica.* Kingston: 1978.

4) Tocatlian, Jacques. Information for development: the role of UNESCO's General Information Programme. *UNESCO bulletin for libraries*; 1981; 3(3):149.

5) UNESCO. VII, Information systems and access to knowledge. In: *Draft medium-term plan 1984–1989*. Paris: UNESCO; 1982: 1.

6) UNESCO. IX, Science, technology and society. In: *Draft medium-term plan 1984–1989*. Paris: UNESCO; 1982: 1.

USE OF DATABASES BY DEVELOPING COUNTRIES: USEFUL TOOLS OR PANACEA?

by Murilo Bastos da Cunha
Universidade de Brasilia
Depto. de Biblioteconomia
Brasilia, Brazil

RESUMEN

¿El Uso de Bases de Datos por los Países
en Desarrollo: Herramienta Útil o Panacea?

Las bases de datos no son una panacea, sino herramientas útiles. La información es la base de una sociedad pos-industrial y por eso una ingrediente o factor de negociación en la política y el negocio internacionales. Hace falta reducir la dependencia informático de los países en desarrollo, mejorar los servicios bibliotecarios del tercer mundo, mejorar los sistemas de acceso informática, y ajustar los modelos informáticos a las necesidades y circunstancias locales. El uso de bases de datos fomentará estas tendencias; el crecimiento de la cooperación internacional en la creación y administración de bases de datos, cambios en la dirección y política de la tabulación hacia incluir más material originario del tercer mundo, una necesidad crecida de técnicos con conocimientos de la región, y una reducción en el costo de la telecomunicación. Incluye bibliografía.

THE GROWING IMPORTANCE OF DATABASES

The introduction of databases, especially in developed countries, may be perhaps the most important event in library and information science in the 1970s. But they are not a panacea for all library problems, just tools a librarian can use to help solve a specific question. Online systems attract because of their novelty, the possibility of receiving information in a variety of formats, and by the speed of access to specific citations. *Time*'s choice of the computer as its "Machine of the Year" demonstrates its growing place in daily life.

D. Bell points out that "a post-industrial society is based on services. Hence it is a game between persons. What counts is nor raw muscle power or energy, but information" (Bell 1973). So he called this new type of society an "information society." In such a society, information plays a vital role and has an economic and political value: it is considered a commodity and can be "bartered, traded and sold between and among nations" (Horton 1978). The control, management and dissemination of bibliographic information extends beyond the librarian's world, involving new types of professional and other, different organizations such as telecommunication companies, data processing firms and government agencies. Since it is a salable commodity there are legal, technical, political, communication, and even national security implications: United States databases for instance only became accessible to Communist China quite recently, as Sino-American relations improved.

Roger Summit perceived the high significance of the new value of information: "information access services are coming to be seen, not only as economically viable, but also as an essential part of each country's national interest (Summit 1980). In the dialog between developed and developing countries, information can be used as a new weapon. Briquet de Lemos, illustrating how information may be used "as a form of pressure and even as one of the vital elements in the blockade or boycott of a certain country" points out that

> the medical library in Teheran, while the Shah was in power, had access to the MEDLARS system of the National Library of Medicine. After the Shah was removed and the relations between Iran and the United States deteriorated, the supplying of MED-LARS services to Iran was suspended, damaging not only that country, but several others in the region that had access to that service in Teheran (Lemos 1980).

The number of organizations using database services grows annually. Carlos A. Cuadra estimated that in 1974 the "number of users was about 1,400 in the United States and Canada, and probably no more that ten other countries... At the present time [1978] it is well over 5,000 users located in twenty five or thirty countries" (Cuadra 1978). Now with a high level of competition in the North American and European markets and with library budgets diminished by shrinkage and inflation, United States database producers and vendors are starting to worry about markets for their products and services. The cost of transatlantic telecommunication links to online services in North America led European users to implement EURONET, thereby lowering access costs (Brenner 1979) but reducing sales for the United States industry. In 1976, D.H. Barlow, then a director of INSPEC, predicted that the solution would be sought "by trying to penetrate further into markets that we have not tapped, for example in the Middle East, or in the developing countries" (Barlow 1976).

The exact number of database users is unknown but it is clearly a fast growing market involving dozens of countries and millions of dollars.

Access to Databases by Developing Countries

Developing countries, having discussed their concern over access to information separately for years, were able to join together at the Conference on Science and Technology for Development, held under UN auspices in Vienna in August 1979 and "demand a New Global Information Network (GIN) that would facilitate the transfer of scientific and technological information to the Third World," believing that "a global network would reduce their information dependency and provide them with a certain amount of access to the world's scientific and technological information" (Sardar 1981).

Their struggle to achieve a new World Information Order and to reduce the information gap will not be an easy one. Reactions against it have already begun. Thomas Galvin of the University of Pittsburgh opined in 1981 that it "constitutes a major threat both to *our overseas market* [my italics] and to the free flow of information across national borders" (HR 3137... 1981). This shows two important concepts. First, that in information, as in technology, there is a market dominated by a few industrialized nations. With EURONET and the marketing ability of the British and French database producers, the level of competition is increasing, and affecting the United States industry. Even a cartel of online services was foreseen by Cuadra (1978) to eliminate competition and protect their market. Secondly, that this is related to the cliché of the free flow of information. In fact there is no such thing, only rhetoric—as Briquet de Lemos points out (Lemos 1980).

F.W. Lancaster seems to understand the clamors and fears of the developing countries when he says:

> Information is becoming big business and control of access to information is passing out of the government sector to the private industrial sector. In the West, information is increasingly looked upon as a

profit-making exportable commodity. Instead of getting information at nominal cost, developing countries will have to pay rich-nation commercial rates —a big threat (Lancaster & Martyn 1978).

PROBLEMS IN THE USE OF FOREIGN DATABASES BY DEVELOPING COUNTRIES

Rolf Weitzel analyzed the first eighteen months experience of using MEDLINE at the WHO MEDLINE center, Geneva. Searches were processed for seventy countries, most of them from the Third World: Asia, Africa, Oceania. Several problems were noticed. The average lapse from request to the delivery of the bibliography to the requestor was twenty days: "a fairly long delay in the context of an online system" (Weitzel 1976). But not all users shared this problem. Most were impressed by a type of information technology unavailable in their countries. There was also the document delivery problem.

> Everybody knows that the library facilities in the developing countries are inadequate but the degree of this inadequacy is usually grossly underestimated ... in many areas, library facilities are not inadequate, they are nonexistent. Procurement from abroad of photocopies, when they have to be paid for, is difficult because of the lack of foreign currency (Weitzel 1976).

This dramatic situation demands solutions by both industrialized and developing countries.

E.N. Adimorah analyzed the difficulties faced by Nigerian librarians in dealing with scientific information. Some relate to the inadequacy of communication and the poverty of the bibliographic services. He suggests that "in an era of fast development in science and technology in developing countries and in the transfer of technological development from developed countries, information science should play a leading role" in solving those problems (Adimorah 1976).

The need for industrial information in Latin America was analyzed in 1976 by Stella Dextre, who wrote that, in order to resolve the need "it is not enough to set up a computer with telex links and suppose that information will magically flow along them." Most of the largest Latin American companies are subsidiaries of multinationals who usually "do no research but rely on the foreign head office for this and for help with any technical problems" (Dextre 1976).

To provide a current awareness and retrospective reference service in libraries in the less developed countries, Charles Bourne has suggested: (a) "augment present local information services with computer-based reference services"; (b) "...spend more money for each site to improve local collections in a conventional way by increased numbers of subscriptions to printed awareness services and abstracting and indexing publications" (Bourne 1977).

Bourne claimed the former as better in cost-benefit terms, but presented no concrete proof. Selective dissemination of information services would require the preparation of user profiles. Selective dissemination of information requests could be run through local computer centers, or use existing services in developed countries. Wisely, Bourne added "that any good SDI or reference retrieval system generates an increased demand for copies of the actual publications" (Bourne 1977).

Robert Munn has criticized the implementation in developing countries of library and information models originally created in the North.

Reports, proposals and proceedings had much in common. ... Almost all were highly theoretical in nature. Just what information was to be retrieved at what cost and for what purpose was rarely mentioned. ... Most of the proposals involved the use of very large computers, and many assumed the existence of sophisticated communications networks. ... Thus the cost of some proposals, while perhaps reasonable by...United States standards, exceeded the entire higher education budget of many LDCs.

He also mentioned the need to pay more attention to the problems of document delivery, because "in countries where library services range from poor to nonexistent, access to documents is viewed as the critical problem" (Munn 1978).

In 1978, Johan Van Halm created the concept of "information dependence"—the result of technological, economic and educational dependencies. He proposed international cooperation in the information area in order to achieve "full access to information in easily assimilable terms to the user in all nations regardless of their stage of development, their culture, and their political system" (Halm 1978).

To secure access to agricultural information, FAO has set up a modern information system, AGRIS, based mainly on international cooperation. Cooperating countries total 120 and include many LDCs, cataloging and indexing the agricultural documentation of their countries and adding it to the AGRIS database. An evaluation of AGRIS's first two years, done in 1976, found that the attitude to AGRIS of information specialists of LDCs included:

(1) a need for "a single comprehensive database covering the world's agricultural literature, in conventional form, to replace the multiple databases now in existence;"

(2) a desire for "a participatory program ...[and] not... to feel completely dependent on a product fully controlled by one of the developed countries";

(3) a feeling that "AGRIS is already better than most other sources in its coverage of the literature of the developing countries" (Lancaster & Martyn 1978), especially in those subjects related to tropical agriculture.

The LDCs support decentralized international information systems to decrease their information dependency and narrow the information gap due to non-fulfillment of services provided by the developed world. But, as noted by Lee Burchinal, "representatives of some, if not most, industrialized countries are wary of, if not openly opposed to, development of further systems on the INIS model" (Burchinal 1976). Economic reasons make them favor their own profit-motivated private enterprise organizations over international, governmental,non-profit systems like AGRIS or INIS.

The United States has already begun selling databases and their SDI, software and similar byproducts to the LDCs. Louella Wetherbee points out the problems such highly developed technology can face in library-poor environments: (a) "lack of tradition of community-based library or information services"; (b) "lack of state support for general programs and materials..."; (c) "shortage of appropriately trained and allocated information specialists ..."; and (d) "lack of understanding by government decision makers of the importance of information transfer as a component of technology transfer in development plans" (Wetherbee 1979).

A.R. Haarala detailed common information problems faced by "remote countries" as: (a) "limited national research and development efforts which dictate *a great reliance on services from abroad*"; (b) "insufficient staff resources and collections of scientific and technical information"; (c) "a small clientele for scientific and technological information, which make domestic information systems costly"; (d) *"great distance to international data systems and large libraries abroad"*; (e) "great distances within the country between users and suppliers of information"; (f) "and last, but not least, language barriers" (Haarala 1978) [my italics].

Cavan McCarthy reaffirms these points.

We need databases, as well as reference books, journals of current contents, abstracts and indexes. We need information centers in the corporations and research institutes, libraries in universities and schools, and books in the hands of the people... Within this general picture, the perspectives for databases will be brilliant; treated in isolation they can never reach their real potential (McCarthy 1980).

Tefko Saračevic has a similar viewpoint: "...introduction of computer services without library backup is seen by some as counterproductive in that it raises users' appetites and with it the frustration in not satisfying the appetite, thus turning users away from information services" (Saračevic 1980).

CONCLUSIONS

Clearly, the use of databases by LDCs will, despite some complex problems, increase. Some trends can be anticipated:

International Cooperation

INIS and AGRIS will stimulate the creation of other international cooperative efforts. Participation, even on a small scale, has several advantages. It not only increases access to foreign information, relatively cheaply, but also forces the creation, reorganization or modernization of the national information infrastructure, at least in regard to the specific literature. AGRIS, for example, has stimulated the creation of national agricultural libraries in Brazil and Paraguay and of AGRODOC, a Brazilian database with 60,000 citations.

Changes in Indexing Policy

LDC use of foreign databases gives limited satisfaction because of the low input of documents from developing countries. BIOSIS and CA SEARCH are among the exceptions: by including hundreds of titles from developing countries they have attained really international coverage. If they are to attract more Third World clients, other database producers will have to follow their example.

New clients from developing countries

Increasing numbers of clients from the Third World will pose other new problems for database producers and vendors: a need for training manuals in languages other than English; a need for instructors who understand local cultural differences and can communicate in local languages; a need for offices abroad (or at least the appointment of local representatives) to provide closer relations with the new clientele; and a need to adapt publicity to the local market.

Reduction in Telecommunication Costs

The cost of accessing foreign data is still very high: in Brazil, for example, $200.00US per hour for telex or telephone has to be added to the basic fee. In August 1982, a digital data telecommunication network (INTERDATA) connected to TYMNET and TELENET became operative in Brazil, substantially reducing such costs. Such developments have already occurred in other LDCs and will probably soon become common.

REFERENCES

1) Adimorah, E.N.O. Problems of scientific information work in developing countries. *Information scientist*; December 1976; 10(4):139–148.

2) Barlow, Derek H. Abstracting and indexing services as database producers: economic, technological and co-operative opportunities. *Aslib proceedings*; October 1976; 28(10):325–337.

3) Bell, Daniel. *The coming of post-industrial society: a venture in social forecasting.* New York: Basic Books; 1973: 127.

4) Bourne, Charles P. Computer-based reference service as an alternative means to improve resource-poor local libraries in developing countries. *International library review*; January 1977; 9(1):43–50.

5) Brenner, Everett H. EURONET and its effects on the US information market. *Journal of the American Society for Information Science*; January 1979; 30(1):5–8.

6) Burchinal, Lee G. Observation on international scientific and technological information transfer. *Bulletin of the American Society for Information Science*; October 1976; 3:11–12.

7) Cuadra, Carlos A. US-European co-operation and competition in the online retrieval services marketplace. *Information scientist;* June 1978; 12(2):43–53.

8) Dextre, Stella G. Industrial information in Latin America. *Information scientist;* December 1976; 10(4):149–156.

9) Expert fears info tech too costly for Third World. *American libraries;* November 1981; 12(9):598.

10) Haarala, A.R. Online user problems in remote countries, EUSIDIC Conference, Copthorne, United Kingdom, October 3–5, 1978. In: *Information policy in the 80s*. Oxford: Learned Information; 1979: 79–84.

11) Halm, Johan van. International cooperation or national dependence? *Special libraries*; May/June 1978; 69:201–205.

12) Horton, Forest W., Jr. The transfer of information technology to the Third World. In: *American Society for Information Science. Proceedings of the 41st Annual Meeting, New York, November 13–17, 1978*. White Plains, New York: Knowledge Industry Publications, 1978: 162.

13) *HR 3137 proposes information policy institute*. Library journal; August 1981; 106:1465.

14) Lancaster, Frederick Wilfrid; Martyn, John. Assessing the benefits and promise of an international information program (AGRIS). *Journal of the American Society for Information Science*; November 1978; 29:283–288.

15) Lemos, Antônio Agenor Briquet de. A transferência de informação entre o Norte e o Sul: utopia ou realidade. [Paper contributed at the Congresso Latino-americano de Biblioteconomia e Documentação, 1, Salvador BA, 1980]. *Anais*; 1980.

16) McCarthy, Cavan Michael. Bases de dados: vantagens, desvantagens e perspetivas latino-americanas. [Paper contributed at the Congresso Latino-americano de Biblioteconomia e Documen-

tação, 1, Salvador BA, September 21-26, 1980].
Anais; 1980: 593-618.

17) Munn, Robert F. Appropriate technology and information services in developing countries. *International library review*; January 1978; 10(1):23-27.

18) Saračevic, Tefko. Perception of the needs for scientific and technical information in less developed countries. *Journal of documentation;* September 1980; 16(3):214-267.

19) Sardar, Ziauddin. Between GIN and TWIN: meeting the information needs of the Third World. *Aslib proceedings*; February 1981; 33:53-61.

20) Summit, Roger K. The emerging internationalism of online information retrieval. *National Online Information Meeting*, New York, March 25-27, 1980. [Proceedings]. [ERIC ED 190103].

21) Weitzel, Rolf. MEDLINE services to the developing countries. *Medical Library Association bulletin*; January 1976; 64(1):32-35.

22) Wetherbee, Louella V. *North American machine readable database technology: some effects upon library and information systems in developing countries.* [Paper D-7 contributed at the American Society for Information Science 8th Mid-year Meeting, Banff, (Alberta), May 16-19, 1979].

AN OVERVIEW OF AUTOMATED INFOR-
MATION SYSTEMS IN BRAZIL

by Cavan M. McCarthy
Federal University of Paraiba
Joao Pessoa, Brazil

RESUMEN

Un Repaso de los Sistemás Automaticos
de Información en Brasil

Se describe en forma breve varios sistemas de información
brasileños, entre ellos sistemas para la diseminación de índices y bibliografías, bases de datos, catálogos colectivos,
sistemas para procesar datos de origen extranjero, y sistemas para analizar bases de. datos extranjeros. Entre los
problemas de estos sistemas se encuentran la falta de personal técnico, prohibiciones políticas sobre algunas clases
de importación informática, la falta de coordinación entre
las bibliotecas y las fuentes de información, y la dependencia informática en general. Se necesita que Brasil fomente
sus propios sistemas de información. Incluye bibliografía.

INTRODUCTION

A considerable range of automated information activities has been initiated in Brazil in recent years. First came the automation of traditional bibliographic services—union catalogs, indexes and the national bibliography. Now there is an effort to absorb modern database technology, with the importation of magnetic tapes for selective dissemination of information and retrospective search services. This paper covers all automated systems that disseminate bibliographic information beyond the responsible institution. It includes both indexing/bibliography systems and advanced technology systems but not internal library catalogs or internal indexing systems. It is based on information collected for the author's PhD thesis, the field study for which took place in 1980, and an update by mail in 1982. For clarity a few minor systems have been excluded.

SYSTEMS PROCESSING BRAZILIAN DATA

Systems disseminating indexes and bibliographies

IBICT (periodical indexing): IBICT, the Brazilian Institute for Information in Science and Technology, Brasília, has published bibliographies of Brazilian literature in specific subject areas (mathematics, physics, engineering, etc.) since l968, using KWIC or KWOC formats; 14,000 entries were made in 1979, when the total file contained 145,000 entries.

BN: The National Library, Rio de Janeiro, publishes the national bibliography, automated since 1976. Processing is via CIMEC and PRODASEN in Brasília; COM is used as a negative for offset printing 2,000-copy quarterly issues. quarterly issues.

CIMEC: The Education and Culture Ministry's data processing center, Brasília began producing a list of

Brazilian theses in 1976. Twice-yearly volumes, printed in 5,000 copies by a process like that for the national bibliography, are distributed free. Each volume has approximately 600 pages and some 3,000 theses, totaling in the four volumes issued through 1979 12,000 entries.

IMLA: *Index Medicus Latino-Americano*, produced by BIREME, São Paulo, first appeared in 1979, covering 220 Spanish or Portuguese language medical journals; 500 copies are printed. By 1982 the backfile was of 11,000 entries. Processing is on BIREME's own PDP 11/34 and online searches can be made.

FO/USP: The University of São Paulo's Dentistry Faculty has produced a Brazilian dental bibliography since 1966/67. Each volume, offset from printout in 800 copies, covers two years or about 1,000 entries in 200 pages. The backfile totals 5,000 entries.

CBP: The Brazilian Catalog of Publications is a books-in-print service set up by the Nobel book shop, São Paulo, in 1981. Subscribers receive a monthly updated set on fiche. The file of 26,000 titles may be interrogated online.

RFFSA: The Federal Railroad Network, Rio de Janeiro, issues a quarterly 150-page bibliography of railway affairs, reproduced from printout. The complete file of 15,000 items indexed since 1975 is available in printout form in the RFFSA library, which also has an online book catalog.

DATABASE AND UNION CATALOG SYSTEMS

PRODASEN: The Data Processing Service of the Senate, Brasília, operates an extensive and complex legislative database of over 300,000 entries (mostly post-1946 legislation, new bills, Supreme Court decisions) on an IBM 370/158, searchable by over one hundred terminals, using STAIRS/AQUARIUS. Two minor files hold bibliographic data: a 40,000-entry file for the Senate library's monographs, searchable by subject headings, and a 30,000-entry file of articles in its periodicals, with its own thesaurus. As several other institutions are inputting into PRODASEN it is becoming a general government system. Being directly subordinate to the Senate, it is well placed to receive the heavy funding such systems require. PRODASEN has been able to collaborate on other projects, most notable in producing indexes to a list of official publications and to the Official Gazette.

IBICT: The Union Catalog of Periodicals was begun by IBBD in 1968; thirteen regional centers collect data; most submit it on 80-column cards but four use magnetic tape. The file of 71,000 entries is updated quarterly; additions and alterations total 6,000 per year. Outputs include printouts of titles within broad subject areas, printouts of titles by region for the use of the regional centers and some printed catalogs for special purposes such as PETROBRAS libraries. The entire file has been available on COM fiche since 1978; fifty copies are made.

MINTER: The Interior Ministry's information system operates as a cooperative network. Ten large institutions (regional development agencies, for example) input material, mostly MINTER publications, but some members include other documents available in their libraries: monographs, periodical titles and articles. Each member receives a printout of its own input, union catalogs are produced on demand and the entire file (32,000 entries in 1980 increasing by 8,000 per year) may be searched in batch mode for specific subjects.

PLANALSUCAR: The planning organization for the sugar alcohol program, Rio de Janeiro, has an online searchable database of 8,000 items, increasing by 2,000 per year.

A PDP 15 computer is used and communication with the five network libraries is by telex.

DNER: The Federal Highway Department, Rio de Janeiro, has a single file (10,000 entries in 1980) for books in its libraries and relevant legislation, on an IBM 370/148, searchable by terminals in three locations via STAIRS/AQUARIUS.

PETROBRAS: The Brazilian Petroleum Agency, Rio de Janeiro, has 50,000 volumes in its thirty six-library network in a COM fiche union catalog producing cards for the holding libraries; a new cumulation and three supplements are produced annually.

SYSTEMS PROCESSING DATA OF CHIEFLY FOREIGN ORIGIN

Systems Searching Imported Tapes

EMBRAPA: The Federal Agricultural Research Agency, Brasília, being in a major government priority are, has been able to search a wide range of imported tapes. AGRICOLA was the first; CAB, Food Service Technology Abstracts, BIOSIS, Chemical Abstracts and SCISEARCH have since been added, making 7,300,000 entries by 1982. Researchers using the selective dissemination of information system number 3,500, including 200 in the "Southern Cone" countries; 1,500 profiles are searched by entry via computer and processing on an IBM 370/158. The number of profiles has been higher, but EMBRAPA felt this masked inefficiencies, such as several researchers on the same project using different profiles. Major effort is made to secure document delivery, obtaining 200,000 photocopies annually. There is also a retrospective search service: 354 such searches were made in 1979, on subfiles in batch mode.

BINAGRI: The National Agricultural Library, established in Brasília in 1978, searches AGRIS and International Food Information Service tapes. The selective dissemination of information service had 3,400 users with 4,200 profiles in 1979. By 1982, a retrospective search service had been added. Printed publications being considered essential at the current level of development of Brazilian agricultural libraries, BINAGRI produces a number of hardcopy products from the database: specialized bibliographies, both national and international, and the annual Brazilian Agricultural Bibliography, produced in 2,000 copies, offset from printout. AGRIS is a participatory information system and over 300 librarians have received training in preparing its input forms; by 1980 Brazilian items in AGRIS exceeded 12,000.

CIN: The Center for Nuclear Information, Rio de Janeiro, has been offering information service based on INIS tapes since 1970, beginning with selective dissemination of information which has 1,600 users with 1,900 profiles. A comprehensive manual is published, and output is in the form of a concertina of printed cards; considerable care has been taken to offer an attractive-looking product (always an important consideration in Brazil). Retrospective searching began in 1975: in 1979 360 searches were made via terminals at CIN; by 1980 400,000 entries were held on an IBM 370/165. The selective dissemination of information system uses weights but retrospective searching is by Boolean logic. INSPEC tapes have recently been added to the selective dissemination of information service and European Nuclear Documentation System tapes (1,300,000 entries) to the database for retrospective searching. INIS is a participatory information system, and CIN inputs details of Brazilian publications in the nuclear field (about 100 a month in 1980), and in 1981 the data began also to be used to produce the annual Brazilian Bibliography of Nuclear Energy. CIN can offer relatively extensive services because government considers nuclear energy a high priority area.

IPEN: The Institute for Energy and Nuclear Research, São Paulo, has offered MEDLINE since 1974, operating for about six hours per week. Searches are online from BIREME or from terminals in three other cities. A charge is made and 890 searches were carried out in 1979. BIREME is responsible for the indexing of thirty nine South American periodicals: two copies of each are received, one of which is sent to MEDLINE with completed indexing sheets, MESH headings and translation of article titles.

IPT: The São Paulo State's Institute for Technological Research imports COMPENDEX tapes for an selective dissemination of information service and has a backfile from 1973. In·1980, fifty profiles were being run at subscriptions from $100.00 per year. Output was on smartly-printed concertinas of cards.

Systems Searching Overseas Databases via a Telecommunication Link

The Brazilian government severely limits all forms of overseas data processing, including database searching, permitted only to IBICT. In 1980, SDC databases were used; 343 searches, the result of ninety eight requests from forty five organizations, were processed in 1979 at a user charge of about $100.00 per search. A major cost component was the telecommunication charge, Brazil not having access to a public packet-switching network.

(Since this paper was written, network access was established and searching of overseas databases was permitted.)

Comments

Automated information systems in Brazil range from simple list-making systems to full-service databases. A considerable demand has been established. All the essential indexes and bibliographies are produced, and, being on paper can be used in libraries throughout Brazil, without advanced equipment. These products could be improved, in coverage, indexing quality or currency and in the future doubtless will be; the important point for now is that they exist. Distribution is another obvious area for attention. They are usually free and in limited editions. With little tradition of reference information use in Brazil, the potential market is still unaccustomed to buying bibliographic material.

Demand for selective dissemination of information is greater than for retrospective searching: in 1979, 7,500 users of selective dissemination of information compared with 1,800 retrospective searches (Bibliotecas... 1980). Brazilians are not used to using information, so material likely to be of interest is sent regularly, in easily-analyzable amounts. Selective dissemination of information systems are well-publicized, through leaflets, courses or conferences and the user may be given a manual to help draw up the first profile. The three most full-established systems update profiles via a terminal, only one selective dissemination of information service charges its users and all include systems whereby users can complete forms to request original documents. *Revista de biblioteconomia de Brasília* 2(2) was devoted to selective dissemination of information: the first time, I believe, any Brazilian library journal has concentrated on a single subject. Selective dissemination of information is also one of the few library topics with two books dedicated to it, both by EMBRAPA staff (Braun 1982, Brízida 1980). Retrospective searching on the other hand is not an automatic process. The user has to request it specifically, usually (in Brazil) by having to fill out and mail a complex form. A large number of references may be received, many to older material. Retrospective searching is publicized less than selective dissemination of information and more often charged for, with the danger that dissatisfied users will become annoyed and cease to use the service. Brazilian professional salaries are too low for charges for literature searches to be accepted cheerfully. As a basic principle, all Brazilian information services should be free to users. As the government is the ultimate source of all research and development funding, charging for information service is an unnecessary interdepartmental accounting exercise. Bibliographic publications should be distributed free to libraries, but some copies should be held back for sale at a nominal price to the public, foreign libraries and libraries in need of extra copies.

Brazilian systems are often general ones, selecting material by form, origin or both (e.g. theses from Brazil) whereas systems using imported data are likely to be subject specific, and to cluster in certain fields (there are two services in agriculture, two in nuclear science). This duplication guarantees service should one service close; the systems claim to complement and not rival each other. Meanwhile, wide areas of culture and research are without information systems. The government, facing the myriad problems of a rapidly developing country in a world recession, has no time for detailed planning in the information field. The central institutions in the area have themselves had trouble adjusting to the new conditions, especially as some have undergone severe modification recently. So positive planning is lacking.

Interestingly, institutions that started by offering quite specific services have begun to offer much wider ones. Thus EMBRAPA, in agriculture, began with AGRICOLA, later obtaining tapes including *Chemical Abstracts*. CIN, in nuclear science, began with INIS, then added INSPEC. There is both a tremendous demand for an extension of service and a very small number of institutions with capability and experience in tape processing, so that the latter come under heavy pressure to widen their range. My thesis showed the experience bottleneck to be the most serious problem facing automated systems in Brazil.

The lack of integration between libraries and information systems is also notable. Systems using Brazilian data basically emit products for libraries, but the imported systems select the information and pass it direct to users, bypassing the library. This ignores the fact that libraries are well-established and relatively common in Brazil, totalling 15,000, with 30,000 employees of whom 10,000 are graduates (4,500 graduates in library science) and a total bookstock of 48,000,000. They have 7,000,000 readers, using 63,000,000 volumes per year in the library and borrowing a further 20,000,000. These figures are much higher than those for use of information systems. In fact, all Brazilian professionals are close to a library: seven percent of Brazilians are registered library users. So libraries could have an important role as the interface between information systems and their public; their use would avoid the danger of advanced information systems being confined to an élite. Their use as the prime area for information system interface and training would do wonders for the performance, impact and image of the library profession.

In a low-information environment such as Brazil, potential users, unfamiliar with the entire information retrieval concept—even simple indexing—need training. Postal contact and the consequent need to handle complex forms is particularly difficult. Dealing with a trained librarian would help considerably. Long-term it is clear that, as they develop, information systems will want to move online and that libraries are the only institutions where terminals could be installed. So far there has been little pressure to install terminals: Brazil's own packet-switching network has yet to go into operation and foreign systems have been refused access to Brazil as detrimental to national interests.

All seven systems searching imported tapes rely on imported tapes. This has caused much soul-searching by Brazilians concerned with dependence in the computer field. Dependence is an emotive word and a complex issue. One expert, commenting on the semiconductor industry, states that "it was hard to see why dependence in the semiconductor areas should be worse than dependence in any other— energy, metallurgy, plastics, pharmaceuticals, food, machine tools" (Braun 1982). Presumably, because computing is so essential to government control and uses equipment originating from the one dominant power in the Hemisphere, it arouses fiercer emotions. The Brazilian government has taken considerable steps to reduce this dependency. Reserving the micro-computer market for Brazilian companies, the most spectacular of these steps, was the most obviously successful: computer imports have also been severely controlled. The prohibition of overseas processing and of United States packet-switching networks is more relevant to us. To cite one Brazilian official:

> Political frontiers, which until recently limited the physical space and protected the intimacy of nations, are beginning to become diffuse. There can be no doubt whatever that the torrent of data that crosses frontiers, not always in a reciprocal manner, is one of the major causes of the aforementioned lack of definition of these limits (Brízida 1980).

Brazilian law forbids the processing of data abroad. "If complete freedom of data flow were allowed, much of Brazil's commercial data processing would be done outside the country," (McCarthy 1982) and the prohibition extends to searching foreign databases. Only IBICT is permitted to search databases overseas, and only for peripheral subjects; where a subject is of importance to Brazil, policy is to import the tape for local processing. This policy has led to the setting up of the six information systems mentioned above. This is about as close as we can get to government planning in this field, but it is not positive planning, merely the negative impact of a general policy that happens to affect the information field.

(It is a telling comment on Brazilian planning that as noted above, policy has changed and overseas searching is now permitted.)

Nor are these six services information systems in the full sense. Receiving ready-made tapes they are responsible for technical but not for intellectual aspects (except insofar as they input local information to an international system). Scientific and technical information in Brazil is run on exclusively computational and mechanistic lines (McCarthy 1982). As systems that use Brazilian input are intellectually much simpler, there is no place where Brazilians are gaining large-scale experience in abstracting and indexing. This serious deficiency reflects similar deficiencies in library schools, where information analysis is rarely taught and where classification is a routine, not an intellectual operation (e.g. students are asked to find classification numbers for predetermined subjects, not to classify books).

The only reasonably satisfactory international information systems today operate on participative lines. One unit in each country collects and analyzes local information, submitting it to a central unit, usually in an industrialized country, which processes the information, combining it into a single tape. All participants then receive the complete combined tape.

These are the minimum conditions for an international system; nothing less can be acceptable to developing countries. Indeed a further condition is valid: the technology used at the center should be available to all participating units. And practice in Brazil has brought about a further modification: national units publish local information in hard-copy for local use. This already happens with the Brazilian input to AGRIS and INIS and the South

American input to MEDLARS (published as *Index Medicus Latino-Americano*).

Computer professionals are proud to be considered important by government, and fan the flames with patriotic advertising: "Computers are like crude oil, it is dangerous to depend on others." The Brazilian government is fully aware of the potential of databases. One official became almost ecstatic:

> The most relevant symptom of the expansion of tele-information is the birth among us of a new service sector: database consultation, which becomes possible when specialized public telecommunication networks exist. Database services should become one of the major business areas; there are forecasts that the potential return in this sector will equal that of telecommunications and crude oil (Costabile 1981).

The great fear is that if computers, and by extension databases, are like oil, then someone, somewhere, could just turn the tap off. There is a clear implication that the United States might use such pressure, although Brazilians are too polite to cite the United States by name. I do not share such fears and have gone on record as saying:

> A more healthy attitude would be to state that if the North Americans do not want to sell information to us, we will work things out with the Europeans, Japanese, or even find our own way. ...North Americans can cut off our supply of scientific and technological information; they can equally well boycott our coffee, iron ore, etc., and refuse to make further loans... All these actions are possible, but only make sense in a context of unimaginable politico-economic convulsions, a situation of semi-warfare. ...All modern politico-economic systems, capitalist or communist, are. based on strategies of world-wide market integration. It is of extreme importance for

North American capitalism that Latin America remains within its market, within the technological patterns established in Chicago or California... Turning off the tap would be extremely harmful to North American interests, because it would force Latin America to discover its own technological direction, and thus the subcontinent would become isolated from overseas markets and models. A more convincing scenario would be to turn off the tap of scientific and technological information at the Latin American end. A nationalist leader might well restrict or prohibit access to foreign information ... simultaneously economizing foreign exchange and forcing his country to develop a national technology (McCarthy 1982).

Given the global trend for the North to switch industrialization to Southern countries while it concentrates on service industries such as information, the southward transfer of selective dissemination of information will be essential, both as the tool of such a development and as its result. Brazilian official policy meanwhile is to encourage cooperative use of databases, as well as to set up purely Brazilian ones:

As information is a resource which has an economic value, the concept of protection or stimulation of a similar national product will be applied or adapted to its case. A tendency has also been noted for cooperative structures in the use of information networks, a tendency that the SEI (Brazil's Special Secretariat for Information) intends to accompany, stimulating all initiatives which lead to the establishment of databanks in Brazil, and their use, on a reciprocal basis, by other countries. Apart from the development of Brazilian databases, we intend to maintain in the country local copies of foreign databases, thus reducing its vulnerability to interruptions in the supply of information (Costabile 1981).

The linguistic precision is notable: local copies of foreign databases will *reduce* vulnerability, not eliminate it: a hypothetical "turning the tap off" will mean the loss of future information, the most up-to-date information, leaving Brazil with a backfile, rapidly losing its value as it becomes older. Participative systems apart, the approved solution is acquisition from a variety of sources. Brazil has set up a minicomputer industry using Japanese and European technology; when and if databases become available from two or more sources worry over loss of supply can cease.

A major cloud is a possible worsening of the recession and of Brazil's balance of payments deficit, and their effect on information imports, causing the profession to face a period in which the major objective will be to set up Brazilian systems operating on Brazilian equipment. These will be small-scale systems using microcomputers, owing more to existing indexing systems than to large information systems. Such a turning inward would be somewhat (although not wholly) negative, so it is to be hoped that Brazil's finances will let her remain intellectually open to the world.

If they do, we shall probably soon see the first attempts to set up large-scale, purely Brazilian, information systems, beginning in those areas where the international systems have had most success and impact and where the potential user group will be large, viz. agriculture, energy (both government priority areas) and health. Of the first two, agriculture has most experience of large-scale systems; the energy field has a number a people experienced in automated systems but they are more scattered and have operated on a smaller scale. As much of Brazil's foreign exchange comes from agricultural exports, an indigenous agricultural information scheme would contribute directly towards her economic priorities.

Brazilian institutions might become the central elements of Latin American participative information systems. This would be welcomed by the profession as enhancing its image, and by the government as a move towards the use of Brazilian databanks on a reciprocal basis. But there are two serious practical problems. Portuguese is spoken nowhere else on the subcontinent, and Brazil has, unfortunately, minimal experience of cooperation with other Latin American countries. In fact, the major advantage of Latin American systems with Brazil playing the central role would be precisely that they would encourage such cooperation.

REFERENCES

1) *Bibliotecas Brasileiras.* Rio de Janeiro: IBGE/INL; 1980.

2) Braun, Ernest. Electronics and industrial development. *Bulletin of the Institute for Development Studies*; March 1982; 13(2):19-23.

3) Brízida, Jourbert de Oliveira. Posição brasileira sobre fluxo de dados transfronteiras. *Boletim informativo da Secretaria Especial de Informática*; November/December 1980; 1(2):9-17.

4) Costabile, Henrique. Política nacional de informática. *Boletim informativo da Secretaria Especial de Informática*; March/April 1981; 1(4):4-10.

5) Gomes, Hagar Espanha. Informação ontem. *Revista de biblioteconomia de Brasília*; January/June 1982; 10(1):33-42.

6) Longo, Rose Mary Juliano. *Sistemas de recuperação de informação: disseminação selectiva da informação e bases de dados.* Brasília: Thesaurus; 1979.

7) McCarthy, Cavan Michael. *The automation of libraries and bibliographic information systems in Brazil.* [PhD thesis]. Loughborough, England: University of Loughborough; 1982.

8) McCarthy, Cavan Michael. *Bases de dados: vantagens, desvantagens e perspetivas latino-americanas.* [Paper contributed at the Congresso Latino-americano de Biblioteconomia e Documentação, 1, Salvador BA, September 21-26, 1980]. Anais; 1980; 593-618.

9) Nocetti, Milton A. *Disseminação seletiva de informação: teoria e prática*. Brasília: ABDF; 1980.

10) Rosenberg, Victor. Information policies of developing countries: the case of Brazil. *Journal of the American Society for Information Science*; July 1982; 33(4):203–207.

THE NEED FOR THE ENGLISH-SPEAKING CARIBBEAN TO ADOPT AN AGGRESSIVE INFORMATION ACQUISITION POLICY

by Barbara Gumbs
Caribbean Industrial Research Institute
Trinidad

RESUMEN

La Transferencia de Información a la Industria:
Algunos Tópicos Caribeños

La infraestructura informática del Caribe de habla inglesa es muy inadecuada. Existen numerosos planes, pero, con la excepción de Jamaica, se encuentran mínimamente en vigor. La mayoría de la transferencia de la información ocurre informalmente por contactos personales. Existen varios sitemas, como CARISPLAN, CARIRI, UWI Libraries, SRC, y otros, y todos se encuentran con problemas serios, como el intercambio de moneda, la proliferación de servicios informáticos comerciales de eficacia no igual, y la falta de información ajustada a las necesidades regionales y a la industria regional. Se debe crear un servicio informático centralizado para la región. Incluye bibliografía.

INTRODUCTION

> The systematic and purposeful acquisition of information and its systematic and purposeful application are emerging as the new foundation for work, productivity and effort throughout the world (Drucker 1968).

The application of modern technology to the acquisition and processing of information has provided access to more data than was ever available before. Not only is more data available, but the format is likely to change from hardcopy to end products of the electronic media in the long term. These new developments in information, acquisition and processing present a serious dilemma for developing countries, most of whom are still in the process of planning and talking about a basic information infrastructure, including library networks and manpower training.

The information gap is becoming wider—the North is becoming richer and the South poorer. For the South to progress and develop, the gap needs to be narrowed. While several international organizations are assisting in the establishment of mechanisms for information transfer in the English-speaking Caribbean, it is also necessary for these territories to adopt a more aggressive policy for the acquisition of scientific and technical information for regional and national development. This acquisition could be achieved through the building of national databases, utilization of national embassies in developed countries, establishment of specialized information centres in areas of national and regional priority and participation in cooperative information schemes.

INFORMATION SERVICES

The Caribbean region needs to develop the capabilities for serving its technical information needs despite deficiencies in the basic information infrastructure. The More Developed Countries (MDCs) in the region with larger cores of scientists, technologists and better physical facilities need to take lead roles under the aegis of the Regional Bodies in acquiring information which is of critical importance to the region at large. A recent study on information flow in science and technology in the Caribbean revealed that existing information centres in the MDCs neglected to market their services to the region's LDCs, where fifty percent of the categories of information defined as difficult to obtain could have been provided by MDC information centres (Wiltshire, Gumbs & Durant 1982).

In the information transfer process, the local information services need to be supplemented by information services in the North. These services have assisted in bridging the information gap and have provided valuable information on specific topics. However, in the long term, use of these services in themselves does not strengthen and build local information expertise. Enzo Molino, while seeing this channel as an opportunity for the acquisition of information, sees it as "limiting in the sense that it does not create the facilities for national development in the field of technology or information; it does not solve the problem of local information; the supply of information is subject to restrictions; there is a continual outflow of foreign currency; and it leaves the country dependent on foreign sources of data" (Molino 1982).

Active consideration should be given to other avenues which in the long term will assist in building a foundation for local expertise.

NATIONAL DATABASES

The goal of the English-speaking Caribbean should be to attain some measure of self-reliance in the acquisition of information. In the first instance, priority should be given to the collection and organization of local information in each territory. Information generated from research studies, inventories, development projects, consultancy reports, project reports and annual reports constitute a valuable national resource for development of the region.

Local information has been neglected largely because of the fugitive nature of the material. Local consultancy reports are produced in small quantities and forwarded directly to clients for whom they were prepared. In the absence of a policy for declassifying material, these documents can be considered lost. In addition, local research findings are not published in local journals but in international journals where scientists achieve recognition and through which academic promotion is sought. Tracking and organizing local reports and identifying local research is at least the first step towards the establishment of a national database.

A first attempt is being made to organize socio-economic information at the regional level with funding provided by the International Development Research Centre, Canada. Under this cooperative programme, the sub-regional office of the Economic Commission of Latin America trains indexers in each participating territory and promotes the collection and preservation of all development planning information. The result is a core of trained indexers and a nucleus of a national database of socio-economic information in each territory. This programme should be extended to cover all types of local information since with the limited resources available, the Caribbean territories cannot afford to set up individual systems to handle different types of information necessary for development.

UTILIZATION OF INFORMATION TECHNOLOGY

·"When information is a priority—online is a necessity" shouts an ad in one professional journal (American Society... 1982). This slogan typifies the attitude to information access in the developed world. Low telecommunication rates, extensive coverage of relevant material in commercial databases and an adequate network for the provision of hard copies have encouraged widespread use of online systems.

Unfortunately, most of the English-speaking Caribbean territories lack the required telecommunication infrastructure to implement the use of online systems. Entrepreneurs in the developed countries seize this situation as an opportunity for business. They aere willing to acquire the local data, load it on computers in the Nort and sell online access through specific nodes. They provide a necessary service and a short cut to propel the developing countries into the information technology era. This approach would provide no foundation for future development.

It is now expedient for governments in the region to give a firm commitment to the establishment of telecommunication facilities to encourage online access of local information and to provide cheap access to foreign databases both in the North and the South. Any delay in doing so would perpetuate the weak negotiating position in which we find ourselves due to unequal access to information.

CONCLUSIONS

The building of national databases and the establishment of the telecommunication infrastructure are major thrusts to assist in the acquisition of information. However, while these are being developed, information requirements proceed apace. Information policies need to be put into effect to ensure rapid access to information.

Search centres should be established in developed countries either as a separate entity or as part of national embassies abroad. There is no reason why staff of national embassies should not be expanded to include information intermediaries whose responsibility will be to facilitate the acquisition of information—scientific, technical and economic—in areas of national interest. Developed market economies already utilize such centres, for example, the Society for Information and Documentation (GIB) of the Federal Republic of Germany has liaison offices in Bonn, Washington, D.C. and Tokyo, with headquarters in Frankfurt. One of the functions of the Washington office of GIB is to carry out liaison activities for scientific and technical information between the United States and the Federal Republic of Germany. (Strengthening... 1982)

Specialized regional information centres such as the Technology and Energy Unit of the Caribbean Development Bank should be established and strengthened to provide all types of information on specific areas of regional importance.

> If the developing countries remain recipient nations in ever-increasing quantity of scientific knowledge and technical information, their dependency will grow in ratio to the time and magnitude of the material they receive. ... Hence it is imperative that the developing countries create mechanisms for the capture, ordering, storage and dissemination of their indigenous knowledge and information related to national priorities and interests. (Policy Group...)

REFERENCES

1) *The American Society for Information Science bulletin*; October 1982; 9(1):5.

2) Drucker, P.F. *The age of discontinuity*. New York: Harper; 1968.

3) Molino, Enzo. Databases: considerations of relevance to developing countries. *UNESCO journal of information science, librarian and archives administration*; October-December 1982; 4(4).

4) Strengthening information resources in developing countries. *Information services and use*; November 1982; 2(3-5):100.

5) Policy Group on Scientific Information (POGSI), International Council of Scientific Unions. *Science information and development*: a POGSI report. [n.d.].

6) Wiltshire, W.W.; Gumbs, B.; and Durrrant, F. *Information and communication flows in priority areas of science and technology within the CARICOM Region – 1982*. [Study done for CARICOM Secretariat under the aegis of the United Nations Interim Fund for Science and Technology].

THE PRESENT STATE OF INFORMATION SYSTEMS AND BIBLIOGRAPHIC DATABASES IN LATIN AMERICA AND THE CARIBBEAN: FINDINGS OF AN OAS-CONTRACTED STUDY

by Marietta Daniels Shepard
Consultant
Bedford, Pennsylvania, USA

RESUMEN

La Situación actual de Sistemas de Información y Bases de Datos Bibliográficos en la America Latina y el Caribe. Los Resultados de un Estudio Contratado por la OEA.

Por medio de un cuestionario, se hizo un estudio de las bases de datos y sistemas informáticos en varios países latinoamericanos. Se describe los servcios en Argentina, Colombia, Brazil, Chile, Costa Rica, Ecuador, Jamaica, México, Peru, Venezuela y en algunos sistemas regionales, como AGRINTER, BIREME, CELADE y otros. Detallados en breve son los recursos humanos, la cooperación internacional en adquisiciones, catálogos colectivos, la catalogación, control de autoridades, índices, bases de datos automáticos, y otras funciones. Se recomienda, entre otras cosas, más cooperación entre y más normalización de sistemas automáticos, más transferencia de información, más índices, etc. Las bibliotecas de INBINA y UNAM tienen programas exelentes, que pueden servir de modelos para otros. Incluye bibliografía.

INTRODUCTION

The OAS has been active for over a decade in technical aid toward the creation of national library systems and laying the groundwork for an eventual inter-American information network. More recently, various OAS bodies have called upon the General Secretariat to promote information systems for economic and social development. Funds were consequently made available for a series of studies, beginning with investigation of the present status of information systems and the telecommunication aspects of information transfer.

A questionnaire was devised on national and regional systems, their human and technical resources and the services provided. A checklist covered 155 databases of general interest: thirty-seven on education, forty on energy, twenty-eight having information on Latin America and the Caribbean and six international bases from Europe (FRANCIS, INSPEC, etc.).

Finance limited the study to five countries, involving forty information systems and subsystems and nineteen library networks (sixteen in Colombia, two in Costa Rica, nineteen in Mexico, ten in Peru, eight in Venezuela and four regional).

The information obtained is not definitive, even for these five countries, but it illustrates the present situation in a segment of Latin America that includes some well developed systems. No single pattern emerges, but there is consistent emphasis on certain fields essential to national development.

NATIONAL INFORMATION SYSTEMS AND SUBSYSTEMS IN THE REGION

The creation and maintenance of national information systems in Latin America and the Caribbean has been found to be most successful in medium-sized and smaller countries having an active and vocal group of specialists, information users and purveyors, involved in promoting legislation in support of a national information system, and possessing an adequate and diverse information infrastructure: for example, Colombia, Venezuela, and Jamaica. In larger countries, there have been difficulties in creating and maintaining national systems, despite the existence in all of them of national councils for science and technology, and despite the efforts of international organizations to aid in their creation.

Even in countries lacking national systems, subsystems or networks, specialized information centers may exist to support teaching and research that can serve as national focal points for national systems—many already provide some services nationwide—and also as national nodes for regional and international systems.

What follows derives from both the questionnaire returns and a literature search.

Argentina

Although long discussed, no national information system exists in Argentina, even for scientific and technical information, although CAICYT (part of CONICET, the National Scientific and Technical Research Council) carries out many activities appropriate to the center of such a system: a published union catalog of periodicals held by Argentina's principal libraries and information centers, selective dissemination of information services to industry, support for accessing foreign databanks, a Telex network for inter-library loan, and work on thesauri and indexing language.

Other centers that could eventually become components of information subsystems include INTI, CNEA, DIGID, INTA and various institutes of the University of Buenos Aires such as IBUBA.

Brazil

Brazil has displayed great interest in forming a national library and information system and although none yet exists, many of its essential elements are maintained regularly, often as the result of agreements between various government and academic entities with IBICT (formerly IBBD), the information coordinating arm of the National Research Council (CNPq). Brazil's subsystems include PRODASEN (an automated data system for the Senate), CIN (which contributes to and receives INIS tapes), EMBRATER (developing SNIR, a national system of rural information), EMBRAPA and BINAGRI (both linked to AGRINTER and CARIS), and others in the fields of transportation, shipping, petroleum, patents, education, mining and sugar and alcohol production.

Brazil is working toward the automation of its national bibliography through the BIBLIODATA project at the FGV in cooperation with the National Library.

Chile

Chile's policy for science and technology, closely linked to economic development, is the responsibility of its National Scientific and Technological Research Commission (CON-ICYT) which liaises with the universities, the scientific and technical institutions of the state, and the private sector.

Under CONICYT is CENID, the national scientific and technical information coordinating agency.

The 1975–80 five year plan envisaged the creation of subsystems in agriculture and forestry, technology, medicine, energy, oceanology, education, social sciences, mineralogy and metallurgy, and of regional subsystems. There is also a subsystem for nuclear energy and plans for automating the national bibliography using the Venezuelan adaptation of NOTIS-3, which will also produce catalog cards.

Colombia

Colombia is among the few countries where a national information system (SNI) is functioning well, thanks partly to the decentralized nature of the education ministry and the existence of decentralized institutes with specific responsibilities as part of the governmental structure. The SNI, which doubles as the scientific and technical information subsystem, is operated by the national science foundation (COLCIENCIAS) in collaboration with the higher education institute (ICFES). In turn, ICFES maintains the university library network (Sistema Colombiano de Bibliotecas de Instituciones de Educación Superior) with automated cooperative cataloging using Mexico's LIBRUNAM. The national library and archives and the public library network come under the cultural institute COLCULTURA, but school libraries are under the education ministry.

Subsystems in health and education function in the corresponding ministry offices, one in agriculture (SNICA) is in the Colombian Agriculture Institute (ICA), one in economics and administration (SNICEA) in the Chamber of Commerce, one in industrial information (SNII) in COLCIENCIAS, one in energy resources (SNIRE)—partly automated—in the National Oil Undertaking (ECOPETROL), one in natural resources and the environment (SNIMA) in INDERENA, and one in maritime information (SNIMA) in the Navy. Additional subsystems are planned for popular culture, for tourism (in the National Tourist Corporation), in population (in the National Planning Department, DNP, and its population division), in anthropology (in the National University's Anthropology Department) and in telecommunications (at the National Telecommunication Office). Connection to MEDLARS is provided by the computerized Medical Information Program (INFORMED) of FUNOPA as part of the national medical information network.

Besides the national information subsystems, there are six regional committees and a Banco de Series Estadísticas Continuas in the DNP, as well as regional groups of specialized units in Medillín, Valle and on the Atlantic coast.

Costa Rica

It was hoped that a decree creating a National Information System for Development might be implemented in 1982 by the National Planning Office for Economic Policy (OFIPLAN). Developing a national scientific and technical information subsystem is the responsibility of Costa Rica's CONICIT. Subsystems exist in industry, agriculture and health, and educational information services are provided although there is no information service as such. Services of energy and industrial information form part of the subsystem of the Executive Secretariat of Planning of the Economy, Industry and Commerce Sector (SEPSEIC) and are partly automated using an imported package program. The University of Costa Rica maintains its Libraries, Documentation and Information System for its various campuses—soon to adopt MINIMARC—but this is unconnected to the other, newer, universities. Networks also exist of school and specialized libraries.

Ecuador

Recommendations have been made to set up a national information system with subsystems in agriculture, industrial and technical standards and in library development; that in agriculture has been partly achieved. CENDES in its Guayaquil Center for Industrial Development is an effective information service center in technical information for industry.

Jamaica

Jamaica's National Information System is a well planned one, supervised by the National Council on Libraries, Archives and Documentation Services (NACOLADS) and supported by adequate legislation. Its operation depends on the National Library, created in 1978 on the basis of the former library of the Institute of Jamaica, the Jamaica Archives and Records Center, the JAMAL Foundation and the Jamaica Library Service (school and public libraries). National centers linked with international and regional systems include the Network of Social and Economic Information (SECIN). The regional systems in which Jamaica participates include CARISPLAN (and *CARISPLAN Abstracts*), CARDI, CARICOM, AGRINTER and CLADES.

Mexico

Mexico's CONACYT was created in 1971, with legal responsibility for developing a national information system and a science and technical information subsystem, the latter under its Scientific Development Directorate which supervises the activities of the OAS-sponsored Multinational Center for the Transfer of Automated Bibliographic Information for MARCAL: MARCAL is the basis for a current project to automate the national bibliography at the National

Library. A service to industry, INFOTEC, has also grown out of CONACYT's scientific and technical information activities: it is now a semi-autonomous agency and a model for other countries. Another important agency set up by CONACYT is SECOBI, created to provide and coordinate online access to national, North American (DIALOG, ORBIT, BRS) and European (FRANCIS, INSPEC, PASCAL, INFONET) databases.

In its early years, CONACYT also developed a fellowship program to train university librarians at United States library schools, developed plans to improve provincial library holdings, for automating a union catalog of twelve scientific libraries and for a national union serials catalog. Recent administrative changes, however, have given CONACYT new priorities, lessening its concern with information systems.

The OAS survey revealed subsystems in statistics, geography and informatics (SENEGI), programming and budget and administrative sciences (SPP/CTCCD), health (CENIDS and its regional centers CRIDS), labor (INET), industrial promotion (SEPAFIN), agriculture (SNIA) and the sea, and also one covering Mexico City (SID). As in other countries, a library may provide the basis of a sectorial subsystem without having any official status. Mexican instances occur in chemistry, metallurgy, cattle production, telecommunications, transportation and *zonas áridas* (desert ecology). One of the most effective is that of the National Nuclear Research Institute's information center (ININ/ CIDN) in the field of nuclear energy, which has online access to INIS, as well as through its tapes, thus giving access to twenty different databanks in the energy field.

UNAM/DGB developed the LIBRUNAM automated system to centralize cataloging for the 165 UNAM libraries, using MARC. There are plans for other Mexican libraries and library systems to use the LIBRUNAM system and database: UAM for example. Its use in Colombia has already been mentioned. Another university library network is that of the provincial public universities (REBIMEX) which has an agreement with the National Library for cooperative cataloging of 16th-19th century books.

The Publications and Libraries division of the Secretariat of Public Education (SEP) is developing a public library network, centralizing acquisition, cataloging and building construction programs. A national archives system is being developed on the basis of two subsystems: historical and administrative archives. There is also a network of school libraries.

Peru

After some years in the planning stage, a national network of information for development is now included in the government's national plan for 1980–85. It is also hoped that the CENIDCYT of the National Science and Technology Council (CONCYTEC) may have resources in this period to begin developing a scientific and technical information network (RENICYT); a national union serials catalog, a national inventory of information resources, disseminating information in microform, training courses and continuing education in library and information science, newsletters in scientific and technical information and the creation of specialized subnetworks are the activities envisaged.

The government has demonstrated its commitment to information systems by creating SISNIDE in the education ministry with regional information centers (CENDIE and CREDIES, now called CEDDIES) and by the recent creation of a national network of school libraries and of professional training. A network of public libraries has existed for many years, the responsibility of the National Library's Public Library Office (OBIPU).

Other subsystems are petroleum (PETROPERU), industrial standards (Institute of Technical Research in Industry and of Industrial Standards), mineralogy (Mineral Enterprise of Peru), fishing (PESCAPERU), nuclear energy (Peruvian Nuclear Energy Institute, with links to INIS), productivity (CENIP), medicine (Information Center of the Colegio Médico de Perú, linked with BIREME), agriculture (Redagnigo, the subsystem REDINA of the National Agrarian University's National Agricultural Library in coordination with ABYDAP; and also REDAGRYCO of the Documentation Center of the AGRARIAN sector—both networks contributing to AGRINTER), housing (CENDIVIC's REDINAHVI network), telecommunications (RENIDTEL of the National Institute of Research and Training in Telecommunications—with automation being developed using packaged programs from abroad) and economic and social information (ABIISE).

The Peruvian Librarians' Association's University Library Group is active in promoting a university network through liaison between CONICDYT and CONUP. Lastly, an educational statistics system operates as a subsystem of the National Statistical System as a function of INE.

Venezuela

Decrees of 1976 and 1978 set up SINASBI, a national library and information service system on the NATIS concept, with the national library (now INBINA, an "instituto autónomo") as its secretariat. INBINA was made responsible for public library development, improving its Venezuelan holdings and automating its services, including the national bibliography (on a MARCAL format), through a contract with Northwestern University to use NOTIS-3. The first automated number of the national bibliography came out in September 1981. In 1982, however, SINASBI was left without an operating budget and CORDIPLAN was seeking funds to keep it going.

School library development is a function of the education ministry and the privately-supported Banco del Libro, with technical support from INBINA. Archives are under the Archivo General de la Nación.

A parallel (and partially automated) national scientific and technical information system (SINICYT) is the responsibility of CONICIT. Subsystems have been developed in medicine, agriculture (REDINARA), housing, construction, petroleum (at INTEVEP), urban development and social and economic information (REDINSE). Venezuela also has information services in ethno-musicology and folklore (INIDEF) being automated with OAS assistance.

REGIONAL INFORMATION SYSTEMS

The forty years of library, information and networking activities of the IICA in San José de Costa Rica have cumulated in the AGRINTER database (published as the *Índice agrícola de América Latina y el Caribe*), supplying regional bibliographic data to FAO's AGRIS in Rome through a network of agricultural libraries in every country.

The PAHO's Regional Medical Library in Sãa Paulo has developed BIREME, in cooperation with the United States National Library of Medicine for South American use of MEDLARS and MEDLINE.

Lima has the Andean System for Technical Information (SAIT), the Education Information Network (RIDECAB) of the Andrés Bello Convention countries, and ALIDE'S RIALIDE (development finance), plus a system for water and sanitation information (REPIDISCA) being planned by SENAPA whose database will use ISIS's CDS program.

Santiago de Chile has two United Nations regional systems—CELADE (demography) and CEPAL/CLADES (economic and social development)—and a third, that of UNESCO's Regional Office for Education, under development.

Other systems being formed are RITLA (technical information), SILADE (a UNESCO-sponsored documentation system) and OLADE (energy) in Quito. Subregional systems being formed include CEPAL's CARISPLAN and Caribbean Information in the Caribbean, and the OAS-supported ICAITI (industrial technology) in Guatemala.

MARCAL is already implanted in Mexico, Venezuela, Colombia and Brazil, and is being adopted by Chile on the basis of Venezuela's adaptation of NOTIS-3.

HUMAN RESOURCES

Statistics are incomplete but at least 3,365 persons are employed in the systems and subsystems of the five countries in the survey. Of these, thirty-eight are graduates in library or information science and there are 772 other information professionals and 343 professionals in other fields. Only 230 are known to read English well.

Mexico and Venezuela have provided foreign study fellowships. Seven systems and subsystems in all the most of them tenable with the country, and nine have funds to bring in outside experts to give courses and workshops.

COOPERATION

Acquisition and Storage

Only one system in the five countries reported a centralized acquisition plan, although others are known to be operating and there are seven cooperative acquisition plans in the proposal stage.

Some five systems and subsystems report cooperative storage for little-used materials; six subsystems have programs for cooperative transfer of blocks of material to other units where use will be greater; and three have such programs in development.

Union Catalogs

Colombia has five union book catalogs (one automated using LIBRUNAM) and is planning the automation of a regional union catalog. Costa Rica has two union book catalogs and Mexico has five (one printed, and one—that of UNAM—automated and on microfiche). Peru has five (one printed) and a sixth being planned. Venezuela has two automated union book catalogs and a third projected.

In Colombia, six union serial catalogs have been published by automated means. Costa Rica has two printed union catalogs of serials. Mexico reports six union serial lists, all but two printed; three have used automated means but as each used a different program, merging them is impossible. Peru has four union serial lists (two printed) in national systems and three in regional systems. Venezuela has five union serial lists: two printed, two automated and another with automation in prospect.

Nine systems reporting union catalogs indicated the percentage of members participating: Colombia 45–90% of three systems; Costa Rica 64–90% of two systems; Mexico 30% of one system; Peru 100% of two systems; and Venezuela 60% of one system.

Centralized and Cooperative Cataloging and Standardization

Of seventeen systems in the five countries giving detailed information, eleven have centralized cataloging and six have cooperative cataloging. The University of Costa Rica has a cataloging service for libraries of the other Central American countries.

Most Latin American and Caribbean libraries use AACR; increased conformity should follow the forthcoming publication by the University of Costa Rica of AACR2 in Spanish.

All seventeen systems use the Dewey Decimal classification system (in English, in Spanish or both), five of them use the Library of Congress (LC) classification system too. Another four systems use LC exclusively.

Authority Control and Subject Cataloging

National authority control is being achieved in Colombia, Mexico and Venezuela but there are programs in all five countries. Most Spanish American libraries and systems use the Carmen Rovira list of subject headings and a new edition, produced by OAS with participation from librarians throughout the region, will shortly be published by ICFES in Colombia. The list by Gloria Escamilla of the Mexican National Library is used in seven systems and that of the Library of Congress (on which both Rovira and Escamilla are based) in another seven. Sears is used in two systems. Locally produced lists, mostly adaptations of the foregoing, are used in nine. University networks in Colombia and Venezuela also use the National Library of Medicine's Medical Subject Headings (MeSH) for medical terms.

Thesauri used to supplement these lists include some from UNESCO, OECD, and ERIC. Some eight use other thesauri and five produce their own; seven are microthesauri, two (OECD in social sciences, ERIC in education) are macrothesauri. A few are bilingual, but most are monolingual.

Automated Cataloging

MARC has aided enormously in automating cataloging and several instances have already been given. The Catholic University of Chile has developed a centralized cataloging program using a minicomputer. MARCFICHES are in use at the Monterrey (Mexico) university library. The Universidad Iberoamericana in Mexico City is using MARC through AMIGOS contact with OCLC. UNAM began connection with OCLC in early 1983, and OCLC has been recommended for the Trinidad campus of the University of the West Indies and other Caribbean libraries.

Periodical Analysis, Indexing and Abstracts

In respect to journal indexing, questionnaire returns seldom distinguished between national and foreign titles. Duplication of effort (and cost) was seen in Colombian, Costa Rican and Mexican projects, caused by a wish to have the contents of recent journals available locally with least delay. These same countries all provided indexing services in the humanities, the three plus Peru in education, the three plus Venezuela in science and technology, and the three plus Venezuela and Costa Rica all indexed in the social sciences. Colombia, Mexico and Peru indexed agriculture. Colombia and Mexico both indexed energy and higher education, Costa Rica and Mexico both covered jurisprudence. Besides these, Colombia indexes in medicine, Venezuela in pharmacy, Mexico in labor, Peru in telecommunications, sanitary engineering and finance. All these are in file form and most of them in print.

The journal article databanks of ICFES (Colombia), UNAM/CICH (Mexico), INBINA and SINICYT (Venezuela) are automated. "Bancos de analíticas" are maintained in automated form in Colombia and in card files in Costa Rica and Peru. The INBINA records are to form part of its monograph database.

Indexing of national journals is done in all fields in Colombia, Mexico and Peru, and for literary journals in Venezuela. One Mexican project covers official journals. UNAM/CICH indexes articles on Latin America or by Latin Americans appearing in non-Latin American journals. Many of these indexes are published.

Abstracts are published on energy (Colombia), school libraries (Colombia), education (Peru) and economics (Venezuela).

SERVICES FOR USERS

Information

Analysis of information services is offered in twenty systems in the five countries: as compendiums in Mexico; as abstracts in four systems in Mexico and Peru; as analytical cards in seven systems in Costa Rica, Mexico and Peru; as miscellaneous publications in Costa Rica, Mexico, Peru and Venezuela; and by other means in Costa Rica, Mexico and Peru.

Bibliographic searches are made at users' request by twenty systems, in Colombia, Mexico, Peru and Venezuela: in manual form in at least ten, online in seven in Mexico and Venezuela, primarily through DIALOG, ORBIT, BRS AND INIS. Two systems produce lists from the computer.

Bibliographies are compiled by fourteen systems: four of these (in Colombia and Mexico) use automated databases for doing so.

Manual selective dissemination of information (SDI) is provided by thirteen systems. SDI from international databases is given by five (in Mexico and Venezuela). Four systems use information from user studies in providing SDI.

Current awareness service—usually photocopies of journal title pages, paid for by the center or by the components of the system—is offered by twenty-one systems. Most services relate to agriculture, education, energy, finance, housing, petroleum, technology or telecommunications.

Patent information is given, in some fields at least, in all five countries. Exchange of services at the international level occurs in ten systems. Question and answer service is offered by thirteen systems, and another is in project form; five are online to national databanks, two to international databanks.

Translation

Twenty systems offer translation service, most often from English, French and Portuguese, although Mexico's SECOBI covers many more languages with the aid of embassies and the Benjamin Franklin Library.

Copying

Most information units own photocopiers. Six systems have microform equipment. The number of requests received annually ranges from fifteen to 20,000, and the number of pages copied from twenty-five to 150,000 a year.

Loan Service

Home loans are generally allowed except from the Mexican National Library.

Interlibrary loan, almost unknown thirty years ago, prevails in most systems, on a library to library basis rather than through a national center. International loans are usually requested from the Library of Congress, BLLD, the National Library of Medicine or BIREME. Photo- and microform copies often substitute for interlibrary loan and may be obtained additionally from the retrieval systems of DIALOG, ORBIT and BRS, and , at times, from INIS, NTIS, ISIS and PASCAL.

Patron interests are identified by user studies in fourteen systems, of which ten (in Colombia, Mexico and Peru) make user profiles.

Access to Automated Databases

Databases most frequently used in the five countries are those in the fields of agriculture, medicine, education, social sciences, energy (nuclear as well as petroleum), science, industrial technology and news (NYTIS). Many databases are used in their printed form, where this is available, and by search requests sent to the sponsoring agency. Some tapes are imported (e.g. INIS). Online access in Mexico has already been mentioned but little is known of the extent this is used, except in the field of health, where access is available for nine hours and about fifty questions are received each day.

COMMUNICATIONS

National

The traditional means are the most used: mail accounts for 5-100% of all communications, telephone for 10-95%. Telex is used by one subsystem in Colombia, by two in Peru and by two in Venezuela.

International

International telephone calls go mainly by cable; four subsystems use microwaves and eight use satellite. Telex is more frequent than for national communication. TYMNET and TELENET are becoming more frequently used, in Mexico at least, for online access to databases.

PUBLISHING AND STANDARDS

National Bibliography and its Automation

International organizations, as well as librarians in the different countries, have long been concerned to achieve prompt and regular production of national bibliographies. Mexico, Peru and Venezuela among our five countries have undertaken to do so. Much will depend on effective legal deposit.

Besides books and periodicals, national bibliographies often include journal articles, these, official publications, non-conventional documents and audiovisual material. In Colombia, Mexico and Peru there are specialized national bibliographies in education, migration, popular art, nuclear energy, statistics, geography and agriculture.

Automation of Venezuela's national bibliography using NOTIS-3 and its adoption by Chile have already been mentioned. Colombia's National Library may also use this system.

Experimental MARC tapes for the *Bibliografía mexicana* were produced for January-February 1979. It may be possible to coordinate it with the LIBRUNAM system.

National Bibliographic Control

OAS has joined UNESCO in promoting national bibliographic control as essential to achieve IFLA's ideal of Universal Bibliographic Control (UBC). Various institutions have been given national responsibility for assigning ISBNs and ISSNs, for legal deposit, and for the study and acceptance of the International Standards Organization's ISBD standards. Colombia has accepted thirty-three ISO documentary standards and Peru twenty-seven.

Bibliographic Inventories Maintained

Besides union catalogs of different types of material, inventories are maintained of: research-in-progress in different systems and subsystems of all five countries; of technical reports (Mexico, Peru, Venezuela); and of resources (Colombia, Mexico, Peru, Venezuela).

Production and Publication of Directories and Guides

Directories are produced, irregularly, of libraries and information units (all five countries); of specialists (Colombia, Mexico, Peru, Venezuela); of translators (Colombia, Venezuela); or research institutions (Mexico, Peru); and of natural resources (Venezuela).

Other Products and Publications

Most systems and subsystems produce acquisitions lists, bibliographic bulletins, manuals, periodical catalogs, statistical annuals, and journals of articles and abstracts. Some, particularly in Mexico and Venezuela, also produce catalog card sets, magnetic tapes, microfiche and microfilm catalogs.

EQUIPMENT USED

Most system members have access to photocopiers. Microform readers exist in fifteen subsystems; seven subsystems have equipment for making microforms; sixteen have card duplicators; three have mimeograph, multilith or offset equipment; six have other reprographic equipment; and nine have binding or document repair equipment.

Fifteen subsystems have access to computers, six to mini- or microcomputers; seven have key punch equipment, eight have terminals, five have computer printers, and one has other computer equipment. Make of equipment varies greatly: IBM, Burroughs and Digital are the most popular for computers; Data General, Ohio Scientific and Wang are popular for minicomputers. Capacity and language (COBOL-ANSI, AEC-FORTRAN, PL/1 Assembler, BASIC and RPE) also vary a lot. For some systems complete documentation exists, but not for others. Products include thesauri, catalogs and lists, microfiches, and publications such as REPIDISCA's REPINDEX. Some programs could be applied in other countries.

INFORMATION SUBSYSTEMS OBSERVED TO BE NEEDED

In Mexico and Peru, at least, need was expressed for systems and subsystems in: agriculture; commerce; construction; education (higher as well as technical); energy; the environment; fishing; health and medicine; industrial property; metallurgy; mining; nutrition; social sciences (including economics and politics); and technology and its transfer.

OBSERVATIONS AND RECOMMENDATIONS

Our report shows the great strides made in recent years to improve Latin American access to the world's information, particularly where there has been thorough planning, adequate financing, effective standardization, appropriate legislation, cooperative effort and the avoidance of wasteful duplication.

Those involved must continue to strive for more effective national and regional information systems; automating in accord with international standards; creating new databases and increasing the use made of the existing ones; achieving bibliographic control in a way to ensure that the record of a work shall be created once only and in its country of origin; planning new networks based on "centers of excellence" that will serve as regional, national and sectorial foci of information systems; training users in identifying their information needs and in using databases and information systems; training the human resources needed to exploit the new technical advances; and making the necessary manuals and studies available in Spanish and Portuguese.

But information flow must be two-way: making information generated in the region known abroad is also important.

Provision of the infrastructure for effective information transfer is patchy: no one country of Latin America possesses every element. These include current and regular national bibliographies; union catalogs of books and serials; centralized cataloging to international standards; indexing of articles appearing in national journals or written by nationals and appearing abroad; interlibrary loan; and document delivery services.

Automation has been successfully applied but the need for standardized forms and compatibility of format has often been overlooked. With such equivalence, data in different bases can be merged for greater access at less cost than by developing individual unmergeable systems.

Access to Lain American journal contents, virtually non-existent twenty years ago, is improving: many indexing services have been mentioned. But duplication is evident. Coordination and automation can lower costs and increase availability.

Two outstanding programs mentioned in automation of bibliographical control and library collections are those of INBINA and UNAM: their experience ¡and the systems themselves can be of use elsewhere. Merging them with the other MARCAL databases being created in Brazil, Chile, Colombia and, in the planning stage, in Costa Rica, could make a Latin American database available in all countries, either online, as magnetic tape, on microfiche or in printed form. This would need conversion programs and translation of those MARC formats not yet put into Spanish.

The computer equipment currently is underutilized, thus in many countries additional programs could be mounted without more hardware. Chilean and Cost Rican applications of minicomputers to library automation should be significant.

Mexico is the country making most use of United States databases: proximity lowers telecommunication costs. Use of European bases may increase following a survey by Cuadra Associates to coordinate a project whereby twenty information brokers in the United States and Mexico will provide access to forty more such bases.

Remote online access to Latin American databases needs investigations. It is not clear how far AGRINTER, BIREME, REPIDISCA or CLADES are available online outside or even within their respective countries. In Brazil, national policy favors the importation of tapes over direct access to foreign databases; it is not known to what extent such policies may exist elsewhere.

OAS has been recommended to seek means to create additional regional information systems and databases in education (a Latin American ERIC?), energy (based on INIS), popular culture (based on INIDEF) and of national bibliographic control (based on the Venezuelan and Mexican systems). In these fields, development would be relatively easy because Latin America already has services in place on which they could be based and because there are international systems whose experience could be applied.

RECOMMENDATIONS

Some of the goals we seek:

1. *Information systems and their development:*

- National scientific and technical information systems and subsystems;

- Regional networks and systems in such strategic areas as Education, Energy, Popular Culture and National Bibliographic Control;
- An Inter-American network of information systems.

2. *Databases:*

- New automated databases in: Latin American and Caribbean bibliographies; Translations, National bibliographies, a Latin American database merging the national bibliographies, located in the region and in the Columbus Memorial Library;
- National union catalogs and serial lists, and the merging of existing ones.
- Creation of a Latin American OCLC for cataloging and interlibrary loan.
- At the OAS, a database of activities in education, science and culture, including research in progress and technical reports.

3. *Databases and their usage:*

- Wider use of existing databases by online access as well as in printed form and by requests sent to sponsoring institutions.
- Better knowledge of databases maintained in Latin America and the Caribbean and how they can be used.

4. *Databases and improved access to them:*

- Means of achieving access to European databases.
- Means of making databases in the region more accessible.
- Lowering telecommunication costs for online access, or developing alternative means of obtaining information from databases.

- Facilitating the use of databases through the world needed by such national level services in the region as SECOBI.

Coordination needed to achieve these goals covers the following areas:

- Union catalog production in standardized form; current awareness publications; periodical indexing; automation of the national bibliography programs now in progress in Venezuela, Mexico, Brazil, Colombia, Chile and Costa Rica, and the conversion programs developed for the merging of records; UNESCO and other United Nations development programs; OAS and its specialized organizations (IICA, PAHO, etc.) OECD, government agencies such as Canada's IDRC.

Standardization needs also to be achieved for merging information, in:

- Formats for union catalogs and serial lists with holdings according to MARC;
- Terms in subject heading lists and thesauri for subject analysis of materials;
- MARC formats for monographs, serial titles, periodical articles (analytics), technical reports, etc. and for authority records;
- Format for research-in-progress to be developed;
- Use of AACR2 for cataloging and MARC formats for automating bibliographical records;
- Compatibility of MARC formats and ISIS system for bibliographic records;
- Developing conversion programs to merge information from Venezuela's NOTIS-3 and LIBRUNAM, etc.

The development of certain mechanisms is recommended to achieve these goals;

- Creation of a multinational body responsible for clearing house services and for planning, coordinating and developing the various elements involved in creating an Inter-American Network;
- Strengthening the OAS Integrated Project of Library and Information Services in Education, Science and Culture to provide advisory and development services in these areas, including adequate funding for personnel and technical assistance projects;
- Assistance to member states in achieving UBC and UAP at regional level.
- Increased standardization of forms used in recording data and compatibility of information and data systems for more effective merging.

Instruments to be used in creating the mechanisms needed for achieving these goals:

- Technical assistance – by experts experienced in developing information systems and their automation, using standardized methods and forms, in missions by individuals or teams;
- Technical meetings – on indexing services for coordination purposes; of the directors of information services in selected fields such as education, energy, and national bibliographic control, to plan for systems development;
- Studies to be made: (a) of the information services of individual "centers of excellence" as a basis for developing sectorial systems in standardized and coordination fashion; (b) an inventory of automated databases in the region, online or not, and the products and services provided; (c) an updating of the studies of individual countries done by OAS a

decade ago on scientific and technical services, and of that of Scott Adams on selected countries, and the preparation of new studies on those countries not covered before.

The experience gained not just in Latin America, but throughout the world, in individual, national and regional projects for information storage and retrieval can be marshalled for the benefit of those who desire access to the world's information and knowledge.

REFERENCES

Author's note: This paper has drawn on over 200 works, in addition to interpretative reports on the questionnaires by Estela Morales (Mexico), Peregrina Goñi de Morgan (Peru) and Robert Vitro (Colombia and Venezuela). Among the more significant were the following.

1) Adams, Scott. *Scientific and technical information services in eight Latin American countries: developments, technical assistance, opportunities for cooperation; a report to the Office of Science Information Service, National Science Foundation.* Louisville, Kentucky: 1975.

2) Arias Ordóñez, José. *Centros y redes de información científica y tecnológica en la comunidad iberoamericana.* [Paper submitted to REUNIBER 78, Bogotá, 1978].

3) Bronsoiler, Charlotte et al. *LIBRUNAM: sistema automatizado para bibliotecas.* Mexico City: UNAM; 1982.

4) Carvalho, Abigail de Oliveira et al. *Informação científica e tecnológica: levantamento de situação no Brasil.* Versão preliminar. Brasília: CNPq; 1980.

5) *Computer-readable data for use in Latin American studies.* Princeton, New Jersey: Princeton University; 19—. [Computer printout].

6) CONACYT. *Consulta a bancos de información (SECOBI).* Mexico City: 1976. [Serie Servicios].

7) Escorcia S., Germán. *Redes: coexistencia conceptual y tecnológica.* [Paper submitted to IFLA Con-

ference, Montreal]. Bogotá: 1982. [141/PLE/10-Sp.].

8) Fundação Getúlio Vargas. *Sistema BIBLIODATA/ CALCO: trabalho realizado pela Biblioteca Central/ Centro de Processamento de Dados.* Rio de Janeiro: FGV; 1982.

9) Garcia, Maria Lúcia Andrade. A informação científica e tecnológica no Brasil. *Ciência da informação*; 1980; 9(1/2):41–81.

10) Goñi, Peregrina Morgan de. *Estudio sobre el estado de las redes y systemas de bibliotecas y de información en Perú: informe final.* Lima: 1982. [Typewritten].

11) Goñi, Peregrina Morgan de. La experiencia del Perú en su proyección al enfoque de la información aplicada al desarrollo. *RUCIBA*; April/June 1981; 3(2):136–143.

12) Gietz, Ricardo Alberto. El Centro Argentino de Información Científica Tecnológica. *RUCIBA*; April/June 1981; 3(2):113–117.

13) Guardia, Flor Oliver de. *Sistema Nacional de Servicios de Información Científica y Tecnológica en Venezuela.* [Working paper submitted to ACURIL XII, May 1981]. 1981.

14) INBINA. *Venezuela's National Library and Library Serices, 1974–1979.* Caracas: 198–.

15) Lampart, Sheila L. *Jamaica: the National Information System.* [Working paper submitted to ACURIL XIII, Caracas, 1982]. 1982.

16) McGinn, Thomas P. The automation of technical services in Venezuela's National Library: aspects of

transfer of library technology. *Library resources and technical services*; April/June 1982; 26(2):170–176.

17) Martínez C., V.D. La problemática de la transferencia de información técnica entre las fuentes y los usuarios en la operación de un servicio de información a la industria en las condiciones de un país en desarrollo. *REUNIBER*; 78:219–255.

18) Martínez Arellano, Felipe. *Perspectivas de catalogación cooperativa entre OCLC y LIBRUNAM*. [Working paper submitted to Seminário ABIESI Automatización 81, Mexico City, 1981]. Mexico City: 1981.

19) Martínez Gutiérrez, Marco Antonio. *Sistema de diseminación selectiva de información del ININ*. Mexico City: ININ; 1981. [Serie 4, Divulgación].

20) Matza, Morris. Una nueva etapa de la información para los investigadores venezolanos. [Working paper B-14, *SALALM XXIV*, Los Angeles, 1979]. Caracas: 1979.

21) Medina McLeod, Yola. The role of national libraries in Latin America: the example of the Biblioteca Nacional of Venezuela. *International cataloguing*; April/June 1982:22–23.

22) Monte-Mor, Jannice; Cysneiro, C.R. *BIBLIODATA*. Rio de Janeiro: FGV; 1981. [SIAC-81. Sessão D: Geração de bases de dados nacionais].

23) NACOLADS. *Plan for a documentation, information and library system for Jamaica*. Kingston: NACOLADS; 1978.

24) Ortiz O., José Rafael. *El Subsistema de Información en Recursos Energéticos: informe de las actividades de coordinación del estudio de factibilidad presentado a COLCIENCIAS y al PNUD por medio de ICFES.* Bogotá: Fondo Colombiano de Investigaciones Científicas y Proyectos Especiales "Francisco José de Caldas"; 1980.

25) Primus, Wilma J. *The Caribbean Information System for Economic, Social Development Planning (CARISPLAN).* [Working paper submitted to ACURIL XIII, Caracas, 1982]. San Juan, Puerto Rico: ACURIL General Secretariat; 1982.

26) Reina Matallana, Manuel José. *Base de datos de autoridades bibliográficos.* [Paper contributed at the III Reunión de Coordinación del Proyecto OEA para la Normalización de Técnicas Bibliotecarias y la Transferencia de la Información]. Bogotá: IC-FES; 1982.

27) *REPIDISCA: Red Panamericana de Información y Documentación en Ingeniería Sanitaria y Ciencias Ambientales, Lima, Perú.* Informaciones FID/ CLA; September/December 1979; 34.

28) Sambaquy, Lydia de Queiroz. *Brief report on library automation and scientific information systems in Brazil.* Rio de Janeiro: FGV; 1981.

29) Saracevič, Tefko et al. Information systems in Latin America. *Annual review of information science and technology (ARIST)*; 1979; 14:249–282.

30) Shepard, Marietta Daniels. *La infraestructura bibliotecológica de los sistemas nacionales de información.* Washington, D.C.: OAS; 1972. [Planeamiento nacional de servicios bibliotecarios, 1. Estudios bibliotecarios, 8].

31) Sistema de información del Caribe: sector de planeamiento económico social. *RUCIBA*; April/ June 1981; 3(2):151-152.

32) Tomé, Martha V. *La OEA frente a la problemática del control, procesamiento y diseminación de la información.* [Paper contributed at the Primera Reunión del Comité Interamericano para el Análisis del Formato MARCAL, Mexico City, February 25-27, 1980]. 1980.

DATA COLLECTION BY DEVELOPMENT PROJECTS
AS A NATIONAL INFORMATION SOURCE

by Marta L. Dosa
School of Information Studies
Syracuse University
Syracuse, New York, USA

RESUMEN

La Colección de Datos para Proyectos de Desarrollo
como una Fuente de Información Nacional

Los proyectos de desarrollo internacional son fuentes generalmente ignoradas para datos demográficos, sociales, económicos, y ambientales. Esto crea la posibilidad de crear redes nacionales de datos para adquirir, evaluar, y ajustar la información a las necesidades nacionales de planeamiento e investigación. Hay una tendencia reciente hacia la determinación de necesidades básicas en los proyectos de desarrollo, y esto afecta la naturaleza y utilidad de la información adquirida. Por eso, se necesita tomar muy en cuenta las circunstancias socio-culturales de cada región que se estudia ·y evaluar factores como la relación de confianza que existe entre investigadores y los individuos investigados. Se propone la creación de una red para la sistemización de pequeñas fuentes de datos. El problema no es tanto la falta de datos, como la falta de acceso a los datos que ya existen. Incluye bibliografía.

INTRODUCTION

The importance of human capital is now widely recognized as a major contributory factor to the growth process. Data on human capital require adequate information on matters related to education, health and housing (United Nations 1979).

Recent decades of international development assistance have brought disillusionment, critical searching and reflection to those involved. Investment in building physical infrastructures and industrialization dependent on capital flow and technology from the North has not helped alleviate poverty. One specialist expressed the anxiety of many:

> ... a quarter century of experience has placed some constraints on our thinking, in the form of facts on how the process has gone. Sometimes these facts are summarized by saying that development has been disappointingly slow: poverty still persists, and because of the rate of population increase, is numerically greater than it was at mid-century (Keyfitz, 1982).

A joint study of the Dag Hammarskjøld Foundation and the International Foundation for Development Alternatives, in concert with numerous other efforts at reassessment, warned that capital flows to developing countries "will bypass the nearly 800 million people living in absolute poverty. Most of these people live in the thirty-eight low-income countries which have little or no capacity to participate in the world's economy." This new realism led to the recognition that

> ... development cannot be reduced to economic growth; it is indeed a human-centered process aiming, through structural transformation, at the satisfaction of human material and nonmaterial needs, built from within the

society on the basis of self-reliance and in harmony with the environment (DFA/IFDA 1981).

The trend indicated by such observations implies that assistance policies are increasingly concerned with improving social conditions. As this requires an understanding of needs, methods of assessing poverty and developing standards for satisfying basic human needs have become a serious problem for developmentalists, summed up in the United Nations report on improving social statistics: "In developing countries, masses of people live in appalling and not quantified social conditions and a major concern should be measuring problems relating to them" (United Nations 1979). Although one cannot but shudder at the organizational lingo and the juxtaposition of human suffering and quantification, one must recognize that gaining information is the first step toward understanding the magnitude of a problem.

This paper investigates one resource for demographic, social, economic and environmental data: the international development assistance project. Such a project normally accumulates much scientific, technical and socio-economic data relevant to the population and conditions in the area, but data files produced for it are seldom known and used beyond the staff, organizations and consultants involved. Three broad issues concern us regarding the potential inventorying and utilization of these files and related documents: (1) international development strategies as a policy framework of projects and their information activities; (2) the nature of project-related data, and barriers to their dissemination and wider applications; and (3) the potential of national networks of project-generated data pools and their use for planning, policy making and research.

DEVELOPMENT ASSISTANCE PROJECTS

Financing assistance projects is undertaken by a wide variety of national and international agencies. The widely used term "donor agency" is misleading; many make loans, not donations. Projects may be identified, and consultants selected, by an international organization, one of the many consultant and technology transfer firms, a national government, or a particular ministry or private institution in the "host" country. Project teams may serve on reconnaissance missions, feasibility studies, project planning, design and implementation, or may be employed for specific tasks of data collection for assessing needs, monitoring project performance or evaluating the entire impact of a development program. Technical assistance may be targeted on economic and technological improvements, on health, social, educational or communication infrastructures, on urban, regional or rural development, or on introducing changes in a particular sector such as agriculture, energy, forestry or water supply.

A technical assistance project usually evolves a three-way communication pattern determined by the relationships between the project team, the local counterparts in the "host" country, and the donor agency. The attitudes of project management and technical advisors towards their local counterparts and the target population, as well as their understanding of the particular needs of the sociocultural environment, usually have a decisive impact on the outcome of development efforts (Dosa (in press)).

Experience shows that knowledge generating and informing activities are interwoven with almost all processes of planning, implementing and evaluating development projects, although there is usually no systematic effort to coordinate information flow. A literature review identified at least four broad categories of information processes:

(1) Manage Decision Support Information —
These activities may include reconnaissance, feasibility and planning surveys, administration data collection, policy analyses and reports, management information systems, and occasionally a more advanced decision support system. Normally these activities are carried out by managers and information specialists.

(2) Applied Scientific Investigation —
These may include environmental assessments, agricultural studies, rural sociological studies, industrial applications of technological research and development, or the social and economic analyses of existing conditions. Usually this type of information is produced by consultants and technical advisors who might be either foreigners or indigenous researchers.

(3) Local and International Bibliographic Resource Identification —
Projects may secure access to international bibliographic information systems and use the bibliographic search capability of the donor agency; in addition to building up its own documentation, a project may draw on information clearinghouses and libraries in the region or in the donor agency's home country. An information professional would be in charge of these activities.

(4) Interpersonal and Organizational Linkages —
A project often develops both formal and informal linkages with government agencies, provincial and local offices and institutions as well as with private bodies (farmers' associations, trade organizations, educational programs, etc.). Projects might hire consultants in nonformal education or communications to carry out such information activities. information activities.

This overview of project-related processes, although far from comprehensive, will serve as a backdrop for focusing the present paper specifically on data resources. "Information" and "data" are elusive, controversial concepts, abundantly used but seldom defined in project management documentation: interpretation depends mainly on the professional or methodological concept. Thus, a report on designing rural projects explains that

> the rationale underlying the reconnaissance survey assumes that it provides a way of synthesizing *data* rapidly into *information*, drawing on the analytical skills of the rural development specialists. "Data" are further described as "specific data points, such as those used to complete entries on a questionnaire..." In contrast, the report defines "information" as "data analyzed in a form that can be used in decision making" (Weisel & Mickelwait 1978).

In the following discussions, the terms conform to this interpretation. "Knowledge", a term often used synonymously with "information" (e.g. knowledge systems, knowledge explosion), will be referred to only sparingly and as information fused in the human mind with creative intuition and experience.

TRENDS IN DEVELOPMENT STRATEGIES

In the late 1970s, three forces affected the approach of international and national organizations to technical assistance for developing countries. First, changes in the world economy drove up inflation rates, thereby reducing investment and employment and encouraging protectionism. Developing countries face in consequence a decrease in capital flows, in exports to industrial countries and in technical assistance. Secondly, Third World countries, especially those dependent on the import of oil, are carrying an increasing burden of national debt and becoming increasingly aware of their dependence on external capital. With the emphasis on self-determination and sovereign rights to protect national cultures, the relationship between industrialized and aid-recipient countries is strained. Finally, past experience with development assistance adds little to the trust people in low-income countries place in projects and consultants. In some areas the changes introduced in agriculture, health care, family lifestyles or public administration by technical aid projects, have been abandoned after the foreign advisors have left. Inequitable distribution of the benefits of development and the lack of the recipients' involvement in planning are among the reasons for this (Independent Commission... 1980, Ingle 1979, Kilby 1982). Analysis of the relation between economic development and income inequality has found no evidence of the "trickle-down" process by which the poor are supposed to benefit from overall economic growth (Stack & Zimmerman 1982).

Although advances in science and technology are seen as means to rapid improvements in socio-economic conditions in Third World countries, the technological imbalance between them and the industrialized countries causes a growing frustration. An ODC report (Overseas Development Council 1979) estimated that 90% of innovations take place in and for the industrial countries with only 30% of the world population. Technology transfer to low-income countries is hampered by insufficient indigenous scientific and technological capabilities, the problems of adapting technologies to local needs and conditions, and the lack in some countries of acknowledgement of patent rights (United States... 1982). Another view holds that "...many scientific discoveries and technological innovations were initiated, and may be controlled for a long time to come, by a small number of countries and by a few transnational firms" (International Commission... 1980).

Changes introduced in development strategies in the mid-1970s by domestic legislation and international policies mandated aid to the poorest populations in developing countries and more determined efforts by project management to mobilize local participation in planning and implementation. It was hoped that such local involvement might motivate people to support, adapt and continue new agricultural, health, business and educational practices beyond the life of a project (Uphoff 1979). One of the basic conditions for involving beneficiaries is their capacity to make decisions on the selection of technology and to adjust foreign know-how to their own cultural and social needs. Today, developmentalists see information processes not only as a supportive technical factor in project planning and management, but also as a way to reach and interact with participants. For example, a research study of local social conditions conducted for a development project may become a vehicle for communication with local people (Bhatt, 1978).

The literature of rural development stresses the need for indicators that gauge the impact of social innovations and the involvement of local beneficiaries in projects. A survey by Cornell University Rural Development Committee evaluated land reform measures in Nepal ten years after their introduction, collecting data on land tenure, agricultural production, economic income and political participation, including participants' views of local government expenditures and taxation. Mexico's PIDER, an integrated rural development project made identifying measures to evaluate its social impact one of its priorities (Cernea 1979). Researchers are increasingly using social and socioeconomic factors in developing countries to measure disparities in the quality of life (Arief 1982, Oyebanji 1982). In fact, the entire "basic needs" movement, advocating international aid for adequate food, shelter, clothing, essential services and freely chosen employment to the poor, rather than for overall national income growth which normally tends to favor the elites, struggles with problems of identifying uniform standards and measurements. Hicks and Streeten are not the only sceptics when they write that "...any measure of poverty income, no matter how carefully derived, will be inadequate for measuring basic needs" (Hicks 1979).

Both research and managements reports stress that only a two-way communication flow between developers and local participants can assure the effectiveness of information dissemination as a development tool. Probably the most positive change in recent intercultural communication activities was the recognition that neither development planning nor the diffusion of innovations can be successfully imposed from the top down (Rogers 1978).

Information processes may explore the perceptions of local officials and population on what changes are needed and feasible and their results can be assessed from the viewpoint of those whose life and work have been affected. but for this a basic trust-relationship must exist. The relationship between researchers and information disseminators is crucial. As Lele has pointed out, "it is only when an effective two-way dialogue between research and extension is established that the current rural development effort will have a noticeable impact" (Lele 1975). Highly bureaucratized large-scale donor organizations find it much harder to mobilize local participation than small private voluntary ones (PVOs) with their more flexible and informal approaches (Sauerwein 1979).

THE CULTURAL ASPECTS OF TECHNOLOGY TRANSFER

The exchange of information and data is an inseparable element in the transfer of technology between countries. In the case of international technology brokerage firms it is often the only form. In a policy review. paper for the World Bank, Stewart states that "defining technology very broadly to include all knowledge related to economic activity naturally means that it encompasses a very wide range of types of knowledge, and that there are, correspondingly, very many mechanisms of transfer associated with it" (Stewart 1979). Weiss distinguishes between "hardware" innovation and social or "software" innovation, suggesting that "an intervention focused purely on technology ... is doomed from the start. In such cases, the introduction of hardware should be accompanied by and integrated with a package of policy and institutional changes" (Weiss 1979). Newly industrialized developing countries which are simultaneously building industrial and information infrastructures are importing, together with the hardware, computer process control systems and communication systems (Porat 1978).

These examples show the need to distinguish clearly between three interrelated processes: (1) *hardware transfer* (machinery, technical equipment, systems, parts); (2) *information transfer* (data and documentation, guidelines, standards, specifications, legal documents, policy statements, training manuals and maintenance handbooks); and (3) *knowledge transfer* (an understanding of the origins and potential impact of the technology, the ability to plan organize and manage applications, technical skills and know-how, training programs and materials.)

Knowledge transfer often strains the adoptive capacity of government officials: "they have to deal with indigenous issues largely with tools exogenously developed. The adaptation of those tools to their unique problems is dependent upon a sense of creativity and an innovative outlook" (Heper 1974). One of these new tools of administrative practice which is gradually finding its way to state and provincial offices, regional development organizations and social service agencies is the ability to convert administrative data into information for planning and program assessment. The creation of new data collection programs to support policy making is costly, cumbersome and seldom seen as justified even at the national level.

A prototype program created for a donor agency, thousands of miles from the project, often turns out to be oversized, overly complicated and inflexible. Often the cultural and technological gap between the developers and the would-be appliers cannot be bridged. Cultural and psychological distance can exist, too, between a member of a younger, urbanized and westernized generation and a more traditional provincial society within the same country, and then implanted information gathering methodologies may turn into barriers between project management and local populations rather than into opportunities to interact.

Sometimes innovative technology has been introduced that was not sufficiently integrated with the country's overall development goals and indigenous culture. A series of World Bank studies concluded that the transfer of inappropriate technology has contributed to serious dislocations and sometimes increased the hardship of the poor (Weiss 1979). Valid as this concern is, similar warnings have been exploited by technical advisors using them as justification for selling outdated equipment or condescendingly teaching oversimplified methods.

To safeguard against repeating past mistakes, adaptive field testing has been developed as a management tool, allowing for experimentation with new approaches without drastic consequences. Olsen (1978) suggests consideration of the following issues before field testing a proposed innovation: the availability of capable or trainable data collectors; the money available to pay personnel; the attitudes of host country officials toward a field testing program; and ethical concerns about experimentation.

Most factors that may influence the field testing are sociocultural. Rather than think of them as "barriers" or "problems" in people's adjustment to model transfers, we should consider them "opportunities": it is the model that must be adjusted to the cultural environment, not vice versa. Such sociocultural factors include:

(1) cultural heritage and the historical approach to communication (oral or written tradition, openness to, or mistrust of, foreign influences);

(2) societal values and beliefs, language(s) spoken or written;

(3) political ideology and dynamics, geopolitical alliances;

(4) the economic and social systems as they bear upon development priorities;

(5) educational programs and their relation to development programs;

(6) level of urbanization and bureaucratization;

(7) existing informal communication links in the region and the country; and the

(8) capability to work with, absorb and use information.

Some of these may have only an indirect effect, but keeping them in mind when testing a prototype should help build flexibility, tolerance and adaptive capability into the final plan.

PROJECT MANAGEMENT AND DATA COLLECTION EFFORTS

Reviewing a typical project cycle followed by the World Bank will help identify the processes that generate as well as require information (Baum 1978).

The phases include:

210 — Marta Dosa

Identification: Study of a problem and need, generation and selection of project and site.

Preparation: Examination of the technical, institutional, economic and financial aspects of the proposed project.

Appraisal: Review of the proposed project and preparation of the appraisal report.

Negotiations: Discussions with representatives of the borrowing country; preparation of the agreement and loan documents.

Implementation: The borrower is responsible for implementation and the preparation of progress reports for the Bank.

Evaluation: A department of the Bank reviews staff reports, prepares an audit and conducts field visits.

Similar guidelines, varying in emphasis, are maintained by other international agencies: United Nations Development Programme (UNDP), United States AID, OAS, the International Development Research Centre (IDRC), etc. Examples also exist of the integration of several projects into development programs, often systematizing programs within a sector such as agriculture, forestry or the building industries (Raman 1978).

To justify a project, management has to collect much technical, institutional and economic data about the project site and conditions in the host country. The World Bank and its International Development Agency require mainly investment-oriented managerial decisions and data. Other organizations stamp their own policy orientation on data collection priorities. In the past far greater attention perhaps has been given to economic and technical aspects than to social problems (Oyebanji 1982), but the World Bank has indicated a. new policy emphasis on human development in the fight against poverty (World Bank 1980), and it has recognized that "any development project that ultimately degrades the human environment is not a sound investment" (World Bank 1979).

Each phase within a project may be further analysed for steps requiring managerial decisions. Weisel and Mickelwait (1978) suggest, as "critical decision categories" in planning:

(1) specifying project objectives, including indicators of success;

(2) specifying project components;

(3) determining project management arrangements, and

(4) specifying project resource commitments.

Overstructured and inflexible projects leave no room for on-site adjustments, but decisions made in the course of implementing the actual development interventions matter even more. Dawson recommends that "an initial survey of local resources, potentialities and problems−not too time-consuming−should show where to start towards short-term results and longer-run improvements without risk of technical errors" (Dawson 1978). Certain indispensable processes beyond implementation are often overlooked; Rondinelli emphasizes the following:

(1) post-evaluation;

(2) diffusion and demonstration of results;

(3) transfer of resources to operating agencies;

(4) follow-up action (assistance of output users and identification of further investment opportunities;

(5) adapting appropriate technologies used in project implementation to other development activities;

(6) training of personnel for new projects.

The data gathering and manipulation activities usually connected with these processes are seldom integrated into
a system that would allow each action to draw on the
resources and experience of the others.

DATA COLLECTION FOR MANAGEMENT SUPPORT

I have set out in this paper to look at the characteristics and potential uses of data files generated by technical
aid projects in developing countries. One cannot expect to
locate data files and hope that today's users will be able to
benefit from them without problems or doubts. Some data
might be several years old, tabulated in incompatible ways
or uneven in quality, but might still represent a unique
resource for a given geographical or cultural area and for a
certain population. To understand the characteristics and
potential uses of development data, we should ask who collected them originally and for what purposes.

Smith (1974), formerly management systems advisor
to the MASAGANA 99 small farmer and rice production
project in the Philippines, defined a management information system as "a modern development of a more familiar,
but less glamorous process known as 'reporting'..." From
simple card files to computer systems, the reporting process
has undergone spectacular changes in recent years, expanding with the increasing complexity of development itself,
processing ever larger amounts of data. As the systems approach gained territory, "planning information systems",

"evaluation information systems" and "policy information systems" split off the management information system (MIS) model. Different teams on different phases of a project at different sites constructed their own information bases, often with little coordination, but MIS remained the dominant approach, spawning a large volume of literature (Delp et al. 1977, Hageboeck et al. 1979, Stewart 1979).

The information support that project managers received has been criticized for needless complexity, lack of selectively collected and evaluated date, and emphasis on efficiency rather than on effective decisions. A series of studies of rural development projects in several countries by Mickelwait and others (Information... 1979) showed MIS producing much under-utilized data and a failure to feed back information to the local population.

Occasionally a project will draw on government-university cooperation to produce an experimental decision support system (DSS) and computer modeling. A DSS may include a number of functions to allow the manager to analyze problems and study alternative ways to attack them. It is most appropriate for project decisions, because it can serve specific needs, provide data evaluation selectively, and perform comparisons and projections. Consequently, data sets assembled for this kind of flexible information support are usually more relevant and better evaluated.

Adelman and others (1979) compared two large-scale modeling efforts for the analysis of policies on income distribution and employment, one by the ILO, the other by the World Bank, which attempted to discover whether a set of policies could be identified which would, in time, lead to the satisfaction of basic needs for the majority of poor populations. National accounts, household expenditure surveys and censuses had served as data sources. Data sets used included information on prices, taxation, farm management and flow of funds. Uncertain data quality might be a problem in using such resources for secondary analysis, but they could have great potential usefulness. Thus the World Bank undertook to identify, for several countries, existing data sets for the analysis of income distribution patterns (Visaria 1979).

RESEARCH STUDIES AND PROBLEMS OF MEASUREMENT

The difficulty of assessing existing conditions and changes introduced to alleviate poverty is widely discussed. It is uncertain what information should be collected, and by what means, to understand local needs; whether it should be purely factual or should include people's subjective perceptions. Data on rural working conditions, urban plight or changes in family life styles are far more difficult to obtain than those on economic relationships.

Specialists have identified problems of social measurements in many different contexts (Hicks 1982, Hursch-Cesar & Roy 1980, Pearce-Batten 1979, Rush 1977). The issue of construction and use of indicators is seen mainly as that of methodology rather than of conceptualization. Those trained in a specific methodology may be reluctant to accept other approaches and collaborate with researchers of other methodological backgrounds. Definitions are controversial ("absolute" and "relative" poverty lines, basic needs, equity, etc.) and data collection is difficult because many concepts cannot be expressed in monetary values. Interpretations change with the situations and even international standards may fail when used in a different cultural context.

Methodologies designed for large-scale cross-national projects are not readily adaptable to local projects sponsored with modest funds. Technical skills for field research are often lacking, and the application of techniques must include extensive training.

Much primary data collection has been initiated where creative insight could have identified the existence of data files constructed by previous projects.

Cultural distance between researchers and indigenous populations may vitiate research. Gulhati argues that

> while the quick, airborne missions of international staffs were very appropriate when the focus was on modern, organized, high technology segments of Third World societies, they may prove quite ineffective in the context of designing poverty redress schemes requiring long and patient study (Gulhati 1977).

In considering reuse of research data files and reports, we must consider the possible impact of the researchers' background on the credibility of data in culturally alien regions.

ACCESS TO LOCAL INFORMATION RESOURCES

Today many projects are mandated by donor agency policies to direct their efforts at the poorest regions and to involve the local population in development choices. Assessment of local economic and social conditions by formal survey or information interaction is necessary. Advisors bent on introducing new disease control practices, water supply improvements or local public administration procedures similarly would make efforts to find out about existing customs and resources. Information thus gathered may be the only available intelligence on the area.

Projects collect local data by statistical surveys and the records of local governments and institutions. The former encompass reconnaissance surveys, "area frame sampling," population sampling and farm record surveys. Mickelwait, Sweet and Morse (1978) indicate that the amount and type of information collected for certain projects "differed according to the existing information base and the design team's mandate and resources." They describe several "existing information bases" that the analysts were able to locate and use, so saving both time and funds.

Mayfield (1977) reports on a study of financial administration of Egyptian villages. Face-to-face interviews with local officials were supplemented by the administrative records of the Organization for Reconstruction and Development of Egyptian Villages. A University of Wisconsin team (1979) relates similar experience in Tunisia.

Contrary to the frequent assumption about non-availability of data on local populations, etc. in developing countries, Woodward (1980) argues that

> by far the most important type of information, both in volume and value to any one country, is the locally produced information, and it is also this type of information which poses the biggest problems in organization and utilization. It consists of resource inventories, consultancy reports, project reports, studies of all types and, very important, annual and other administrative reports.

Woodward, then a technical cooperation officer at the National Agricultural Documentation Centre in Kenya, explains how new techniques and products introduced by assistance projects need local testing and evaluation, dependent on feasibility studies, analyses and reports of local researchers which hardly ever appear in the open literature. Their portrayal of local conditions could be extremely useful to subsequent projects.

Local documents are often unique means of access to information on town and village institutions. For thirty years aid projects accumulated extensive experience with community development, producing a large number of records (Holdcroft 1978). Local organizations are interlinked by a variety of activities and modes of communication (Korten 1979, Uphoff & Esman 1974). Projects intent on mobilizing participation managed to recruit local leadership and acquire important social and technical information about the community by contacting such organizations.

A NEW INFORMATION RESOURCE IN DEVELOPING COUNTRIES

Thus managerial, research and extension work related to technical aid projects include data collection efforts that may produce unique information embedded in data files and largely published reports. But while donor agencies and national governments have invested considerable energy and funds in creating these data pools, development specialists continually deplore the lack of data on local conditions. The present paper argues that these fugitive data resources could be used by a wide range of planners, policy makers and researchers provided their location and terms of availability were widely known.

Evaluation reports document not only problems but also positive experiences with project management information (Brinkerhoff 1979, Morss et al. 1976, Rush 1977, Sobhan 1976).

(1) Several MIS were designed for local and provincial governments; their databases have information on structures, processes and intergovernmental relations.

(2) Many systems collected and archived income-related socioeconomic data of use for secondary analysis.

(3) Information systems created for fairly recent projects probably have information in their databases about local participation and resources, a starting point for other projects.

(4) As several donor agencies and national governments are concerned with energy problems, relevant scientific and social data may be embedded in their project documentation.

(5) Demographic, household, farm employment and health-related information in local areas is almost certainly present in the data files of former projects.

Since both surveys and MIS are said to be least effective when handling data on such "squishy" problems as the participants' reaction to new cropping practices or their preferences in choice of health services, a constructive outcome of bringing these problems to the attention of planners, project managers and researchers might be some renewed efforts for improvement. Measuring and quantifying human conditions merit such careful reflection that attention drawn to their ethical implications would be a great benefit.

NETWORKS OF SMALL DATA POOLS: A PROPOSAL

Meyer and Smith (1978) report the following effort to identify the location of data resources:

> During the course of our examination of off-farm employment among farm household members in Taiwan, Korea and the Philippines, we found that there appears to be a growing interest in both the conceptual and the methodological issues related to rural development and off-farm employment. Unfortunately, we also found that many researchers were unaware of similar or complimentary studies complete elsewhere... Many of the researchers that were responsible for collecting the data have completed or are working on studies that will improve our under-

standing... In the autumn 1977, we sent a questionnaire to several researchers that could be identified... The responses identified yet other persons...

The network concept has been used in interpersonal, organizational and technological contexts. But definitions are conflicting and very vague. Progress toward synthesis of the various meanings was made by Pritchard (1978). Unpublished information sources are often shared among peers through personal contact. A trend toward systematic use of formerly informal channels emerged in the mid-1970s when organizations and interdisciplinary research groups began to compile directories of consultants, specialized programs and resource persons.

There are numerous reasons why information professionals in a developing country would want to initiate a pilot project for inventorying and linking data pools of local information. Although development planners and others may benefit from the network, information professionals have the expertise to effect a needs assessment, implementation and evaluation. The cost would be modest: no attempt would be made to remove data sets from their original locations and access would be through network referrals. The smaller the area covered, the more effective will be the referral service.

Negotiations with government departments and institutions storing the data would be necessary. An inventory of resources would be to indicate not only location, content, scope, coverage dates, collection dates, storage medium and related documentation, but also the terms of access. Questions of ownership, jurisdiction, primary users, possible confidentiality and service charges might arise. In fact, a pilot project to locate underused data might have the added benefit of identifying and raising some very timely policy issues.

THE NEED FOR EXPLORATION

Despite the alleged "shortage" of data, the real problem is one of lack of access. Crowther observes that

> a basic problem in Latin America is that we do not know presently how much is documented but not readily accessible. No country in the region has a well-functioning system of bibliographical control or data inventory, and the bibliographies and inventories which are prepared are bound to be extremely incomplete as long as such a system does not exist (Crowther 1979).

International organizations may occasionally evaluate large-scale databases, but there is no hope for the many smaller data files housed—but often not maintained—by various ministries and private institutions being given the same treatment. Nor is their integration into national or regional data centers a realistic option. Organizations develop proprietary feelings toward information they house, even if it is hardly ever used by the few officials or academicians who know of its existence. Politics, finance and logistics would defy any attempt to bring desperate data resources together, which, if achieved, would have no effect on the quality of the files short of an enormous evaluation effort.

The choice for national information planners is between the total neglect of such sources and inventorying them in their current imperfect state. Information professionals have always striven to organize information resources into near perfect order before making them available, but this principle needs rethinking. Awareness of possible difficulties with project-generated data should help users exercise critical thinking and caution, but not deter them from tapping the resource when hard-pressed for specific locally-relevant information. An education and training program for intermediaries who would maintain and update the network and handle referrals to data resources in an individualized mode seems a more realistic approach than condoning waste. As development strategies continue to emphasize human capital, it would be ironic to ignore the potential of human resources in the utilization of information.

REFERENCES

1) Adelman, I. et al. A comparison of two models for income distribution planning. *Journal of policy modeling*; 1979; 1:37–82. [World Bank reprint 81].

2) Arief, Sritua. Regional disparities in Malaysia. *Social indicators research*; 1982; 11:259–267.

3) Baum, Warren C. The project cycle. *Finance development*; December 1978. [World Bank reprint].

4) Bhatt, Vinayak Vijayshanker. Decision making in the public sector. *Economic and political weekly*; 1978; 13(21):30–35. [World Bank reprint 96].

5) Brinkerhoff, D.W. Inside public bureaucracy: empowering managers to empower clients. *Rural development participation review*; 1979; 1(1):7–9.

6) Cernea, Michael M. *Measuring project impact: monitoring and evaluation in the PIDER rural development project, Mexico.* Washington, D.C.: World Bank; 1979. [Staff Working Paper 332].

7) Crowther, Warren. *Information, development styles and environmental problems in Latin America.* [Paper prepared for CEPAL/UNEP Project Styles of Development and Environment in Latin America, Santiago de Chile, Instituto Centroamericano de Administración Pública, 1979].

8) DHF/IFDA. The gap in international resource transfers, parts 1–2. *Development dialogue*; 1981; 1:5–27.

9) Dawson, A. Suggestions for an approach to rural development by foreign aid programmes. *International labor review*; 1978; 117:391–404.

10) Delp, Peter et al. *Systems tools for project planning.* Bloomington, Indiana: PASITAM; 1977.

11) Dosa, Marta L. The consultant as information intermediary. In: *FID Congress, 41st, Hong Kong, 1982: Proceedings.* The Hague: North-Holland. [In press].

12) Gulhati, Ravi. A mandate on behalf of the poor? International agencies and the New World Order. *The round table*; 1977:268.

13) Hageboeck, Molly et al. *Manager's guide to data collection.* Washington, D.C.: Practical Concepts Inc.; 1979.

14) Heper, Metin. Training for potential bureaucratic elites of the transitional societies. In: Swerdlow, Irving; Ingle, Marcus, eds. *Public administration training for the less developed countries: Maxwell School Conference proceedings.* Syracuse, New York: Syracuse University; 1974: 4–12.

15) Hicks, Norman L. Sector priorities in meeting basic needs: some statistical evidence. *World development*; June 1982; 10(6):489–499.

16) Hicks, Norman L.; Streeten, Paul. Indicators of development: the search for a basic needs yardstick. *World development*; June 1979; 7(6):567–580.

17) Holdcroft, Lane E. *The rise and fall of community development in developing countries, 1950–65: a critical analysis and an annotated bibliography.*

East Lansing, Michigan: Department of Agricultural Economics of Michigan State University; 1978. [MSU Rural Development Paper, 2].

18) Hursch-Cesar, Gerald; Roy, Prodipto, eds. *Third World surveys: survey research in developing countries.* New Delhi: Macmillan Company of India; 1980.

19) Independent Commission of International Development Issues (Brandt Commission). *North-South: a program for survival; report.* Cambridge, Massachusetts: MIT Press; 1980.

20) *Ingle, Marcus D. Implementing development programs: a state-of-the-art review.* Washington, D.C.: USAID; 1979.

21) International Commission for the Study of Communication Problems. *Many voices, one world: report by the Sean McBride Commission to UNESCO.* London: Kogan Page; 1980.

22) Keyfitz, Nathan. Development and the elimination of poverty. *Economic development and cultural change*; 1982; 30(3):649–670.

23) Kilby, Peter. Evaluating technical assistance. *World development*; 1982; 30(3):649–670.

24) Korten, David C. *Community social organization in rural development.* [Resource paper given at A and P Agricultural and Resource Staff Seminar, Yogyakarta, Indonesia]. Manila: Ford Foundation; 1979.

25) Lele, Uma. *The design of rural development; lessons from Africa.* Baltimore, Maryland: Johns Hopkins University Press; 1975.

26) Mayfield, James B. *The budgetary system in the Arab Republic of Egypt: its role in local government development.* Washington, D.C.: USAID; 1977. [Field report].

27) Meyer, Richard L; Smith, D.A. *Data sources for the study of off-farm work.* Columbus, Ohio: Department of Agricultural Economics and Rural Sociology of Ohio State University; 1978. [Economics and sociology occasional paper 495].

28) Mickelwait, Donald R. et al. *The "New directions" mandate: studies in project design, approval and implementation.* Washington, D.C.: Development Alternatives; 1978.

29) Mickelwait, Donald R. *Information for decision making in rural development.* Washington, D.C.: Development Alternatives; 1978. [2 v.].

30) Morss, Elliott R. et al. *Strategies for small farmer development.* Washington, D.C.: Development Alternatives; 1976.

31) Olson, C.V. *Adaptive field-testing for rural development practice.* Washington, D.C.: USAID; 1978.

32) Overseas Development Council. *The United States and world development: agenda, 1979.* New York: Praeger; 1979.

33) Oyebanji, J.O. Quality of life in Kwara State, Nigeria: an exploratory geographical study. *Social indicators research*; 1982; 11:301–317.

34) Pearce-Batten, Anthony. Indicators of development; the search for a basic needs yardstick. *World development*; June 1979; 7(6):587–580.

35) Porat, Marc Uri. Global implications of the information society. *Journal of communication*; 1978; 28(1):70–80.

36) Pritchard, Roger. *Information networks and education; an analytic bibliography.* Paris: UNESCO; 1978.

37) Ramam, Pattabhi. Project implications in the context of a plan: the missing links. *International development review focus*; 1978; 20(1):5–7.

38) Rogers, E.M. The rise and fall of the dominant paradigm. *Journal of communication*; 1978; 28(1):64–69.

39) Rondinelli, Dennis A. Implementing development projects: the problem of management. *International development review focus*; 1978; 20(1):8–11.

40) Rush, W.H. *Application of comprehensive computerized surveys in the collection and analysis of farm data in developing countries.* Washington, D.C.: American Technical Assistance Corporation; 1977.

41) Sauerwein, V.T. United Nations restructuring: new challenges to PVOs. *International Council of Voluntary Agencies news*; 1979; 83:3–5.

42) Smith, Kenneth. *The MASAGENA 99 management information system.* Manila: USAID; 1974.

43) Sobhan, Igbal. *The planning and implementation of rural development projects: an empirical analysis.* Washington, D.C.: USAID; 1976.

44) Stack, Steven; Zimmerman, Delores. The effect of world economy on income inequality: a reassess-

ment. *The sociological quarterly*; 1982; 23(3):345–358.

45) Stewart, Frances. *International technology transfer: issues and policy options.* Washington, D.C.: World Bank; 1979. [Staff working paper 344].

46) United Nations. Department of International Economic and Social Affairs. Statistical Office. *Improving social statistics in developing countries: conceptual framework and methods.* New York: UNO; 1979. [Studies in methods. Series F, 25].

47) United States of America. National Science Foundation. *The five-year outlook on science and technology 1981.* Washington, D.C.: GPO; 1982.

48) University of Wisconsin, Madison. Regional Planning and Area Development Project. *Opportunities for development: a reconnaissance of central Tunisia.* Madison, Wisconsin: University of Wisconsin; 1979.

49) Uphoff, Norman Thomas et al. *Feasibility and application of rural development participation: a state-of-the-art paper.* Ithaca, New York: Cornell University Rural Development Committee; 1979. [Monograph series, 3].

50) Uphoff, Norman Thomas and Esman, M.J. *Local organization for rural development analysis of Asian experience.* Ithaca, New York: Cornell University Rural Development Committee; 1974.

51) Visaria, Pravin. Demographic factors and the distribution of income: some issues. In: *Economic and Demographic Change, Issues for the 1980s: proceedings of the conference.* Liege: 1979.

52) Weisel, P.F.; Mickelwait, D.R. *Designing rural development projects: an approach.* Washington, D.C.: Development Alternatives; 1978.

53) Weiss, Charles, Jr. Mobilizing technology for developing countries. *Science*; 1979; 203:1083–1089. [World Bank report 95].

54) Woodward, A.M. Future information requirements of the Third World. *Journal of information science*; 1980; 1:259–265.

55) World Bank. *Environment and development.* Washington, D.C.: World Bank; 1979.

56) World Bank. *World development report 1980.* Washington, D.C.: World Bank; 1980.

THE INFOPLAN SYSTEM AND THE TRANS-
FER OF PLANNING INFORMATION
IN LATIN AMERICA AND THE CARIBBEAN

by Ximena Feliú
Centro Latinoamericano de Documen-
tación Económica y Social
Santiago, Chile

RESUMEN

El Sistema INFOPLAN y la Transferencia de Información
de Planeamiento en América Latina y el Caribe

En 1979, se formó INFOPLAN para centralizar y distribuir información sobre experiencias de planeamiento de desarrollo en la América Latina y el Caribe, para crear una base de datos, y para desarrollar personal técnico y actividades educativas. El sistema es utilizado por una gran variedad de instituciones y individuos. Se ha analizado la selección y adquisición de información para el sistema en un manual para el use de personal. INFOPLAN también tiene un servicio de publicación de abstractos, y prepara bibliografía especializadas. Incluye bibliografía.

INTRODUCTION

A desire among Latin American and Caribbean planning authorities to be better informed about the planning experiences of each other's countries led to the creation at the April 1977 Primera Conferencia de Ministros y Jefes de Planificación de América Latina y el Caribe in Caracas of the Sistema de Cooperación y Coordinación entre Organismos de Planificación de América Latina y el Caribe, with ILPES as its technical secretariat. The objectives were to promote and implement the exchange of national experiences in economic and social planning and establish formal methods to strengthen cooperation. Subsequently the Technical Subcommittee of ILPES meeting in April 1978 at Panama City recommended that ILPES (a) undertake the broadest possible dissemination of research and studies on planning, and (b) maintain records of the results of work done by planning organizations. To fulfill these twin objectives, CLADES and ILPES, with financial support from IDRC, began in January 1979 a joint project to create an Information System for Planning, INFOPLAN.

That same month the first Meeting of Caribbean Planning Experts took place in Havana. Its report established that Caribbean planning cooperation should become the basic subregional instrument for the better functioning of the Sistema de Cooperación and Coordinación entre Organismos de Planificación de América Latina y el Caribe. At the same time, the Caribbean Documentation Centre (CDC) of ECLA's Port of Spain office (created in 1977 to support and coordinate the activities of the CDCC (CLADES. Guía... 1982) became the Caribbean Community's focal point for INFOPLAN, responsible for making information available to countries within the Caribbean and outside.

It was thus envisaged that INFOPLAN would consist of two regional groupings—Latin America and the

Caribbean—permitting adaptations to the characteristics and needs of each.

The nature of the planning process and the diversity of documents it creates have led CLADES to develop a special methodology to meet the information needs of the professionals involved. One very complex problem is the diversity of views on the very concept of planning, which stem from differing notions of society, particularly as regards the role assigned to the State. These theoretical differences and their practical effects lead to difficulties in the classification, control, processing and retrieval of documents. ECLA has striven to standardize the concept of planning, seeking an integrated approach that would define it as a continuous process designed to guide a social system toward a desired objective. The conception of the INFOPLAN system has been based on this approach.

Experience teaches that it will take at least five years to attain full efficient operation of a regionally decentralized information system such as that proposed for INFOPLAN, especially when the information structures of the cooperating national institutions and the professional training of the staffs involved are so various. For this reason, CLADES is giving particular emphasis during INFOPLAN's initial period (1980–82) to promoting the cooperation of member governments, to training staff to operate the system at national and subregional levels and to creating and organizing National Planning Networks (Redes NAPLAN), aiming first at controlling the documentation within each individual country and organizing national collections on planning recorded in internationally compatible databases. compatible databases.

The system has already created its own working tools (handbooks on information analysis and processing and for identifying and selecting material on planning, guides on methodology for training courses, manuals on the participation in NAPLAN of the coordinating national centers, etc.)

and this will allow a more rapid rate of development to be implemented in late 1984.

STRUCTURE

Definition of the INFOPLAN system

INFOPLAN may be defined as a decentralized, user-oriented network made up of cooperating centers coordinated by a General Coordinating Center, a Subregional Coordinating Center and National Coordinating Centers.

ECLA/CLADES, responsible for developing the project, acts as the General Coordinating Center. ECLA/CDC in Port of Spain, Trinidad, is the Sub-Regional Coordinating Center for the Caribbean. The roles of national coordinating centers should be played by the information centers of the respective national planning ministries or other authorities. In most countries these have been the respective national focal points of the project.

The participant centers are the information units of the national planning agencies, or where no such agencies exist, they are the information units of such private or university organizations as carry out equivalent functions in gathering and providing the literature on national social and economic development.

The cooperating centers are information units or systems within institutions whose activities relate directly or indirectly to economic or social development. They can be national, regional or international.

Objectives

The INFOPLAN system intends (a) to contribute to strengthening economic and social development planning in

Latin America and the Caribbean through the control, analysis and dissemination of documentary information generated in the region by national, regional and international agencies for planning or related subjects; and (b) to support ILPES programs for cooperation and coordination between participating planning agencies, by means of an information service on planning experiences in the region.

Specifically it plans (a) to develop the most suitable mechanisms and methods to make the region's documentation on planning accessible; (b) to coordinate and develop technical support and training activities as required by participant and cooperating centers; and (c) to maintain in CLADES, as the General Coordinating Center, an up-to-date regional bibliographic database on planning.

Geographic Coverage

The region covered by the system includes all countries in Latin America and the Caribbean (Map 1).

MAP 1

GEOGRAPHICAL COVERAGE OF THE INFOPLAN SYSTEM

◎ REGIONAL CO-ORDINATION
□ SUBREGIONAL CO-ORDINATION
● NATIONAL CO-ORDINATING CENTRE OF
   OF THE NAPLAN NETWORK
○ FOCAL POINT
▽ CONTACT

CLADES also maintains links with the information activities of other regional agencies and regionally based international agencies with subject interests relevant to development planning, to establish joint programs of information exchange, etc. (Map 2). INFOPLAN will also be linked to kindred information systems in other parts of the world, such as PADIS in Africa.

Map 2

**REGIONAL AND INTERNATIONAL BODIES
WORKING IN THE FIELD OF ECONOMIC AND
SOCIAL DEVELOPMENT AND BASED IN THE
REGION**

CIDE*
UNEP/ORPAL*
Mexico
ASIP

*CENTRAL AMERICAN BANK
OF ECONOMIC INTEGRATION

ICAP* IICA/CIDIA*
CSUCA* Costa Rica

UNESCO*
LATINAH* SELA
Venezuela
CLAD* ASIP*

*Bogota
INDERENA/INFOTERRA

OLADE* UNDP*
Ecuador INIS*

ECIEL
BIREME Brazil

ALIDE/REALIDE
Lima

WHO
* CELADE/DOCPAL
Chile

*Bodies with which the System
has been linked in the period
1979-1982

Subject Coverage

The general field is the planning process, defined as the record of planning experiences in economic and social development in Latin America and the Caribbean (Figure 1).

Figure 1

Planning Process

Stages

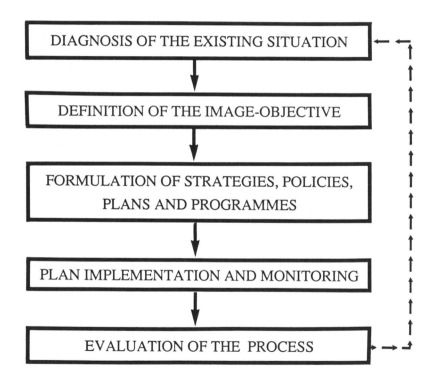

The planning process so defined cannot be separated from its institutional framework, constituted by the national planning agencies (both as users and producers of information), central banks, national statistical agencies, sectoral ministries or agencies, departmental planning agencies, planning and development research centers, etc.

Types of Documents

The documents most typically required and generated within the institutional framework have been identified according to the characteristics of each stage of a program and classified according to the DEVSIS Study Group's "development action" categories. For example, the documents generated and required during the "diagnosis" phase include basic statistics, financial statistics, national accounts, integrated studies of natural resources, reports on production sectors or factors, descriptions and analyses of society or the economy, and relevant legislation. In the phase of "establishing strategies, policies, plans and programs" the documents required and generated include: development strategies and plans; recommendations and resolutions; commentaries and observations by government and international agencies on global, regional, national and local policies and activities; and official statements.

To secure the broadest subject coverage and the comprehensive inclusion of all documentation required and generated by the planning process, CLADES has prepared and adapted methods and instruments for control, selection and processing of planning literature to be used by participating information units. INFOPLAN has also prepared a training program.

Documentary input into INFOPLAN should increase as new cooperative agreements are made with other systems covering subjects of interest, such as AGRINTER, ECIEL, ERIC, IREME and PADIS, permitting regular information exchange in compatible formats (tapes, disks or computer outputs).

Institutional Users of Information

The institutional function carried out within the process of development planning created specific information needs, independently of the person performing the function. Institutional users therefore include ultimately institutions themselves: the national planning ministry or agency; the national statistics office; the finance ministry and other ministries according to importance of their sectors in national development; the central bank; and government research organizations concerned with priority development sectors, etc.

Through cooperative agreements and information networking the institutional user also becomes a source of planning experience and therefore a producer of planning literature for its counterparts in other countries.

Individual Users of Information

Information needed by a minister of planning or the head of a national planning office differs in form and scope from that needed by a professional carrying out a sectoral development program or that developed by an economic advisor to project a medium- or short-term policy. Since individual users function within the institutional framework of the planning process, they can be grouped, for the operational purposes of the system, into broad categories and their interest profiles identified with greater precision.

So far six such categories have been identified and these have guided the methodologies adopted for information processing and in INFOPLAN's publication distribution policy. Further study will allow this categorization to be perfected. (See Figure 2.)

Figure 2

THE PLANNING PROCESS AND THE
DOCUMENTATION GENERATED IN IT

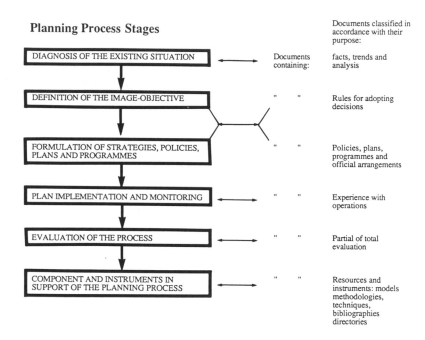

Planning Process Stages

Documents classified in accordance with their purpose:

DIAGNOSIS OF THE EXISTING SITUATION	Documents containing:	facts, trends and analysis
DEFINITION OF THE IMAGE-OBJECTIVE	" "	Rules for adopting decisions
FORMULATION OF STRATEGIES, POLICIES, PLANS AND PROGRAMMES	" "	Policies, plans, programmes and official arrangements
PLAN IMPLEMENTATION AND MONITORING	" "	Experience with operations
EVALUATION OF THE PROCESS	" "	Partial of total evaluation
COMPONENT AND INSTRUMENTS IN SUPPORT OF THE PLANNING PROCESS	" "	Resources and instruments: models methodologies, techniques, bibliographies directories

Information Systems as Information Users

Planning as an agent of change cuts across all fields and uses knowledge generated in all disciplines. INFOPLAN has to be linked with every information system or unit that gathers, processes or disseminates information in any development sector or in any discipline affecting economic or social planning matters or subjects. At the same time, all such systems and units need access to all information that could be relevant to their own field. In this way they become both users and providers of information. Contacts so far established with regional and international organizations have been made to promote this user-provider relation with the intention of making it before long a formal program of inter-system cooperation. Such inter-agency and inter-system cooperation will make it possible to satisfy complex information needs with "integral information packages", i.e. a set of statistics, projects, theories, models, etc. related to a single subject or specific problem required as input for each phase of the process.

Working Languages of the System

Spanish, Portuguese, English and French coexist in Latin America and the Caribbean, all actively producing economic and social planning documentation. Bibliographic data, abstracts and descriptors are fed into the CLADES database in the original language, but the abstracts disseminated through PLANINDEX include subject descriptors from the OECD *Macrothesaurus* in Spanish, English and French, to which Portuguese will be added as soon as the Portuguese translation of the *Macrothesaurus* has been published.

Administrative Organization and
Phases of Implementation

Although INFOPLAN has been defined as a regional and decentralized information system, its decentralization is an aim to be reached in successive phases depending on the level of development of each national information infrastructure. The first phase has necessarily been one of centralization in CLADES as executor of the project with overall management responsibility as the General Coordinating Center. How soon the second stage can be embarked upon will depend on the extent of commitment and support at national and subregional levels.

NAPLAN NETWORKS

The main reason for having national networks is not just INFOPLAN's commitment to decentralization, but the very nature of the planning process. This, because it cuts across so many disciplines and affects so many spheres of activity, involves almost every branch of public administration and some private agencies too. A lot of the material circulates outside conventional publishing and escapes normal bibliographic control, making it hard to identify. It is often confidential and subject to official restrictions. And the very size of the task makes decentralization imperative for efficiency.

The information unit of the national planning agency has to be strengthened to act as the national focal point, its staff trained and its information processing standardized. The other bodies directly or indirectly related to the country's planning process have to be identified, and their cooperation and participation obtained.

The objectives of each NAPLAN network are (with INFOPLAN support) to maintain and keep up to date a national collection, national union catalog and national bibliography on planning, to contribute to PLANINDEX through contributing to the database, and to exchange information on their country's planning experience with other member states of INFOPLAN. When all the various NAPLAN networks reach the same level of development, the system will have achieved the purpose of its creation.

FUNCTIONS

Technical Support

CLADES, as the central coordinating component of INFOPLAN, backs up the regular operation of the system in everything affecting the efficiency of its operation and of the services it offers at national, subregional and regional levels. Its studies of techniques and methodologies have led to standardization of information processing in the member states. It is hoped soon to embark on in-depth studies of user needs: INFOPLAN's decentralized structure will make it possible to carry these out simultaneously in different sub-regions using a common methodology.

The complexity of the subject field has called for the preparation of special staff handbooks to effect the systematization of such tasks as literature selection and acquisition. A preliminary edition in 1982 addressed itself to problems in identifying and collecting planning literature at national level. Staff training has also been furthered by courses at ECLA headquarters and others in individual countries; these have treated both the conception and design of INFOPLAN and the use of its special tools. A textbook has been prepared for those teaching such courses.

Technical advisory work with individual units has aimed at helping them organize collections and retrieval systems to operate with the ISIS system. Emphasis has been placed on the transfer of guidelines that will aid national control of planning literature, the organization of a basic collection at the national planning agency and the creation of a system for information management suitable for the available personnel and equipment. As these are scarce, the UNITERM system has been promoted as flexible and easy to operate.

The UNITERM bibliographic record card (BRS) master sheet includes the same fields as the analysis worksheet for electronic data processing of the ISIS system used by INFOPLAN, making it possible to convert a manual system into an electronic one without additional cost and work.

CLADES' advisory work has confirmed its earlier findings regarding the dispersion of information within the same institution. Registry offices, libraries, data processing units, statistical units, press offices, publishing departments, etc. function independently and with a total lack of coordination. The information collected by any institution is never available as a whole when decisions are made and it is difficult for information units participating in INFOPLAN to keep proper track of the documentation their institutions produce. CLADES is therefore very concerned to create a mechanism to coordinate "the internal institutional information system."

Selection and Acquisition of Information

The complexity of planning documentation makes traditional methods of selection and acquisition inappropriate. The need to create a special methodology and the need for staff to have a good grasp of the literature at the national level have led to the preparation of the draft manual *Seleción y adquisición de documentos para el sistema de información para la planificación.*

Information Analysis

To facilitate information exchange, INFOPLAN has introduced methods and techniques to standardize the analysis of information fed into the various local and regional databases. Classification follows the DEVSIS categories for development, adapted to the planning process. Description conforms to CLADES's *Manual de descripción bibliográfica*. An indicative-informative abstract is prepared in natural language. Indexing uses the OECD *Macrothesaurus*, to which special planning terms are added as necessary.

Information Storage and Retrieval

Worksheets have been designed for both bibliographic description (BDS) and content analysis (ACS) with descriptive and analytical data being recorded in independent fields, corresponding to the requirements of the services offered and codified according to ISIS programs. Data is entered online into the CLADES regional database; information is extracted by batch searching. Compatibility with other regional and international information systems has been consciously striven for.

Publications and Services

Information in the regional database is disseminated through *PLANINDEX*, a six-monthly abstract bulletin arranged by categories representing the various phases of the planning process and with subject, country and personal and institutional author indexing. Its coverage is representative of the most significant planning experiences of the region, but it is not exhaustive. It is hoped however that similar publications to be produced by the individual national coordinating centers will be exhaustive.

Distribution of *PLANINDEX* is based on an IN-FOPLAN study which identified all institutions in the region connected with planning. Currently 418 copies are produced: 387 are distributed inside Latin America and the Caribbean and the remaining thirty-one go to Europe, Africa and Asia.

Since July 1982, INFOPLAN has been given a special section in each issue of the *Boletín de planificación del IL-PES*. This gives news on INFOPLAN activities and lists the latest planning publications of the region.

Other services include the preparation of specialized bibliographies and retrospective searching upon user request, and the obtaining of photocopies.

Evaluation

Progress reports are regularly submitted to ECLA's executive secretary and to IDRC (the project's financing agency). Periodic technical meetings with the national coordinating centers discover how far the system's procedures have been imparted to local personnel. The first of these took place in Panama City in November 1981, with attendance from Honduras, Guatemala and Panama, and led to the launching of NAPLAN networks in these countries.

REFERENCES

1) CLADES. *Guía conceptual y metodológica de capacitación para operar el sistema INFOPLAN.* Santiago: 1982. [In preparation].

2) CLADES. *La información catalizador del proceso de integración de América Latina.* Versión preliminar. Santiago: E/CEPAL/CLADES/R.7; 1980.

3) CLADES. *Manual de análisis de información: barrador para uso del curso-seminario, Santiago de Chile, 14 de julio-1 agosto 1980.* Santiago: E/CEPAL/ CLADES/R.8; 1980.

4) CLADES. *Manual de procedimiento: uso y registro de datos en hojas de análsis bibliográfico.* Santiago: E/CEPAL/CLADES/R.6; 1980.

5) CLADES. *Manual de selección y adquisición de documentos para el sistema de información para la planificación (INFOPLAN).* Santiago: E/CEPAL/ CLADES/SEM.1/R.4; 1982.

6) CLADES. *El proceso de planificación, la documentación que genera y la problemática de su clasificación.* Santiago: E/CEPAL/CLADES/R.14 and ADD.1; 198?.

7) DEVSIS Study Team. *The preliminary design of an international system for the development sciences.* Ottawa: IDRC; 1976: annex 9.

8) OECD. *Macrothesaurus para el tratamiento de la información relativa al desarrollo económico y social.* Nueva edición española. Paris: OECD; 1979.

DEMAND FOR, AND SUPPLY OF, BRAZILIAN GOVERNMENT DOCUMENTS IN NORTH AMERICAN LIBRARIES

by Laurence Hallewell
Ohio State University Libraries
Columbus, Ohio, United States

RESUMEN

La Demanda de y Abastecimiento de
Documentos Brasileños Gubernamentales
en las Bibliotecas Norteamericanas

La adquisición de documentos gubernamentales en general es difícil, y el caso de Brasil no es excepcional en esto. Hay una gran variedad de publicaciones oficiales brasileñas, y se han hecho numerosos ensayos de compilar guías, catálogos, y bibliografías para organizar' ese material. Por medio de un cuestionario, el autor ha conducido una extensa investigación de bibliotecas en los Estados Unidos y Canadá para averiguar su interés en, y adquisición de documentos gubernamentales de Brasil. Los resultados de esa investigación se presentan en detalle, y llevan a la conclusión general de que sólo las bibliotecas que tienen programas de adquisición intensivas se dan cuenta de la gran cantidad de material que *no* pueden adquirir debido al control bibliográfico inadequado,

ediciones pequeñas, y distribución desorganizada. Incluye
bibliografía.

INTRODUCTION

The difficulties of dealing with government documents, the documents of *any* government, are well known. The boundary between what is for internal use and what is to be made accessible to a wider readership (i.e. the distinction between purely departmental circulation and actual publication) is often vague. Between what are definitely classified as secrets of state and what are conceived *ab initio* as propaganda (using the word neutrally), there is a large gray area often bereft of any consciously planned circulation policy at all. When in doubt, most bureaucrats prefer to play it safe and be restrictive of access to their department's papers. Often there is simple incredulity that any outsider should be interested in, for example, the internal workings of government. An American documents librarian, James Bennet Childs, quotes the instance of a pamphlet on the control of public receipts and expenditures printed by His Majesty's Stationery Office for the United Kingdom Treasury which was virtually unobtainable for research for just this reason (Childs 1967).

Even when deliberate secretiveness or restriction does not apply, access is still often difficult because the process of making publications available is ill-defined or undeveloped. A department may have a printing office, but no sales office, or one geared solely to dealing in over-the-counter transactions in cash. If mail orders are accepted, there may still be no way to deal with a customer unable to provide a check drawn on a local bank in the national currency. Sometimes even the would-be purchaser who attends in person may be frustrated by limited office hours or other difficulties. Nor are such problems a peculiarity of the less developed countries. An account of London publishing in the 1970s remarks that "the Greater London Council also showed a tendency to enter publishing, which, considering the haphazard way they went about it, might have been better delegated to someone else. There was nothing wrong with the actual publications; only with the inadequate organization for selling them..." (Mumby 1974).

The basic principles of government accounting themselves create obstacles. Instead of treating publishing as a commercial process, production costs are considered independently of sales, and financial accountability, in so far as it exists, is limited to ensuring that these costs stay within the original estimate, regardless of receipts. The all too frequent result is a print run far below demand, so that many publications go out of print before the interested foreigner ever hears of their existence. In other cases, a publication may receive a production budget so out of line with sales possibilities that money is wasted on unwarrantably large editions. Pricing policies may be equally remote from normal commercial practice. Some countries include so much overhead in calculating the selling price that one feels the government may be using the pricing mechanism to restrict availability. At the other extreme, one meets government agencies where it is felt somehow undemocratic to require the customer to pay a commercially realistic price, which is seen as a hindrance to the circulation of information prepared in the public interest and for which the citizenry has already paid through its taxes. Sometimes this attitude reaches its *reductio ad absurdum* in a policy of totally free distribution. And all too often, when distribution is free, it is purely arbitrary. The issuing agency simply decides who is worthy to receive a copy, effectively consuming the entire print run, but at the cost of being unable to respond to requests from those who really need the work.

When, as in most Latin American countries, official bodies have difficulty obtaining foreign exchange with which to acquire the publications they need themselves from abroad, they usually try to obtain them by exchange. Often their entire publishing output beyond that needed for national distribution will be committed to their exchange programs. A North American librarian, on the other hand, may be unable to participate in such a program because his institution has no suitable publications to offer or he may find the administrative and labor costs of participation make this in fact a very expensive method of acquisition.

Most frustrating of all, perhaps, from the viewpoint of the person really interested in consulting government publications, is the lack of information as to what has been published and what is currently available. Although Her Majesty's Stationery Office (HMSO) in London and the Government Printing Office (GPO) in Washington were issuing regular listings of their output in the 1890s, these two organizations were exceptional. Things began to improve, in the more developed countries at least, only in the 1920s. Soon after Mussolini came to power in Italy, that country published a retrospective *Pubblicazioni edite dello stato o col suo concorso, 1861–1923* (1924). This aroused the interest of the young Childs at the Library of Congress and led him to write *An account of government document bibliography in the United States and elsewhere*, which the Library of Congress put out in 1927. As a direct result of this work, the national governments of several countries were stimulated to begin current listings of their official publications: Japan from 1927; Germany from 1928; the Netherlands from 1929; and Sweden from 1931. The work was revised in 1930 and in 1942, and is now in its fourth edition as *Government publications: a guide to bibliographic tools*, prepared by Vladimir M. Palic (Library of Congress, 1975). Childs also did a special *Guide to the official publications of the other American republics* (Washington, 1948). Volume 3, by John De Noia, was devoted to Brazil, covering its publications to 1946.

Part of the difficulty of securing proper bibliographic control of government publications has been the great number of sources from which they emanate. Even within the same ministry there may be inadequate control (or even awareness) of what its subordinate departments and agencies are publishing. And government operates at more than one level—federal, state and municipal (i.e. county) in the case of Brazil—and hardly any country in the world has yet devised an effective means to keep track of *local* government publishing. Even at the national level, coordination has proven difficult. The Anglo-Saxon nations seem to have had the most success. In the 1930s, herculean efforts by the Controller of His Majesty's Stationery Office achieved almost total centralization of United Kingdom national government publishing by the end of that decade; but the enormous expansion of official publishing since then, plus the policy decision that Her Majesty's Stationery Office shall only deal with publications likely to prove viable commercially, has reduced the proportion of United Kingdom government publishing issued through Her Majesty's Stationery Office to under 20% of the estimated total central government output.

BRAZIL

When printing was first permitted in Brazil in 1808, total control was simple: there was only one printing shop, the government's own. For many years a bibliography of this early period was the only published guide to Brazilian national government documents in existence (Cabral 1954). With independence came not only the end of the *Typographia nacional*'s monopoly but also such an increase in the volume of government printing that more and more of it had to be put out to commercial firms. Sometimes a private printer was preferred for the quality of his work; at other times he got the job through friends in high places. The very constitution of the new nation came from a private printer, Pierre Plancher. Later in the century much official printing was done by Georges Leuzinger, who also secured a near monopoly of government binding contracts. No sales catalog seems to have been issued until the *Catálogo das obras que se acham á venda na Imprensa Nacional* of 1928 and the possibility of any retrospective bibliography disappeared with the press's records in the fire of 1911.

An attempt to centralize all federal government printing at the *Imprensa Nacional* followed the 1937 establishment of the *Estado Novo*. A formal agreement with the United States for inter-governmental exchange of official publications in June 1940 resulted in a marked improvement in Library of Congress holdings from about that date. In April 1941 the press began an monthly list, the *Boletin bibliográfico*. This did not survive beyond March 1945 but a complementary and less frequent *Mostra de livros* began in 1942. The first *Mostra* covered publications of the year ending May 13, 1942; later issues appeared annually until the March 1964 Revolution. It has been less frequent since then. One issue covered 1964–1968, but by then the *Imprensa Nacional* was no longer printing more than a fraction of the federal government's total publishing output. Since 1969 the *Mostra* has been appearing in two parts, covering works printed by the *Imprensa Nacional* in Rio and those printed in Brasília (at its new main plant), respectively.

Many government agencies have issued catalogs of their own publications from time to time, but there has been no uniformity and little regularity. The National Archives has put out a catalog almost every year since 1886, supplemented by occasional subject indexes and by listings of recent publications in some issues of its monthly *Mensário do Arquivo Nacional*. The Foreign Ministry's Divisão de informações (formerly Seção de publicações) has been providing regular lists of publications, at varying intervals and under various titles, since 1939; it has also issued, in 1951, a retrospective listing from 1826 to 1950. The Education Ministry issued a catalog of the books in its series *Os cadernos de cultura* in 1959 and again in 1965. In 1970 the now defunct series was listed in full in the Ministry's *Revista do livro*. Dependencies of the MEC, notably the National Book Institute, the National Library and the Casa de Rui Barbosa have also issued catalogs of their own output from time to time, but there appears never to have been a complete catalog of the Ministry's current output.

Best organized, both bibliographically and in their distribution and sales methods, are those semi-autonomous agencies with the status of *fundações*, in particular the Fundação Getúlio Vargas (a teaching and research institute in administration and the social sciences) and the Fundação Instituto Brasileiro de Geografia e Estatística (responsible for coordinating official statistics and for administering the national census). Both issue regular catalogs, with the IBGE's giving prices in dollars for the convenience of foreign purchasers. The FGV functions practically like an ordinary good-class commercial publisher, while the IBGE maintains a chain of offices throughout Brazil that provide both a library and a bookstore of its publications. Another fundação is the University of Brasília with easily the most active publishing program of all Brazilian federal universities; so active and so efficiently distributed (with a nation-wide advertising campaign) that it has been attacked in the Brazilian trade press as competing unfairly with commercial publishers.

State and local government publishing is far more haphazard, although the *Arquivo público estadual* of Pernambuco managed a retrospective catalog of that state's output for 1926–1966 in 1967, the year in which the State Printing Office issued Leduar de Assis Rocha's *Meio século de imprensa oficial em Pernambuco*.

Deficiencies in bibliographic control by the issuing bodies themselves would matter less if there were an adequate and current national bibliography. Despite a long history, going back to the 1860s, of a variety of efforts to this end by government, by the booktrade and by individual bibliographers such as Antônio Simões dos Reis, this has only been achieved for quite brief periods. The last occasion was from 1967 to 1972 when the National Book Institute's *Bibliografia brasilerira* became a monthly, ably administered by Aureo Ottoni de Mendonça Júnior and helped by both a tightening up of the copyright deposit law and by access to the resources of the Library of Congress office in Rio de

Janeiro. Unfortunately, a new education minister, feeling with some justification that his department's publishing was too diffuse and uncoordinated, undertook its complete overhaul. As a result, he became aware of an overlap in bibliographic responsibilities between the National Book Institute and the National Library. His solution was simply to scrap the *Bibliografia brasileira mensal*, and order the National Library, whose *Boletim bibliográfico* was four years in arrears, to ignore the years 1967–1972 and proceed immediately to the production of its volume for 1973. Unfortunately the *Boletim bibliográfico* has fallen behind again, largely because it also includes foreign publications acquired by the Library. And even if if should manage to achieve prompt publication, its quarterly frequency would prevent its ever being truly current.

North American librarians have been particularly aware of the deficiencies in the bibliographic control of Brazilian official publications and the problem has, over the years, provided the subject of a number of working papers of the Seminar on the Acquisition of Latin American Library Materials. James B. Childs and John H. Thaxter contributed a paper on "Bibliographies of official publications in Latin America and their utility" to the Sixth (1961) SALALM; the Brazilian Laura Garcia Moreno Russo dealt with the difficult (and allied) problem of catalog headings for Brazilian government agencies in the Eighth (1963) SALALM; and Jerry James, then director of the Library of Congress Rio office, addressed the Fifteenth (1970) SALALM on "The acquisition of current Brazilian social science publications." The interest of SALALM, expressed by the formation of a permanent working party on government publications, led to Rosa Quintero Mesa's listing official documents with details of holdings in two hundred United States and twelve Canadian libraries in *Latin American serial documents* (Ann Arbor, University Microfilms, 1968) of which Volume Two was devoted to Brazil. Five years later, Mary Lombardi produced an extensive listing by issuing agencies, *Brazilian serial documents: a selective and annotated bibliography* (Indiana University Press, 1974).

In 1979 the working party's chairperson, Nelly S. González, Latin American bibliographer at the University of Illinois, wrote to every publisher listed in the *Catálogo dos editores oficiais brasileiros: área federal* (Brasília, Câmara dos deputados, 2. ed., 1977) to request catalogs of their publications. The response rate was high (100 percent from the five agencies of the Judicial branch, 80 percent from 60 agencies of the Executive branch, 50 percent from the two agencies of the Legislative branch and 53 percent from the nineteen federal university presses), but only 35 catalogs were available, representing 31 agencies (Gonzalez 1981).

Within Brazil, it was the librarians catering to the Legislative branch who were most sensible of the need for better bibliographic control of official publications, and regular lists began to appear in the *Boletim da Biblioteca da Câmara dos deputados* from 1952 onwards, mainly the work of Edson Nery da Fonseca. Later the House of Deputies Library issued the most useful and necessary list of official publishers.

An important landmark was the article, "Publicações oficiais brasileiras", by the senior reference librarian of the House of Deputies library, Juracy Feitosa Rocha, in January 1974, which stressed the importance of official publications and the great need to make them more accessible bibliographically (Revista... 1974). This article seems to have been largely instrumental in initiating the current series of biennial Seminars on Brazilian Official Publications. These began as sectional meetings within the Brazilian National Conference of Library and Information Science in 1975, but the Fourth Seminar was held independently of the national conference, at the Imprensa Nacional headquarters in Brasília, July 27–31, 1981, and attracted many publishing staff and other non-librarians involved with or interested in official publishing. The Directora da Subsecretaria de Edições Técnicas of the Senate, Senhora Leyla Castello Branco Rangel, presided over the conference, which also provided the occasion for the publication of the first *Bibliografia brasileira de publicações oficiais: área federal*, 1975/1977, a hefty tome of 846 pages: 538 pages of full catalog entries arranged by departments, followed by full indexes of authors (82 pages), titles (174 pages), series (36 pages) and periodical titles (16 pages). Some 6,605 items are included, of which 500 or so are periodicals and 435 are co-editions of the National Book Institute with commercial publishing houses.

There is hope that resources will be made available to continue this invaluable bibliography on a regular basis. Volumes for 1978/1980 and 1981/1982 did in fact appear during 1983. But even this can contribute nothing to the even more difficult problem of bibliographic control of non-federal publications and the larger of the Brazilian states probably publish more than some individual Spanish American independent countries.

RECENT SURVEY

I had the pleasure of contributing to the Fourth Seminar on Brazilian Official Publications a paper on the probable extent of the demand for Brazilian government publications from libraries and information centers outside Brazil. An unexpected degree of interest was shown and I was invited to undertake a more detailed investigation.

Late in 1982, I mailed a questionnaire to 122 libraries in the United States and twenty-two in Canada to discover the extent of their interest in Brazilian government publications and to find out what special difficulties they might be experiencing. The libraries were selected, on the basis of their possible interest, from the *American library directory*, 35th edition (Bowker, 1982) and *Subject collections*, edited by

Lee Ash, 5th edition (Bowker, 1978), after consultation with Nelly González and with Peter Johnson (Latin American bibliographer at Princeton). The questionnaire was submitted for approval to the president of the Comissão sobre publicações oficiais brasileiras, Senhor Ubaldino Dantas Machado. The survey was later extended to libraries outside North America, but this part was completed after April 1983 and is referred to only incidentally here.

Of the 144 libraries, 60 (50 in the United States and eleven Canadian) had replied by mid-April 1983 and fifteen replies (nine United States, six Canadian) indicated no current interest in the acquisition of Brazilian official publications. Since it seems fair to suppose that many of the libraries failing to return the questionnaire would have done so from lack of interest in the material, it could be that the 46 positive replies come close to the totality of North American libraries with a definite commitment to Brazilian government documents.

Three libraries made no reply respecting the levels of government featured in their acquisition policies. All the other forty-three claimed to include federal government publications. Some twenty-eight collected the output of federally funded universities, one library professing itself unable to distinguish this category from other universities. Para-governmental organizations are extremely important in Brazil, where such direct intervention in the economy is probably greater than in any other non-Communist country; twenty-six libraries collected their publications. State government publications were of interest to only eighteen libraries and municipal government publications to only thirteen.

Four libraries claimed to collect comprehensively within their areas of interest; six said they collected "in depth"; twenty-five collected selectively; and twelve only occasionally. The breakdown of respondent libraries' interests by subject follows:

	General works	*Statistics*
All subjects	6	14
Administration	8	2
Agriculture	19	10
Bibliography	20	2
Biology	3	2
Cartography	12	4
Demography	24	18
Ecology	21	0
Economics	23	16
Education	13	5
Finance	12	11
Geology	12	4
History	1	0
Industry	15	13
Law	10	2
Politics	21	6
Social conditions	22	5

"History" was a "write-in" by one library. The intention of
the questionnaire had been to elicit information in respect to
publications directly connected with the process of government, but this was nowhere spelled out. Clearly any attempt to include *all* subjects covered by the output of official
presses would have had to include many other non-
administrative topics: literature, biography, school
textbooks, etc.

264 — Laurence Hallewell

Responding libraries' collection policies by format were:

Census returns	3
Maps	24 (3 marked "seldom")
Microform publications	24 (5 marked "seldom")
Monographs	38
Official gazettes	20 (2 marked "seldom")
Other periodicals	37
Patents	1
Reports	27

"Census returns" was a "write-in" (it was thought to have been adequately covered by demographic statistics above); "Patents" was a category inadvertently omitted from all but a few questionnaires.

The most frequently mentioned source of information was the Brazilian book trade. Eleven respondents mentioned "Brazilian book dealers" without further qualification; fourteen mentioned Susan Bach by name and nine mentioned José Heydecker (Atlantis Livros). One library said that its collecting had become more haphazard recently, precisely because of a decline in the number and quality of booksellers' catalogs received, which was attributed to economic problems (a reference, presumably, to the Brazilian booktrade's present difficulties or the impact of fewer foreign orders due to budget cuts by North American universities or both). Four libraries cited "current bibliographies" without further specification; five cited the Library of Congress's *Accessions list—Brazil*; five cited Library of Congress proof sheets; and twenty-three cited the catalogs of Brazilian government publishers. Two libraries mentioned United Nations lists and two, *BOLSA*. The *Bibliographic guide to Latin American studies*, the *Handbook of Latin American studies*, *Hispanic American historical review*, ISO's *International labour documents*, the *Population Index*, *APLIC census network*, the *Joint Bank-Fund catalog* and *Current Awareness* were all mentioned by a single library. Two libraries said "journal reviews," four said "retrospective bibliographies," two said "faculty members," one said "other library accession lists" and one "advertisements in Brazilian periodicals." The *Bibliografia de publicações oficiais brasileiras* received just three mentions, one with the hope that it would appear regularly and promptly in the future. Four libraries gave no indication of their sources of information.

Somewhat to my surprise, sixteen libraries said they were satisfied with the currently available information sources and two more said they were "fairly satisfied". Perhaps this reflected the superficial nature of their interest? Of the other respondents, fifteen found their sources not comprehensive enough, fourteen found them not sufficiently up-to-date, nine found them insufficiently detailed ("especially for serials", said one), six complained of a failure to give prices and one wanted more regularity in publication. There was one "don't know" and seven admitted to dissatisfaction without giving a reason. One specifically exempted the Library of Congress *Accession list* from such strictures.

As expected, purchase was the most common acquisition method; thirty libraries used Brazilian book dealers (for ten of these this was their main source, for a further five it was their second source); twenty-eight bought directly from the publishing agencies (a main source for ten libraries, a second source for five others); and nineteen used North American book dealers. Fourteen libraries used Brazilian subscription agents (one as its first choice, one as its second) and six used subscription agents in North America or Europe. Six libraries (four in the United States, two Canadian) had sent staff on book-buying expeditions to Brazil; for the Library of Congress this was the main acquisition source and it has maintained its own office in Rio for this purpose for over fifteen years. One United States university library mentioned using the services of a Brazilian resident in the United States who has long-standing personal relationships with many government officials in Brasília and who makes regular visits to Brazil. It is understood that this person also obtains material for a least three other large United States research libraries but none of them mentioned her in their replies to the questionnaire. One library with a vigorous collection policy, which deals directly with the publishing agency (for acquisition by purchase, gift or exchange), volunteered the information that some fifteen hours weekly was spent on drafting correspondence, it being their experience that form letters were unproductive and that individual personalized communication was essential.

Twenty-three libraries said they obtained material by exchange with Brazilian libraries and eighteen exchanged directly with the publishers. There was one special mention of exchanges with EMBRAPA and EMBRATER; USBE got eight mentions and the Centre d'Échange Canadien de Livre, the Library of Congress Gift and Exchange division and the National Library of Canada were all mentioned once each.

Twenty-six libraries received material as gifts from the publishers, twenty-five as gifts from other Brazilian government agencies in Brazil and ten from agencies of the Brazilian government in North America. Two received material from the United States State Department, one from Canadian government representatives in Brazil, one from Brazilian libraries, five from individuals (students or faculty) and one from other personal contacts. Two failed to indicate any source of the material or any method of acquisition.

Ten libraries did not indicate whether they were satisfied with their means of supply or not. Among the reasons given by those who were not satisfied, delay was cited sixteen times (whereas only four libraries indicated positive satisfaction with the time taken to supply material). Reaction to comprehensiveness of coverage was mixed: fourteen libraries indicated dissatisfaction, ten said they were satisfied. (One wonders whether some of the latter were not in the position of a European respondent who said that, following recent budget cuts, comprehensive coverage was no longer a problem; he learned of as many publications as his reduced funds allowed him to acquire!)

Generally, cost per item seemed not to be a problem: seventeen libraries were happy on this score and only three dissented: one of the latter made an explicit distinction between the prices charged by the publishing agencies (regarded as reasonable) and those charged by dealers (which were not). Seven found their suppliers reliable; one said "in part"; ten found them unreliable. Only two were happy about continuity in the supply of periodicals (but two others were "mostly satisfied"). Of the ten who were dissatisfied in this respect, one wrote that it was his most serious problem.

The actual process of effecting payment was a problem to only three libraries: two objected to having to make prepayment (a legal impossibility under state law); the other complained of delay in supply once prepayment had been made. Yet another library said it had given up trying to obtain material directly from the publishers: either correspondence produced no result at all or the material took six to ten months to arrive.

Only seven libraries regularly correspond in Portuguese. Twelve reported using English and Portuguese. Of these, one admitted a preference for English, while one said they used English in corresponding with Susan Bach and Atlantis Livros but otherwise used Portuguese. There were twenty-two libraries who normally correspond in English; one among them, with a very active acquisitions program in all Latin American fields, claimed that little correspondence was necessary, most matters being adequately served by form letters (presumably in English). Four libraries used English or Spanish. Six libraries made no reply or misunderstood the question. Two libraries admitted to linguistic difficulties: in one the Latin American bibliographer had as yet no ability in Portuguese or Spanish; in the other the Latin American bibliographer was the only library staff member with Portuguese competence, so correspondence was delayed by his absence. One assumes that most libraries claiming to correspond only in English could understand communications in Portuguese, but only in one case was this made clear. (A respondent from the extra-American part of the survey admitted to the common-sense solution of "routine correspondence in English, queries tackled in Portuguese.")

Perhaps the most significant finding of the survey was the high degree of reliance on one source, the bookseller Susan Bach. (Even taking the extra-American part of the survey into account, there would be only four mentions of any Brazilian book dealers other than Bach and Heydecker: Basseches, Kosmos, Livroceres and Veras, all cited once each). This was not unexpected. Bach's business is devoted wholly to the overseas market for Brazilian publications, particularly the academic library market. She has been in the business a very considerable time, and, by attendance at SALAM, is personally known to many of her customers. One wonders, however, to what extent library stocks may have been biased in their collection building by their reliance on this one dealer. For commercial publications she offers no doubt an excellent service, but government publications could be something else. Although she may well be almost the only Brazilian dealer making a serious effort to include a wide selection of government publishing in her regular book lists, this must, of necessity, be weighted towards what is easily obtainable in Rio. Several of the larger states maintain offices there, but these cannot be expected to have more than a small selection of their publications on hand; some promise to obtain any not in stock but my personal experience does not rate their efficiency high in this regard. Transferring most federal departments away from Rio when Brasília became the new capital has also limited the selection available to Susan Bach, since they too cannot be expected to have all their publication on hand at their Rio branches. Susan Bach is doubtless willing to hunt for specific items requested by her regular customers, but such hunting is limited: it necessarily costs much more than most libraries are willing to pay.

Overall, the impression received from the questionnaire was that only those few libraries with a really intensive program of acquisition in the area were aware of how much valuable material was escaping their acquisition net through inadequate bibliographic control, short print runs and poorly organized distribution methods. One commented:

> Our major problems center on official publications from agencies with which we lack direct contacts and which aren't covered by our blanket order dealer (Susan Bach); lack of current, comprehensive bibliographies makes it difficult to fill gaps before works become unavailable.

Another wrote: "Judging from publications obtained last year in Brasília, many valuable titles aren't listed by regular dealers or obtained by LC." One of the country's major collections reported:

> Most official government publications ... are received through our blanket order with Susan Bach... Gift arrangements are of primary importance in acquiring publications of semi-official agencies, and exchanges are the most important source for many academic institution publications. Serial subscriptions and gift arrangements are particularly difficult to maintain... Many titles are missed."

Yet another library stated: "Most of what we get is either on serial standing order or the blanket order we have with Bach. [But] she can't, or doesn't, get a lot of things from outside Rio. When she tells us to order direct ... most often we get no response." A large map collection mentioned, as a special difficulty, the failure of book dealers to describe maps adequately.

One of the respondents, who admitted to a long-term interest and concern in collecting Brazilian government publications, took the trouble to accompany her returned questionnaire with a long and detailed letter in which she admitted to longing for the day when some single Brazilian—or perhaps North American—clearinghouse, patterned on the ERIC system for education, would "conscientiously collect all current Brazilian documents at all administrative levels and put each on a microfilm numbered and indexed, ERIC style, which could then be put on a database for machine searching..." If this were achieved for Brazil, she muses, it could set a pattern for all of Latin America.

REFERENCES

1) Cabral, Alfredo Valle. *Annaes da Imprensa Nacional do Rio de Janeiro de 1808 a 1922*. Rio de Janeiro: Typographica nacional, 1881. Suplemento, 1823–1831. Rio de Janeiro, 1954.

2) Childs, James B. Government publications. *Library trends*; January 1967; 15(3):378.

3) Gonzalez, Nelly S. Acquisition of official publications from Argentina, Brazil and Mexico: three case studies. In: *Library resources on Latin America: new perspectives for the 1980s; final report and working papers of the 25th Seminar on the Acquisition of Latin American Library Materials*. Madison: SALALM Secretariat;1981:203–222.

4) Mumby, Frank Arthur; Norrie, Ian. *Publishing and bookselling*. London: Cape; 1974: 520.

5) *Revista de biblioteconomia de Brasília*; January/June 1974; 2(1):1–14.

INFORMATIONAL DEVELOPMENT:
THE THIRD FRONTIER
FOR THE SURVIVAL
OF LATIN AMERICAN COUNTRIES

by Michel J. Menou
Consultant
Gentilly, France

RESUMEN

El Desarrollo Informacional: La Tercera Frontera
para la Supervivencia de los Países Latinoamericanos

Hay algunas ideas comunes sobre el desarrollo informacional
que no tienen bases científicas sólidas, tales como la idea de
que el acceso a, y mayor integración de sistemas de información son requisitos del desarrollo socio-económico, y la
idea de que todas las sociedades deben pasar por etapas
evolucionales específicas del desarrollo informático. Al con-
trario, los países en desarrollo suelen contener varias etapas
de desarrollo simultáneamente. Hay tres fronteras del
desarrollo que deben considerarse de igual importancia: lo
económico, lo social, y lo informacional. Se debe crear una
política informacional nacional entre todos los partidos y las
instituciones interesados, y los servicios informacionales que
contienen deben ser mejor financiadas. Idealmente, deben
ser economicamente   auto-suficientes.   Los   servicios

bibliotecarios e informáticos pueden, más de lo que se ha pensado, pasar por alto algunas tecnologías manuales tradicionales y entrar directamente al uso de tecnologías modernas. Esto se debe al desarrollo reciente de sistemas de tamaño reducido, portátiles, y de costo reducido. Se debe utilizar hasta lo máximo las tecnologías modernas, adaptándolas a las circunstancias socio-culturales de los países en cuestión. Incluye bibliografía.

DEVELOPMENT OF INFORMATION IN-
FRASTRUCTURES VERSUS DEVELOP-
MENT OF AN INFORMATION SOCIETY

In the early 1960s, the transformation that the more industrialized countries were undergoing gave rise to the concept of the "post-industrial" society (Bell 1973), characterized by the central and predominant role of information-
related activities, accompanied by a decline in those to do
with the transformation of materials, and economic analysts
achieved the first measurements of the weight of
information-related activities in the economy (Machlup
1962). Such concepts as the information society, or its
economic model the information economy (Ito 1978), were
long disregarded by library and information science studies.
When at last in the early 1970s they were considered, their
novelty and the allegedly loose connection between the components of the information sector as defined by Porat and
Rubin (1977) led more often than not to an at least partial
rejection, as, for example, in Anderla's study (1973). The
overwhelming majority of librarians and information scientists continues to ignore these concepts when considering
national information policies and plans, but the computer
community has been much more open-minded, and able to
gear these concepts towards the satisfaction of its own expectations.

The library and information science community has
elaborated two main propositions regarding the development
of its field. One is that information, unconsciously equated
to printed matter and bibliographic records, is a necessary
ingredient in the socio-economic development process. This
assumption not only lacks supporting evidence, as Saracevič
has pointed out (1980), but it tends to isolate information as
an independent factor, evolving from its own particular
starting point yet contributing to the overall process of
development. Studies of the information society, however,
show that information is not just an object that facilitates

development, but is the very subject of development. The other proposition, popularized in particular by the NATIS program (Unesco 1974) is that the development of the various components of the so-called information infrastructure should be integrated. However desirable for more effective management and use of available resources, it is questionable whether establishing closer links between various types of information institutions would bring about any change in the nature and prospect of the process of socio-economic development or any greater level of "informationalization."

In the case of the less developed countries, the use of the information society or economy concepts may be objected to on the grounds that this transformation, being the most recent one in human societies, can only apply to the more advanced countries. Such a view assumes a linear development of society through agrarian, pre-industrial, industrial and post-industrial stages in succession. In fact, however, the simultaneous coexistence of various types of societies and conflicts between them is a fundamental aspect of the less developed economies. This is particularly true of the most advanced among them, such as those of South America, where the dichotomy between various sectors of the population at differing stages of socio-economic development is a key factor of imbalance (Fonseca 1980).

Few studies of the information economy in the developing countries seem to have been attempted so far. Their results and the average figures for the size of the various components of the information sector suggest that the latter accounts for ten to twenty-five percent of the gross national product (GNP) of a typical developing country (Karunaratne & Cameron 1981, Vitro). So high a figure justifies our attention, especially if the expansion of this sector is going to be the characteristic feature of the coming decades.

Specialized information services are not widely available in most developing countries. Other forms of information (oral history for example) tend to be overlooked, and an absolute lack of information is reported. A synthesis of the information society and Dedijer's "social intelligence" (Dedijer) concepts would probably provide a most powerful tool for the analysis of the situation and of the evolution of societies from an information standpoint.

On the other hand, a simple look at the working of any information system in the restricted sense in which the library and information science community uses the term shows that it cannot perform its most basic and specific functions without adequate participation by most other components of the information sector. What could an agricultural information system do without agricultural research, paper, office furniture, mail, computers, etc.?

SCOPE AND USE OF A COMPREHENSIVE NATIONAL INFORMATION POLICY

This author therefore feels that the concept of the information society provided the only framework for organizing and orienting large-scale information activities.

The challenge all countries face is not just that of making more bibliographic information available and used, expanding the application of computers and robots, increasing telecommunication capacity or producing more books or films. It is all this and much more. It is how well countries can engineer the flow and use of information among individuals and groups; information is becoming the major component of the value of goods and services while at the same time it is ceasing to be stored in the memory of individuals and groups. A country's prospects will depend on how effectively, speedily and comprehensively it achieves this socialization of knowledge.

To avoid an increasing dependence on the more industrialized world without creating an information gap that will worsen their relative position, the developing countries will have to consider seriously how to "informationalize" their societies. For a long time, economic development—creating more goods for the needs of the population—has been the only frontier. More recently a second frontier, social development, has been recognized: improving conditions of life and minimizing the harmful consequences of economic and other changes. However, development is primarily the consequence of integrating new knowledge with the original culture, a process requiring the greatest possible production, mobilization, dissemination and use of information. This is the third frontier: informational development. These three frontiers are equally important and should receive equal priority. Informational development, within a broad cultural perspective, may even deserve to be regarded as the main issue, since it determines society's ability to produce goods and services and to solve problems.

The basic national information policy—valid for almost all countries—can be defined as a "sustained effort to create as quickly as possible a strong, *integrated* and *balanced* information sector." Integration and balance cannot be overemphasized. So often isolated initiatives from one segment of the complex information sector or imbalances between its components, jeopardize all other efforts—as when poor postal services limit secondary information services. Such an approach may also prevent the various segments in the information sector from equating their share with the whole, as so often happens.

The components of the information sector are in fact spread over the whole societal fabric. Responsibility for them is distributed among most government agencies and private interest groups. An information policy, therefore, to be effective, cannot be left to a single entity (the national coordinating agency for library and information services, the national computer center, the telecommunications ministry, etc.). It must be formulated so as to orient the policies and activities of all the parties involved and provide a common yardstick for evaluating projects and results. In Brazil, IBICT has recently taken steps towards the application of such principles (Menou 1982).

Such an approach promotes information from the status of a secondary support activity within each area, often at the lowest level of priority (e.g. as a byproduct of science and technology), to a self-contained high priority topic. It also implies the use of a language and perspective familiar to high-level decision makers, appealing to them in a way the usual preaching about the supposed goodness of a vague "information" never can.

Establishing an information service industry

Many segments of the information sector are already established as specific industries (mass media, manufacture of information processing goods, telecommunications, printing, etc.) or as fully committed areas of activity (e.g. education or research and development). These segments are economically and socially visible and, more importantly, are managed as industries. Library, information and similar services are in this respect the weakest component of the sector. Outside a few Western countries where such an industry is emerging, they remain largely a low-level segment of other activities, without visibility or autonomy. This may be partly why they are often poorly managed.

Karunaratne and Cameron (1981) have noted a basic structural difference between developed and developing countries in regard to their information sectors. In the former, a much larger share is taken up by information generation and distribution. In the latter, basic infrastructures are the main component. This may apply less to the major countries of Latin America, where a number of information-related industries have enjoyed noticeable development. The risk management industries for instance are growing with promise, as are, more recently, telecommunications and computing (at least in Brazil). But information services still offer a very traditional picture, with a paucity of national bibliographic data bases and indexing and abstracting services in general.

It is unlikely such services will reach a satisfactory level of development if they remain fully subsidized support activities. Such a situation implies not only managerial limitations, but also exposure to budgetary cuts, policy changes and turnover among executives in the parent organization, all particularly prevalent in difficult times such as the present.

The concept of information as a public good that should be provided free has all too often been taken to extremes. Other no less important public services—health, education, clean water, recover at least part of their costs from the user. To support information services wholly by taxation means that the entire community, including the poor, subsidizes the users—inevitably the better off—so they may benefit from resources likely to reinforce their social position. Undoubtedly some, adequate, information services have to be provided free for the citizens who need them most, the underprivileged majority—especially in the form of reference, advisory or extension services (which are not, by the way, the most commonly provided). It may well be that such services would operate much better if there were a certain level of direct contribution (financial or in kind) by the user community, accepted by it in advance, as happens, for instance, in Mali's rural library network (Vallet).

Information policy for the library and information service should aim primarily at establishing it as a self-sustaining industry able to support its operation from revenues generated by the sale of its products and services. Government funding should set up the initial service on a firm basis, but costs should then be progressively shifted onto the users. Demand could be stimulated by government through direct subsidies (e.g. distribution of coupons for use in payment for searches or document copying) or indirect ones (e.g. tax exemptions or grants). Such a strategy is likely to facilitate a much better management of information services and operation of this subsystem in the information sector. The services would be stimulated and sanctioned by actual demand and so be forced to adapt, innovate and respond rather than pursue the fulfillment of organizational idiosyncrasies in collection building, technical processing or capital investment.

Building an information service industry also means concentrating dispersed information units around a few poles to meet user demand more effectively. It is also important to establish in each country specialized institutions capable of becoming partners with their counterparts abroad, so as to promote fair conditions of international information exchange, making the North pay for what at present it gets almost for free, and then resells back to the South at eighty dollars an hour.

Full use and adaptation of modern information technology

It is generally thought that in building up library and information services in developing countries reliance must be mainly on traditional (manual) techniques: resources of all kinds, especially of qualified personnel, are scarce and technology is seldom available or difficult to maintain or both. This is true but not inevitable. Things have begun to change, although a "realistic" approach satisfies those who feel that change must be progressive.

Incrementalism, as advocated by Cochrane (1979), may be necessary in traditional areas of economic or social life, such as agriculture or the position of women. In areas that are relatively new and exogenous, and where the world's technological evolution leaves only a short while for the developing countries to build up enough strength to avoid being left out altogether, it may be a luxury. So, unfortunately, it is with information activities. With the generalization of interconnected intelligent computers and with data bases of all kinds available to all educated people, Northern societies are likely, within a decade or so, to reach a capacity enabling them to ignore any society that has failed to attain the minimum level of informationalization needed to preserve its identity and its bargaining position.

On the other hand, information technology is rapidly moving towards small scale, flexible, portable and low cost systems and approaches, thereby eliminating a number of contrary indications of the earlier stage of its development. In most developing countries computerization, telecommunications and reprography are spreading into all sectors of activity. Some in Latin America and Asia are building up their own industries in these fields. If information technology is applied only slowly and reluctantly in the area of library and information services, their backwardness and poor image compared with other activities will only worsen. Also, the more limited the use made of modern information technology, the less likely is its adaptation to local conditions in such matters as power supply autonomy, tropicalization, etc. This technology might also solve various persistent problems: information might for instance be gathered from illiterate populations by recording with voice-driven microcomputers.

In satisfying many national information needs, the size or urgency of a problem often makes traditional techniques ineffective or prohibitively costly in money or manpower. The cataloging bottleneck in many Latin American libraries leaves much of the collection unprocessed while staff spend time in technical processing at the expense of user services. A cooperative scheme with access to MARC for English-language material and automatic allocation of Spanish or Portuguese subject headings could provide a much more effective solution than vain attempts to upgrade the size and qualifications of the staff.

Traditional approaches will also maintain, if not reinforce, the low status of information services. In many instances, "premature" introduction of advanced technology has been the catalyst needed for a real development of information services, exemplified by the early work of Brazil's IBBD on national data bases or that of UNAM's Center of Information on Science and Humanities (CICH) in the area of secondary sources. The use of such technology creates problems, but so do traditional techniques. Where various projects in different countries have collapsed this has been due not just to the inadequate use of advanced technology but also to the mix of organizational, managerial, political and other factors that could have affected any kind of development project.

This author feels strongly therefore that there is no alternative, in terms of national strategy for the development of the information service industry, other than to make the fullest possible use of modern technology. The range of practical possibilities depends on the overall level of technical and industrial development. This means more scope for the larger Latin American countries, considered on their own. A regional strategy, however, by widening the markets for locally produced information handling equipment and systems could well change the picture for Latin America as a whole. With such a choice, the countries of the region would embark upon a dialectic process by which they would take a jump across to the most advanced application of information technology and then progressively adapt it to their own mix of socio-economic and technical conditions, preparing for another and more effective advance.

Overcoming socio-cultural barriers

Having discussed these problems at length elsewhere (Menou 1981), this section will just summarize the main points of this extremely important component of any strategy for developing information activities.

Although the socio-cultural implications of the rise of the information society and the consequent obstacles are similar throughout the world, the developing countries face specific constraints which should be considered carefully in implementing the kind of policy we are proposing.

The propensity to use information depends on the social desire to change the existing state of affairs. Effective change should be rewarded, but the societies of the developing countries are predominantly static. Personal loyalty to one's superior is the supreme virtue; professional effectiveness, however useful, is not indispensable and many even prove positively dangerous.

Knowledge should no longer be considered as an established cultural asset, but as a fundamental input to any activity, and one in constant change. This goes against the traditional perception of knowledge shaped over millenia of man's history. More specifically, social structures and educational systems in most developing countries tend to solidify knowledge.

Far reaching changes are likely to be resisted more strongly in societies that are still little diversified and where the instruments of power remain in the hands of a small segment of the population.

A national information policy based on the concepts of the information society will be better able to take such aspects into account and integrate them into a process of global dynamic development.

REFERENCES

1) Anderla, Georges. *Information in 1985: a forecasting study of needs and resources.* Paris: OECD; 1973.

2) Bell, Daniel. *The coming of the post-industrial society: a venture in social forecasting.* New York: Basic Books; 1973.

3) Cochrane, Glynn. *The cultural appraisal of development projects.* New York: Praeger; 1979.

4) Dedijer, S., ed. *Knowledge for development: the social intelligence approach.* [In press].

5) Fonseca, V. *L'industrie du savoir et le dialogue Nord-Sud.* Meeting on the Knowledge Industry and the Process of Development, Paris, June 9–12, 1980. [Proceedings]. Paris: OECD Development Center; 1980: Document 28.

6) Ito, Y. Cross cultural perspectives on the concept of an information society. In: Edelstein, Alex S. et al., eds. *Information societies: comparing the Japanese and American experience.* Seattle: International Communication Center of the University of Washington; 1978: 135–145.

7) Karunaratne, N.D.; Cameron A. A comparative analysis of the information economy in developed and developing countries. *Journal of information science*; 1981; 3(3):113–127.

8) Machlup, Fritz. *The production and distribution of knowledge in the United States.* Princeton, New Jersey: Princeton University Press; 1962.

9) Menou, Michel J. *Anteprojeto de documento básico de política nacional de informação para o desenvolvimento.* Brasília: IBICT; 1982.

10) Menou, Michel J. *Cultural barriers to the international transfer of information.* [Paper contributed to the VIII Cranfield Conference on Mechanized Information Transfer, Cranfield, United Kingdom, July 20-24, 1981].

11) Porat, Marc Uri; Rubin M.F. *The information economy.* Washington, D.C.: Department of Commerce; 1977. [9 v.].

12) Saracevič, Tefko. Perception of the needs for scientific and technical information in less developed countries. *Journal of documentation;* September 1980; 36(3):214-267.

13) UNESCO. *National information systems (NATIS): objectives for national and international action.* Paris: UNESCO; 1974.

14) Vallet, D. [Private communication].

15) Vitro, R.A. [Private communication].

TRANSFERENCIA Y DESARROLLO

por Ofelia Rodríguez de Supelano
La Oficina Central de Estadística e Informática
de la Presidencia de la Republica
Caracas, Venezuela

ABSTRACT

Transfer and Development

The lack of transfer of information from developed to the developing countries retards the latter's development and prolongs their dependence. Developing countries lack the resources necessary to create their own information technologies and systems, and thus the solution to the problem must be seen in a global context. There must be increased cooperation between public, private, and international institutions to foment informational and technological development and policies must be adopted to facilitate this.

La índole cambiante de la información y del conocimiento parece requerir un examen más hondo y permanente, especialmente a raíz de los adelantos de las ciencias y tecnologías asociadas en el marco conceptual de la "informática." El impacto de esas tecnologías en los individuos y sociedades no es solamente directo, sino que obra también indirectamente, mediante alteraciones de lo que se ha dado en llamada "ecología del saber."

El acceso a la información, así como su uso adecuado, confiere reputación y poder. El ambiente informativo en transformación, debido a su complejidad y a los instrumentos utilizados en su manejo y explotación, agudiza el problema de las desigualdades o brechas existentes entre individuos y grupos dentro de las sociedades, así como entre países. Es una cuestión seria, a todo nivel de proceso de la información: generación; producción; distribución; acceso; manejo y "punto de acción"; y acosará cada vez más las relaciones entre los países industrializados y el Tercer Mundo. El llamado "diálogo norte-sur" es, ni más ni menos, una cuestión de redistribución de información y conocimientos. Las actitudes, disposiciones y técnicas que podrían mitigar el problema, incluso las comunicaciones opcionales y la utilización popular de tecnologías avanzadas merecen ser estudiadas, discutidas y puestas de relieve.

PROBLEMAS EN LA "ECOLOGÍA DEL SABER"

Sobre todo a partir de la primera Conferencia Intergubernamental sobre Estrategias y Políticas en Informática (1978), dirigentes públicos y privados han recalcado la necesidad de mejorar la capacidad de las organizaciones gubernamentales y extragubernamentales para la gestión de las informaciones y su comunicación. Tal gestión mejorada se considera necesaria en varios aspectos: para tratar de la problemática mundial; para remitir que los pueblos se liberen de la dependencia y sean dueños del propio desarrollo; para fortalecer su autonomía; para solucionar difíciles problemas sociales causados, por ejemplo, por la urbanización; y, en general, para encarar la complejidad y el cambio.

Debemos estar conscientes de que los países en vías de desarrollo se encuentran inmersos en un trama, en una problemática cada vez más creciente y compleja, como es la de encontrar vías y soluciones que permitan en plazos razonables, superar algunas de las dificuldades que surgen en el proceso de transferencia de información de los países más avanzados. Estos limitantes hacen precisamente mucho más dificil enfrentar los escollos conéxos del propio desarrollo en el ámbito económico y social.

Tales obstáculos no sólo entorpecen la modernización y la inserción de tales países a la dinámica de la sociedad actual, sino que además restringen las posibilidad de integración a los sistemas evolucionados de comunicación y la armonización a los avances en el orden cultural, económico y social en que están comprometidos como una responsabilidad prioritaria. Tambien estamos convencidos de que la información, como parte del proceso social, se encuentra aún indefinida y que su impacto e influencia en la sociedad moderna sólo comienza a comprenderse parcialmente.

El proceso de asimilación y de actualización en el área de la transferencia de información se ha hecho lento y complicado hacia los países de desarrollo y será aún más díficil y compleja en el futuro en la medida en que no se adviertan síntomas de comprensión y de cambios en las actitudes por parte de los países más avanzados, ya que la tranferencia se hace distante, a veces inaccesible, no sólo por los costos, carencia de recursos y diferencias socio-culturales, sino también por los intereses en juego tanto político como económicos.

LA TRANSFERENCIA DE TECNOLOGÍA

La posesión de conocimientos científicos y técnicos y las capacidad de los países para su utilización, tienen una afluencia significativa en la orientación y la realización de un desarrollo económico y social integral. En el Tercer Mundo la falta de tales conocimientos retarda la posibilidad de desarrollar en forma autónoma un proceso social armónico, equilibrado y sostenido. Por ello, el fenómeno de la transferencia de tecnología, con su incorporación al comercio internacional, reviste particular importancia desde el punto de vista de las estategias y políticas nacionales de desarrollo de los países menos avanzados, para armonizar la recepción de nuevas técnicas con las condiciones estructurales del país y con los intereses y necesidades identificables en un momento histórico-político determinado.

La transferencia tecnológica no es un fenómeno de generosidad, sino de intereses de comercialización internacional, casi monopolizado por los países altamente desarrollados, por lo cual se mantiene o se agrava la situación de dependencia de las economías del Tercer Mundo.

La concentración del conocimiento determina que las soluciones tecnológicas que van surgiendo respondan a las características, condiciones y necesidades de los países desarrollados y no se adecúan a los intereses de los países receptores de tecnología extranjera, ni resuelvan en forma eficaz los problemas para cuya solución la adquiere. Una técnica nueva estructurada y desarrollada sin tener en cuenta las características propias y el tipo de desarrollo del país receptor agrava sus dificultades económico-sociales y ahonda la brecha tecnológica ya existente respecto de países más avanzados.

Por otra parte, los países en vías de desarrollo carecen en su mayor parte de condiciones y recursos para desarrollar la investigación acorde con las tecnologías autóctonas de base y que respondan a los problemas planteados por cada desarrollo económico particular. Los altos costos de la investigación y la necesidad de evitar la repetición de las etapas intermedias del progreso técnico ya realizados por otros, para adecuar el propio desarrollo al ritmo de la evolución tecnológica mundial, colocan a los países menos desarrollados en la situación de compradores de tecnologías extranjeras en condiciones desfavorables de negociación y de recepción.

Por lo consiguiente, el desarrollo de un país como tal no puede entenderse sino desde un punto de vista global, de conjunto, como un entorno integral mediante el cual la población no solo llegue a encontrar un relativo bienestar económico y social, sino también a alcanzar una evolución y un progreso sotenido y autóctono en cuanto a ciencia y tecnología, una disminución de la dependencia en sus diferentes manifestaciones.

POLÍTICAS DE INFORMACIÓN

Se deben, en consecuencia, establecer políticas, programas y estrategias muy objetivas y concretas tendientes al incremento de la cooperación entre instituciones públicas y privadas con miras a desarrollar las capacidades de aquellos menos desarrollados. Por tales consideraciones, se hace necesario dentro de un conjunto de medidas inmediatas detectar elementos indispensables para que el proceso de tranferencia tecnológica tenga sentido y efecto en el tiempo, entre las cuales se pueden destacar como relevantes la generación de instrumentos normativos y de negociación, y el desarrollo de la capacidad de inversión, de recursos humanos y de investigación.

El aprendizaje y la asimilación tecnológica sólo son alcanzables cuando se perfeccionen estos mecanismos y las condiciones de adquisición de la tecnología auspicien y permita la transmisión de los conocimientos y su absorción.

Por todo esto, en numerosos simposios, foros, seminarios y otros eventos nacionales, regionales e internacionales se han examinado los problemas que afectan a los países en desarrollo en materia de transferencia y dependencia tecnológicas. Se ha avanzado bastante en el examen general y específico de la situación, pero no lo suficente en términos de reducir la brecha y alcanzar metas relativamente satisfactorias para las partes involucradas. La problemática es tan dinámica y mutable como el progreso científico y tecnológico que es característico del mundo actual.

Otro aspect que se puede mencionar es la facta de autoridades nacionales u organismos superiores de coordinación y administración, lo cual impide que se lleve a cabo una política coherente respecto de la transferencia de tecnología que debe basarse en la adecuación de las decisiones de adquisición de material y procesos, o de patentes para ejecutar y utilizar nuevas técnicas, a los reales intereses del país, sus condiciones estructurales y sus recursos humanos y financieros.

Asociada a la acción política nacional que se caracteriza por el esfuerzo de la planificación de las condiciones de recepción tecnológica adquirida en el exterior y por la necesidad de desarrollar la capacidad negociadora frente a las grandes empresas productoras a fin de contrarrestar la dependencia tecnológica de tales empresas y de mantener un adecuado progreso técnico-científico en el país, se encuentra la acción internacional llevada a cabo por los organismos internacionales especializados.

La cooperación prestada por dichos organismos tiene como objetivo principal el favorecer la capacidad de independencia de juicio de los países menos desarrollados en el marco de las negociaciones para la obtención de transferencia de tecnología.

LA NECESIDAD PARA UN CONVENIO INTERNACIONAL SOBRE TRANSFERENCIA TECNOLÓGICA

Finalmente se debe considerar la importancia de estimular los esfuerzos de los estados y organismos internacionales en favor de la elaboración de un convenio internacional sobre transferencia tecnológica dirijido a favorecer la colaboración bilateral y multilateral, al establecimiento de normas que garanticen mayor justicia y equidad de los contratos de adquisición, como así mismo, un trato preferencial en las negociaciones internacionales hacia los países en vías de desarrollo.

OTRAS BARRERAS

Existen otras barreras específicas que dificultan el flujo de la transferencia, el intercambio y la similación de tecnología, como son el diferente lenguaje, la escasa disposición de bibliografía de textos, documentos y otros elementos de comunicación, las fallas del sistema educativo, la falta de sistemas organizados de informática y de bancos de información, las limitaciones del mercado, la movilidad profesional y la ausencia de política y estrategias para el mediano y largo plazo. Hacen falta, por otra parte, diagnósticos objetivos que conduzcan a una toma de decisiones enmarcadas en realidades y en sentido riguroso de prioridades. De otra manera será imposible avanzar sólida y armoniosamente, difícil utilizar los recursos disponibles y consolidar el escaso progreso que se ha alcanzado.

THE FLOW OF INFORMATION WITHIN VENEZUELA IN RELATION TO ITS AVAILABILITY INSIDE AND OUTSIDE THE COUNTRY

by Thomas P. McGinn
Biblioteca Nacional
Caracas, Venezuela

RESUMEN

El Movimiento de Información dentro de Venezuela
en Relación a su Disponibilidad dentro y fuera del Pais.

El movimiento de información y materiales monográficos
dentro de Venezuela es sintomático del movimiento de información en la América Latina en general, y de su dependencia informática. Entre los problemas se encuentran la falta
de intercambio informático eficaz dentro de la América
Latina, control bibliográfico inadecuado de publicaciones
venezolanas, la mala distribución de publicaciones, y la poca
coordinación de información. Se ha iniciado algunas ges-
tiones correctivas, como las creación de bases de datos e índices. La creación en Venezuela de una base de datos
cooperativa nacional es muy preferible a la adquisición de
bases de datos extranjeros. Se ha empezado a desarrollar
planes para extender este sistema a otros países
latinoamericanos, especialmente a Chile. Incluye
bibliografía.

INTRODUCTION

Scope

This paper briefly examines some problems concerning the availability both locally and abroad of academic and scientific information produced in Venezuela. Since it is impossible to describe here all types of information flow, I will concentrate on monographs, without implying that these predominate in present-day communication; they are at any rate definitely sought by the research institutions of other countries. In this general context I will comment on developments in the technology of information processing and on the flow of information into Venezuela from the developed countries.

Venezuela as symptomatic of information flow in Latin America

Venezuelans have criticized the insufficiency of the country's production of scientific and scholarly publications (Penalver 1975). Its information dependency has been likened to its economic dependency. Such criticism is not applied to information imports from Spanish-speaking countries: the desire to foster cultural interdependency among Latin American countries is evident in the many existing bilateral agreements and in such regional ones as the Andrés Bello Treaty (Fernández Herez 1973). What is not favored is the degree of dependency existing in relation to North America and Europe.

Mechanisms to exchange information with Latin America have not, however, functioned well. No single institution in the region has resources adequate for studying Latin America as a whole and Latin American researchers find it necessary to attempt this in the United States. It ought, however, to be possible to remedy this: if all the exchange agreements between the Venezuelan National Library and its continental counterparts were functioning, it would be such a center.

THE AVAILABILITY OF PUBLICATIONS IN VENEZUELA

Distribution of Venezuelan publications: problem areas

In 1970, there were no single institution in Venezuela with research resources adequate for national studies. No adequate list existed of what the country had published and there was no union list of holdings of the most important libraries. The country's intellectual output was dispersed in various libraries, many of them private. Major studies commissioned by government often remained in officials' desks, not even reaching the library of the sponsoring ministry.

Monograph distribution

Venezuela's current annual monograph output is 4,000–5,000 titles, a large proportion of them scholarly or scientific. A random sample from the 1978 *Bibliografía venezolana* (listing mostly receipts by the Legal Deposit Office at the National Library) divides thus:

175 or 43.8% are university publication or theses;

102 or 25.5% are government publications;

80 or 20.0% are from commercial publishers;

43 or 10.7% are privately published by their authors.

The Legal Deposit Office assigns these into the following sequence in order of difficulty of acquisition:

(1)   Works privately published by the author: the most difficult to acquire because most difficult to identify and having a high rate of noncompliance with legal deposit. Many important historical, literary and legal works come in this category.

(2)   Government publications: also often difficult to identify. Printing and publishing is often decentralized even within individual ministries. Little effort is made to sell government publications. There is no general policy on confidentially and some items are unnecessarily restricted.

(3)   University publications: easier to identify as several important universities have centralized publishing and issue regular catalogs. These are not strictly publications and are uncoordinated although the National Library is striving with some success to acquire them.

(4)   Commercial and other private sector publishers: few in number and most issue catalogs. The low percentage in the sample above is probably a fair estimate of their role.

Corrective Measures Taken in Recent Years

Inadequate distribution mechanisms hamper the flow of information from Venezuela to its potential users. Efforts by the National Library's director led to a 1980 decree obliging government agencies to inform their libraries of their publications and these libraries in turn effect compliance with the Legal Deposit Law. A more recent decree directs all government agencies to reserve 25% of their publications for the National Library to distribute. The bulk then goes systemically to public and university libraries. Some are used in the National Library's exchange program, hitherto hampered by lack of Venezuelan material to offer. Others are to be sold in the Kuai-Mare bookstores, a chain established by a special administration under the National Library to sell exclusively Venezuelan publications. These stores have been so successful that some may be opened abroad.

The Legal Deposit Law has been widely publicized and public-sector libraries may not buy from publishers who ignore it.

The Processing of Information Held in Venezuela

In Venezuela as elsewhere information subject to internationally defined bibliographic standards (books, periodicals, maps, films, sound recordings) are usually processed by librarians. Information in freer formats (journal articles and unpublished documents) has not been widely indexed in Venezuela and very little of such indexing has been done by librarians. Traditional manual indexing (e.g. of journal articles) has been done by persons trained in a subject area, most often literature. Almost all indexing done with the aid of automation has been done by computer scientists.

In the last few years computer scientists and librarians have made serious efforts at coordination, as at the National Seminars on Library and Information Systems (SENASBI) at Mérida (1979) and Caracas (1980, 1982). Automation at the National Library, the National Science and Technology Council (CONICIT), the Technical Institute for Petroleum Research (INTEVEP) and the Universidad Central (UCV) has also seen very productive cooperation between the two groups. What follows relates mainly to these four institutions, all in Caracas. A complete report would need to include the activities of various government bodies and of some important research centers outside the capital.

Bibliographic control of publications

There being no unified catalogs of either trade or official publishing, the national bibliography has tried to list national publications of all kinds. Being dependent on the Venezuelan acquisitions of the National Library its coverage has been affected by lack of compliance with legal deposit. Publication has been delayed by the Library's cataloging backlog and by holding up publication of each annual volume until most imprints of that particular year could be included. Volumes for 1982 onward, however, cover whatever the cataloging division processed during the previous year. processed during the previous year.

Aware how inadequate bibliographic control had been, the National Library in 1976 began a project to identify Venezuelan publications retrospectively. Foreign library catalogs were searched, and titles found were entered in a database and then acquired—minimally in microform from the library holding the work. Compilation and input was carried out at Northwestern University until 1979, but everything is now on the National Library's computer, making its records of Venezuelan material the most complete in the world.

Extending automated processing to technical services has facilitated the communication of the national bibliography in non-traditional forms. Library of Congress MARC tapes have been acquired since 1979; since 1982 they have been exchanged for the *Bibliografía venezolana* on tape.

All this has led to better bibliographic control of all types of material held in the country. Since 1979, all National Library monograph cataloging has entered the database, including much foreign (but mainly Spanish-language) material. The Hemeroteca Nacional (serials center) has been entering its material since 1980. In 1982, non-print materials began to be included and the UCV main library went online, sharing the National Library database. UCV additions are important for areas not given priority by the National Library, notable the sciences.

Such automation has been an enormous leap forward. A union catalog of participating institutions is in existence for the first time: continuously updated and easily accessed. The catalog cards produced daily from the database and supplied to non-participating libraries constitute Venezuela's first centralized cataloging service.

Some institutions automated control of publications prior to the National Library or concurrently with it. CON-ICIT has been collecting holdings information on periodicals since the mid-1970s, printing two versions of the national union list of serials and continuing to update the information. As participating institutions are not online, direct access or updating is not possible. An interface currently being prepared between the CONICIT and National Library computers will permit online access. The NOTIS system used by the library is well designed for control of serial holdings information and so is particularly suitable for a union serials catalog.

INTEVEP and the Venezuelan Institute for Scientific Research (IVIC) have also agreed to enter the database online. INTEVEP has a database of petroleum information and gives an online service to various documentation centers throughout the country. IVIC has not automated but wants to link its library with INTEVEP, which will in turn serve as a bridge to the National Library's computer. The National Library is anxious to include scientific and technical information to avoid any fragmentation of information services.

Besides the online input from participating institutions, CONICIT and the National Library will continue inputting data from institutions that are not online with the system.

How far should Venezuela process its own bibliographic information?

The exchange of tapes with the Library of Congress illustrates a mutually beneficial exchange of processed information. But larger questions enter when Venezuela considers online information importing.

INTEVEP has had a direct line to DIALOG for many years, inherited from the international petroleum companies. Although an important instrument for importing technical information, it has not been generally available to scientists outside the National Petroleum Company.

In 1980, CONICIT began using a commercially available link to DIALOG, since extended to all available European and North American databases. This gives a service to any Venezuelan researcher and a link with the National Library's computer makes it part of the national information system.

These foreign databases include much non-bibliographic information, but the basic question of whether to tie into a science or technology database is similar to that of whether a Latin American country should link up online with a foreign bibliographic service such as OCLC.

This writer feels it would be a mistake for a country that does not have automated bibliographic processing to plan its information system with too great a dependence on sources that are only available online at a great distance. It is often cheaper to import manufactured goods than to make them locally but would any country forego industrializing just for that?

The Venezuelan pooling of information in a shared database offers an alternative to importing it. It would be faulty logic to equate importation of hard-copy with importing the cataloging and indexing from bibliographic services. Having the book is real possession but we do not really "have" a bibliographic record on our screen unless we have the tape or disk on which it is recorded. Exchanging tapes, although less attractive for a completely up-to-date service, is more analogous to the real importing of information in the traditional print media.

Distance is also still a factor in the economic evaluation of imports. Mexico and perhaps Venezuela are near enough to consider importing information online from major United States databases by dedicated telephone line. But costs rise as we go south. Satellite communication is possible, but complex to negotiate, and libraries come too low in official priorities.

An even greater potential barrier lies in the restrictions governments may place on data transmission. It is therefore important for Latin American countries to develop modern national networks. These can most easily begin with automated processing of national publications. Sophisticated software for bibliographic processing exists within Latin America and with it the necessary technical capacity. But the small existing databases should be pooled through already established cultural exchange treaties. Regular and frequent exchange of tapes will suffice at present.

It is important to note that Venezuela has shown no bias against collaboration with the North on these issues. Technical cooperation with Northwestern University continues: the National Library was the first institution outside Evanston, Illinois to use the NOTIS software, which has been adapted for use by technical processors who speak Spanish. But there is no wish to change the basic programs. This permits the library to enjoy a maintenance contract with Northwestern by which all innovations and program improvements are regularly incorporated.

Can a database be prepared which various Latin American countries would share?

This adaptation of NOTIS, and its technical versatility, led the Chilean National Library to seek the system for Northwestern through the good offices of the National Library of Venezuela. An agreement between the two libraries provides for technical assistance for setting up the system in Chile, and for regular interchanges of records of all cataloging in all formats.

The director of Venezuela's National Library is seeking funds to permit the use of NOTIS by other Latin American national libraries. This could lead to the establishment of a Latin American database, of obvious importance for all researchers on the region.

Indexing and processing of non-bibliographic materials

The predominant interest of scientists in sophisticated subject access tends to submerge the bibliographic aspects of indexing and leave librarians out of the process. The slowness of librarians to give adequate subject access to much of their material has left the field open in North America to indexing and abstracting services organized as profitable commercial enterprises. In Venezuela, little indexing has been done. The *Hispanic American Periodicals Index* (HAPI) is an important start in Spanish-language indexing, but it omits many of the Hemeroteca Nacional's most heavily used titles.

The need for indexing was first felt in law, especially in respect to documents of the Venezuelan Supreme Court. These are not well served by traditional cataloging rules, which are the basis of NOTIS. Latin America lacks even such quasi-standard controlled vocabularies as Library of Congress subject headings. And few thesauri have the comprehensiveness of those developed by United States science and technology databases.

The lack of standardization required the development of a free-format style for this non-bibliographic information. The National Library was also aware of an increasing tendency to use MARC format databases for information retrieval more than for technical processing. In 1982, it acquired software for NOTIS for online searching through Boolean combinations of key words. This new capacity and the possibility of entering the full text of documents stirred new interest among scientists. The Supreme Court was the first user of the new software, followed by the Patent Office. These organizations can enter records in any convenient format and, if desired, enter the full text, so suppressing the manual paper record system. Each user decides whether to develop a thesaurus or search a free vocabulary through various concept-linking techniques such as truncation and synonym tables which the system provides.

The system was originally designed for newspaper indexing and the three main Caracas papers are considering its use. The National Library has been able to go ahead with certain long-delayed projects. The Division of Studies and Research has entered the results of a survey on research projects in humanities and social sciences being carried out in the country. CONICIT will input a similar survey on scientific research.

The system also permits the continuation of the journal article indexing done during the Venezuela Project at Northwestern, which can now be done without the restriction imposed by MARC, and articles may now be accessed through title key words. The National Library's first project is indexing Venezuelan *Time/Newsweek* — style news magazines.

The new software also permits the development of selective dissemination of information services, using the whole database or any file in it.

OBSERVATIONS

Latin Americans have a great incentive to share all data in their information systems among themselves. The obstacles to exchanges with Northern countries are mainly economic and political. The world price of raw materials fluctuates but that of manufacturers remains stable or increases. Printed indexes have increased greatly in price and we may expect prices of database leasing and the use of on-line facilities to behave similarly. Even government-subsidized databases, such as those of European national libraries, are under pressure to recover costs completely. Latin American countries are thus likely to remain in a negative balance of payments situation. If exchanges on a one-for-one record basis become mandatory—the present trend—the economics of North-South exchange will be unfavorable for the foreseeable future.

Venezuela has made considerable investment in equipment and personnel. The total economic impact has not been studied, although shared cataloging is an obvious saving.

The need to import computer hardware implies continuing dependency. Unlike Mexico, Venezuela imported much of her software too and this has permitted a very rapid take-off of automation. Several of her computer professionals have mastered software design and can explain it elsewhere in Latin America, and make improvements while respecting the basic design. In this sense there has been an emerging independence.

Perhaps the greatest achievement so far has been the use of imported technology to produce and process information that would not have been produced in another country with the same technology. National needs vary: the .database produced would not have been done otherwise.

The chance of increasing the North-South information flow and making it more reciprocal seems to lie in the continued development of these activities in Latin America. More information exporting will benefit Latin America economically. The real values at the level of human consciousness which come through the process of intercommunication as such cannot be quantified.

It might be best for Latin American countries to do independently some of the indexing currently imported. An advantage would be the non-commercial climate for such indexing. Various users of a national information system could cooperatively divide up the work. Venezuela has a very inefficient multiplication of small libraries and information centers, which, if unified, could free staff for indexing.

Venezuela's current situation calls for increased importing of all kinds of documents. More local technical processing and indexing could avoid an increase in costs while giving a better information service based on greater document availability. There will still be much information importing from the large overseas databases, but these will become secondary resources after the national database has been consulted. Over time the most frequently sought monographs and serials will be cataloged or indexed directly, leaving non-regional databases as a last resort for less sought-after materials. If the hopes and plans of many Venezuelan information professionals are realized, North Americans and Europeans will be searching Latin American databases. These would be basically national in administration, but relatively similar in content through an exchange of information by the countries of the region.

REFERENCES

1) Fernández Herez, Rafael. *El Convenio Andrés Bello: la integración educativa, científica y cultural de los paises de América Latina.* Caracas: Ministerio de Educación; 1973.

2) Penalver, Luis Manuel. *Hacia el desarrollo por la ciencia.* Caracas: Ministerio de Educación; 1975.

INFORMATION TECHNOLOGY
AND THE
COMMONWEALTH CARIBBEAN

by Winthrop W. Wiltshire
Caribbean Industrial Research Institute
Trinidad

RESUMEN

La Tecnología Informática y la Comunidad del Caribe

En general, los países del CARICOM no tienen buenos centros informáticos, expertos profesionales, y no se da suficiente cuenta de la importancia de la información al desarrollo nacional. Para reducir la dependencia informática se debe fomentar programas de investigación para producir información de importancia nacional, crear bases de datos sobre sectores nacionales críticos, y establecer sistemas informáticos que pueden identificar información pertinente en bases de datos del Norte. Todas estas medidas son importantes para fomentar industrias y mercados en la region del CARICOM. Hay varias categorias de información de acceso difícil en el Caribe, especialmente en las áreas de la tecnología y el comercio. Incluye bibliografía.

INTRODUCTION

The Commonwealth Caribbean comprises 12 states: Antigua and Barbuda, Barbados, Belize, Dominica, Grenada, Guyana, Jamaica, Montserrat, St. Kitts, St. Lucia, St. Vincent and the Grenadines and Trinidad and Tobago. Jamaica has the largest population (2,000,0000), Trinidad and Tobago, a petroleum exporter, is the wealthiest (*per capita* income over $3,000). Seven states have populations under 150,000.

This paper focuses primarily on aspects of information technology relating to the storage, retrieval and dissemination of bibliographic information. This includes, but is not limited to, the use of computers in conjunction with modern telecommunication technology.

Weak information infrastructures

Scientific and technological information is increasingly being recognized internationally as an indispensable ingredient for development, even as a resource as important as many natural resources (Jaffray & Chandler 1977). Unfortunately this recognition is largely notional. Indeed, a critical constraint in developing countries is not only the low level of information infrastructure *vis á vis* industrialized countries, but also the limited perception of the importance of information (Lancaster 1981).

The term information infrastructure refers to the national capacity to acquire, store and disseminate scientific and technological information, wherever generated, for those who need it to enhance their decisions and choices, including, in particular, state planners and policy makers, public and private sector managers, manufacturers and researchers.

Elements of this infrastructure include: physical resources, such as information centers and libraries in all sectors of national economic and social importance; an adequate supply of trained library and information personnel; facilities for generating and adequately storing information of national significance; telecommunication access to external data bases; and national and regional policies promoting the systematic and rational development of the infrastructure.

Despite the existence of several centers of excellence in the more developed CARICOM· territories (the campus libraries of the University of the West Indies in Jamaica, Barbados and Trinidad, the Technical Information Service at CARIRI and Guyana University library, etc.), no CARICOM country has a strong national information infrastructure. The lesser developed territories, such as Grenada, Dominica, St. Kitts, St. Vincent, St. Lucia and Montserrat have each less than six information professionals.

The prevailing situation is a lack of good information centers, of trained information professionals and of awareness, at all levels, of the vital importance of the information function as an agent for national development. Access to information relevant to problem-solving or decision-making in science, technology, business and government is limited, whether it is generated in the region or outside.

In Jamaica, for example, faltering attempts are being made to establish a union list of serials, but it is being done with minimal resources and with no immediate plans for computerization. In Trinidad and Tobago a similar union list of serials held by parastatal and government agencies was started by one agency on a voluntary basis; not surprisingly it has not been kept up. Due to an absence of clear policies regarding storage and retrieval, it is difficult to locate reports prepared by consultants for public sector agencies. Such reports, often the result of studies costing hundreds of thousands of dollars and containing valuable information about some aspect of an important national activity are frequently lost to the community soon after completion. Often the information they contain is needed as input in planning programs or projects that were not the focus of the original assignment. The problem is further complicated because the consultant, usually a foreign expert, is unavailable for consultation after the report's submission. Such inaccessibility has sometimes led to costly studies being duplicated in the same country by other agencies: either they could not retrieve the relevant report, or they never knew of its existence. This shows how the absence of a simple element of national information policy can have significant adverse consequences. Consultants contracted to undertake studies that will result in an information product such as a report should have, as a term of their contract, the obligation to supply at lease one copy, with related documents, to a designated information center, as well as those for the client agency. The issue of confidentiality could be managed by providing appropriate guidelines for storage and use.

Dependence

All countries of Latin America and the Caribbean depend on the industrialized countries, especially the United States, for much of their scientific and technological information, a dependence not unexpected, given the vast resources available in the North for information generation and processing. It would however be shortsighted for countries of the South simply to remain passive. Development is not an inevitable process; underdevelopment is also a process. No country is necessarily always in process of development.

Quite apart from considerations of growth in a given national economy, as measured by such indices as the GNP, several factors determine whether the dominant dynamic is one of development or underdevelopment. Information is certainly one of these. Although the countries of the Caribbean (and Latin America) have very limited human and financial resources, there are many actions they themselves can take in respect to information to reduce dependence and minimize its negative effects.

Thus, in acquiring technology from the North, the size of the information gap between the Caribbean buyer and the Northern seller will largely determine the terms on which a particular technology is acquired. To get the most favorable terms and the most relevant technology, the buyer must be able readily to procure information on alternatives. The implications for Caribbean information services are clear: they must be able to reduce the information gap between buyer and seller in respect to both (a) the negotiation process itself and (b) the specific technology being acquired.

In considering the services of foreign consultants, it should be noted that information itself is not necessarily knowledge. In cases where a Caribbean country lacks the local expertise to evaluate or assimilate the information relevant to achieving any specific development objective, it may be valid and cost-effective to purchase the services of external experts. But often local expertise is available and the missing factor is information which is already in the public domain.

If local mechanisms to gain independent access to the relevant information sources are not developed, Caribbean countries will be perpetually dependent on the foreign expert, without being able to determine when such expertise is genuinely warranted.

Related initiatives that need to be taken to reduce levels of dependence include:

(1) Initiation of research and development programs to generate needed information on various issues of national significance;

(2) Identification of national sectors and sub-sectors of critical importance to the particular country and developing comprehensive information databases with respect to such sectors;

(3) Establishing information systems and services that will allow for ready identification of information stored in databases in the North relevant to decisions and choices in the Caribbean.

Clearly, before Caribbean countries can take advantage of the opportunities provided by developments in information technology, several initiatives need to be taken at the local and regional level.

The 1975 Lima Declaration (Lima... 1975) from the UNIDO General Conference is one attempt to reduce levels of the Third World's dependence. It proposed, as a major objective of the New International Economic Order, that developing countries should increase their share of the world's industrial output from the 1975 level of 7% to 25% by AD 2000.

Third World states, in attempting to build industrial plants and increase their markets to reach this objective, need to recognize the critical role of information. If national information infrastructures in Third World countries are not systematically strengthened, irrespective of whatever other measures are taken, the year 2000 will see little progress towards this objective!

DATABASES IN NORTH AMERICA

Advantages of external databases

Databases in industrialized countries accessible directly from the Caribbean are an important information source for the region as they contain a vast amount of information on various aspects of science, technology and other fields. They could provide policy makers, private and public sector managers and researchers with timely information on a range of important topics.

Limitations of external databases

These databases are not a substitute for developing databases in the region itself. Many issues of specific interest to the region will be of marginal concern in the United States and other industrialized countries, so local and regional databases must be established to cover them. CARISPLAN, the database on social and economic issues being developed by ECLA's Port of Spain office, is such an initiative. Brazil (Rosenberg 1982) is, undoubtedly, on the correct path in emphasizing the development of national databases in that country.

A vast amount of important information is not contained in accessible databases: proprietary information (except for registered patents) and information considered sensitive for security reasons are examples (An ominous... 1982) has recently drawn attention to pronouncements of United States government officials indicating the existence of strong pressures to place stricter limits on disclosure of results of government-funded research "to keep US technology from falling into the wrong hands."

The high cost of telecommunications, especially in countries that have not set up special facilities for data transmission, is another constraint on widespread use of external databases. Shortage of trained information personnel and foreign exchange difficulties are other limitations.

Use of external databases in CARICOM region

The use in the region of online interaction with commercially available United States databases is very much in the embryonic state. As of January 1983 only Barbados had set up centralized facilities for accessing them. In 1981 the local telecommunication company, Cable and Wireless (West Indies) Ltd. established the "International Database Access Service" for Barbados users at a cost of $0.17US per connect minute plus $0.45US per kilo character transmitted (exclusive of database charges). These charges appear reasonable, but only three institutions have yet installed the computer terminal and modem needed for regular use of the service.

This limited utilization probably results from two factors. Many potential users are unaware of the technology, and secondly, the local company lacks specific expertise on the information contained in the various databases, which hinders effective marketing.

In Trinidad and Tobago the local telephone company, a state enterprise, has entered into agreement with GTE TELENET to establish a public data packet switching network with a node in Port of Spain and concentrators in outlying districts. It should be operational by mid-1983.

No other CARICOM state has established a public data network.

COST OF INFORMATION PRODUCTS

Information costs money. This may not be readily recognized by university researchers in the region used to getting the information they need merely by borrowing a journal from a library. Commercial selective dissemination of information services are not well known here. But industrialists who have to sign a license agreement to import a technology are fully aware that that information has a cost.

It should be self-evident that bibliographic information products of value cannot be free. It costs money to generate a database. Database vendors who provide access to the information in the computer are in business to make a profit. But the costs of some information products seem artificially high. The print-on-paper version of a journal such as *Chemical Abstracts* has risen phenomenally over the last 10 years. This results it seems from the information industry being in a transition period when many traditional products are being replaced by their computerized equivalents. Lancaster (1981) points out that as more centers acquire online access to centralized databases, the smaller the market becomes for many print-on-paper products. It is not surprising that database producers of such products, in order to retain their profit margin, raise unit prices to offset falling demand. So, in the case of *Chemical Abstracts*, by 1983 only large libraries can afford to buy print-on-paper editions. Of course, in a perfect market, the charges for the equivalent computerized database project should fall over time as the number of users increases. This may however not happen.

CATEGORIES OF INFORMATION FOUND DIFFICULT TO ACQUIRE IN THE CARIBBEAN

A recent study (Wiltshire, Gumbs & Durrant 1982) commissioned by the CARICOM Secretariat revealed that scientific and technical information found most difficult to acquire by a cross section of professionals in the region included:

(1) Availability of small-scale equipment and machinery;

(2) Evaluation of alternative manufacturing processes;

(3) Effectiveness of different pesticides;

(4) Alternative sources of equipment and machinery;

(5) Process technology for alternative energy;

(6) State-of-the-art information on projects under study including information on work already done on similar projects regionally and internationally;

(7) Disaster preparedness information that has been adapted for use in the Caribbean region;

(8) Regional trade information;

(9) Sources of technical data on selected packaging materials;

(10) Information from Latin America concerning experience on the adaptation of technology.

Some of this information is in the public domain, but the main reason for the difficulties experienced is the absence of appropriate information-gathering mechanism at local levels. Quite apart from the infrastructural developments alluded to earlier, many of the difficulties now encountered can be overcome by the creation of networks of personnel in similar disciplines across CARICOM countries and beyond. A limited degree of networking exists already, but there is potential for wider application.

CONCLUSIONS

The Commonwealth Caribbean could benefit significantly from the use of aspects of modern information technology. The most important contribution that international agencies and industrialized countries such as the United States can provide is with respect to the development of national information infrastructures in CARICOM states.

REFERENCES

1) Jaffray, J; Chandler, J. *Proposals regarding the establishment of a national scientific and technological information network in Ecuador.* Report to OAS. Washington, D.C.: 1977.

2) Lancaster, Frederick Wilfred. *Latin American workshop on the automated retrieval of information.* Mexico City: March 9–20, 1981.

3) *Lima declaration and plan of action in industrial development and cooperation.* UNIDO: 1975.

4) An ominous shift to secrecy. *Business Week*; October 18, 1982:115.

5) Rosenberg, Victor. Information policies of developing countries — the case of Brazil. *Journal of the American Society for Information Science*; 1982; 33:203–207.

6) Wiltshire, Winthrop W.; Gumbs, B.; and Durrant, F. *Information and communication flows in priority areas of science and technology within the CARICOM region — 1982.* [Study done for CARICOM Secretariat under the aegis of the United Nations Interim Fund for Science and Technology].

THE STATE OF LIBRARY RESEARCH IN THE CARIBBEAN AND LATIN AMERICA[1]

by William J. Cameron
University of Western Ontario
London, Ontario, Canada

RESUMEN

La Situación de la Investigación Bibliotecaria
en el Caribe y América Latina

Hace mucha falta más análisis sistemático de la condición de la investigación bibliotecaria e informática. En agosto de 1982, había una reunión del Comité de Educación Bibliotecaria de la ACURIL en Montreal. Allí se hizo varias resoluciones en pro de fomentar la investigación bibliotecaria, la instrucción bibliotecaria, la traducción, y la creación de redes informáticas.

---

[1]Prepared for the Library Education Committee of the Association of Caribbean University, Research and Institutional Libraries (ACURIL) Conference, Montreal, Canada, 1983.

INTRODUCTION

It is difficult to provide the synoptic analysis of research projects and completed projects implied in this title. The bibliographical control of publications in the field of library and information science in the region is far from properly established and those publications that can be categorized as "research reports" or "articles and books based on research" are not easily accessible. There is a crying need for improvement in the bibliographical control of the literature. Such an improvement would be the result of professional activity and not in itself a research activity.

This leads me to a second point. Perusal of the unrepresentative sample of the literature available to me suggests that a clear distinction needs to be made between professional and research activities. The distinction is worth making, but the connections between the two kinds of activity should also be made clear.

Someone has said that the literature of the profession in North America is made up of "glad tidings" or "how we run our library good," current factual reports and opinion papers, and reports based on the systematic application of reliable research methods. Analysis suggests that the first category is most common, the second less common and the third rare. The same observation could doubtless be made about the literature of Latin America and the Caribbean. The first category is an essential ingredient of professional literature, for communication of news and information about professional activities, institutions and people is vital to the everyday work of everyone in the profession. It can also help researchers identify problems to be solved, to home in on experience-based opinions and myths to be tested and discover areas of ignorance or doubt to be addressed. But much of the research needed to resolve, test or dispel these problems, myths and dubieties cannot be carried out without a great deal of professional work in the second category.

Compiling catalogs, bibliographies, directories, publishing accumulated operational date (annual reports, statistical summaries, etc.) and disseminating conference proceedings, seminar results, etc. form an important foundation for investigative research. Such research may require the gathering of further data, but the formulation of projects nearly always begins with existing data.

This present report falls, I hope, within the second category rather than the first, but I would rather have been able to provide a contribution firmly in the third category. The methods would have been those characteristically employed by historians and social scientists who endeavor to reach a level of informative generality by analyzing and comparing reliable samples of gathered data: it is the absence of representative data that prevents the research from being done. So I propose to discuss what may prove to be an important initiative leading to improved professional data-gathering and encouragement for research-oriented treatment of the data supplied as a result of professional activity.

IDRC/IFLA PRE-CONFERENCE SEMINAR 1982

ACURIL's Library Education Committee was actively involved in proposing, planning and carrying out the IDRC/IFLA Pre-Conference Seminar on "Education for Research and Research in Education" in the week before the 1982 Montreal IFLA Conference. The Seminar, held August 15–20 in the Sheraton Centre Hotel, was a major attempt to bring library school professors and notable researchers of Latin America and the Caribbean together with North American library educators on a matter of particular concern for the improvement of library education in our hemisphere. This concern, the provision of research-oriented librarians to supervise or carry out research in our field, is of great relevance to ACURIL as evidenced by the theme of its 1983 conference.

The Seminar was conducted in Spanish and will be so published, in Bogotá, under the auspices of ALEBCI and IDRC. As no funds for simultaneous translation were available, seminar participants without good Spanish may have encountered difficulty during some sessions.

Eight organizations participated as sponsoring, initiating or supporting bodies. ACURIL was among the supporters and five of its members took part: William J. Cameron (University of Western Ontario); María Casas de Faunce (University of Puerto Rico); Hazel Bennett (UWI); Jean Wilfrid Bertrand (Institut Français d'Haïti) and Sheila Lampart (National Council on Libraries, Archives and Documentation Services, Jamaica).

Besides the three in this list, six library school professors from Latin America also participated: Nice Figueiredo (Biblioteca Nacional, Brazil); Rocio Herrera (Prof. Directora del Departamento de Investigaciones Bibliotecológicas de la Escuela Interamerican de Bibliotecología, Universidad de Antioquia, Colombia); Lidiette Diez Solano (Universidade de Costa Rica); Yoshiko Moriya de Freundorfer (Universidad Nacional de Asunción, Paraguay); Laura Apitz de Taborda (Universidad de Zulia, Venezuela)—and two from the United States: Edwin S. Gleaves (Peabody College, Vanderbilt University, Nashville, Tennessee) and William V. Jackson (University of Texas at Austin).

Research institutes were represented by two of the ACURIL participants and by five others: Emilio R. Ruiz y Blanco (Centro de Investigaciones Bibliotecológicas, Argentina); Regina Celia Montenegro de Lima (IBICT, Brazil); Lucila Martínez de Jíminez (CERLAL, Columbia); Julio Cubillo (CEPAL/CLADES) and Rosario Gassol de Horowitz (Venezuelan National Library).

Observers included a library school professor from the Philippines (Rosa Vallejo, University of the Philippines), an IDRC representative (Claude Boivin, IDRC, Ottawa), an IFLA liaison representative (Jean Lowrie, Western Michigan University) and a representative of the IFLA local arrangements committee (Miriam Tees, McGill University, Montreal).

Participation was thus very broadly representative of library educators and research institutions and the work of the group during the week was productive and interesting. A draft directory of research in Latin America and the Caribbean was published for use in the Seminar: a more complete version will appear with the proceedings. The survey was undertaken by ALEBCI and the results entered into a database at the University of Western Ontario. The library school of the Pontificia Universidad Javeriana, Bogotá, and the University of Western Ontario, London, Canada are cooperating to help ALEBCI maintain and develop this database, collecting additions and corrections with a view to publishing new editions of the directory from time to time.

Keynote addresses on the Seminar's first morning by Julio Cubillo and Octavio Rojas-León set an excellent background for discussion of the topic of research for the rest of the week and provided a basic classification scheme for analysis during the afternoon of research projects reported on in the directory. This provided concrete evidence for the nature, type and variety of research currently being done within Latin American and Caribbean library schools, and, to a certain extent, outside. But coverage needs to be extended before generalizations about the state of research and of education for research can be made authoritatively. Discussions on the first day centered on the practical difficulties the schools face both in conducting research and in teaching research methods. Mobilizing human and financial resources for research is very difficult in Latin America.

Tuesday morning was devoted to papers on the research or the coordinating activities of CERLAL, CLADES, NACOLADS and FID/CLA/ET and the afternoon to reports of research in library schools of four countries. Wednesday focused on possibilities for mutual support between the library schools of North America and those of South America. The issues of the first three days were intensively discussed on Thursday and their results put together on Friday. Of the final resolutions, those that I have suggested that ACURIL might like to take further follow:

1.1. ACURIL, through its Library Education Committee, could sponsor a regional seminar on methods of instruction for library school professors to improve the teaching of research methods;

2.1. ACURIL could reinforce the recommendation of the Seminar that IFLA support a feasibility study for implementing a regional information network on library and information science;

2.2.1. A Committee of ACURIL might be established for identifying international professional literature that ought to be translated into languages of the region, and possibly to initiate a program for undertaking translation of the material of greatest relevance to the region;

2.5. As is evident in the program this year, ACURIL is already promoting the use of the results of research and raising the consciousness of libraries about the importance of research. But some follow-up activity might be worth considering.

Other recommendations will, we hope, be taken up by one or another of the organizations mentioned in the document, and I can report on at least two initiatives already undertaken.

The University of Western Ontario, with the cooperation of the Deans and Directors of Canada's six other library schools, has begun an opinion survey of professors in these schools. The results and methodology used will be supplied to the International Library Education Committee of AALS (now ALISE). ALISE may then attempt to replicate, or to improve on, the Canadian survey. A practical outcome may be a list of important articles and books to be considered for translation into the languages of the region, as well as materials for aid in teaching research in its library schools.

The possibility is being explored of an initial meeting between members of the International Library Education Committee and representatives of the three Colombian schools in late 1983, with a view to a limited Delphi study for defining priorities for research on library and information education in Columbia. If this materializes, the study could later be replicated or improved upon for the whole region with support from appropriate organizations.

INFORMACIÓN TECNOLÓGICA EN EL SALVADOR

por Francisco Salvador Batres M.
Centro Nactional de Producividad
San Salvador, El Salvador

ABSTRACT

Technological Information in El Salvador

Due to problems of economic dependence and the country's socio-political crisis, there has been a lack of funds for and coordination of technological information in El Salvador. There is a government agency, CENAP, which has the function of fomenting and coordinating technological development, but it operates under serious limitations. There are three areas of government activity that have held back development: credit policies, legal policies, and tariff policies. There have also been problems with technological investment, where private investors operate free of adequate central planning, and where foreign investors are primarily interested in taking any profits out of the country. Several conclusions may be drawn: there is lack of effective information coordination, a lack of capacity to generate technologies suited to the country, there is a lack of sufficient funds for technology, there is a lack of promotion and stimulus for scientific research, there are inadequate credit arrangements for raw material purchases, there are numerous legal problems including the lack of adequate patent protection, there is a lack of a national technological information system, and there is a lack of personnel in all technical areas. In spite of these problems, CENAP has been doing a good job of compiling and distributing information. Includes bibliography.

EL DESARROLLO TECNOLÓGICO
EN EL SALVADOR

Practicamente todos los esfuerzos realizados en pro del desarrollo tecnológico por El Salvador se han planteado en forma desarticulada, no logrando resultados consistentes. Se encuentra limitado por la capacidad con que cuenta el industrial, el empresario, la organización o el país; tanto para generar tecnología, como para escoger dentro de la oferta tecnológica mundial aquellas tecnologías que mejor se adecúen a necesidades y objectivos nacionales. La actual debilidad tecnológica del país resultó de anteriores negociaciones de tecnología extranjeras que permitieron que quedaramos en desventaja con respecto al oferente, sin que lográramos un completo acceso a la tecnología en cuestión. Y la falta de un poder de negociación se agrava aún más con la carencia de instituciones gubernamentales o privadas que aporten los conocimientos tecnológicos necesarios.

En anteriores estudios o conferencias presentados por OEA o UNESCO se formularon una serie de políticas que buscan orientar las actividades de creación, difusión y utilización de conocimientos científico-tecnológicos con el propósito de contribuir al desarrollo economico y social (Lancaster 1978) y que el gobierno de El Salvador ha tratado de incorporar en sus planes de desarrollo, pero que sin embargo tienen grandes limitaciones. Actualmente el plan contempla las siguientes políticas: (El Salvador n.d.) (a) la creación de un Fondo Nacional de Desarrollo Científico y Tecnológico; (b) desarrollo de proyectos tecnológicos locales prioritarios tales como: agro-industriales; agro-químicos genéricos; medicamentos básicos genéricos; y minerales metálicos.

La UNESCO estima que las naciones en vías de desarrollo deben gastar en la investigación el 1% de su producto territorio bruto (PTB), y según datos estadísticos proporcionados por el Departamento de Ciencia y Tecnología de MIPLAN se gastó en 1979 en investigación y desarrollo la cantidad de $12.4US millones de dólares o sea un 0.4% del PTB (en su mayoría aportado por el gobierno). Aunque no disponemos de datos más recientes, podemos afirmar que ese procentaje ha disminuido. Las actividades de investigación científica y tecnológica son desarrolladas casi exclusivamente por el Estado y en la mayoría de ellas el CENAP las ha apoyado con información técnica completamente gratis.

Junto con la falta de inversión en la investigación nacional, existen otros factores que contribuyen al actual estado de desarrollo científico-tecnológico de nuestro país.

(1) La gran mayoría de las investigaciones básicas las realiza el sector universitario pero si bien la investigación es necesaria, la falta de institutos de investigación aplicada limitan los beneficios que se harían al sector de la producción.

(2) Existe escaso desarrollo de algunas redes de la ingeniería (y de servicios de ingeniería), que contribuyen al desarrollo y aplicación del proceso tecnológico, por lo que hay que recurrir a firmas extranjeras de servicio consultorio ya que, las firmas nacionales en su mayoría, se dedican a realizar estudios de factibilidad, anexando siempre en los aspectos técnicos del proyecto, una tecnología extranjera, incrementando más el estado de dependencia tecnológica.

(3) Una de las políticas de gobierno busca coordinar todas las actividades científicas y tecnológicas en función del desarrollo por lo que últimamente se ha formado una Comisión Interinstitucional para el Desarrollo y Transferencia de Tecnología, la cual comienza a caminar en dicha actividad, pero todavía no existe una verdadera conciencia sobre su importancia y trascendencia.

(4) El potencial científico y tecnológico no está dirigido hacia el sector industrial que el país incurre en gastos

por pago de derechos para importar patentes y tecnologías, cayendo cada vez más en una peligrosa dependencia económica, científica y tecnológica de otros países.

(5) Falta de una infraestructura (material y equipo experimental), necesaria para la investigación científica y tecnológica.

(6) Falta de fomento y promoción a la investigación científica y tecnológica.

CENAP Y EL SERVICIO DE INFORMACIÓN TECNOLÓGICA

Al Centro Nacional de Productividad (CENAP) se le ha encomendado la tarea de coadyuvar el desarrollo tecnológico del país, principalente a la pequeña y mediana industria, a través de la captación, procesamiento y difusión de toda aquella información técnica y tecnológica y el adecuamiento de tecnologías en las áreas prioritarias, buscando con ello incrementar la producción del país mediante la formulación de alternativas de solución a problemas tecnológicos de cada industria asistida, ya sea para mejorar el producto, proceso, maquinaria, equipo, materia prima, proveedores, mantenimiento e insumos específicos para sus actuales y futuras necesidades y que abra la posibilidad de ampliar sus mercados, buscando siempre que las decisiones en la selección de las tecnología sean adecuadas a los requerimientos reales del país. Además apoyar las investigaciones locales y evaluar las necesidades que el proceso de desarrollo requiera.

FALLAS EN EL PROCESO DE
DESARROLLO TECNOLÓGICO

Debido a que el CENAP ha enfocado sus esfuerzos hacia el sector industrial, le ha permitido determinar una serie de fallas en el proceso de desarrollo tecnológico, las cuales se han presentado a nivel gubernamental, privado, a nivel de país o internacional.

Fallas a nivel gubernamental

Existen tres formas de políticas que el gobierno ha generado y que son un freno al desarrollo.

1. *Políticas crediticias*

En el Plan Trienal 1981–83 del Ministerio de Planificatión (El Salvador n.d.) incluyen: (a) la ampliación del crédito de mediano y largo plazo, a través del Banco de Fomento Industrial; (b) la ampliación del crédito a los subsectores de la pequeña empresa artesanía y la manufactura doméstica, en condiciones preferenciales; (c) apoyo a la rehabilitación de empresas; (d) apoyo crediticio, complementario del crédito internacional, para la obtención de materia prima importada. Estas políticas financian capital de trabajo para la consolidación de deudas por adquisición de materia prima, maquinaria o equipo que en su mayoría procede de países desarrollados, pero no se preocupan de que los prestatarios tengan capital de negociación de contratos que en cualquier momento afectan al país, ya que además de ser una fuga de divisas, no son realizados en función del desarrollo económico nacional.

2. *Políticas legales*

El marco legal existente en el país adolece de una serie de vacíos y obsolecencias que colocan en desventaja a los intereses nacionales. Cualquier empresa extranjera puede inscribirse en el registro de la propiedad industrial sin garantizar a los nacionales el acceso a esa tecnología. Por otra parte se ha legislado sobre productos de interés social (farmacéuticos, alimentos), sin considerar su impacto en la economía y especialmente en el desarrollo tecnológico. De esta manera se impide que un nacional con diferente proceso llegue al mismo producto, pues la actual ley permite que la patente o marca sea un instrumento de monopolio en un mercado.

3. Políticas arancelarias

El gobierno con el ánimo de proteger la incipiente industria nacional creó una ley de incentivos fiscales que benefician especialmente a la gran industria sin que exista una exigencia legal que promueva la investigación o por lo menos, una adecuación tecnológica. Dicha ley ayuda a las empresas a mejorar sus niveles de rentabilidad, con lo que podrían financiar dicha investigación y mejorar sustancialmente sus procesos y el valor agregado. Por otra parte con el objeto de atraer la inversión extranjera se crearon las zonas francas, las que significan una serie de servicios e infraestructura, pero que no garantizan una transferencia de tecnología, porque dichas industrias sólo ocupan mano de obra a nivel obrero cuyo trabajo no requiere especialización; esta afirmación se basa en que muchas empresas de este tipo radicadas en el país tuvieron que irse por la crisis que atravesamos y al intentar reactivarlas con personal nacional, han encontrado dificultades en el sentido de no conocer todo el proceso tecnológico necesario. Esta situación tiene que forzar al estado a legislar de acuerdo a las necesidades que presenta el desarrollo económico nacional, brindando a la transferencia de tecnología un especial interés.

Fallas a nivel privado

La empresa privada presionada por la competividad del mercado y de acuerdo a su condición microeconómica, toma decisiones sobre la tecnología a usar, que acentúan y mantienan las condiciones de sub-desarrollo, ya que descuidan la estrecha relación, que existe entre el nivel de empleo, la procedencia de las materias primas y la balanza de pagos. Esto se agrava aún más debido a los diferentes intereses existentes entre el estado y el sector privado, que busca las máximas utilidades a través de nuevos procesos y maquinarias, de ser se posible automatizada y en general nuevas combinaciones de los factores de producción que buscan un incremento en la productividad y que abran la posibilidad de ampliar sus mercados. También el empresario concentra su atención en el nivel político gubernamental, con miras a asegurarse la protección aduanera y la fijación de precios internos favorables. Además no es de interés del empresario, ahorrar divisas, las cuales el Estado debe garantizar por algún medio, ni hacer uso de las materias primas del país o de la abundante mano de obra. En resumidas cuentas la descoordinación existente entre el Estado y los empresarios, permite que estos negocien tecnología sin tomar en consideración otros factores de la producción provocando dichos contratos efectos adversos en el desarrollo económico nacional ya que aumentan el grado de dependencia.

Fallas a nivel de inversión extranjera internacional

Las compañías transnacionales están estrechamente relacionadas con el actual desarrollo tecnológico del país. Dominan entre un cuarto y una tercera parte de toda la producción mundial, controlando especialmente el procesamiento y el mercado. Su inversión directa en los países en desarrollo fué en 1975 de aproximadamente $68,000US millones, y se ha dirigido a un número limitado de estos, principalmente los países que pudieran ofrecer estabilidad política, y un ambiente económico conveniente, incluidos incentivos fiscales, mercados grandes, mano de obra barata, fácil acceso al petróleo y otros recursos naturales (Brandt 1981): las Bahamas, Barbados, Bermudas, Islas Caimán, Antillas Holandesas, Panamá, Hong-Kong, Brasil, México, Argentina, Perú, Venezuela, Malasia, Singapur y la India.

En realidad existe una relación triangular entre los intereses del país sede, el país anfitrión y los de la compañía transnacional. Evidentemente, el país sede y la compañía tienen la meta de elevar al máximo sus ganancias mundiales y por consiguiente no tendrán los mismos intereses del país anfitrión cuyo deseo es obtener el máximo beneficio nacional. Po lo tanto el país debe buscar cooperación internacional con aquellos países que tengan un interés humanitario en la tranferencia efectiva de capital y tecnología.

Fallas a nivel nacional

A nivel nacional el primer problema que frena el desarrollo es la carencia de un sistema nacional de información científica y tecnológica. Existen varias instituciones que prestan servicios de información que si bien no duplican esfuerzos, sus acciones no cumplen la coordinación necesaria para conformar un verdadero sistema. Intentos en esta dirección no han alcanzado sus objetivos por no considerar la importancia de la transferencia de tecnología como variable económico, sino como alternativa sectorial.

Otro problema es la excasez acentuada de personal nacional capacitado en negociación de tecnología. Para que esta se desarrolle en condiciones óptimas debe contarse con un buen servicio de información tecnológica que permita que la información fluya ágil y oportunamente y que cuente además con un respaldo legal que opere en función nacional.

SITUACIÓN ACTUAL DE LA INFORMACIÓN TECNOLÓGICA EN EL SALVADOR

Antecedentes

La presente crisis socio-política en el país tiene como consecuencia un decremento en el ingreso y en el empleo. Una solución sería el fortalecimiento del sector productivo, que se puede obtener con la conjunción de esfuerzos de los sectores públicos y privados, a fin de rehabilitar empresas y de elevar la producción en los planteles educativos.

El CENAP ha venido trabajando desde 1980 en esto, a través del Departamento de Información, Investigación y Adecuación Tecnológica, suministrando todos los elementos técnicos que sirvan de herramientas adecuadas al empresaio y gobierno salvadoreño a fin de contribuir a una mejor toma de decisiones para el desarrollo de sus empresas, implementando además canales de información que permitan a los estudiantes superiores, investigadores, técnicos y personas dedicadas a la producción industrial o cualquier actividad afín, tener acceso a documentos técnicos y de gestión empresarial, con el único objeto de desarrollar el sector industrial, también a través del Servicio se pretende poner al alcance de la industria y gobierno, todas aquellas tecnologías existentes que le permitan resolver sus problemas en este campo, mediante una efectiva adecuación de las mismas. Además el CENAP busca una efectiva coordinación con otros organismos que disponen de centros de documentación técnica existente en El Salvador.

El CENAP es una institución semi-autónoma del Ministerio de Economía, teniendo como objetivos generales: (a) contribuir al desarrollo de las sectores económicos del país por medio de la asesoría y consultoría técnica a las empresas, especialmente las usuarias de la banca de fomento industrial; (b) coadyuvar al desarrollo de los sectores económicos del país a través de la captación, procesamiento y difusión de toda aquella información técnica y tecnológica, así como con el adecuamiento de tecnologías en áreas prioritarias; (c) promover el incremento de la productividad del país y su desarrollo económico mediante la capacitación y adiestramiento de los recursos humanos nacionales.

El Departamento de Información, Investigación y Adecuación Tecnológica tiene actualmente los siguientes objetivos específicos: (a) contribuir al desarrollo del sector industrial facilitando todos los aspectos tecnológicos necesarios para la mejor selección o adecuación de tecnologías en función de los recursos de cada sector; (b) contribuir al desarrollo tecnológico nacional mediante las diseminación de información a estudiantes, investigadores, técnicos y profesionales dedicados a la investigación, producción industrial o cualquier actividad afín, mediante el suministro de la información tecnológica que el proceso de desarrollo demande; (c) coadyuvar al desarrollo tecnológico a través del establecimiento de una biblioteca, un centro de documentación tecnológico en los cuales se procese, almacene y actualice permanentemente toda la información técnica y tecnológica que el proceso de desarrollo requiera; (d) fomentar el desarrollo tecnológico del país, mediante el establecimento de mecanismos que procuren la difusión y aplicación sistemática de las normas, del control de calidad y metrología; (e) coadyuvar el desarrollo tecnológico del país, a través de la utilización de la propiedad industrial como una herramienta que promueva la investigación científica-tecnológica y que estimule la inventiva y creatividad del salvadoreño.

Descripción de las actividades del SIIAT

Las áreas industriales atendidas por el SIIAT son las siguientes: alimentaria, del cuero, maderera, del caucho y plástico, papelera, del embalaje, gráfica, textil, de confecciones, química, de cerámica y vidrio, metal-mecánica, siderúrgica, y eléctrica y electrónica. Los servicios que se ofrecen son: (a) consultas técnicas (incluyendo un análisis del problema, sus soluciones y recomendaciones así como la información de apoyo útil al usuario; (b) búsqueda de información tecnológica, sobre pedidos específicos (tecnología de procesos, identificación de nuevas oportunidades industriales, normas técnicas, control de calidad, bibliografía y literatura técnica); (c) diseminación de información a través del boletín de noticias técnicas *Informador tecnológico*, el cual se edita mensualmente en las áreas química, electricidad, mecánica, ingeniería industrial, administración y mercadeo, alimentos, normas tecnológicas, control de calidad, anunciantes industriales, patentes de invención (desde el segundo semestre de 1983), mas un boletín informativo de la Biblioteca y el boletín AMTID (Aplicación de tecnología moderna para el desarrollo internacional) a través del cual se promueven títulos de documentos NTIS; (d) biblioteca y centro de documentación; (e) enlace industrial, un programa permanente de visitas a empresas industriales, con el objeto de determinar necesidades tecnológicas, administrativs o de capacitación.

COMENTARIOS

El desarrollo de CENAP ha estado acompañado de una intensa cooperación internacional, realizada como miembro de la Red de Servicios de Información Científica y Tecnológica que patrocina el Programa Regional de Desarrollo Científico y Tecnológico de la OEA en coordinación con el ICAITI, el IDRC del Canadá y el NTIS de los EUA. Tal cooperación es vital para que cada país logre sus objetivos nacionales y debe aprovechar todos los recursos existentes que garanticen los bajos costos del servicio, la eficiencia, efectividad y los beneficios. Las labores de almacenamiento y recuperación de información que actualmente el CENAP realiza así como otros miembros de la Red de SIATES, principalmente para el área centroamericana y el Caribe, se han desarrollado en gran parte, debido a aportes de la OEA, el ICAITI y el IDRC, pues fué a través de ellos que se elaboró el tesauro de información industrial para el uso de los banco de datos de CentroAmérica y la República Dominicana.

La eficiencia de un servicio de información tiene como parámetros principales la rapidez y bajo costo, y defineremos como efectividad del servicio cuando se considera también la calidad. Una evaluación debe tener en cuenta los recursos asignados al Servicio de Información principalmente del recurso económico (para la compra de información, suscripción o publicaciones periódicas), como de los recursos humanos y materiales con que se cuentan. El económico es de gran importancia ya que la demanda de la información está de acuerdo a la actualidad del documento y por regla general la demanda disminuye en relación directa a la fecha en que se generó el documento.

Otro aspecto muy importante es la relación que existe entre el costo y beneficio de un servicio que consiste en la relación entre el costo de proveer un servicio y los beneficios que se derivan de contar con este servicio, el servicio es justificado si los beneficios superan los costos. También es conveniente denotar que los servicios se ven positivamente afectados con la edición de publicaciones periódicas como son publicaciones de alerta, boletines de noticias técnicas, los cuales estimulan los servicios de información.

Una vez aclarados los anteriores conceptos y conociendo los servicios que el CENAP ofrece en coordinación con los lineamientos que conforman; los programas de reactivación económica del actual gobierno, así como de las necesidades del sector industrial, podemos enumerar una serie de limitaciones internas de CENAP para el ofrecimiento de un buen servicio para la actual y futura demanda de información tecnológica en El Salvador.

(1) El sistema de procesamiento y recuperación de información es obsoleto a parte de que se dispone de un limitado personal técnico en esas actividades.

(2) El accesso a bancos de datos extranjeros se realiza generalmente por correo, por lo que el servicio se ve limitado por el tiempo que tarda la comunicación.

(3) El sistema de almacenamiento de documentos es en papel copia lo que limita grandemente el espacio físico, pues se carece de máquinas que resuelvan el problema.

(4) Las bases de datos de los SIATES son muy limitados, por lo que se busca tener acceso a otras fuentes europeas, suramericanas y americanas, pero que requieren mucha inversión.

(5) Se dispone de un número de técnicos que necesitan capacitarse y especializarse con el propósito de mejorar la calidad y efectividad del servicio.

(6) El Centro cuenta con un presupuesto exiguo que es originado por las políticas de austeridad del actual gobierno. El actual recurso financiero solamente le permite satisfacer las necesidades de funcionamiento, pero no de modernización y ampliación.

CONCLUSIONES

Do todo lo anterior podemos sacar las siguientes conclusiones:

(1) En El Salvador existen diferentes centros que manejan información tecnológica en diferentes áreas, pero no están coordinados, por lo que el almacenamiento, recuperación y diseminación de la información tecnológica no se hace eficazmente.

(2) Se carece de una capacidad para gestionar la tecnología más adecauda a las necesidades del país, tanto en el sector público como en el privado que tráe a veces como

consecuencia la subutilización de la tecnología, así como el desplazamiento de la mano de obra.

(3) La inversión que se ha venido haciendo para la investigación y el desarrollo tecnológico en El Salvador ha sido insuficiente, lo que ha traido como consecuencia el atraso en esta área para el país en relación con otros países.

(4) Hace falta fomento y promoción para la investigación sistemática científica y tecnológica en todas las áreas técnicas; así como infraestructura (material y equipo experimental), necesario para la misma.

(5) Las políticas de crédito en el país para la compra de materia prima, maquinaria y equipo, no contemplan la garantía necesaria para las tecnologías adquiridas sean las más adecuadas para el país.

(6) Se hace necesario que las políticas legales se renueven y actualicen sobre todo en lo concerniente a la inscripción y uso de patentes de invención, de tal forma que se protejan los intereses nacionales y se promueva la invención y desarrollo tecnológico en el país.

(7) Se carece de un sistema nacional de información tecnológica, por lo que la información generada en el país y la transferida de otros países no se encuentra debidamente procesada y organizada, lo que viene a obstaculizar su divulgación tanto a nivel nacional como internacional.

(8) Se hace necesaria la capacitación de personal en las áreas de gestión tecnológica, procesamiento y clasificación de la información, procesamiento computarizado de información, administración de servicios de información, investigación científica y tecnológica, transferencia de información tecnológica, etc.

A pesar de los problemas que se han presentado y con fuertes limitaciones económicas el CENAPA a través del SIIAT ha venido realizando un buen trabajo de recopilación, tranferencia, procesamiento y divulgación de información tecnológica, entre los empresarios nacionales y de otros países de la región. Contando para ello con el apoyo económico de la OEA.

REFERENCES

1) Brandt, Willy. Participación en inversión y tecnología; transnacionales: nuevas dimensiones. *Revista perspectivas económicas*; 1981; 33:34-40.

2) ICAITI. *Tesauro de información industrial de Centroamérica y República Dominicana.* Guatemala: [n.d.].

3) Lancaster, Frederick Wilfred. *Guidelines for the evaluation of information systems and services.* Paris: UNESCO; 1978.

4) OEA. *Documento de trabajo CACTAL/doc. 5.* Rev. 1, 20 de Abril, 1972.

5) El Salvador. Ministerio de planificación y coordinación del desarrollo económico. *Plan trienal 1981-1983 de la República de El Salvador.* [n.d.].

EXPERIENCIA EN LA TRANSFERENCIA DE INFORMACIÓN CIENTÍFICA Y TÉCNICA A TRAVÉS DEL CENTRO DE INFORMACIÓN INDUSTRIAL DEL BANCO CENTRAL DE HONDURAS (CIIBANTRAL)

por José Ricardo Freije M.
Depto. de Investigaciones Industriales
Banco Central de Honduras
Tegucigalpa, D.C., Honduras

ABSTRACT

The Experience of Scientific and Technical Information Transfer through the Center for Industrial Information of the Central Bank of Honduras (CIIBANTRAL)

The functions of the CIIBANTRAL in distributing industrial information include coordinating national and foreign institutions with respect to information access and providing library and publication services. The service cooperates with the Universidad Nacional Autónoma de Honduras. Its principal publication is the *Boletín de noticias técnicas* which is widely distributed in the industrial sector and in Latin America.

INTRODUCCIÓN

El objeto de este artículo es el de presentar la experiencia en una forma breve sobre la transferencia de información científica y tecnológica a través del CIIBANTRAL.

Para identificar y seleccionar una tecnología, es necesario conocer la información disponible, quién la tiene y cual es la más apropriada para un propósito en particular. Además proveer la información necesaria y los datos para negociar y adquirir la tecnología con éxito del proveedor industrial. La aplicación de los resultados deberá convertirse en un poderoso instrumento para el dessarrollo general del país.

El Departamento de Asuntos Científicos de la Secretaría General de la OEA, consciente de la alta prioridad que tiene la aplicación de los conocimientos técnicos que en una gran proporción se manifiestan a través de la información técnica, impulsó en 1976 como una estrategia común para la aplicación de la ciencia y la tecnología al desarrollo de los países centroamericanos y del Caribe, la creación de los servicios de Información y Asistencia Técnica a las Empresas (SIATES), incluídos dentro del Programa Regional de Desarrollo Científico y Tecnológico de la OEA.

Al mismo tiempo el Banco Central de Honduras, a través del Departamento de Investigaciones Industriales contribuyó a que este proyecto fuera posible, creándose entonces en esta Institución el Centro de Información Industrial (CIIBANTRAL) a quien se le asignó el Proyecto Especial de Servicios de Información a la Industria, trabajando en dos áreas específicas, la industria química y la de alimentos. Esta decisión se hizo en base a la infraestructura ya existente en este Departamento.

La Universidad Nacional Autónoma de Honduras (UNAH) también entró a formar parte del proyecto, creándose el Centro de Información Industrial de la Universidad (CII-UNAH) quien trabaja en las áreas relacionadas con la construcción, madera, metal-mecánica y eléctrica.

El organismo de enlace para ambos proyectos lo constituye el Consejo Superior de Planificación Económica (CONSUPLANE).

ACTIVIDADES

Las acciones llevadas a cabo en CIIBANTRAL para el desarrollo del proyecto se han encaminado a lograr una mayor disponibilidad de información para transferir a la pequeña y mediana industria, contribuyendo de esta manera a aumentar la eficacia de aspectos técnicos y administrativos del sector productivo del país. Son: (a) fortalecer el CIIBANTRAL en lo que se refiere a la formación de recursos humanos y adquisición de información técnica y equipo; (b) procesar, almacenar y recuperar la información adquirida; (c) canalizar información tecnológica directamente a las pequeñas y medianas industrias; (d) diseminar información específica a través de publicaciones especiales; (e) hacer uso de los mecanismos de coordinación, comunicación e interrelación con los demás centros de información que integran la red Centroamericana y del Caribe; (f) asistir al sector público y privado que ejecutan acciones de Asistencia Técnica y Financiera a la industria, que solicitan información técnica apropiada disponible en el CIIBANTRAL o recurriendo a fuentes nacionales o del extranjero para su adquisición.

A manera de crear un clima favorable para la innovación, la difusión de la información científica y tecnológica se verifica a través de: (a) servicio de consulta técnica; (b) servicio de enlace industrial; (c) publicaciones del *Boletín de noticias técnicas*; (d) diseminación selectiva de información y (e) servicio de biblioteca. El servicio de consulta técnica recibe solicitudes del sector industrial, ya sea por iniciativa propia o por el servicio de enlace industrial. La información proporcionada puede cubrir procesos de manufactura, métodos de manufactura, control de calidad, reportes de investigación, etc:, que permiten el uso efectivo de la tecnología. Sobre este servicio el sector industrial del país consitutye el 70 de los usuarios. El servicio de enlace industrial es el medio para promover los servicios del CIIBANTRAL. Por medio de visitas a las industrias se trata de establecer contacto personal con los gerentes de pequeñas y medianas industrias, tratando de identificar problemas técnicos de las empresas, y tratar de hacer conciencia en ellos de utilizar la información como una herramienta útil para sus empresas. A través de este servicio se ha visitado la mayor parte de las empresas industriales del país, afines a nuestras áreas de trabajo, realizandose tranferencia de información en forma directa.

El *Boletín de noticias técnicas* permite al sector industrial mantenerse al día con los advances tecnológicos. Para su elaboración se hace uso de la información existente en CIIBANTRAL, así como de los boletines de INFOTEC-CONACYT de México y del Centro de Desarrollo Industrial del Ecuador (CENDES) y en algunos casos los boletines que se reciben de otros centros de información de Centroamérica. El *Boletín* es enviado también a estes, en forma gratuita, asimismo a solicitud de ellos se hacen envíos de los artículos contenidos en él. Estos centros centroamericanos (y del Caribe) constituyen un 3.7 de los usarios de este servicio.

A fin de poder dar un servicio eficiente de tranferencia de información, se cuenta con una biblioteca en la cual se reciben numerosas publicaciones periódicas, libros, folletos, documentos, etc. seleccionados a base de las necessidades de información detectadas en los usuarios de CIIBANTRAL o por iniciativa de su personal.

Asimismo como apoyo a los servicios de información se cuenta con la colaboración de distintas instituciones del país y del extranjero a quienes se recurre para distintas demandas de información.

Para la formación del personal de CIIBANTRAL en los principales aspectos de la ciencia de la información, se ha contado desde el inicio con la colaboración del Banco así como de la OEA, quien planificó desde un inicio el desarrollo de programas de entrenamientos básicos sobre servicio de información a la industria. Colaboran con nosotros también otros centros del extranjero quienes ya cuentan con una amplia experiencia en el campo de información y que de alguna forma tienen vinculación con la OEA. CENDES ha facilitado entrenamiento y asesoría al personal del CIIBANTRAL, así como también ha suministrado numerosas publicaciones (perfiles industriales, consultas técnicas, noticias técnicas), que en gran parte han servido de base para tranferir información técnica al sector industrial de nuestro país. Otras instituciones de las cuales el CIIBANTRAL ha aprovechado sus experiencias han incluido: INFOTEC-CONACYT (Mexico); INDOTEC y ICAITI (Guatemala); CIAT (Colombia); INTEC (Chile); NITS, EPA, United States AID y Patent Unlimited (EUA); Brace Research Institute (Canadá); Intermediate Technology Industrial Service, Appropriate Health Resources and Technologies Action Ltd. y BLLD (Inglaterra) y GATE (Alemanha).

THE DISCUSSIONS OF THE CONFERENCE

Monday Morning, 11 April 1983

The Role of Scientific and Technical Information in Aiding Development

Victor Rosenberg:

I would like to dispense with formality and to have this Conference be as much as possible an informal discussion. We're going to be spending four days together discussing a number of issues and I'd like everyone to feel free to speak to these issues and to deal with them.

What I have set as our goals for this conference are some rather high goals indeed. What I hope will come out of this Conference is first of all a renewed understanding and a renewed motivation to deal with the very difficult issues that Dr. Chen spoke of last night. Secondly, I would like to see developed a set of recommendations that we can take back to various respective government agencies, professional societies and organizations, so that we can in fact do something about the problems and issues that will be discussed here this week.

Consequently we have designed this Conference so that there will be a discussion of ideas. There will be no formal presentation of papers. The papers have been prepared in advance and you have all received copies. This also dispenses with the difficulty of when papers are presented at a conference, very often the person presenting the paper has a vested interest in defending the points of that paper. I'd like this to be an open discussion, an open Conference, so that we can in fact modify our thinking and modify our positions, as we deal with these very difficult problems.

Each session will deal with a specific topic. I suspect that we will range from that topic to others, and that there will be an interplay between the topics. At the last session I would like to have us formulate a series of recommendations that can come out of the Conference. We expect to publish the proceedings of the Conference in the form of the papers that have been submitted and edited, the edited deliberations, and most importantly the recommendations. I hope that this volume will go a long way to try to deal with these issues.

I'd like to turn to Dean Bidlack of the University of Michigan School of Library Science, for some welcoming remarks.

Dean Russell E. Bidlack:

My task is very simple this morning. It is a genuine pleasure to welcome you to Ann Arbor, to the University of Michigan and to the School of Library Science. The University of Michigan frequently entertains visitors from abroad, and the Library School itself has a long tradition of bringing guest speakers from around the country and once in a while from overseas. But I do not believe that the Library School has ever been associated with a program with quite as many guests from as far away as this one. Thank you, Victor, for adding this to our list of accomplishments.

I am especially pleased that among the participants we have four of our own graduates. You heard one last night, Ching-Chih Chen. She received her Master's degree in Library Science here a number of years ago and has gone on to achieve great recognition and thus bring honor to our School. We recognized that in 1980 when we brought her back as part of of our annual Alumni-in-Residence Program, wherein we bring back a number of alumni to mingle with our students to inspire them. Ching-Chih certainly did that.

We also have with us today three of our PhD's, Marta Dosa, Juan Freudenthal, and Murilo da Cunha. It is a real delight to welcome you. They are all library educators, bringing distinction and honor to us. To them I would say welcome home.

We are most grateful to the Tinker Foundation for supporting this Conference, and it is a pleasure to recognize Melinda Pastor as representing the Foundation. Not only do I express our gratitude to the Tinker Foundation for making this Conference possible, but also for supporting a number of research projects in which Victor Rosenberg has been involved. I should like to also acknowledge the support of University Microfilms International, and that of the Organization of American States. That support is greatly appreciated.

Our Library School is one of the older library schools in the country, but not the oldest. We began in 1926. We are one of sixty-nine library education programs in the United States and Canada, accredited by the ALA and one of 23 in the United States and Canada offering the doctorate.

At this point I should like to share with you a letter that I received a few years ago. We have a custom in this country that in the elementary schools, at about the fourth grade level, students are expected to write something on their career goals. This is a lot to expect of a child of ten or twelve, so it is not unusual for people in universities to receive letters from children seeking information for what they call their first research paper. Little Debby Brown, in 1971, from a town in Michigan called Lapeer, wrote to me and included several lines which I have taken to heart. She said, "Dear Sir, I am a student of Irving Elementary School. I would like to know some information on the library. We are studying the library. If you don't have much, don't send much." When my secretary received this, she said, "Here's a motto for you, Dean. When you don't have much to say, don't say it." This is what I often think about welcomes. There really is not much to say, once one has welcomed you. Now that I have done that, and, taking Debby Brown's advice, I shall close.

Victor Rosenberg:

Now I would like to turn over the proceedings to Dr. Cavan McCarthy, who is here from Brazil. He is chairing the session this morning on the role of scientific and technical information in aiding development. We set this as the opening topic for the Conference because it is so very fundamental to look at the basic question of how and in fact whether information does indeed aid national development.

Cavan McCarthy:[2]

The world we live in is dominated by two major and often conflicting forces, integration and nationalism. The level of global integration of commerce and industry is high, and constantly increasing. Because of world-wide competition and the desire of multinational companies to produce products as cheaply as possible, industrial production has spread rapidly, especially to the Pacific rim and some southern countries, and it is rare to find products whose manufacture is the monopoly of just one country.

One very interesting point is that scientific and technical databases were, and to a large extent still are, the monopoly of a single country. This is due to clearly identifiable and linguistic factors, but they have been responsible for much of the heat of recent debates on information transfer.

---

[2]Remarks submitted after the Conference took place.

Up to now the amount of technical information necessary for industrialization in the Third World has been fairly low, and could be imported in the form of equipment and foreign engineers on secondment. This explains the existence in countries such as Brazil of large factories which have no visible information supply facilities. But industrialization is becoming increasingly complex, and this will inevitably involve more sophisticated and organized forms of information flow than at present.

Many commentators foresee a strengthening of the trend of transfer of basic industries to the south, while research, development and design continue to be concentrated in the north. It is difficult to know how far this process will go, because it is not necessarily wholly advantageous for the North, and is also politically highly explosive. Should it continue, an essential element would be the southward flow of large quantities of scientific and technical information.

But the worldwide spread of industrialization has been accompanied by an equally pronounced rise in nationalism, and in attempts to maintain and give further emphasis to national cultures and identities. It is important to remember that library science, although theoretically an activity susceptible to a high degree of standardization on worldwide levels, is in practice firmly culturally dependent. Probably the greatest lesson of comparative library science is the wide degree of contrast between practices, even in adjoining countries, and the low level of international communication between libraries. The most intriguing question, it seems to me, is how far scientific and technical information and databases will be standardized world-wide, and how far they will be modified to the particular cultural requirements of each country.

What we appear to be witnessing is the growth of a hybrid system, whereby a few large databases are backed up by an increasing number of smaller local systems. Such an arrangement is perhaps the only one which is both practical and likely to gain acceptance from all sides. Local systems can be more responsive to local needs and to the information requirements of small and medium-sized industries, thus avoiding the dangers of the formation of an information elite. Another important consideration is horizontalization, the use of local systems on a regional rather than a national basis, to compensate for the more usual vertical or north-south communication. South American countries are notorious for their lack of intercommunication and contact, but there is much to be gained from interchange in the scientific and technical information field.

Finally, we must face the very real possibility of the financial collapse of South America, or of at least a decade of zero industrial growth on that continent. In that case there will be very little money to pay for foreign information systems and the development of local systems will be severely limited.

Victor Rosenberg:

I would like to repeat that these are most difficult issues to come to grips with. At one time during some research, I proposed to write a book on the role of scientific and technical information in national development. I was quickly discouraged from the project. There simply is little, if any, evidence of the relationship, and it's so very ill-defined that it is almost impossible to get a handle on it. And yet, it seems to me that of all the topics that we will be discussing it is one of the most central issues because almost all of us believe as an article of faith that information does relate to national development. But the question is, does information relate to development, or is development simply the production of toothpaste and soap for the markets of the nation? This is the issue that we are trying to address this morning—taking the most difficult one first!

Juan Freudenthal:

Shall we start by trying to define what we mean by information? "Information" is so broad. Can we define what kind of information, and how it differs from level to level? Information for whom? Are we talking about only scientific and technical information? When we say scholarly, what does that mean? What about the humanities? In our papers there are numerous undefined terms.

Victor Rosenberg:

I think that is sort of unfair, Juan, to ask for a definition of information from information professionals!

Juan Freudenthal:

Not at all!

Victor Rosenberg:

I've yet to hear information adequately defined. But we could in fact come up with some operational definitions.

Juan Freudenthal:

That's what I'm talking about.

Victor Rosenberg:

We are limiting this somewhat artificially to scientific and technical information. The line between what we commonly consider as that and cultural or social information is very narrow indeed. In fact I think it could be very strongly argued that the forty million viewers (one third of the population) of Brazilian news programs are in fact watching a version of scientific and technical information in the form of the mass media. So, it think it will be very difficult to arrive at some definitions.

Cavan McCarthy:

If we say, for example, "information is the information needed for specific developmental goals," you have the problem that very often Latin American countries are not working toward very specific goals.

Armando Sandoval:

My impression is that, in spite of the difficulties in defining information, it is not necessary to know what kind of information we want to talk about. One of the points that Dr. Chen mentioned yesterday was, information for whom, for what?

It happens that we are working and investing a very large amount of effort for a very small minority, and one finally wonders if the effort is proportional to the use of the information we are providing. Despite this question, for me it is necessary to provide information, no matter for whom, whenever it is requested. It has to be provided.

Let me mention for me what is one of the paradoxes of modern society in the third world. The large effort invested in providing information is viewed by a very small minority, but in our large cities, surrounded by immense slums, where millions of people live, the slums are covered with a forest of tv antennas. There is a real contrast between the information we provide for a very small minority, who may be really working for the development of the country, and those masses of people who are receiving another kind of information. For them, no matter what the cost, buying a tv set is more important than buying food. This is the real paradox that we should worry about. In this context, how should we approach the problem of providing the kind of information that we have in mind?

Winthrop Wiltshire:

I would like to venture a description, rather than a definition, of the term information in our context. It's very loose, and very broad. Information, I suggest, is one necessary ingredient for effective decision-making and taking of choices.

Alma Jordan:

At what level?

Winthrop Wiltshire:

At any level.

Alma Jordan:

Then we are throwing the ball back into the open court. That makes it very general information. When you were framing the description, I was thinking that you were relating it to government and policy-making, but in point of fact we could also be talking about information for decision-making for the man in the street, in the context of what Armando said.

Winthrop Wiltshire

I'm including that.

Marta Dosa:

I would like to try to offer a very modest description of national development first, and then a very modest description of what I mean by information. I think information can be defined only in the context of a purpose, and the purpose today for our discussion is national development. And I like to think of national development in terms of the economic, political, cultural, and social progress of the country. That kind of progress in development has been in the last twenty years expressed in two different ways. One is economically measured by the gross national product (GNP), and the second, in social terms, is measured by basic needs of the poor, in every country. The measurement of poverty.

Now following this description of what I feel development tries to achieve, that is, overall national economic development plus the social development of people, then I would like to suggest that information in these terms could be described as textual and bibliographic information which helps the scholar and supports those who like economic scientists and legal experts work on the overall national development of the country. Numeric data may also be described as information. Many countries are trying to survey their social conditions, and often this results in numeric data. I feel that librarians would benefit by recognizing the need and value of scientific and technical information in bibliographic and textual form, as well as raw data. Let us not overvalue it, by giving data an undue recognition, but recognize that national governments do use social science data and maybe include that notion in our discussion.

Laurence Hallewell:

I would like to remind the group that there is a type of flow of information which has got very little to do with development. This was in fact the first type of information flow between North and South in which I had personal experience as a student. Desiring to eke out my income I started translating for a pharmaceutical multinational, and most of the reports that I translated were on the trying out of new tranquilizers, mostly in a large hospital in Sao Paulo. This is the typical case of the developed world exploiting the developing world, trying out things which they could not or would not find advisable to try out at home. When one is actually reading these reports and discovering what the terrible side effects could be of these new drugs, one is made very much aware of something that has very little to do with development, but it certainly is a flow of information, in this case from South to North.

Armando Sandoval:

The difficulty in defining information is that information is everything that creates new knowledge, no matter at what level. If we are really interested in the development of our people, we should address our efforts toward those who make decisions, and to those who influence the decision-making, the executives, university people, researchers, teachers, technicians and so forth. Those are the people in whom we are interested. And those who influence or influence their decisions.

Beatriz de Carvalho:

I am Brazilian, and also I know something about what's going on outside Brazil. Ten years ago I worked in a Brazilian institute, and belonged to the government, because, as Cavan said, most information people in Brazil work for the government. At that time this institute was working in information policy. Later, I came to be Head Librarian, and I am now involved with problems of every day having to meet users' needs, to respond to requests from everyone in the institute at every hierarchical level. This experience makes me think that if we go on trying to define information, we will spend much time trying to do so. Maybe it would be useful for us to continue discussing what information is.

But remember that in countries like the United States or Europe, before the science called information science existed, people were trying to find solutions to problems that dealt with bibliographic information, because they needed to have people with knowledge, knowledge that is acquired through reading. It is by reading that people can develop their minds in an analytical and critical way, to develop how to think and how to find solutions to the human problems of society. After the main problems of access to bibliographic information were solved, then a science—information science—appeared, and people could think of defining information in a more profound and wider way, trying find the concepts of the many approaches given to information, the nature of information. Books and articles were written about that subject in the United States and the countries of Europe.

The experience in developing countries, in Latin America, is quite different. We have in our countries both kinds of activities going on. We have people struggling to provide access to bibliographic information to users, any kind of users. And we also have people doing research in information, within the concept of information science. This new science sees everything that is involved with the communication of information, and that includes tv, and this increased the scope of the science we are dealing with.

I think there are two different facets to the subject we are discussing. One is directly related to our countries in Latin America. It is that we still have problems of access to bibliographic information. We still have people who are not used to reading, and this is a problem relating to education. But it is a problem. It's not easy to obtain bibliographic information for all kinds of reasons, including economic, but we have large parts of the population who don't read so the problem with these groups is that they are not acquiring the information through reading that would lead them to a critical position in life. This is the second facet. They all have tv sets, so they are receiving information passively all the time which makes them go on being passive. It doesn't develop their critical minds, critical ways of approaching the problems of the country. It won't help them very much in learning how to solve problems of everyday life. and even the political problems. They won't learn how to vote better, for instance. So maybe these two ways of approaching things would be useful, because information is too great, too wide a concept.

Barbara Gumbs:

I'd just like to add that I think that as information professionals generally we have been very occupied with aspects of and dissemination of bibliographic information primarily to people who already have an appreciation of that kind of information. But if you are going to look at scientific and technical information for development we need to pay attention to information for the masses. And it's more difficult and more challenging to disseminate this type of information to them because it has to be repackaged for them.

For example, in St. Lucia, an island in the West Indies, the predominant industry is bananas. There was a need for the dissemination of scientific and technical information to the people who actually grow the bananas. They needed to know how to plant them and protect them against diseases which attack the banana plants. They spoke French Creole—how are you going to provide the information to them? One of the agencies was disseminating text and bibliographic information in English. A study was done which showed that it was not being used. The whole program had to be rewritten in Creole. They had to use early morning radio programs and Creole speakers in order to get this scientific and technical information to the farmers so that it would aid in the development of the banana industry in St. Lucia. They also wrote brochures in Creole with many diagrams and illustrations.

This is necessary if we are going to disseminate scientific and technical information to aid in development. I think we have to work for the general masses, not only in providing scientific and technical information for the researcher in the form of bibliographic records. We have to get much deeper than that.

Armando Sandoval:

In the third world countries there are tremendous education problems. There is no question that development of information resources is related to education. But, that's a real battle. We should start by considering that in your country where the educational level is so low, like in my country, it is considered that the average educational level of Mexicans is 3 years. There is a tendency to confuse the problems of providing information for those minorities which really are helping the development of our country in the sense of making decisions, with the problems of information for the masses. The real problem may be to educate our rural population. It is very difficult to separate one problem from the other. But at this moment, it could be a handicap to consider our educational problems.

Cavan McCarthy:

Are decisions taken by a large group of people in Mexico, or are decisions the privilege of a very small elite?

Armando Sandoval:

By a very small minority. But the country never makes a decision!

Laurence Hallewell:

Surely this depends upon what kind of decision you are talking about. A fishing industry can be improved, or changed at any rate, merely by the decision of individual fisherman to start buying outboard motors, instead of relying on sails. This is a decision, but there are probably thousands of decisions in an economy, whatever the economy is, that are taken at a relatively low level.

Cavan McCarthy:

If the government gives them credit to buy those motors.

Laurence Hallewell:

To take an example of this, consider the fishermen of Cabedelo.[3] Someone said that they've all put in outboard motors because once he has put one in, fisherman can get to the fishing ground so much quicker than anyone else. And therefore, although it doesn't really benefit the economy that that one particular fisherman should get there quicker, you have everyone using precious imported fuel to get there quicker. But it is certainly a decision. The same effect could be reached if they were taught new methods of making much lighter-hulled vessels, in which they could sail more efficiently and they could get to the fishing ground just as quickly. But no one has the same incentive to stimulate this as they have to stimulate the use of outboard motors. But certainly the decision can be at a quite low level.

Cavan McCarthy:

There seems to be a feeling that we need to have information at all levels but we don't know quite how to go about getting the information to the lower levels. Is this going to be too much for our profession?

Marietta Daniels Shepard:

I'm wondering about the structure of information services in Brazil for instance, not only for the fisherman but for the other people who are involved in the industrialization of Brazil. How do they get their information now? In Brazil, I think the element of how they can get agricultural

---

[3] The port of João Pessoa, Paraíba, Brazil.

information and biomedical information and nuclear information is pretty well resolved by having structures in Brazil that can provide it. Do the services of the IBICT serve the industrialists or the possible users of industrial information in other areas of the world to develop the industrialization of Brazil?

Cavan McCarthy:

I think the industrialization in a lot of Latin American countries has consisted of information that is brought in in the form of equipment and foreign engineers.

Marietta Daniels Shepard:

How do they know about the equipment?

Cavan McCarthy:

They use it in the United States and then they're sent down to Brazil for two years, either as a present or a punishment, I don't know which. They set up a factory in Brazil and teach the nationals. These are multinationals, yes.

Marietta Daniels Shepard:

What about the industrialization of Brazil that isn't being done by multinationals? How do they get information about the equipment they might use? How do the fishermen find out about outboard motors? Does someone by chance get one, and then they all decide they are going to use that outboard motor?

Laurence Hallewell:

Presumably the local distributors are well aware that they can increase their sales if they can persuade the fishermen to buy them. The point that I was trying to make is that the outboard motor is something in which the technology-use can be expanded by commercial means, but the completely new method of making hulls might not because in this particular case the industry is organized for pleasure boating. There is a good deal of demand in many middle class homes in Brazil for a boat that they can make a noise outside the yacht club in. So the infrastructure is set up for that type of boating, and it spreads to the fishermen because this is an obvious way for the local distributors to increase sales. But revolutions in the methods for building boats would need government, consciously, I think, to decide that this was an idea to propagate. For instance, the agricultural ministry produces programs in comic strip form for the south of Brazil and uses the a chap book format with rhymed verse for the same purpose in the Northeast. I think that they are fairly well aware of how most effectively to get the message across. The problem is simply the decision to spread the message.

Alma Jordan:

I think we are coming around to the point of my greatest concern, and that is that we in the profession have tended to carve out territory to suit specific needs and purposes at different times, but quite unrealistically in relation to the overall total need.

We are identifying the fact that the need for development is not only at the level of the decision-makers or the people in government. But yet in the profession we have tended to identify scientific and technical information and concentrate on the fact that if we got the right technology over to the engineers then the right thing would happen.

Yet we are recognizing in our discussion here that the technician who may have to maintain that equipment, who is at an entirely different level, has a need for information which the mechanisms of publishing scientific and technical information may not meet at all. I think it was in this overall context that slowly the profession has been trying to unite itself. And I mean the entire profession—librarians and information scientists and the rest—trying to resolve the dichotomy between the UNISIST program as Unesco first set it up, and the NATIS program as Unesco subsequently came up with it, recognized that information for development has no real limits or dimensions or boundaries that we can carve out. Whatever we may want to call ourselves in the profession, whatever we may want to call the documentation centers, and whatever we call the dissemination of the information through all the media channels, it is a total complex which we are grappling with and which we are going to have to recognize is one total field which we attack in different ways, in unison. We can recognize that it is all one, even though no one of us can handle the whole of it. It is one profession trying to grapple with the same problem at all these levels. And I think this is in a sense the difficulty we are encountering in trying to define information.

I know for an example, in Trinidad and Tobago, when we were proposing what I suppose we would call in our jargon an information policy to the government, or when we were just using the term "information", the government was very wary because they were thinking of information quite differently. While we were talking about information in the library and information service sense, they didn't want to see "information" anywhere in the title at all. "Information" to them meant their Ministry of Information which was getting across, well not to say propaganda, but "information" in the government sense, telling the citizens what they wanted them to know. And they didn't want to confuse the two. In a sense, the two are confused anyway. But the essence of the point that I want to make is that we have tended to lead ourselves astray, and others indirectly, by the multiple terms and jargon and the distinction between the levels of scientific and technical information and users. Really it is all one puzzle in which we have to try to put all the pieces together.

Cavan McCarthy:

I think this is the kind of problem we have had in certain South American countries. A scientific information center was distributing medical information. Then there were minor political upsets and the telephone was tapped because it was an information center. They didn't realize it was just medical information. In one way you are saying that we need to go back to the good old public library principle that we serve all forms of society.

Alma Jordan:

I'm saying that in national information policy one needs to recognize the need for all the alternatives. That does not say that we at this conference cannot address one area of need, but we must recognize that the other areas exist and need to be meshed with the ones that we may address in any specific mode at any specific time. But we've tended to feel that scientific and technical information is an entity all by itself. So, I'm putting forward the case for the public library, the case for the media, the case for an integrated approach, so that we are getting across the kind of information that was described by Mrs. Gumbs.

Cavan McCarthy:

Information professionals, as a profession, have a general responsibility for information at all levels.

Alma Jordan:

Having recognized that, we can then distinguish between what kinds of information we want to transmit in which forms to which experts, professional societies or whatnot. But there will be another level, and other kinds of information, repackaged and so on, that we should also be concerned about, even though we don't do it ourselves. We

374 — Discussions, Monday Morning

should be concerned about seeing that it gets done at another level somewhere by someone else.

Ching-Chih Chen:

It is true that when we talk about the kinds of things that are the concerns of this Conference, information is very general. I think information is going to be very difficult to define, unless we look at it from the point of view of information needs we are trying to meet. Information needs cannot be measured unless we identify the situations in which people need information.

From the information seeking point of view, whether in the developed or developing countries, we may be artificially separating out coping needs of people and situations in which there are professional or decision-making needs. The coping needs are felt by the masses, and they have every right to expect these needs to be met. In developing countries, for example, the farmers, the workers, whether in non-scientific areas or not, are going to have information needs to be met from the scientific and technical information area. The problem with the developing countries is that the people do need scientific and technical information but they may not have the ability to articulate this need. Here, information professionals have the obligation to repackage the information so that it can help them with these coping or day-to-day needs. On the professional side, we have different levels, such as the beginning technician, the professional, the academic researcher, each with quite different needs. This approach gives us a model, with an obligation to each group. It is artificial, but may be useful. Then, we can consider the role of scientific and technical information in serving the needs for each group.

Ximena Felíu:

I work in the UN Economic Commission for Latin America.

As Dr. Rosenberg has said, one of the official languages of the Conference is Spanish. I would like to exercise the privilege of using it.

Se ha hablado mucho respecto a lo que es información, lo que debiera ser información, o lo que no es información.

Tengo la impresion que nos bastaría como hipótesis de trabajo que información es conocimiento en vías de ser comunicado y que todos los conocimientos en vías de ser comunicados a través de la imagen, del sonido, del escrito son información, y que por razones del desarrollo económico y social de los países toda la información, es decir, todo conocimiento que pueda llegarnos es importante porque lo necesitamos, y debe de alguna manera ser controlado, procesado, entregado a quien lo necesita.

Ahora, respecto a que tipo de información es el más necesario para los problemas del desarrollo y la toma de decisiones para la planificación del desarrollo económico y social, naturalmente que es un tipo de información muy variable, muy heterogéneo, muy cambiante. Se necesita una información estadística, una información conocimiento, es decir se necesita información histórica, información social, información de todo tipo. Y todo el conjunto de esta información y otros tipos de información ... ¿Quieres bailar conmigo?

¡Información también es baile!

Decía entonces, coincidiendo con Marta y con algunas otras personas que han hablado, que tal vez lo importante no sea saber lo que es información, sino quién la necesita. And who is that who?

Pienso entonces que el problema con la información científica y tecnológica para ayudar a los paises en desarrollo no es lo de definirla ni es tampoco lo de para quién, sino que es lo de crear un mecanismo, un mecanismo que permita llegar a constituir un paquete integral de información que sirva a quien lo necesita, un grupo de información, un paquete que permita tener tanto la información estadística, como la información conocimiento, como la informació dato, como la información histórica en un solo mecanismo, en un solo paquete que se entregue a quien lo necesite. Ese mecanismo que pueda entregar una información integral, llamémosla así, es lo que debemos proponer a buscar.

Sabemos que la información estadística puede estar en bancos de datos, como en institutos de estadística internacionales, etc.

Sabemos que la información que se está elaborando o reelaborando está en determinadas instituciones gubernamentales, que se está generando en esas instituciones gubernamentales es una información importante que puede ser de todos estos tipos. Lo importante es llegar a tener esta información integral a través de este mecanismo que toque esos lugares a donde se está generando esta información. Yo creo que todos sabemos qué es información, quién la necesita y porqué. Lo importante es que, sabiendo que está, que existe, que se necesita, la busquemos y la entreguemos integralmente, es decir, de acuerdo a una toma de decisiones que requiere tanto de información histórica, como de información estadística, como de información apretada, digamos así, sintética, respecto a determinadas tendencias que adquieren de repente ciertas lineas de planificación económica o social.

Según los niveles de la demanda de información será el tipo de información integral que entregaremos. Hacia eso es que debemos de proponer dada la moderna tecnología que nos permite tener bancos de datos, bases de dato; y un mecanismo que debiéramos crear que cruzara todas estas fuentes generadoras de información para extraer de ellas este paquete integral de información. Perdón, es una inquietud que tengo, por eso es que la expongo. Muchas gracias.

Defining information, for me, is not the problem. The problem is that we have to know what kind of information exists, and what kind of information the users need. Another problem is that policy makers need all kinds of information. We have to give the policy maker an integrated information package, including statistical, historical, and social information. We have to find a mechanism to coordinate the sources of this information, where it is generated and where it is processed, and repackage it for the user. We have to analyze the problem not in terms of the definition of information, or definitions of user needs. We have to find a mechanism to coordinate and integrate information, more than find an intellectual or scientific definition of information.

Marta Dosa:

Do you envision that the coordination would be at the policy level, rather than at the level of the developing infrastructure?

Ximena Felíu:

The problem is that in the developing countries, we already have institutions that generate information. But in these institutions, especially government agencies, there are archives, databases, libraries, documentation centers, all working independently from each other. In making an institutional information system, we can manage all the information that the institution generates. That would be part of the national information structure. The national information policy must integrate all these institutional information systems.

Marta Dosa:

In my experience in several developing countries, the governments of many are now becoming aware of the need for information policies, and this is the right time for information professionals to meet that need.

Ximena Felíu:

The governments are interested in information, but they think that information is only informatics.

Marta Dosa:

Some governments have a broader view.

Ximena Felíu:

But before they realized that, they thought it was only computers.

Winthrop Wiltshire:

Last week in Jamaica, the ministers of science and technology from the Caribbean had their first meeting. They defined two priority areas for the Caribbean. One was agro-industry, the other was information. There was much discussion of information, and they had no problem with definitions. They discussed issues and actions to be taken.

Armando Sandoval:

It seems to me that we are sorting out the riddle of this morning. Beyond the conceptual problems, as professionals we are facing a conceptually very complex problem. But what really matters is that we have to understand that as professionals we have to desire to be prepared, to be useful and to deliver the needed information. We should focus here on the development of the infrastructure of documentation and information. In every country it will be different. We need to stress the need to develop libraries and librarians and information scientists, because there simply are not enough of them to meet our country's information needs.

Victor Rosenberg:

It's interesting to me to see how little understanding there seems to exist in the developed countries, like the United States and Canada, of the role that information has played historically in the development of these countries. It is clear that information and education have had a significant role, but it is not so clear how directly that information was used in the economic development of the country. I've seen very little information on this.

Second, looking forward, one of the things that we see in the United States now is that we are clearly in the middle of an information revolution, and no one can assess the dimensions of that revolution at this point because it is so new. The levels at which information of all sorts is becoming available and necessary, is staggering. I include here the microcomputers, computers generally, and telecommunications. One of the results very clearly is that there are major dislocations in the economy of the United States. We are seeing them here in Detroit, in the automobile industry. Companies are divesting themselves of major industrial plants and becoming involved in information-related industries. How will this affect the development of other countries? And the United States?

One of the ironies of the developing countries is that the developed countries can afford a lot more mistakes and inefficiencies of trial and error, but other countries cannot and must have even greater efficiency. This efficiency depends upon providing this integrated information to decision-makers at all levels. This is important to understand, so that we can plan for a future that includes these absolutely revolutionary developments. I don't use that term lightly.

Cavan McCarthy:

Efficiency is generally treated in terms of developed countries, making it even more difficult for the developing countries.

Thomas McGinn:

I think we must consider the production of information, which is severely limited in many areas of developing countries. For example there is not sufficient scientific research. Many governments have become very conscious of this. In Venezuela it is an old theme now, and the government has spent a lot of money on scientific research, but we can't do it just by spending money. It involves the whole educational system itself. However in other areas, for instance the news media, journalists create a great deal of information, and Latin America is in a good situation. There are some excellent newspapers in Venezuela, and this is material that is subject to scholarly investigation. In some areas, therefore, there is a good production of information, but it is insufficient in others, especially those areas most closely related to development, such as science and technology.

However given the problems of production, which are there, and must be addressed in a very wide developmental context, we have a second problem, of the organization of information, which many of us are dealing with. Given the information that exists already, what access is there to it? Here you can take the two cases of scientific information and that produced by journalists. There is not an adequate organization of scientific information produced in the North or the developing countries, nor is there adequate organization of the information produced by journalists. I know of no newspaper index in the country, for example.

Where there is already information, which is very widely sought, in many countries where research is done on

Latin America, you can't find out what has been said on a subject without reading the newspaper every day. So here, people who are concerned with communication and the organization of information can make a very strong contribution.

When we try to address the problem of the production of information, scientific research, it is such a wide ranging problem that it is hard to attack it in the specific terms that information handlers like to work. It is an important area for the economic development of the country since I've heard the organization of information in economic terms compared to the building of roads. Sr. Sandoval used the term "infrastructure." The roads of a country do not produce wealth, but they are an essential condition for the economic functioning of a country. If you don't build good roads, you can't have industrial development.

I think the organization of information is similar. It doesn't create wealth, but you can't create wealth without it. The general areas of the production and organization of information are mutually interrelated, and you can't have one without the other. If we attack the organization part, we are doing something which will eliminate obstacles to the production of information. We're working on an essential part of development, but it doesn't solve the whole problem. It's a starting point, but without it you don't have development.

Cavan McCarthy:

There is a great lack of periodical indexing throughout Latin America, but there is no great attention being paid to it. There is a tendency to jump straight from no indexing into databases. Is this a good thing? I am not at all sure.

Alma Jordan:

I think we have been worried a good deal about indexing in the Caribbean. ACURIL, an association of Caribbean university research institution libraries, has taken this up for a number of years and has been responsible for the production of an indexing service for some Caribbean journals and newspapers. It is a cooperative effort crossing several national borders. People are inputting from Jamaica, Barbados, and Guyana, which may make it unique. It may be possible to soon put this manual service into a database through the Unesco ISIS program in Barbados. What worries me is that some of the people involved in the production of the index are a little bit reluctant to revolutionize the way they have been working. While they have been busy talking about PRECIS indexing and looking at ways of doing the index manually, now they are talking about a thesaurus and things they had never discussed before, which would mean practically starting all over! Which is better? Should we encourage people to develop indexes which are convertible, if we are going to have manual systems? They have had a thesaurus of a kind before, but the database will impose quite different restrictions. I would like to hear more comments on Cavan's point because it seems to me that it ought to be possible to start with a database even though you have nothing. Sometimes converting from a manual one is harder than starting from nothing.

Cavan McCarthy:

I get worried by analysts who come along and see a situation and they say Right, we are going to put everything into a database. If you are producing a hard-copy index, that index can go into libraries all over the country. If you put it into a database, that index will be available to only the very small number of libraries which have a terminal.

Alma Jordan:

But you can produce hard copy indexes from the database. This is where the technology is just becoming exciting.

Cavan McCarthy:

There are cases where the manual system has been deactivated because someone is going to set up a database, and then the database never materializes.

Alma Jordan:

I'd like to say one thing more, in the context of what we have been saying this morning. I think we need some kind of planning that will enable us to integrate systems and projects and initiatives that are now isolated, and put them into a total framework that enables us to move in the same direction, however separate our activities might be. I think that so far we have tended to all go our own ways, with whatever seems feasible with the resources available, but we are really at the stage now where if only we could work more closely together, whether it's North America and South America or within South America, we would be able to do much more, particularly with the new technology.

I don't know what the mechanism would be, but one would hope that at the end of this we could be talking about some possible mechanisms, for example in the area of indexing or information policy, for developing a formula for each area to lead us all in the right direction. If each country, for example, were to have as a part of its national policy a policy for indexing its newspapers, and if the indexing were done in this or that framework, then the indexing would be regionally or internationally salable and compatible.

Cavan McCarthy:

I think we are facing some quite severe historical problems here. In library science, countries have traditionally been separate. One of the major contributions of comparative librarianship is that although librarianship can be standardized on a high level, it is in general culturally dependent and varies from country to country, even between those which are quite similar, such as the United States and Britain. There is isolation at the national level, and in Latin America especially there is a very heavy isolation between libraries. They do not have very much contact with each other. This I think has been avoided in the Caribbean, in that you have set up very good networks very early, and you avoided the isolation.

Marietta Daniels Shepard:

My paper reports on an attempt to discover the present infrastructure for information services in Latin America. We found that in the five countries a lot is going on, but it is isolated, and there is much duplication even within a country. For instance two different institutions in a country may be carrying out current awareness services, covering the same journals in the same field, but each is ignorant of the other. The lack of coordination is a very serious problem.

Mary Jane Ruhl:

We've talked about the organization of information, development, and infrastructures, and repackaging information, but I'd like to know if any of you or your organizations have any experience in promoting information in ways that have generated a pull for that information by the various publics that we serve. It seems to me that we can organize our information and plan for it forever, but until people are used to using information, they probably won't demand it.

On top of this, it can be so difficult to obtain the information. Sometimes when I am working in a developing country, I will remember a document, such as a thesaurus, that is at home, but since it would take two months to get it, it is easier to simply begin a new one. This is done often, but it does not need to continue. I think it will, though, until there is sufficient demand for the information. Does anyone know of any shortcuts?

Beatriz de Carvalho:

Referring to Mrs. Shepard's report, there was a comprehensive Latin American and Caribbean study done by the Latin American Center for Social Development in Chile. The report of the survey was published some time ago.

Juan Freudenthal:

The concept about volume is an interesting one. It makes me nervous, because it may be one of our great problems. In the United States, you do need volume. In many of the developing countries you do not need volume demand, and what we get is an enormous amount of information which those countries didn't need in the first place. I think this has been raised directly and indirectly throughout the morning. I think the question is how can we produce not necessarily volume demand and still be able to offer it. It seems that you are saying that we can only offer important information if there is a volume of it. It's obviously a business proposition, but it is one of the major concerns of many of the papers. We are getting an enormous amount of information which is not usable, because it comes in volume. Dr. Chen spoke of it last night as well.

Mary Jane Ruhl:

I've used a term incorrectly. I meant enough flow of documents from one country to another, to cut costs. We can get a document from here to Southeast Asia in a couple of days if we are willing to pay the price, but it will be expensive. I was thinking of something that would allow documents to be sent by air at reasonable cost, as part of the infrastructure. I doubt if it would happen until a volume is reached.

Juan Freudenthal:

In Merline Smith's paper, she says that the result is that more information is generated in these countries than the societies can absorb, and consequently information is transferred into other countries. Her implication is that there is so much information being created in certain countries that they can afford to just send it out. I refer to it as vast pools of information that are being forced on limited information systems. That is the problem. How relevant is the information? Are we able to foresee what people want? When we talk about information it is not a question of having it, because we do have it. We have to also find out when the information will be needed. There is a lot of information which is not needed. I think that what happens in developed countries is that they have lots of information, so that when the problem is there they can immediately look at the information and determine the emphasis, but in the developing countries there is much information, but unnecessary information, so that when you need information it simply is not there.

Laurence Hallewell:

My reference to the drug company using the developing country was not a case of the developing country being exploited as an information source, purely for the needs of that the developed country, but the company was trying out new drugs because there were plenty of sick people who were prepared to be experimented on, and there would be no repercussions from home public opinion should anything go wrong.

Cavan McCarthy:

Note that this is one of the few cases where the research takes place in the South.

Winthrop Wiltshire:

We were talking earlier about definitions, which lead us to a dead end. I would like to highlight the point that when we are talking about information for development, we are talking about not necessarily kinds of information, but about two different focii. We are talking about information that is generated or ought to be generated in our own countries or region, as well as information that is generated externally, in the North, for example, and we are talking about devising systems and mechanisms to generate the information that we need to generate ourselves. We are talking about putting the mechanisms in place for storing, for disseminating that information to the people when they need it. We are talking about sensitizing those people to the awareness of that information and about the sources of that information. We are also talking about insuring that at all levels of the system when we are making decisions that might have national impact or a limited impact that our people are aware of the information that is available from external sources that might have an impact on the outcomes that we are to achieve.

For example, we might be in our scientific research organizations where the industrial research deals with issues that have international implications. We are talking about having access to information which would have impact on that research, not only dealing with the history of a country, where the information may be available only locally. In many cases we do research and it is not necessary at all. The information is already in the public domain: we just don't know about it. So we are talking about devising appropriate systems for knowing what information is available externally. We are talking about having that awareness that that information exists, and knowing where to get it, so that it can have impact, at whatever level.

We are also talking about knowing the appropriateness of the delivery systems. For instance if there is an engineer in a particular factory, I might be able to give him a document to solve a particular technical problem, and he might be able to solve a technical problem on the basis of that, but if there are no documents I might have to send a technical consultant to spend two hours in the factory to solve the problem. So we have to know about the relevance and the appropriateness of the delivery systems.

If we have to confine ourselves to bibliographic information in our deliberations, we have to be aware that that is just a subset of larger systems. I spoke of a program in the Caribbean to sensitize public officials to computers and what they can do, because international agencies and others are making all kinds of decisions about computers and buying mainframes, and micros, and minis, and have bought them only for accounting, when they could be used in a much more versatile way. This kind of program is necessary so that the individual buying the computer can ask the right questions.

Marta Dosa:

I fully support what Winthrop has said. I would like to link it to what I mentioned earlier, that bibliographic information, and librarianship as the main, traditional, and classic branch of the information profession, which has been handling bibliographic information for many years, needs to develop links with other information handlers, even if they are not formally and directly connected within the infrastructure. I hear from my colleagues that what is needed is to be aware of the current programs and research and development programs in any sense, whether bibliographic, or statistical, technological, or industrial, and so on.

To conduct such a survey would take time, because even surveying the bibliographic services available is a problem. Perhaps it should be a goal to find out what other kinds of information and data handling projects are currently going on. The second problem is then for libraries to develop their links with the non-library types of information projects.

The third problem is communication. I have participated in some conferences at which, in addition to librarians, there were scientists, engineers, and technologists, and the theme of the conference was information for national economic development. The need within and outside of librarianship is communication. For years, there has been a stereotype of librarians. Librarians are 'humanistic,' 'traditional,' 'resistant to change.' Social scientists are 'number crunchers,' 'quantifiers,' 'resistant to humanistic values.' Technologists are 'machine-oriented,' 'automation-oriented,' 'unaware of human needs.' Journalists are 'superficial,' 'quick in decision-making,' 'sensationalists,' and so on. These create barriers within the information-handling groups which are as dangerous as the political and technological barriers. While we have less impact on politics and while we can work toward influencing transborder data flow and other national policy issues, I think we could work miracles in inter-professional communication, to break down the stereotypes, and to try to see the non-library information and coming from growth as important, groups with which we can interact effectively. We should be working toward a mechanism for this. Perhaps professional organizations such as FID, which has a strong Latin American commission with very interesting projects, would be one way to start interacting with these various groups. It would be tangible and productive.

Thomas McGinn:

I would like to present a problem for which I have no solution. Most scientists in Latin America prefer to publish in English in United States journals from what I have seen, or those in England, or Europe, rather than in their own country in Spanish. In the Venezuelan Institute for Scientific Research, you are required to publish in a foreign journal, as a part of your contract. I attended a meeting of editors of medical journals a few months ago, and they noted that none of their journals were indexed in any of the international indexing services. The reason is that all the doctors that make an important discovery publish in the United States, so why index Venezuelan or Latin American medical journals? All the good research is being reported elsewhere. The international language of science seems to be English. People want to be read all over the world if they make an important discovery. This damages our development. If governments are going to require that the country's researchers publish in a developed country, how are we going to attack the question of retaining our information? We export the information and then re-import it when we buy the indexes, such as *Chemical Abstracts*. The Venezuelan researcher is doubly dependent, then, not only to publish, but in re-importing the information when he's doing research, even for information on what has been done in his own country. This is a theme which will pervade the Conference.

At the medical editors meeting we did talk about getting the people who publish outside the country to get permission to publish their papers within the country, in Spanish. With the amount of research that is being done, the country could support one, perhaps two, excellent medical journals. It seems that the information handlers could help here, because knowing that your article would be indexed in a source which would be consulted internationally might provide an incentive for publishing in-country. Then the researcher doesn't feel obliged to publish outside of the country and contribute to the double-dependence situation.

Laurence Hallewell:

Regarding indexing in the developed countries, to satisfy my own curiosity regarding databanks, I did some comparisons on the subject of Brazilian book publishing. I identified 43 recent and relevant items, and I tried to see what was available through LISA and PAIS. The latter came up with three items, none of which were of any importance, and LISA came up with five. Both omitted the most important items. They also omitted articles published in a well known English-language journal. This is some measure of the amount of material that escapes traditional nets.

Cavan McCarthy:

To sum up before lunch, the Conference is off to an excellent start and is finding its own voice. We began by trying to define information, and decided that it was best to define it in terms of its use and user needs. The key words after this discussion were integration, especially of the profession at all levels, the total complex of information, coordination within a total framework which includes bibliographic and numeric information, and information both at the coping level for large numbers of people and at the decision-making level on a higher level.

Monday Afternoon, 11 April 1983

Library Acquisitions: The Problems of Acquiring Foreign
Materials by Libraries in both North and South America.
Existing and Future Exchange Programs

Juan Freudenthal:

We are going to be talking today about some of the problems
associated with the acquisition of foreign materials by
libraries. It is obvious that we cannot isolate this topic from
any other that we have discussed already.

The major problem associated with the acquisition of
foreign materials by libraries and information centers in
South America is the lack of acquisition and current awareness tools, such as up-to-date bibliographies and indexing
and abstracting services, compiled and produced in Latin
America. Beyond this there are numerous other obstacles,
which have been identified in the papers such as the one by
Cunha.

Laurence Hallewell, writing on Brazilian government
documents, surveyed over 100 libraries in the United States
to discover the extent of their interest in these materials,
and received 37 positive replies, which he believes
represents the definitive number of libraries with an explicit
policy of collecting Brazilian government documents. Two
important conclusions emerge from the study. One, libraries
in the United States with an intensive program of acquisi-

tion are aware of how much valuable material escapes the acquisition net through inadequate bibliographic control, short printing runs, and poorly organized distribution methods. Two, many United States institutions employ aggressive acquisition tactics.

Merline Smith's paper points out that one of the major obstacles to acquiring important scientific and technical information produced in less developed countries stems from the fact that these fields are poorly organized, and the information is usually contained in national publications, journals and reports that are generally not included in the various databases.

Maria Oyarzun declares that most national information remains unrecorded, and thus it is difficult to locate and obtain. Most reports produced by the government, research institutes and universities are not published, and valuable information is lost.

In the first part of my own paper, dealing with problems of the scientific community in Chile, I addressed the problem of scientific monographs and journals, which must be imported at high cost, and the perennial problems caused by incomplete periodical files. This is one of the great complaints of the scientific community, at least in Chile. Informally, Lawrence Hallewell and I have discussed the extent to which periodicals are not used because they are incomplete files. Just because they are incomplete doesn't mean they should not be used.

Armando Sandoval addresses the important issue of the need for Latin American countries to purchase foreign specialized journals, and mentions the dire need "to create a central repository of journals as a point of departure for all scholarly and scientific information activities." I would like for us to discuss this in more depth, because that is one of the most essential things for Latin America. The idea is not new, we have such repositories in the United States.

Marta Dosa addresses the problems related to the identification, organization, and utilization of locally produced information, and how this information should be linked to the more traditional types of libraries in which many of us work.

Finally, Marietta Daniels Shepard raises the question of possible centralized acquisition plans for Colombia, Peru, Costa Rica, Venezuela, and Mexico.

It seems to me that instead of analyzing and discussing the problems mentioned in the papers, we should discuss the underlying issues. I have four:

(1) There seems to be a need in Latin America and the Caribbean for more carefully formulated collection development policies . and guidelines, which would provide the framework and necessary standards for information acquisition, organization, and dissemination—in other words, what to acquire and for whom.

(2) We should explore further the creation of central repositories of scientific and technical information journals in different Latin American and Caribbean countries.

(3) We should elucidate what seems to be a contradiction in many of the contributed papers. Several contend that national information remains underutilized. On the other hand, they say that we need to acquire more information. I would like to see if we could explain what it means to have so much information which remains underutilized, and at the same time we want so much more information.

(4) Several authors have raised the question of "obstacles to the absorption and effective use of information." It behooves this Conference to discuss the implications of

information overload, caused by information-saturated societies, and the impact of this overload on less developed countries.

It occurs to me, from our discussion this morning and other comments, that perhaps we should also discuss how libraries interact with non-library institutions. How can they be brought together?

Marta Dosa:

I would like to offer a synthesis of what I have observed in the process of working with some development assistance agencies and some national governments. I would like to propose it as a discussion topic and as a question. Should libraries be concerned with relationships between users, specialized information centers, scientific and information councils, and all the organizations and people who are disseminating scientific and technical information outside of the library?

In most developing countries (although I do hate to generalize), the national government with the aid of different assistance agencies, mainly the World Bank, United Nations Development Program, and so on, are developing technology transfer centers. They have different names, but essentially they are importing patent information, licensing information, trademark information and other industrial information relating to technology transfer. We are all familiar with the scientific and technical information councils, and recently we have seen in some countries the emergence of social science data and social science information centers. I would like to emphasize that this is not true of all countries. Fortunately countries are very individualistic, and therefore this an example and not a definitive model. In the center of the model we have the subject specific information centers, such as agriculture, rural health, and housing, which development people call sectoral. The United Nations has its Habitat Agency and in each country they are trying to develop a center for housing information and public administration.

Then there are research libraries including university, special, and public libraries. I would like to suggest that on the two sides of libraries are user groups. The scientists and technologists are on one side and on the other are the urban and rural people, who are currently receiving information partially from public libraries, and partially from agricultural extension services, non-formal education services, literacy programs and the like. If we look at the user groups, then we also see that there are the information rich, who have problems which are not comparable with those of the people in urban slums who really have no idea where to turn for advice, counseling, and information. The information-poor are ethically as much the responsibility of our profession as are the scientists, the scholars and the technologists.

Then, you can draw lines from the scientists and the technologists to the research libraries, and also draw a line from the scientists and technologists to these national centers which are emerging. I believe that much is going on here already to link these groups with networks, telecommunication systems, and non-bibliographic data. My question is, are the scientists and technologists turning to both libraries and these other national information and referral services in an equal way, or are they turning to libraries for documents and journals and printed material, with all other information handling is occurring outside of libraries? Are rural people turning to public libraries, or are they also turning to agricultural extension services and other information dissemination services? Should libraries become aware of, and maybe develop links with these non-library information services? How should that be done? Is it something which is a concern for us? If this is what Armando Sandoval and Unesco refer to as "infrastructure," then what is the role of libraries in this total information picture?

One more example. Many of these national information centers develop networks and rosters of experts, directories of human sources. Are these of interest to libraries? If so, how can these links be developed?

Laurence Hallewell:

I think that we should keep in mind that research suggests that in any society, developed or underdeveloped, and regardless of level of education, information is diffused by a very small proportion of people. Most people depend upon colleagues, friends, and relations, from whom they gather information informally. The few who are actually the effective distributors of information will use all means of obtaining it available. We are dealing with a small proportion of any group, whatever human society we are thinking of.

Marta Dosa:

It is not a question of who uses informal links.

Laurence Hallewell:

We are concerned with who actually gathers the information to be then distributed informally.

Marta Dosa:

This provides for privileged information, and these groups are the information elite.

Laurence Hallewell:

They may be elite simply because they have made the effort or they have the intelligence or the interest to gather the information.

Marta Dosa:

Don't we have the responsibility to extend it to the information-poor segment of society?

Laurence Hallewell:

The natural situation is very inefficient. But the basic problem is human psychology.

Armando Sandoval:

For me also there is evidence that psychology plays an important role. Those who work in libraries in Mexico eventually conclude that the main source of information is not libraries and information centers, except for private libraries. What is important is contacts and relationships with colleagues.

At the other extreme, the urban and rural people may be supposed to depend on the public libraries for information, but, to begin with, the public libraries are even poorer than the people, or just non-existent. The majority of these people do not know how to read, and so they must be informed in a very different way than through traditional libraries.

Marta Dosa:

I can see the problem, and I understand that public libraries, with the resources that they have at their disposal, cannot possibly enter into new roles and new activities. But I see some possibility for international agencies taking an interest in the role of the public library, as one cooperating with extension services and literacy programs, and actually taking on even oral communication and cultural heritage-based projects. For example, a university in Nigeria has a public library program and they are working with non-literate people, collecting information from rural areas on the local heritage.

Victor Rosenberg:

I'd like to bring up a project that was recently initiated in Brazil, the COMUT project. This is to my knowledge one of the first efforts to deal with the problem of selected acquisition of materials and shared resources in Latin America.

Ximena Felíu:;

Pienso que existe un problema en relación al planteamiento que hace la doctora Dosa, y es que nos lleva a pensar en la generación de la información dentro de estos grupos donde se genera una información científica, tecnólogica, también dentro de los aspectos sectoriales, la cultura, educación, etc., las instituciones y las personas que están dentro de las instituciones generan un tipo de información que es fundamental para su propia toma de decisiones. Pienso que antes de llevarnos al problema de la adquisición para servir a determinados usuarios hay algo que resolver antes, y es que seleccionemos para quién. Lo cual nos lleva también a pensar que hemos de seleccionar un tipo de información específica para una específica necesidad de un usuario, se requiere conocer el campo temático sobre el cual se está generando información y requiriendo información. En el caso por ejemplo de la tecnología, mejor dicho de lo científico y tecnológico, no podemos entregar un servicio de información con este contenido científico y tecnológico sino tenemos muy claro el como en determinado campo de ese amplio campo se genera información.

Por ejemplo, tendríamos que conocer el como se genera conocimiento y porqué. Supongamos el caso de una institución relacionada con educación y en el caso de las instituciones gubernamentales el ministerio de educación. El

ministerio de educación tiene como fundamento principal el
crear una política de información.

Para crear esa política de información para el país requiere saber qué ha ocurrido con la educación antes, necesita
información histórica que seguramente la va a encontrar en
bibliotecas, pero requiere también información estadística de
cuanto analfabetismo hay en el pais. Seguramente ahi va a
requerir información de instituciones más lejanas del campo
temático—educacional pero posibles de recolectar. Eso ya no
está en bibliotecas pero puede estar en unidades de información de bancos de datos, unidades de información como
centros ó simplemente oficinas estadísticas. Ahora, para
poder llegar verdaderamente a tener ese acopio de información dentro del campo temático, tenemos que saber qué
seleccionar, cuándo, desde cúando vamos a requerir estadística, cúanto de la historia de la educación vamos a tenerla
controlada para que sirva a esta toma de decisión. Entonces
creo que es más importante antes de adquirir y poder establecer quienes van a entregar qué a quiénes, establecer
qué se genera dónde y cúanto de lo que se genera es útil
para el momento en que se requiere; es decir, si conocemos
la forma en que se va a utilizar la información vamos a
poder seleccionarla y para poder seleccionarla tenemos que
saber cómo se ha generado y quién la va a ocupar en que
momento. Creo que es un problema de selección y de conocimiento del campo temático determinado en el cual se
genera determinada información que va a ser requerida. Sin
duda este planteamiento ha hecho la doctora Dosa en el sentido de hablar ya de información sectorial, de hablar ya de
información technólogica, que indudablemente va a estar
tambien generándose en todo lo sectorial. Es un comienzo de
pensar que las técnicas de selección enseñadas clásicamente
no sirvan y que los índices tampoco sirvan en este momento
porque hay mucha documentación que se genera en las instituciones gubernamentales que no se han controlado jamás
a través de ningún mecanismo.

Si tenemos el concepto de que la selección tiene que hacerse en las fuentes generadoras si vamos a obtener entonces por parte de nuestros profesionales una comprensión de qué herramientas construir para que podamos verdaderamente registrar esa información útil y entregarse al usuario.

Marietta Daniels Shepard:

Certainly one of the problems that is fundamental to all of this is that we have arrived at the Computer Age without having been able to control the flow of bibliographic production from Latin America. There are very few countries in Latin America which normally produce a national bibliography which is in any way complete. Very few national bibliographies have been produced which cover more than a small percentage of what is published or what is produced in the country in mimeo form or any other form. In many instances these mimeo materials are more important than what is published in printed book or journal form. So we are faced primarily with this lack of information services in Latin America, which we still have not been able to bring under control.

Maria Oyarzun de Ferreira:

Siguiendo la idea de Ximena, yo trabajo en un centro nacional de información y nosotros dentro de las actividades que realizamos hemos pensado que es una responsabilidad del centro nacional de información el detectar justamente las fuentes de información pueda seleccionar de esa fuente. Y eso yo creo que es importante, empezar por detectar dónde, tener registrado dónde, para que después hacer posible la selección de cuanta "información" tenga.

Beatriz de Carvalho:

I think that our discussion brings us to one fact: the need, particularly in the developing countries, for an institution to deal with the national information policy, and national coordination of information activities. It should be one institution because that one can observe what is going on in the country, study and survey it, and analyze what is needed by the country as a whole. This cannot be done by isolated individual institutions.

In Brazil, the problem of official publications is being addressed by a group of librarians who have formed the Brazilian Commission on Official Publications. One of their main tasks, a difficult one, is to collect what official organizations are publishing, and compile a bibliography of this material. This is just one example of an approach at the national level. The creation of this Commission was an independent initiative. I believe that in our countries we need the coordination of information activities that deal with the whole field that Marta Dosa described. They would see all the activities in the country as a whole and know what is needed. They would study the solutions to problems such as the need for a central repository of publications, or alternatives such as the COMUT program in Brazil. Instead of a physically centralized repository such as the British Library Lending Division, the idea was to select collections that were as complete as possible, and have them used by all the libraries in the country through the union catalog of serials and through a system that makes it easy to pay for the copies and easy for libraries to request copies from each other without centralizing the request or the management of the system. In Brazil I think this is a successful project. It would be very difficult to find the resources to create a centralized project. It is an alternative. We have come to the point where there is a need for centralized coordination in the country, to solve the problems that we are discussing.

Armando Sandoval:

In Mexico we have been partly centralized. We have been collecting Latin American journals for 5 years. It is a difficult problem. Part of the problem is communication between the different countries. We send an average of four letters for each title we buy before we get the subscription initiated. It is difficult to keep in contact with the publishers. Assuming that the journal begins arriving regularly, then the problem is still far from over. You need a great deal of labor to follow each Latin American title. You never know what is happening with it. Maintaining a repository of Latin American journals is very difficult. I don't know what the experience of others has been; we have two people, full time, to maintain the correspondence with Latin American publishers. I discussed this further in my paper.

Victor Rosenberg:

When I visited Brazil, staff at a large library said that COMUT was really not doing them any good because they were just lending the materials to everyone. This is a classic interlibrary loan problem everywhere. Did the system build in any incentives, for example financial ones, to the net lenders to lend their materials?

Cavan McCarthy:

In the original plan, each library was to keep records of its activity, and a carbon was to be sent to the central agency. At the end of the year, the agency would make a payment to the net lenders. I don't know if this functioned as a real incentive.

Victor Rosenberg:

It is a classic interlibrary loan dilemma that the larger libraries end up loaning far more than they borrow, and the smaller borrowing far more than they lend. Usually these systems have difficulty unless there is an incentive built in for the lenders.

Murilo da Cunha:

The whole idea of the network in Brazil was to share the resources of the country, and not to have a unique central library such as the British Lending Library. That type of cooperation would be very difficult to convince the authorities to fund. The cost of 900,000 titles would be prohibitive. At the same time we have had the national union catalog for about 20 years with about 95,000 different titles built from the contributions of 1000 libraries. This union catalog is kept up to date using a computer and was used in the past as a resource to find out what libraries had what title.

But it was very difficult to request copies because of red tape, such as payment in advance. A group of librarians in Brasilia decided to start a different type of interlibrary loan. They selected 150 good libraries in different areas and these libraries became what were called "bibliotecas basicas," basic libraries. They were chosen by the nature of their collection. Instead of preparing a huge union catalog of one thousand libraries now they are preparing a smaller one of 150 libraries that in reality covers 6 or 7% of the holdings in the union catalog. And they began to sell coupons like the British and French, which solved a lot of problems. You buy a certain number of coupons, and use them when you need copies. Using a basic library is easy because now we have up-to-date catalogs, updated every seven months on COM. COMUT is a new source of revenue for large libraries who receive a large number of request. The charge is not trivial. Of course it is a new program, completing its first year in September of 1982.

My department has signed a contract with COMUT to do an evaluation study, and we hope to have some results in the next six or seven months. It is increasing the number of requests all over the country, because now you have a reliable service. The average time lag is about 15 days. By Brazilian standards, this is marvelous.

Alma Jordan:

I'm not clear about the procedures. Having bought a coupon, you send it to the library and they supply the copy. That library then is reimbursed by the Center?

Murilo da Cunha:

By the Secretary of COMUT. And the reimbursement is more than the lending library's internal cost of producing the copy.

Beatriz de Carvalho:

The group that works at COMUT is very small. It just sells the coupons, receives them, and manages the payments. The staff is about six.

Murilo da Cunha:

There is another good thing about COMUT. We have had about 25,000 transactions during the first year, and we can study these to discover which titles are in greatest demand, and by what libraries, which regions are more information dependent, and which subjects are in demand. In a few years we will have some of the data necessary for a national acquisition policy for periodicals.

Beatriz de Carvalho:

There is a program at FIDCLA, the Latin American commission at FID, which had a meeting two months ago in Argentina, to try to expand COMUT to other countries in Latin America. There is just the beginning of the idea.

Cavan McCarthy:

When COMUT was planned, it was said that Brazil was spending a half a million dollars overseas buying photocopies, mostly from the National Library of Medicine, the National Agricultural Library, and the British Lending Library. If you multiply that by the other countries in Latin America, possibly Latin America is paying over a million and a half dollars overseas a year simply for photocopies and searches. That is a large sum in relation to Latin American library and information systems budgets.

Armando Sandoval:

There are some problems which I would like to point out. First, are the basic libraries all over the country?

Cavan McCarthy:

Yes.

Armando Sandoval:

The idea sounds excellent, but what happens when this is extended to all of Latin America? How long should it take to get a document from Mexico, for example, or from Brazil if the document is ordered from Mexico? Communication is a real problem. It may take weeks or months. I have mentioned the problems with publishers, but of course publishers are not the same as librarians. I wonder if it would be better to save some money and wait for a Latin American supplier or to order it from the British Lending Library? Time plays an important role in document procurement. If you are going to wait for a month to obtain a document it will not work. I don't object to the idea, but we have to consider which is better—to pay a little more to obtain the document quickly, or to obtain it locally in two months.

Juan Freudenthal:

The intriguing thing is that if this is recreated in several countries, and if we also begin to index the kind of information that we need to index as was pointed out this morning, then maybe we will begin to exercise the kind of relationship we need to have between Latin American countries. The only reason we don't do something is because we are terribly dependent upon the Northern countries. Somewhere along the line we have to start to not be dependent any more, and one way to start is to create our own tools. It may take ten or twenty years but by the time we have those tools and we have a good interlibrary loan situation, we may begin to decide it is better to get it from ourselves and not to get it from the United States. The problem we have in Latin America is that we do not even have the tools. So, we have to begin to create these tools, including the indexing of materials.

Cavan McCarthy:

The whole system is a load on the technology system. The periodicals catalog was set up in 1967 or 1969. They are now running a COM (computer output microfiche) catalog, which is very easy to obtain. You put the COM into a microfiche reader, a relatively low level of technology which is widespread in Latin America. The actual copies are made on Xerox machines, and these are widespread. The whole project was really a low-technology one, and that is one of the reasons why it went well.

Murilo Da Cunha:

The existence of COMUT does not mean that we cannot use the British Lending Library. In fact, Brazilian libraries still do. Sometimes we do not have the title, or we need the article in a few days. An article I read a few years ago said that American libraries requested 100,000 copies from the British Lending Library in 1980, and most of the articles were published in American journals. Brazilian libraries cannot afford to pay in hard currency as Americans can.

Thomas McGinn:

I am sure we have heard of the 90% library concept, in which an ideal library should be able to respond to 90% of its users' requests. It is not worth the trouble financially to try to acquire the remaining 10% because the amount of use is much reduced. Would it be feasible to supplement the collection? If you determine that libraries are requesting a certain periodical say from COMUT, and it was not in the system, then the central agency acquires it. Then you can achieve the 90% at the national level, even though in most Latin American countries it is very difficult to achieve the 90% at the institutional level. Then perhaps at the national level 90% would be sufficient, cooperatively. This would address Dr. Sandoval's concern. Is this planned in the system?

Ximena Felíu:

My problem is that I think COMUT is a very real solution to our problems in Latin America, and we can build a system like COMUT in our countries. I think that it would resolve the problems that we have of the exchange of documents. But, what happens with the documents that are, for example, official publications, that are not registered with the central agency or are not contained in the basic library? There is no access to these documents that have real information that researchers and policy-makers need. Could we prepare a program, like COMUT, for those documents that are not accessible through traditional libraries or basic libraries? This means that we would have to register all the documents that a country generates, so that those basic libraries could have access to them. This problem, unfortunately, has not been solved yet.

Alma Jordan:

I think that everything that we have been saying is really revolving around different aspects of national information policy. The UAP program that IFLA has been encouraging and promoting, the Universal Availability of Publications, has as its basic idea that every country would have the responsibility for collecting the material in every form that is generated in the country, and there would be some kind of designated library or center of responsibility for identifying and collecting each item and making it available to anyone anywhere in the world that needed it.

The principle of UBC, Universal Bibliographic Control, is to make sure that everything that is generated in a country is recorded bibliographically, and that a copy is available for consultation anywhere in the world. That is an area of national policy, that we should be able to say that every country takes the responsibility for insuring that everything produced is recorded and made available.

This is where infrastructure comes in, where, if you have your centers or special libraries collecting in their areas, then you have a much better chance of pulling in the materials of a particular sector, such as the government report that is sitting in a cabinet rather than in the library, or is in the minister's brief case, or the brief that was prepared for him which he never bothered to give to the information center, even though it was a very important piece of documentation and could be useful later on. With the overall national policy, all of these kinds of things would be identified. You would have a plan, and a designated resource center, a bibliographic collecting system, a system for availability, and so on. All these are areas of national information policy that we need to put together.

In a national plan, you actually take the trouble to identify who your potential users are, the kind of information they need, and the most logical place to supply it and how to get it, whether it is locally generated or generated outside the country. But you are making sure that that information is going to be available somewhere, and you designate a center that is responsible for it.

The system that has been described for Brazil obviously has less application for smaller countries, where there is not so much the need for a national center as there is for identifying the resource centers in areas of strength that already exist and strengthening these. If you have a good university library or other kind of research library, with collections in a particular field, then that logically is your resource center for that particular field. This is your basic library for that area.

Armando Sandoval:

I don't want to give you the wrong impression about our program. It is really very good. We are close to the United States, and communications are very good. It is better for us to depend on United States resources than Latin American. Sometimes North American or European sources are even better than our own university.

Laurence Hallewell:

This sounds like what happened in Britain. The British Lending Library was set up to handle scientific information, but the National Central Library was so inefficient because it was starved for funds, that Boston Spa finally extended its resources and services.

Marta Dosa:

This is in reaction to the relationship between basic libraries and the role of highly specialized collections, such as in agriculture, housing, public rural health, public administration and the like. It seems very effective in selecting and making available the more formal periodicals and serials which are registered, and the government documents, but what happens to the more informally published internal documents? It seems that the very specialized collections are the ones which could emphasize the fugitive literature and ephemera, including scientific and economic and social science data. When it comes to the question of developing not only the library resources but developing a roster of current, on-going research, again, the specialized collections could expand the collection policy from printed and mimeographed materials to registers of expertise. An agricultural information specialist has more credibility with agricultural researchers than the general national collection specialist, no matter how close to the national library they are. The more specialized a collection is, the more closely they relate to the specialized researchers and decision-makers. These expert indexes and networks might be useful especially in the future, when the technology of interaction is improved.

I would also like to mention that we are talking about developing tools, indexes, and the like, for the next ten years. The technology will be developing so fast, and the price for telecommunications will come down. We have to be ready for it. One way is by developing the links between, for example, agricultural information specialists or librarians, in Venezuela, in Puerto Rico, and Chile, and Jamaica, and researchers. This will help when telecommunication conferences will be possible.

Ximena Felíu:

The tools for acquisitions such as indexes will develop, and librarians will have to be aware of these developing tools. The problem of acquisition hinges on selection, in the context of a knowledge of where information is generated and what the users need. Selection and acquisition must go together.

Armando Sandoval:

For me it is quite clear that we have to differentiate between scientific and technical information and humanistic, social and economic information. The humanists get their information in a way different from the way scientists get their information. And the documents themselves are quite different. This Conference covers the field of scientific and technical information. Referring to Ximena's statement that indexes are not useful, that may be true in some cases of social and economic information.

Ximena Felíu:

They are not useful in the case of unconventional documents, because they do not list very many of them. Indexes are useful of course, but they are indexing only the publications that are distributed massively.

Murilo da Cunha:

A good side-effect of participating in international systems like AGRIS is the resulting good bibliographic control of unconventional materials. For example, the Agricola database does not include unconventional materials from the developing countries. But in working with AGRIS, which produces Agrindex and the AGRIS tapes, developing countries can have a good bibliographic control of unconventional materials. For example, now in Brazil, we have started to have very good bibliographic control of agricultural literature, because we are indexing this type of materials for the AGRIS database. A byproduct of the contribution to FAO is a Brazilian bibliography of agriculture with many unconventional materials.

Marietta Daniels Shepard:

The mention of AGRIS of course points out the great importance of having an institutional structure which makes it possible to develop information networks. AGRIS is getting information from the Latin American countries, coordinated through Agrinter, in the Interamerican Institute of Agricultural Sciences, because IICA in Costa Rica now has had 35 years of experience in developing a network of agricultural libraries throughout Latin America, and program for the training of personnel, so that personnel are capable of identifying, acquiring and processing documents of all kinds, conventional and unconventional, throughout the region. This area is probably the best covered, in terms of knowing what has been published. In order to be able to select what a user might want or need, you have to know what has been published. One of the problems here is a two-edged sword. You have to find out what has been published by getting it to start out with (or someone has to), to be able to describe it bibliographically.

The seminars on the acquisition of Latin American materials have had now 30 years of trying to determine how to select what is needed from Latin America for research libraries not only in the United States but in Latin America. One of the problems that we all have is knowing what is going on and where. We have in the Organization of American States tried to assure the participation of Latin American librarians for many years in the SALALM meetings, and one of the policies of SALALM is to have a meeting in Latin America at least once every five years. Every year a report is made for SALALM of all of the bibliographies that a committee can identify that have been published. Regularly about 300 bibliographies come out in Latin America on different subjects, and one of the reasons that there are so many is that there is inadequate national bibliographic control.

This is one of the most essential elements of the infrastructure that is necessary to sustain any kind of information service in the region. It is at the national level that you should be able to identify unconventional as well as conventional types of materials and record them. Unfortunately it has been the national library which has had the responsibility throughout the world of sustaining national bibliographic control, but most of the national libraries throughout Latin America have been so poorly supported that they have not had the funds to produce the national bibliography on a regular and up-to-date basis.

Nor have they been able to even assure that they acquire all the publications issued in the country. The laws for national legal deposit are very poorly followed throughout Latin America and most national libraries have not created a mechanism for people to go to even the formal publishers to assure that the number of copies that are to be deposited legally are indeed deposited. They have not been able to achieve that, much less the unconventional publications. This is one of the problems that has to be attacked before we can be at all assured of having access to information that has been generated.

Juan Freudenthal:

In a recent survey that I did for some national bibliographies in Latin America, I found that some of the materials that were almost never included were audio-visual materials, maps, dissertations, theses, mimeographed materials, scientific reports, variations in newspapers, atlases, printed music scores, films, tapes, recordings, and government publications. These are not included even if they are published regularly. It is amazing how difficult it is to acquire the materials. They simply are not being recorded in national sources.

Laurence Hallewell:

As someone who worked at the British National Bibliography, can I point out that this is not a problem unique to Latin America. Britain had no national bibliography until 1950. Even ten years later it was not including Irish government publications at all, and it was only including British government publications, selectively. Many locally produced materials were slipping through the net. It deliberately excluded maps, music, and songs. One should be careful about criticizing Latin America too much without realizing that there is much ground that has to be made up elsewhere.

One other point is to be made. A Brazilian publisher with whom I discussed this subject was very vehemently against the national bibliography. It was including material which had not been deposited under copyright, so what incentive was there for abiding by deposit provisions if you were going to get into the national bibliography anyway? And, you were providing free advertising for people who were breaking the law.

Marta Dosa:

I would just like to add to the British example an example from the United States. I think you are familiar with what used to be the Smithsonian Institute's Science Information Exchange (SSIE), which was available as a referral source and also as a database and very good series of specialized bibliographies. Currently access to this valuable source is not there anymore because funds were withdrawn from the SSIE and the whole database was added to National Technical Information Service (NTIS), and it is not going to be kept up-to-date. This shows that there are major problems in the United States as well.

I would like to mention that concerning AGRIS, early in March the international conference on agriculture in Nairobi, had the head of AGRIS, Abe Liebowitz, facing the audience for questions and answers. He said that he would like to collect ideas from the audience on how AGRIS could improve. The single major complaint about AGRIS was that it did not give access to what research is going on until the research is published. Once there is a formal or informal publication, AGRIS will report it, but not until.

Alma Jordan:

The CARIS (Current Research in Agriculture) program is supposed to take care of that. This is a parallel program to AGRIS.

Marta Dosa:

The CARIS program is there, but it does not catch up with the current projects until there is a formal expression of the project.

Alma Jordan:

That was the intention of the program. There is not a published format of the project yet.

Marta Dosa:

That is its intention, but it is not being implemented the way people expected. The major outcome of the meeting was the recommendation that AGRIS should come out with a current research and experts inventory.

Alma Jordan:

I thought that another criticism was the lack of abstracts of publications, to give a clue for selection.

Thomas McGinn:

I would like to comment on Mr. Hallewell's observations. Those of us who went to Library School in the United States know that there is no national bibliography of the United States as such. You do have a union list of monographs and serials, the monthly catalog of government publications, the catalogs of large libraries, and a good unified trade catalog, which allow you to find out what is being published. In Venezuela, you have none of those things. You have the national bibliography which is supposed to do all of that, with the deficiencies that Marietta has pointed out. If we had the union catalog, both for serials and monographs, if we had a unified trade catalog, if we had the catalog of government publications, then we wouldn't have to worry about the national bibliography being adequate. But since we don't have those things, the national bibliography has to try to take over all of those functions. Being deficient, we lack the ability to identify the national publications.

Juan Freudenthal:

Marietta, I would like to come back to you for a moment. In your paper you speak about possible centralized acquisitions in Colombia, Costa Rica, Peru, Mexico and Venezuela. Would you briefly expand on that? What do you mean by centralized acquisition plans?

Marietta Daniels Shepard:

I think the word "possible" was used because I was not too sure exactly what they were. We asked in our questionnaire if they had centralized acquisitions plans and they said yes, but I'm not too sure what they are.

In Colombia, for example, at ICFES, the Instituto Colombiano de Fomento de Educacion Superior, they have a plan for a program for centralized acquisitions whereby the government provides funding for university libraries in the country, and the books and periodicals are acquired and selected centrally and are parceled out to the various institutions.

In Mexico, I think now at UNAM, there is centralized automated acquisitions for the 165 university libraries in Mexico City and throughout the country. The Secretaria de Educacion Publica in Mexico has a program for selecting, purchasing and cataloging materials for new public libraries throughout the country which are being created as a result of agreements between the Secretaria de Educacion Publica and the governments of the various states in Mexico. I know that the metropolitan university was hoping to be able to centralize their publications, I don't think they ever got around to it. I know they were talking about having them done in one place.

One of the advantages of centralized acquisitions is that at least in the United States if you are buying in large quantities you may get a larger discount than if you were buying just one copy at a time for twenty-five different institutions. Programs in universities of university libraries, where there has been some centralization, have been able to embark on cooperative and centralized acquisitions, which are more difficult to achieve in institutions where there is no centralization or coordination of activities of the libraries in an institution or in several institutions.

Ching-Chih Chen:

As I listen to all the problems related to the acquisition of library materials in Latin America, it occurs to me that that the problems are not unique to that region, that they are commonly shared in a lot of areas.

I do have a question. Are we emphasizing the problems with library acquisition, with acquisition specifically interpreted as the process of selecting materials and buying them, or do we mean acquisition to meet the needs of whoever is going to consume the information? That is a very clear-cut fine line which will separate the problems into two different types. I can't comment further until I have an answer to this question, because it seems to me that we are jumping around. We have acquisitions which deals with buying, with the tools which help to tell us what to buy, and at the same time we have acquisitions which is concerned with user needs and selection policy development.

Ximena Feliu:

You can't talk about library acquisitions on two levels without talking about selection first: why, for what, for whom?

Ching-Chih Chen:

I really wanted to get to that point, because we seem to be talking about purchasing problems, but selection is very fundamental. Who are we going to be buying these materials for? And then we can work on fundamental library acquisition problems, which include how develop a collection to meet the needs of the people we are serving. That comes back to Mr. McGinn's point, which is very important when we are discussing acquisitions. Whether we want to serve 95% or 75%, the basic idea is that there are a very few items out there, with the mass of material that is available, that can meet a large percentage of the users needs. The real challenge for each institution, each region, each country, is to develop a way to sort out that percentage, that small percentage, which seems to be able to serve most of the needs of the people we are serving. This seems to be the place to start.

Tony Bowman:

I have an observation that is based on the time that I have spent in libraries, from the vendor's point of view. One of the hardest things to articulate is, What is the purpose of the library? It is not an easy question, based on the answers that I am getting throughout the hemisphere. Within an institution, there is not a clear-cut answer to, What is the purpose of the institution? Who are the users? and, Which subgroup of users are those whose needs are going to be served first? It becomes very political. And sometimes I marvel at how well librarians do it, in spite of the fierce challenges to getting the job done.

Juan Freudenthal:

It seems to me that Ching-Chih is raising a very important question, but one that is very difficult to answer. It seems to me that sometimes when we select and we buy, we are not really sure who our users are. It comes from our own experience as a librarian. I am not completely sure when we acquire that we know who our users are, and when it is going to be used and for whom, even in the science and technology areas. It is much more diffused in the humanities. But I am not so sure about that.

Winthrop Wiltshire:

I think that we must consider at the same time not only who our users are, but who our users ought to be. I find too often the library community relates only to its users, and not that 90% out there who need to be using the materials. There are strategies for bring them into the program.

Ching-Chih Chen:

A lot of times in libraries, the non-user is an important group, and people do tend to ignore them. The important question is, Why are they not using the library? Murilo mentioned the data they are collecting, and I think this will turn up some very useful information, but still it will be mainly based on use. When you get into the infrastructure then you get into much more complicated issues such as, Does the library providing services also refer users when information is not immediately available? If we cannot provide information with the collection, the facilities and the sources we have, do we have the ability to refer to the right source? This may not have anything to do with our organization at all. And that part we usually do very poorly. That has nothing to do with Latin America, as something which in the United States I have been pointing out to librarians. We find out that in providing community information services.

One of our major studies completed just recently pointed out that a lot of organizations out there, so-called networks, are doing work which is so similar to librarians, that you could practically call them library services, but they were done by totally non-library people. Librarians were totally unaware of them. These are the kinds of things I think we should think about.

Juan Freudenthal:

I would like to ask Murilo what impact COMUT might have on acquisitions? Is there a direct relationship between what you are doing there and acquisitions?

Murilo da Cunha:

COMUT is a joint project, between the Ministry of Education, the National Research Concil, and the National Institute for Scientific and Technical Information. It is a new program, about one year old. This year they decided to get some money. They selected 10 libraries to fund to complete their collections in titles that the country needs and are important for the whole country, especially from England. In this sense, COMUT is provoking a change in our acquisitions policy. We have begun to think about our need for an acquisitions policy for Brazil.

Victor Rosenberg:

The question that I have about COMUT is, Why this system is finally working, after so many similar attempts have failed because of the rivalries among the various libraries and the difficulties that have existed before? Or is it too early to tell?

Murilo da Cunha:

That is very hard to answer. We need to study the program.

Victor Rosenberg:

It would be a remarkable achievement, if the system actually works as advertised.

Murilo da Cunha:

I agree!

Victor Rosenberg:

What I have observed, in Brazil for example, is that several organizations would acquire the same database and provide services, and there would be very little cooperation. What political reality was underlying that, I don't know. But there was often a duplication of services rather than a cooperative effort. I don't recall any similar kind of cooperation operating in the past. Interlibrary loan systems have been talked about and tried but they have never functioned. The people would not lend their materials. They would not provide the service. It would seem to me that there must be some underlying reason why this particular structure would work when others would not. Now maybe this could be a result of the deep economic crisis which is really preventing libraries from acquiring materials from abroad, or some other sort of political alliances that have been formed. I wonder what the explanation might be.

Beatriz de Carvalho:

I think that the benefits of COMUT were seen, and were so needed. Everyone could see that there were benefits for all, and these benefits were so concrete, so near, so needed. I think everyone was cooperating.

Murilo da Cunha:

It had a real, tangible benefit.

Beatriz de Carvalho:

This was stronger than any kind of political rivalry.

Victor Rosenberg:

Was there any tension among the libraries that were included in the 150 selected?

Beatriz de Carvalho:

No, I don't think so.

Thomas McGinn:

I would like to come back to a point which is a traditional frustration for anyone who is trying to develop information services in a developing country. You must face the fact that sometimes the information just does not exist. The user wants it, but no one has compiled it. It could be compiled, but no one has. Until about 5 years ago Venezuela had no important statistics on many types of information services in the country until the national coordinating level for library and information services developed a research capacity. We had no idea how many school libraries there were in the country for example. We get this type of request at reference desks daily, but this information is never going to be produced in North America or Europe. It has to be produced locally. In the library school at the central university this is the type of information that the students want. They want to study their own country's needs. But we don't have it. So we often put a library school student to work compiling this kind of data, and that little mimeographed report is often more important, as Marietta has said, than what is being published by commercial publishers. It's a limiting factor which other countries don't have to deal with. I think we are talking about three levels, of information that exists but has not been identified, or information is that identified but not acquired, or the information that has been acquired and not used. But that first level is there too, the information that does not exist. It is a constant struggle.

Winthrop Wiltshire:

I think that ties in very neatly with Marta's schema, in terms of the interaction of the library community with the other information-generating agencies and activities in the countries. For example Thomas McGinn says it may not be just a question of collating information to create an information product, it may be the execution of a research project and there may well be agencies in the country which need to do the project. But, they may not identify that as a need or a priority, they may need to be signaled. This is where the question of the interaction comes in.

Cavan McCarthy:

We have library acquisitions written on the board, but to a large extent the meeting is walking around the problem of library acquisitions, or treating it as if it were the same as library acquisitions in North America, where in your office you have your annual acquisitions fund and every month you spend a certain percentage of that. In Latin America it does not work at all like that. The acquisitions numerically are very low in many libraries, very low indeed. The budgets are extremely low and very often, worse than a low budget, you do now know when you are going to get the budget, when it is going to be released, and because of inflation you don't know how much it is going to be worth when you do get it. These are exceptionally serious problems from the point of view of library acquisitions. Going back to what Thomas was saying about statistical information on numbers of libraries, there was in fact in 1976 in Brazil a complete survey of libraries, and this was published. I have heard recently that it is going to be done on a three-yearly basis.

Beatriz de Carvalho:

It's going to be bi-annual. There will be a survey of libraries this year, 1983. The last data we had was 1974. After that, statistics were collected but not processed because of difficulties within the Ministry of Education, including moving the service to Brasilia. Last year an agreement was signed between the Ministry of Education and IBGE, the Brazilian Institute of Geography and Statistics, to reformulate the collecting and processing of data, and to publish the data. The questionnaire was adapted to the questionnaire that Unesco sent member states to collect statistics all over the world. Everything is ready, and IBGE will start collecting this data now in 1983. So, next year the data will be published, and we do believe this will be done regularly.

Cavan McCarthy:

Will these be published separately, or in the annual statistical yearbook?

Beatriz de Carvalho:

In the statistical yearbook, which will be published anyway. Maybe the Ministry of Education will issue separate leaflets which will give statistics on primary and secondary education, and also what they call the cultural statistics which include library statistics, with more details than are in the yearbook. Another study will be done by the INL, the National Institute for the Book, which intends to publish a directory from data being collected now, as well as the 1976 data which you mentioned. There will be much more data than before in the statistical yearbook.

Murilo da Cunha:

I would like to mention a topic that has not been covered in our discussion, and that is the migration from print into electronic form. We know that the use of databases in the United States and European countries and some Latin American countries is increasing at a high speed. Prof. Martha Williams published an article a year ago about the migration from print to magnetic form. The number of subscriptions to the printed form is declining, for *Chemical Abstracts*, for *Social Science Citation Index*, and for *Science Citation Index*. For developing countries, where we don't have good access to databases, we are going to pay more to subscribe to the printed form, and we are going subsidize the people who will use the electronic form of the database. Perhaps we could have a recommendation dealing with this. At the same time there are some databases for which there are no comparable printed forms, and we don't have access to this information. So the technological gap is widening the information gap for us.

Marietta Daniels Shepard:

It seems to me that sometimes for every step forward you take two steps back. As a former acquisitions librarian the problem of library acquisitions in Latin America has always disturbed me. We finally were able through a conference in Mendoza, Argentina in the early 1960's to get a recommendation to the effect that university libraries should have at least 5% of the total university budget for their maintenance. Many library associations reiterated this, and many countries adopted this as a policy, but we still find that even university libraries frequently have no budget whatsoever, and depend almost exclusively on exchange for the acquisition of materials for their university libraries. So the quality of the university libraries is not quite as good as we would hope it might be. Also the techniques of selecting from what is available, when you know you have a budget, is a serious thing to master to start out with, but when you don't know what your budget is, and if you are told what your budget is and the rector of the university decides that he wants to take a trip to Tokyo, to go to a conference, he may use your library acquisitions funds to go to Tokyo, it leaves quite a strain on libraries.

One of the things that we had hoped to be able to accomplish in changing the curricula of library schools in Latin America was to have more attention paid to the problems of acquisitions and the selection of materials, and we managed over the years to get some changes in the curricula so that the topic of acquisitions and selection was introduced as a topic in library schools. Then about five years later they almost all disappeared because no one was really interested in the matter because they had enough problems cataloging the materials that they got on exchange and the things that they got on exchange were not what they really needed but just what someone sent to them. So here we are back again. What do we do about improving even the methods of or capabilities of libraries to handle exchange materials? We have tried over the years to interest countries in Latin America in setting up national exchange centers or interest universities in setting up exchange centers for the university libraries, and I think our success has been absolutely zero in that. I don't think that anyone has ever requested any assistance in improving their local situation or their national situation as far as exchanges are concerned. So we are doing a lot of abstract talking about selection of information for users whom we haven't been able to identify versus what we are capable of doing in individual institutions.

Alma Jordan:

May I just add one or two problems into the melting pot. One is the factor of currency devaluations, which has affected some countries particularly like Jamaica, where you thought you had an adequate budget one day and then the currency is devalued and suddenly your currency is parallel with the United States dollar or whatever and the currency you are buying in is no longer the same. So your budget shrinks overnight, and you have to cope with that.

And I think that that plus the enormous increase in costs for journal subscriptions have shrunk budgets beyond belief. I think these are two problems that you can do practically nothing about, because both are out of your hands. The cost has gone up and you either pay for it or you drop it.

A third problem I think one could identify is the erratic mail system, or communications generally, which tends to nullify the best of intentions in getting something quickly to a user. We have talked a lot about identifying users needs. Frequently we have a situation where we have a perfectly clear picture of what we are trying to get, and we send for it by air freight, but somebody at the other end mucks up the game and for some reason it doesn't come by the system. Everything else is coming, but the particular item that you are waiting for in October comes in March. You have a catalog of reasons but that doesn't help the user who is in front of you, and you know that you have done everything that you can, including telephone calls and all the rest of it, but it just doesn't work. That kind of communication gap I think is a further problem which tends to complicate life in the developing world. There isn't anything that you can do about these things except wail and gnash your teeth, and try again.

Victor Rosenberg:

Since we are nearing five o'clock I think the best idea would be to table these topics. I am sure they will come up again and we can deal with them in more depth. I can't think of more important topics to deal with and I am not quite ready to give up on these issues. I think that there are some things that perhaps could be done in these areas.

Juan Freudenthal:

During our discussions today we dealt with questions such as, Should libraries link with non-traditional information gathering agencies, and if so, how could it be done? What is the future role of libraries in connection with non-library institutions? There was also the topic of the total complex of information.

Point two, we talked about the need for the creation of a national information policy and coordination. We said that we needed coordination of information activities in the country, and tried to elucidate who is in charge of identifying that information.

Point three, we explored further the possible creation of central repositories for science and technology journals, and we discussed the case of COMUT in Brazil. We also discussed the possibility of the universal availability of materials, very briefly.

Finally, we raised some nitty-gritty questions about problems related to acquisitions, and I was a little troubled about bringing out in the beginning of discussions what is happening because we have lived with it for so long, and in all the papers, the problems are listed over and over again. I was not sure that if we discussed them we would be able to solve them, because as Marietta knows, I think they are unsolvable. But if there are anyt problems that you think coul d be solved, then let's tackle them again.

Thank you, and we will see you

Tuesday Morning, 12 April 1983

*The Access of Latin American Scholars to Publication. How
New Technologies Can Provide New Opportunities*

Victor Rosenberg:

Good morning. This afternoon's session will be somewhat
shorter than usual. We will enjoy the hospitality of University Microfilms this afternoon, for a tour of the facility and a
reception. It is appropriate that we have the tour today, because University Microfilms has pioneered many of the techniques of publishing in the electronic age, and you will see
some things this afternoon that I think are marvels of
modern technology. Many of them are unique in the
publishing world. In keeping with that, I'd like to introduce
our moderator for this morning, Tony Bowman, who is
representing University Microfilms.

Our topic for this morning is the access of Latin
American scholars to publication. Tony brought to my attention yesterday the fact that there is some ambiguity in
the phrase "access of Latin American scholars to publication." What we meant by that was the ability of Latin
American scholars to publish their work, to reach as broad
an audience as possible, rather than their access to publications as materials.

Tony Bowman:

I'm delighted to be here with you today.

Many times, I think we live in a very ambiguous world. We are faced with many choices and many opportunities, and it's very hard to figure out who and what we are, and where we fit in. We are information users, and at the same time we are information generators, and many of us also find ourselves in the third category of information facilitators, either editing, making publication decisions, or involved in dissemination. Which are we? To me it is very hard to separate and compartmentalize these processes.

It seems that unless a fact is written and published, only then is it a fact. Yet we have other worlds of information about us and such as oral history, current events, and the tools of dealing with that information break down.

I'd like to relate to you something that Robert Daley wrote in *American Saga*, a short biography of one trip and how Pan American Airways was founded. In the 1930's, he was looking for a way to go from the United States to Asia, and he was using the maps in the New York Public Library. But he had terrible problems. He could get from Hawaii to Guam, but he had a 3000 mile gap, and there was not an airplane in the air that could fly 3000 miles. Because of his inquiring mind he kept pressing the librarians until finally they brought him out some manuscript journals of Clipper Sea captains. He was able to find Wake Island. He knew one ought to be there. He knew that if one wasn't there he did not have an airline. And I'm sure that the keeper of those journals, the captain, in describing Wake Island and recording its location, had no idea that the information he was recording would be that valuable. Because of that event, Daly was able to become successful, and start his airline, and later became very powerful in Latin America.

So the idea of thinking and then communicating is to my way of looking at it, the essence of what publishing is all about. Why do we publish? Why do we want to subject ourselves to publishing something? Well, in the first place, it is a test of ourselves. It is a test of our ideas. We can prove ourselves, we can prove the worth of an idea. We may be in a situation where our job depends on our performance in this way. We may want to influence someone. We might be actually looking for information, and by publishing we have a mechanism to draw that information out of the world at large to help us. We might want just to record something, like the sea captain. We might do it because we enjoy it, or because we hope someone else will also enjoy reading it or using it. There might be a series of rewards for us intellectually, recognition, and perhaps monetary. We might not know exactly why we want to do it.

Who are we publishing for? To ourselves, to some extent; to our close circle of colleagues; to our colleagues at large; to the world at large.

What are some of the factors that influence publishing? That stimulate it, that make it flow a certain way, that make it not flow at all from time to time?

First, there is editorial policy. For example, a publication may be founded by a peer group of researchers, who collectively want to have an organ to publish their views. They are not particularly interested in making money, they only want to cover costs and provide a forum.

Perhaps you didn't have contact with the editorial board when they featured the special section on your area. Many times these contacts are made on a personal basis, not on the basis of a formal publishing policy. You know the editors, you know who is accepting what, and it is a very informal process but informal over a long distance.

What about timing? Many people have written the right article, but they wrote it in the wrong time.

Fourth, what about geography? You know the editorial policy, you have submitted the outline and think you have an acceptance, but you are seven thousand miles away. Your article requires some reworking, but it doesn't get to the printer on time because of the plain limitations of geography.

Fifth, what about the limitations of cost? Submitting the same article to multiple publishing opportunities, particularly if it has lots of graphics, becomes costly.

Sixth, consider cultural factors such as language. Even within one language, such as English, there are enough confusions even within the United States. What about the differences in Spanish? How willing are we to expose ourselves in someone else's culture, and their language, and in essence play by their rules? And how eager is the publisher to accept materials coming in from another culture in another language? There are a number of journals that want the broadest possible inclusion of ideas and they publish other languages regularly. The *Hispanic American Review* for example, accepts publications regularly in German, French, Spanish, English, and Portuguese, in fact they encourage them. It adds a flavor that you would never get only in English, and I think the journals are enriched.

Seventh, what about economics? What about the journal publisher or book publisher who is looking at how many copies he can sell, or the editor or publisher is looking for something that is more what he or she thinks is the trend in which activities should be directed, and your work is not in these areas? How many publishers are willing to take a chance?

Communicating with others is so necessary that most government intelligence communities recognize the need to be able to publish, and the restrictions that need to be placed on their employees, by having an in-house journal that is published completely and only in-house. It never circulates outside. So, people within their own organization can satisfy their desire to publish, and share their original thinking with others.

How widely read are Latin American authors in this country? How widely read are United States or British authors in Latin America? I think that depends very much on the field.

We at University Microfilms have tried mightily for over 30 years to include more Latin American publications within our program. We've had contracts with many publishers, but then suddenly the publication stops coming to us. So we write, or we have royalty payments to send, and the checks come back, undeliverable. Publishing houses open, publishing houses close. Sometimes it is like a revolving door.

I found a Caribbean Basin newsletter two months ago. It promised to have current effective information. So I had my institution plunk down its $150, and a month and a half later I got my check back with a nice letter stating that well, we didn't really have this as a publication to begin with, and after looking at it all we decided that we don't have enough subscribers, so here's your check back. I can't think of how many times that's happened to me. Maybe I have unusual tastes.

What are some of the things that are in our favor? What are some of the factors that are creating the demand and making a publication for every author or an opportunity for every author?

Victor Rosenberg:

I recently had the experience of ordering a computer program, but the check didn't come back, a letter came back saying that it couldn't be delivered because it hasn't been written yet. People are publicizing materials that haven't been completed, just to complicate the whole process.

Marietta Daniels Shepard:

I have a question for Armando Sandoval, who probably has had more experience than many of us with the publication by Latin American authors in foreign publications. Are Latin American authors in the scientific and technical fields more prone to use journals outside their own countries than those in the social sciences and humanities?

Armando Sandoval:

I think that by now it is a well known fact that scientists prefer their foreign vehicles for science, but humanists, sociologists, social scientists and economists prefer their own vehicles. We have compiled bibliographies of what Latin Americans publish outside their own journals, and we have found that there is an average of about 3500 articles written in foreign journals every year. Most of these are scientific articles. In a paper written by yourself and Dr. Lancaster, you have shown the same thing about Brazilian authors. What happens is that the scientists work in a very universal knowledge arena. They want to know what they may find. They want to have prestige. On the other side the sociologists, humanists, historians are very much concerned with local or regional or national problems, so they prefer their own vehicles of communication. But there are some areas which are in the middle, like geology or zoology, in which the authors prefer their own national, regional, or local vehicles. Many times in different meetings in Latin America specialists in these areas have wanted to know if our Latin American journals are a real expression of the quality or quantity of our research, and it has been stated that we couldn't know the real quality or quantity of Latin American research without knowing about the manuscripts going to foreign journals. That's why our center at the University of Mexico started making recommendations to locate these materials.

I want to stress the well-known fact that our scientific journals do not reflect either the quality or the quantity of the research going on in Latin America.

Going a little further, when Tony Bowman asked about why we write, I should say that there are many more reasons. There is a saying in Spanish that a man is not a man until he has had a son, he has planted a tree, and he has written a book. Why? It may be just a saying, but it is there.

Victor Rosenberg:

Murilo da Cunha and I did a study of Brazilian scientists. We found a paradox in the responses to the questionnaire. When the scientists were asked whether they preferred to publish in Brazilian journals or foreign journals, they overwhelmingly indicated that they preferred to publish in Brazilian journals. But when they were asked which would be more effective for reaching their Brazilian colleagues, they said the foreign journals. In other words there was a statement of a preference to publish locally, but an acknowledgement that the most effective channels of publication were the widely-circulated foreign journals.

Murilo da Cunha:

I think it is related to the lack of bibliographic control of our local publications. They would prefer to publish in the local journal, but they know that because of the lack of bibliographic control, their articles or ideas are not going to be assimilated.

Armando Sandoval:

In Mexico, if the scientists said they preferred to publish in Mexican journals, I would not believe them. They prefer to publish abroad. Something very important is happening in Latin America. On the one side there are great efforts to promote our own journals. The social journals and economic journals are rather good, but the scientific journals are very bad. There is constant discussion of how to improve our scientific journals, but even more effort is given to the publication of articles in foreign journals. When our academic councils meet to decide on promotion, they always look at which researchers have published in foreign journals, not in national journals. This is the real contradiction, and a very discouraging one.

Juan Freudenthal:

I think the reason for that has been given by Murilo. I think that it is because of the lack of access to local materials. I am sure that in Mexico people would take pride in publishing in their own country. I can see why a Dean in a university wants you to publish in a foreign country, because others have no access to local articles. Other people have access to the Mexican library because there are indexes which are distributed worldwide. I have heard this from some of my Mexican colleagues. I think Murilo is completely right. The indexing process is the stumbling block to publication.

Armando Sandoval:

But this is not the main reason. The main reason is language. The English language is the *lingua franca* of the modern world. Of science. If you don't publish in English, the world will not read your work. It is a real problem. You see now that some of the best journals in Latin America are written in English.

Barbara Gumbs:

There is another aspect of this. It is generally felt, at least in the Caribbean, that the foreign journals have a better refereeing system. The articles that are submitted by local writers are more thoroughly screened, and consequently also meet a certain standard. In the local journal, the process may not be as rigid.

Another point is that this publishing in foreign journals also has an effect on the type of research that is done in the developing countries, because the scientist will generally not feel that he will have his articles accepted if they conduct research specifically on a topic that is locally applicable to the situation at hand, and would have more practical application. Here again we are short-changing ourselves in the system. So, scientists prefer to publish something that will be of use to scientific colleagues out there and that will be accepted in the foreign journals.

Maria Oyarzun de Ferreira:

Yo también creo que es una cosa de calidad. Cuando un trabajo es aceptado para ser publicado afuera es en reconocimiento a la calidad del autor. Nosotros el año pasado tuvimos una reunión con los científicos de Chile, sobre los problemas en cuanto a la tranferencia de información y sobre los problemas en cuanto a publicar en el pais ó afuera. Llegamos casi a la misma conclusión, quienes trabajan en las ciencias básicas prefieren publicar afuera, y aquéllos que tienen interés local prefieren publicar en el pais. ¿Pero en cuanto a lo que es ciencia basica: con todo aquello que no se puede publicar afuera porque no es aceptado, que pasa? No publican, es un campo de mala calidad, es basura, no lo aceptan. Y yo creo que esto va tambíen mirando un poco al exceso de publicaciones, al exceso de lo que se escribe, es una manera de talizar = discriminar qué debe ser publicado y qué no. Y como les digo ésta fué una opinión que vino de los científicos mísmos, que a mi me sorprendió sobremanera. O sea, si es publicado a nivel internacional, es porque es aceptado un buen trabajo, para ellos eso significa un reconocimiento a su trabajo.

Tony Bowman:

That in a way is surprising to me. We have an example where people in a country accept a foreign judgement over the quality of their publication. This judgement is based on whether it is published in a foreign journal. If I understood you correctly, if it isn't, they themselves will treat it as garbage.

Juan Freudenthal:

Let me summarize briefly what she said. In a conference of scientists in Chile, they found out in general that for those aspects of science which were written locally or which had a local flavor, they were happy if they were published in Chile. But those which had a broader significance, they wanted to have published abroad. When she asked, Why don't we publish in Chile those things which have been rejected abroad? the scientists said no. Anything which has been rejected abroad for us means that it is not good. It is treated as garbage. This was very surprising to her. We are talking basically about intellectual underdevelopment. We have terrible complexes about that.

Tony Bowman:

In a way that is totally shocking, especially when you see that the credentials of these people are from the finest universities in the world.

Juan Freudenthal:

That shouldn't be shocking, not even to my colleagues in the United States. If you are published in certain journals, your are congratulated, and if you are published in other journals, even in English, they do not think it is as good. That snobbishness exists even in our own country.

Merline Smith:

What you find in Jamaica is that there is a great problem as far as prestige is concerned. Our scientists feel, for example, that if they publish in the local journals, circulation is limited and the article doesn't get very far. So they tend to publish in the foreign journals. And they get permission for the same article to be published in our local journal. We publish it locally, because it gets to more of the local people.

Another thing is that they aim to write what the foreign journals will accept, rather than things that are per-.tinent to our own local situation. So we find that the information that is included in the local journals is not really of much practical help in our own development.

Winthrop Wiltshire:

We shouldn't be surprised by this need for external validation. What we are witnessing is a manifestation of Latin American psychological and cultural dependence. In fact you might have very bright scientists who because of this syndrome do not perceive that they themselves must do the analysis, and determine in fact whether their work might do some good in their own country. Even though they might reject it in a foreign country because it does not meet their priority area for their country or international area, it may be very relevant locally. We have to attack that problem I'm afraid from a much broader perspective. This is psychological dependence, which is a hangover of course from colonialism.

Thomas McGinn:

I think that Dr. Sandoval has made some very good points. The linguistic area is very important, in that scientists want to be read in Poland and Thailand where people do read English, and their journals most often will have at least abstracts in English. So the scientific community is dependent on English.

However I think we can distinguish between pure science where that is absolutely true, and applied science. Areas that Dr. Sandoval mentioned, for example zoology, geology, and botany, are applied and area-related. Tropical medicine is much more important in Latin America than it is in North America. There is a great deal of applied research in these areas, rather than pure physics, by Latin American researchers. I think that what Winthrop is saying is true. In these areas we could do a great deal more in Spanish and Portuguese. Venezuela could produce two, maybe more, excellent scientific journals, with the amount of research that has been done and has been accepted in prestige journals in English. In Venezuela we did a project to identify national publications and it included all articles done by Venezuelans in foreign journals, and an extremely high proportion were in English in science.

When you go to the university, our undergraduates in science and engineering and so forth pick up English right away. They have to. They are expected to. However when we go into a documentation center, people who have graduated in engineering and other applied areas know how to read English but they cannot access an article in English very easily. Their lectures are in Spanish. They speak Spanish in daily life. Any computer scientist in Venezuela knows English to read it, but he may not speak it well.

I think that as a sort of counter-attack, as a means of defending our cultural importance (because we are producing in Latin America good quality material), we could index the

English-language journals in Spanish. We are totally dependent upon the foreign abstracting and indexing services. The first step we could take is to make this material accessible in Spanish, certainly, absolutely when it is published in Spanish. But even that is not done. Then also at the same time, to defend ourselves in terms of bounds of trade considerations, having paid enormous amounts of money to the indexing and abstracting services which after all are commercial services, we could get together, at least on a national basis in each country, and index those journals which are most widely used. That will include the journals to which the Latin American scientists are contributing. Here we would take a first step toward certain autonomy in this area, which we are trying to do in Venezuela. Although our first priority is indexing Venezuelan journals, we do want to reduce our dependency on importing totally this type of abstracting and indexing service.

Laurence Hallewell:

In regard to the flow of information North-South, rather than South-North, I wonder whether we should not be wary about too much reliance on the English language. I think that I saw that in *Chemical Abstracts*, 50% of their sources were English, 20% were Russian, and 20% were Japanese. I've been impressed by the extent to which Japanese tend to write in their own language. And there is no trouble in accessing their literature. A Brazilian student of mine came to me very aggrieved because she had spent quite a lot of money on an off-line search of a Brazilian databank to come up with five references, all in Japanese. I think here the problem is making translation available. It occurs to me that more people are qualified to translate from Japanese in Brazil than in the United States. And I think this is something Brazil could possibly take up.

Beatriz de Carvalho:

Just to confirm what Mr. McGinn was saying, in the study we did in Brazil, it was shown that in some subjects, in the biomedical sciences and in physics, the scientist published abroad. We know that, for instance, the information professionals publish in Brazil. I think our professionals are happy to publish in the Brazilian journals. So the subject matter has an influence on it. Again, if the country coordinates information activities, a whole program could be developed to improve the quality of our journals. Now it is a vicious circle. One of the ways to improve our journals would be to publish in Portuguese what is also published abroad. Of course we will never be able to prevent a scientist from publishing abroad, for obvious reasons.

Marietta Daniels Shepard:

On the topic of indexing of Latin American journals in the language of Latin America, the lack of indexes is I think one of the key problems that Latin America has had over the years. In our survey we were not able to determine when we asked a question about the indexing of national journals whether they were actually indexing the local journals or whether they were indexing journals in general. Now we find in the sectoral information systems that much indexing is going on and this indexing is done unquestionably in the language of the country where the system is in effect. This is done because of the lack of published indexes, and because they want to give assistance to their local users. I think the time has come when we have to do more to coordinate all of these indexing activities in Latin America. We need to avoid the duplication of efforts in the same fields, and at the same time to give wider access to users throughout Latin America to the indexing services that are available. The computer of course makes all of this extremely possible, if we can achieve a standardization of indexing methods and the standardization of machine-readable formats. It seems to me that one of the things that should come of this Conference is a recommendation to achieve greater coordination, standardization and compatibility of indexing activities.

Marta Dosa:

I'd like to comment on the intellectual dependency of developing countries in a broader context. I believe that a large portion of the blame has to go to the large scale donor or technical assistance agencies. Technical aid to developing countries has been quite significant in the development of the research and publishing world, especially in publishing rural development research or research in the applied areas. Donor or assistance agencies usually send consultants, who are many times in charge of applied research or social science research projects in developing countries. The consultant usually writes a report, sometimes jointly with indigenous researchers, but sometimes not even jointly. If the research report is joint then naturally it will be published by the donor agency in an industrial country. This I believe very strongly imposes the dominance of assistance agencies on the growth of original research in the countries. There is a slight change now. Many agencies are beginning to realize this, and they are beginning to give more assistance to develop original research by the nationals and to build up a core of researchers in the various countries. I think this is a very significant factor, because research aid is always welcome, but research aid can be a double-edged sword, not always beneficial and sometimes even detrimental. I wonder whether you have seen evidence of this? Do you agree that this is a factor and that there should be a change in the influence of the consultants?

Tony Bowman:

I've seen it in Bolivia, but I don't know how you change it.

Marta Dosa:

I think many consultants today are beginning to give feedback to the donor agencies, and agencies are beginning to see that some of the technical projects introduce an intervention, whether it is building a road or establishing a retrieval system in a developing country. After the project team and the consultants leave, the change or the new intervention will not be maintained. Local people were not involved with its planning, or did not participate originally, or did not provide intellectual input, and therefore they do not feel committed to the new project. This happens over and over again. The World Bank and United States AID are beginning to realize that this is not the right way to go. I gave a paper entitled 'The Consultant as an Information Intermediary' at an international conference last September and the audience was just about equally divided between representatives of industrial countries who felt it was very critical and representatives of developing countries who felt it was very useful.

Thomas McGinn:

There is another activity which might be helpful in correcting the problem of dependence on foreign publication, and it is the question of documenting research projects. I saw in Marietta's study that a great number of countries seem to have information on the research projects being carried out in the country.

Of course this is the question of pre-publication control, and it is my understanding that the scientific community is just as interested in knowing what the scientific research projects are before they are published as they are in actually finding out afterwards. When one is doing his PhD, for example, he wants to know what everyone else is doing, so he doesn't work on something that someone else will beat him to. If we could document nationally all the research projects being done in the scholarly and scientific community, consistently, with some agency in charge, (including the social and natural sciences), then we would attract the interest of the international community in what's being done in the country. They would have to come to that agency to find out what is being done.

This has been done in Venezuela for the humanities and social sciences within the last year and a half, by the Department of Research of the National Library. Every six months it does a survey of all the research projects in the social sciences and humanities. These are now put into the computer, and you can consult the file. We have found that some areas are quite limited, with only a few thousand researchers doing work in these areas. The National Council for Science and Technology (CONICIT) has a similar operation for natural sciences. If we could do these in each country, and perhaps pool them internationally, we would have an extremely important independent source for the publication of scientific information.

Ching-Chih Chen:

I'd like to get back to a couple of points, and also follow up on what Marta said about the consultants. My own personal feeling here is that while it is difficult to generalize, I have always felt very strongly that the consultant needs to go into a country to do a project, and try to meet the local national needs, not to take the view of whatever is happening in their own country. We do see many consultants simply equate "development" to what was happening in the United States or England or in France ten or twenty years ago and say that what you need is what we did twenty years ago. That would be absolutely wrong simply because all the social, economic and cultural backgrounds were very different. I think that is something all the consultants definitely should take note of. There are certainly consultants who would not think that way.

To come back to the funding agencies, it depends on the agencies' main priority. I'm particularly thinking of some of the experiences that I've had with WHO, developing health sciences information networks in certain geographic areas. It ties in very much with developing bibliographic control for locally published journals. It is absolutely true when we talk about the difficulty of bibliographic control. How could you possibly expect your people to use journals published in your own language in your own country if there's no way to get to those articles? So there are some very substantial projects right now which deal with a certain area, for instance Southeast Asia, or a few regional areas. They essentially set up a national focal point, which will sort out the journals published in each country, and start worrying about doing indexing and abstracting of the journals within their own country. Then the countries with similar languages can connect them together. To me that is a step in the right direction, because there is some way to lead to the publications, which probably would enhance the desire of local scientists to publish in local journals.

I think that the tendency for the 'higher' quality' research results to be published in English and in foreign journals is going to continue for some time, for the developing countries. If the top-rated scientists want to be recognized internationally, there is no way they are going to confine themselves to being known just in their own countries. To me it is not bad, rather it is good for the developing countries. The scientists ought to be able to publish in very high-quality refereed journals and have their names there and their countries represented. Then people recognize that those countries do have good people. On the other hand that does not mean that local people ought to be deprived of access to their own local articles, and I would certainly think that if the quality journal in each country could republish them, or at least summarize them, that would be another way to provide access to that information. These problems, also, are not unique to Latin America but are shared by developing countries around the world.

Maria Oyarzun de Ferreira:

Siguiendo un poco la idea, otro sector de la comunidad científica en Chile, que es el sector biomédico, ellos piensan que si lo que ellos publican es bueno, no importa el idioma en que esté escrito si es interesante para la comunidad científica mundial. Y ellos se han preocupado en desarrollar buenas revistas con muy buenos comités editoriales que selecciónan lo mejor de la produccion en el país y mejoran tanto (digamos) la forma como ellos están transmitiendo la información como el medio que la registra, y a través de esto ellos han conseguido mantener muy buenas revistas con muy buena periodicidad, buena presentación, y son revistas que están siendo recibidas por las publicaciones secundarias internacionales, que aparecen en los índices internacionales y llegan los pedidos de fotocopia o tienen conexión con otras revistas. Porque ellos proban que si es bueno no importa el idioma, y lo han conseguido.

Juan Freudenthal:

In a nutshell, what she said was that in Chile, for example, in the biomedical area, whatever is good is published in Spanish. They feel that there is going to be access for everyone who wants to read it, and they feel that people have requested those biomedical articles in Spanish because the biomedical people outside the country are interested in them.

She says that language in itself is not the major problem. I would like to add that I am not so sure that I agree with María on that. I really feel that there is nothing wrong with having a *lingua franca*. Human beings have always dreamed of having an Esperanto. English may have a political connotation for many countries. But there is nothing wrong with trying to write in one language so that we can all understand it. We are talking all the time among ourselves about the need for standards, among other things for bibliographic items. Why don't we standardize the language? I understand that in literature, you have to express yourself in your own language. But when it comes to items in biomedicine and medicine which everyone needs, I don't see why we don't use English. This is my own personal opinion.

Ching-Chih Chen:

I wasn't really advocating standardization of language. English is already an international language. Rather, I spoke of journals outside the developing countries which are already considered to be the top-rated journals in their fields. You can't blame the top-rated scientists for wanting to publish in them.

Marta Dosa:

I didn't mean to imply that all consultants are domineering, I was talking about trends. The trend is actually documented in foreign assistance literature, and planners, sociologists, managers, and developers write about it. As a trend, naturally, it has exceptions, and I would hope that there are many consultants who do not represent this trend. Secondly, I feel that the whole question of publishing in different languages inside and outside of one's country is very much also a question of the invisible college, because the publications are many times passed along in a network of colleagues, of people who cooperate across national borders, and that's why I always like to support the idea of the invisible college. The more support we can lend to it, even formally, the better.

Tony Bowman:

Does anyone have any follow-up comments to this morning's discussion?

Cavan McCarthy:

Dr. Chen was talking about bibliographic control in library science. In Brazil we are doing quite well on that scene. A very simple publication is prepared in which we collect together all the abstracts that are published in various journals, put them in alphabetical order by author, add a manual KWIC index, and print it off as a book which is distributed throughout Brazil. This means that every library school, every library, every practicing librarian can have this book and can have immediate access to Portuguese literature in library science. It costs very little. If you put it into a databank, almost no one has a terminal, almost no one would have access to it. But if you have it in a book, you have immediate access.

Beatriz was talking about translation. There is in fact in Brazil a very strong demand for translations of things I write in English. They want them translated into Portuguese. Perhaps they are afraid I've written something they wouldn't like. But I think we should put as a specific recommendation from the Conference that Latin American scholars who publish overseas should be encouraged as much as possible to publish a translation in their own country.

One of the problems that you have if you publish overseas and then you try to publish the translation in your own country is that normally the journal will ask you to produce a letter from the overseas journal authorizing you to publish a translation. This is an extra step that you do not have when you submit to an American journal. I don't see how you can get around that.

Another problem is that occasionally you have journals and conferences in Latin America which insist upon original work. It is perfectly valid in one way, but this means that you cannot present translations of items you have already published overseas. I got caught on this once!

The paper came straight back from the conference organizers. I think that conferences in Latin America should accept translations of work published overseas as if they were original work. For the country, they *are* original work. The fact that they have been published overseas should not influence this. This could be another specific recommendation.

If you write something, you have to decide where you are going to publish it. Are you going to present it at a conference? Publish in a journal? If you choose the journal, you have more chances of it being picked up in the bibliographic control machinery, such as it exists, and you have more chances of it being known outside the country. If you present it at a congress, very often congress proceedings don't get outside of the country, and very often they are indexed less.

But there are financial advantages in presenting at a congress, because you can write off expenses and you can request your air fare or bus fare to the congress, you can request a per diem for attendance, and you can request your registration fee for the congress. You have quite strong financial incentives thereby to send your work to a congress. If you send your work to a journal, you literally get nothing back. Very often in Brazil you don't even get off-prints. This might sound commercial, and it is not considered good form to bring up such matters in academic circles. But if you are in South America you have to. Who discusses their salaries? But in South America you get low salaries, and this makes a considerable difference. Attendance at a congress can be a considerable addition to your salary, whereas for the journal you get no financial incentive. And possibly, one should consider that journals in South America should be encouraged to pay their contributors. This sounds from the United States and European point of view totally crazy, because the professional in the United States and Europe is paid a higher salary, and is expected to publish. But the situation in South America is different, and a strong case could be made for paying contributors. At the very least if you send in a journal article you have to pay a typist, and it is not that cheap on a low salary.

The final problem: If you are working in a South American university, how do you progress academically? Do you do so by publishing papers, or do you do so administratively? One looks around at administrators, and you find that they actually publish very little. They spend their time administrating. Those are the ones who get ahead academically and career-wise. This is very similar to the situation that you have in government, where you have the politicians on one level, who are getting big salaries and getting promoted, and you have at a lower level the specialists who are doing the specialized work and who remain at the lower levels. The same thing occurs in universities. You have the administrators on the higher level, and the research people who publish, on the secondary level. Famous examples in Brazil include very high administrators who have maybe one publication from 1967. As long as this pattern continues, there is less of a stimulus for you to go out and publish.

Marietta Daniels Shepard:

Previously something was mentioned about translations. I almost always go back to the fact that we need more control of the things that have been done. Of course Unesco did help to create a center, I believe in Argentina, for translations into Spanish made by institutions in the Americas, and I wonder to what extent even those who are here notify the center in Argentina of the translations that have been made in their institutions? In our survey I found that Mexico seems to have a more intelligent approach to translations than other countries. They have used the foreign embassies to make translations rather than have members of their own staff do them. The Benjamin Franklin library in Mexico, supported by the United States government, also helps to find out who translators are. In some of the countries of Latin America there are directories of translators, but I don't see that many of them make any attempt to keep track of what has been translated and make this available to other countries in Latin America. I think that that area is one in which there needs to be greater control.

Merline Smith:

I want to comment on the question of payment to authors in journals. No, I don't think that our Scientific Research Council could do so for its journal. We have found it extremely difficult to get articles for the journals. We normally try to issue three a year, and we are reduced to one this year. I really wonder whether an incentive like payment would help us to acquire more articles. Should we try this approach?

Secondly, the question of translation. I find that when we get publications in Spanish, we tend to put them aside. I know facilities are available for translation in Jamaica, but they are extremely exorbitant. But I also feel that the information in these documents would help us in sharing, in a manner, what is happening in Latin America. We have tried to work on this, by having our members of our staff attend Spanish courses, and I think we will get to the point where we will be able to make abstracts of the documents, but it will be a long time before we begin translating entire documents. We think the abstracts will at least help, because the people are interested. It is really a problem for us.

Mary Jane Ruhl:

At the Pan American Health Organization in Washington they are working on the translation of English to Spanish, and they now will begin working on the translation of Spanish to English. It is really working very well. Machine translation has had a lot of bad press over the

years, but they feel that they are able to do machine translation and save about 60–70% of the effort that has to go
into it. They do go back over the work editorially, and they
feel that this is about 30% of the effort that would have
been required. The last I heard, United States AID was
going to be funding the English to Spanish segment of the
work, and that it would be going on over the next several
years.

Victor Rosenberg:

I'm not sure at what level this exists, but I wanted to
bring up the question of the prejudice that exists, particularly among United States journals, about publishing foreign
authors, and the extent to which this is something that
should be dealt with. Even in the United States the whole
context of getting published tends to be to some extent political. I guess about ten or so years ago someone at the
American Psychological Association decided that with the
new technology for publishing, it would be possible to
publish all the papers that were submitted to the Association rather than having this review process to filter out the
papers that did not merit publication. They wanted to
publish all articles as separates, rather than in journals, and
then disseminate them to those individual members who had
indicated an interest in that particular area, so that each
member would receive a customized journal, if you will, of
papers that were submitted. The person that came up with
this idea was summarily dismissed, and the reason is obvious. The editors of the journals wanted to retain the control that they had over what did and did not get published in
these journals. And many of these editors, it seems to me,
are to some extent, prejudiced against publishing anything
from outside the United States, or even outside their particular sphere of interest.

This is, I think, a problem that has to be acknowledged, in terms of access to publication, in the context
of the extent to which Latin American scientists and authors

are choosing to work on projects that, in my opinion, have no other virtue than the possibility of being published. I recall a large number of papers that came out of Brazil at one point on bibliometrics. It seemed to me, and this is my opinion, that in the United States this whole concept, while not entirely a dead issue, had been pretty much exhausted in publication. Yet these papers were coming out in this area primarily because they would have access to publication abroad. They would have virtually no appeal within the country. Maybe I am overemphasizing this point, but I see that sort of thing happening and it's very unfortunate. You have on the one hand the prejudice of the journal editors against publishing anything from Latin America, and you have the corresponding understandable response of Latin American authors of selecting work simply on the basis of its being able to be published abroad. I think it is an unfortunate set of circumstances that is resulting from many of the conditions that we have been discussing.

Thomas McGinn:

I heard a very interesting statement from one of the heads of conservation at the Library of Congress, whom we invited to Caracas about two months ago, who described a technology which would get us around the editors through publishing on demand, via optical disks. We would pull out from the disks what interests us, and there wouldn't be journals in the traditional sense. He said it is only four or five years away, in terms of the ability to do it on a wide scale in the United States. I don't know how much longer it would be for Latin America. In other words we are going to have all our journals in something like a juke box, and we just push a button for which article we want, and that is its publication. You can get it in print form, but you would not be subscribing to a journal in the usual sense. Isn't that what we want? We don't want a lot of those articles necessarily, but the editors want the prestige that is connected with judging what is good and what isn't.

Of course in large research libraries in the past we have always included a lot of materials that are not prestigious and are only for the occasional user. We don't expect a book, or a large number of them, in the Library of Congress to be used more than once or twice in 30 or 40 years. But they have to be in that size of a library. That is true of a lot of publications. But if you are doing a doctoral thesis, you and a few others may be the only ones using certain materials. And they should be available somewhere. I wish that things had been published in my areas of interest that haven't been. Things come out in mimeographed form, and they are very important. I will just come upon them by chance, or through the invisible college. I've talked to someone who is interested in my area, and can share his work with me.

The cost at present of the video disk technology is far too high for the ordinary library at this time, but the librarian from the Library of Congress said that it would be coming down in four or five years so that you would have on optical disk anything that you wanted to put there. Of course it revolutionizes the concept of the traditional print library, and anyone that is tied to that type of operation is going to be in trouble. We will resolve I think a lot of publication problems in terms of what has been described here by Victor Rosenberg.

Tony Bowman:

I'd like to respond to this area of technology. We have put a lot of futures in technology, that technology is going to solve for us things which we are unable to solve now. Somehow or other the technology will resolve it and we don't have to make decisions.

What this entire system suggests is a system that would peel off the very high demand materials, those which have a demand for rapid transmission, those which need to go from concept to almost instantaneous dissemination.

Unfortunately, economic considerations immediately present themselves. The cost, for example, for mastering the disk is extremely high, as is the cost for a retrieval device. And then you have to talk about setting up nodule centers where the article may be reproduced because the nodule center will have to stand some of the costs of reproducing it. Further, we are talking about the possibility of having a technological interface with the machine, either reading the information as a displayed image, or storing the information on optical disk and transmitting it and reproducing it on paper. The costs for these things are absolutely overwhelming. You can spend over a thousand dollars just to master a single article in a quality way. You can spend ten to twenty thousand dollars just for a receiving device on the other end.

It has a parallel, interestingly enough. In 1839 micrographics was developed. It used a screen with a projected image. It is different from a book, in that you can't take it around, it isn't portable. But in terms of costs, we estimate that micrographics will still be competitive well past the year 2000 in terms of full text retrieval. Now there will always be exceptions of titles that are so much in demand that the transmission of them, the timeliness of them, or the high number of copies needed, in itself will satisfy the economics of doing it. Most of the publishers of journals today are looking very closely at the newer technologies. All of our contracts now have an electronic distribution clause. It took from 1839 until 1929 before micrographics was even viable, in spite of the fact that the first document recorded micrographically was a newspaper and librarians quickly saw the opportunity for storage.

I would caution that technology, as exciting and as wonderful as it is, sometimes causes us to put off solving the problems that we could solve in whatever way, and wait for those problems to be solved in the future. And I would submit that several possible outcomes are, that if we don't actively get involved with the problem-solution, that someone else will be the technology controller, and that they will solve it in their way, in their cost effective way, or in their control of information way. We could wake up and find that many of our basic interests have been excluded from that sort of a system.

It comes down to the technology of the book. You can have them in all sizes, colors, shapes, languages, on almost any type of material. They're portable, and you don't even have to have a flat surface to use them on. They're one of the most brilliant systems yet devised, and this is applicable universally. If we lock ourselves into some type of system that deprives us of that universality, I see all these ideas being tamped down into a funnel, and few have access. In some areas it would open the materials up as has been noted previously. It is a double-edged sword. It could bring a lot of good, but the potential for also bringing a lot of very negative things is also there.

Thomas McGinn:

I don't want to be the devil's advocate for the Library of Congress, and I speak from attending the conference and having read a paper, but they don't predict the disappearance of the print form at all. If anything is going to remain widely used it will be print, because the book has to circulate, and the public will need materials through public libraries. Primarily research materials will go into this form. Why *should* such materials be printed? It is more expensive to print them. Why shouldn't it be just available when someone needs it? And that will be the type of material suitable for publication on demand. At least that is the explanation that I heard.

Ching-Chih Chen:

I would like to comment on technology. What I would say to people from developed countries is very different from what I would say to people from developing countries. The video disk has a tremendous capability in that on one single phonographic-type disk we can store 54,000 different images and make reference to them. I think a recent estimate is $100,000 to master a disk, including filming and labor costs. So when we are talking about a Library of Congress-type project we are talking about a multi-million dollar project grant. Right now, it is something for developing countries to think about down the road, but it not something to solve problems today.

We should consider the newer technologies also for bibliographic control, for producing indexing services or producing national serials lists of journals available locally. Think of the uses of microcomputers, which are certainly not far off. In Brazil, for example, home-made microcomputers have tremendous capabilities, and in terms of costs these are accessible. At a recent conference in Israel on microcomputers, it was clear that all the developing countries are looking into that tremendous capability. It is important to consider the newer technologies, but bring the discussion down to areas that are more easily achievable.

Juan Freudenthal:

She stole part of my thunder! But I'm not sure that the video disk is that expensive. The disk contains 54,000 frames on each side, making it 108,000 images in total, and it is being used in museums all over the country today. The Metropolitan Museum of Art has 400,000 slides on four records which can be distributed all over the world. They are just not that expensive any more. This raises the question which I have heard from many of my colleagues. Why shouldn't Latin America leap-frog the whole area of microfilm and go immediately into video disk, which is much more durable and has much more capacity for information storage? That opens another incredible area beyond this Conference. I don't think it is going to be so expensive in the next 10 to 20 years.

Tony Bowman:

Costs will start dropping in 6 years; in 10 years they will be practical in that we will see a lot of them, but there will still be some areas that will be excluded because of the costs and the demand. There are people today using them, such as in records management.

Victor Rosenberg:

I just saw a journal recently that offered a royalty to authors who submitted manuscripts on diskettes for microcomputers, and specified the format. I think that that technology is very close. The advantage of microcomputers is that they are inexpensive enough to be within reach of the developing countries. You might see in João Pessoa that not every professor will have one on his desk, but there will be enough at the university to be available. And so if you send a diskette, what you have immediately is the possibility of publication on demand, not only at a central location but anywhere. If you want to produce a document from that diskette, it would be a simple procedure to run off 100–150 pages from the diskette and produce a printed document. I have often felt that print is still the most valuable way of communicating, but with these diskettes it would be very nice because you can just send the information much more cheaply and have the material printed later.

Something happened recently that convinced me of this. I have for a long time used terminals to computers, at various places, and more recently at home. Recently a friend of mine wrote a program for my microcomputer. He called, and said that the program was finished. I said Fine, can I come over and get it? This was just one place to another in Ann Arbor. And he said No, I'll just send it to you. And so by telephone, he was able to send it from his microcomputer to my microcomputer, and it took only a couple of seconds. I think that it is this sort of thing that will make it possible to have the kind of publishing that we are talking about. Then comes the question of bibliographic control of *that* kind of publication. And I don't want to even try that one.

Ching-Chih Chen:

I'd just like to add to what Victor is saying about sending information back and forth on floppy disks. It certainly is in the mind of many journal editors for submission of articles. Assuming the systems are compatible, they can simply comment on the floppy and send it back. At the meeting in Israel, one of the presenters had his microcomputer with him, from England, and it was compatible with mine. I just asked for a disk with his article on it, and he made one, saving the trouble of photocopying the article and sending it from England.

Commenting on what Juan said about the videodisk, it is certainly true that copies of the disk are indeed inexpensive, at $15–30. But the production costs are incredibly high. If in developing countries, you feel that the copies available from the developed countries are pertinent to you, then so much the better, but I still submit that many things available from the developed countries are not what you want. In that case you would have to take into account the costs to produce your own disks. Economically it is just not feasible right now.

Laurence Hallewell:

I just wanted to raise the question of taxation, an element of the costs of all non-book traditional materials. Librarians interested in the transmission of knowledge have managed to get very many governments to remove books from taxation, but some governments aren't convinced about removing taxation from non-book materials. Britain for example has had no sales tax on books since 1940. Anything else, including time at consulting a databank, is taxed at 15%. Brazil has allowed free import of books since 1957, but any microfilm brought into Brazil is taxed at 135%. I think that there should be some effort toward having non-book materials treated tax-wise the same way as traditional hardcover books.

Victor Rosenberg:

The confusion in this is also massive. Governments are trying to define what is and what is not information.

Marietta Daniels Shepard:

Sometimes this situation derives merely from the fact that governments have enacted legislation to control the import of movies, and they tax everything that is in film form at the same level. It doesn't occur to anyone that there is a difference. Librarians and scholars haven't worked together to bring to the attention of the country that there is a difference there. I know this has prevented microfilm from coming into many countries in Latin America, because of the confusion over the medium itself. Microfilm and microfiche is a technology that is so well developed that we forget that it exists.

Marta Dosa mentioned the technical reports that have been made by technical missions. Frequently only one copy of the report was made and it is lost in someone's files and no one ever knows that it has been done, so the same technical assistance mission was requested of another international organization, which goes in and makes another report on the same thing and that report too is lost. We've had the same problem in OAS. The technical reports get lost in someone's files and no one ever remembers that they were made. We finally began to do something at OAS about this and began to issue a listing of the technical reports. It is a problem of developing a mechanism for extracting from the various offices of the OAS copies of the reports so that they can be reproduced and kept someplace so that if someone asks for a copy of it a microfiche or hard copy can be produced for them. But the mechanism for doing this is something that takes time. Specialists have a tendency to be involved in so many things that they forget to inform anyone and they don't remember where they put the copy of the report when it arrived. I remember that Venezuela was hoping to be able to control all of the technical reports that had been made for the country. I don't know if they were able to do so.

Tony Bowman:

Some weeks ago Dr. Rosenberg and I had the opportunity of sitting down at the *despachante*, the customs broker, in Santos, Brazil, discussing some of these same issues. We originally looked at it from the premise that Marietta suggested, that it was an oversight, and then as we got into it further we found that it was no oversight. In the Brussels nomenclature, they definitely excluded video recordings, microfilms, and microfiche. The problem goes back to some of the original GATT agreements. I suspect that if we could really get a history of all of this we would find that the politics of the commercialization of all of these industries would be a powerful factor. The politics sneak up on you so many times and have such great influence. It is not the technology, it's not the need, it's the way things are structured. Unfortunately that is the way things are for imports. Most countries follow the Brussels trade agreements.

If there are no further comments, I think we have covered the area.

Victor Rosenberg:

We'll reconvene at two o'clock this afternoon to talk about databases.

Tuesday Afternoon, 12 April 1983

*Coverage of Latin American Materials in Major
International Databases. Improving the Inclusion
of Latin American Materials.*

Victor Rosenberg:

At the crossroads between policies of both North and South
America and the technologies that are either making these
policies rapidly obsolete or causing them to change is the
question of bibliographic and other database systems. One
of the subjects that we wanted to deal with at this Conference was what could be done with the problem of the
representation of Latin American research and publication
in the international databases. Murilo Cunha has recently
completed a study of the use of these databases by Brazilian
libraries, and he will be the moderator for this afternoon.

Murilo da Cunha:

We will talk this afternoon about the coverage of
Latin American materials in major international databases,
and how the inclusion of Latin American materials can be
improved.

I prepared two questions for discussion that I think
will be very controversial. In my paper, I noted that the use
of foreign databases by developing countries can satisfy an
information need only in a limited way because of the low
influence of foreign countries and the low proportion of

foreign documents. In order to attract more clients from developing countries, database producers have to change their indexing policy and try to include more documents related to the peculiarities of developing countries. Michel Menou queries, "Why not go to the international marketplace to sell information which is too often acquired for free by the North and resold to the South at $8 per hour?" Marietta mentions the creation of a Latin American database which is conceived of as a database of materials that are published in Latin America and on the region. Another participant, Thomas McGinn, points out that North Americans and Europeans will be doing searches in the Latin American database. So, my first question is, Should Latin Americans try to stimulate the coverage of its materials in major foreign databases or should they try to create a Latino database? What are the advantages and disadvantages of each option?

Victor Rosenberg:

I think that one of the major problems with the first option, in trying to encourage the major databases to provide more coverage of Latin American materials, is that the major databases are almost all commercial ventures, and as such it is only going to be in the interest of those database systems to include Latin American materials if there is a commercial demand for those materials. I think this is going to be a complicating factor in trying to get greater coverage. We did a preliminary study on the coverage in databases of foreign language materials by questionnaire and telephone and one of the directors of a database, *Sociological Abstracts*, wanted me to be aware of the fact that some of his clients, sociologists in the United States, had encouraged him to have less coverage of foreign language materials because they simply clutter up the database with material that they consider of inferior quality. He said that quoting his clients, not that he was in favor of it. He was quite against it. I think there are some serious problems in getting these database systems to include materials from Latin America.

Thomas McGinn:

I'd like to limit an observation to bibliographic materials. Here, I believe that in Venezuela we cannot wait. Even though, for example, OCLC will acquire through its research libraries a lot of Venezuelan materials, (not as many as we get of course), and could in fact reduce our cataloging costs if we tied into it, we feel it is our responsibility to catalog all national publications. On that basis we went ahead, even though we knew we could get this information by waiting two or three years. And that delay is another problem. In the acquisitions process of a research library in the United States it is a year or two for acquisition and another year for cataloging, giving about a two or three year lag compared to our processing. We don't want to wait that long to make the materials available. We get the material immediately, say within a year or two after it's published. And I believe that it is simply the responsibility of the national library to identify and process its own national materials. Hence, our first emphasis was precisely processing these and making them available through a database.

This permitted then, the exchange of tapes with the Library of Congress to our huge benefit, because the Library of Congress sends us the United States national bibliography. They give us 80-90,000 titles per year and we send them our 4-5,000 titles per year if we're lucky, so the benefit is immensely in our favor. But they are interested in this because they would not get that material otherwise. It is beneficial for them because the countries that they do this with are assuring that they have that bibliographic information available in the Library of Congress, and we are not jealous if it is available in other countries. Our benefit is economic, in that we don't have to pay for that part of the MARC database. We can exchange with other countries that are capable of sending information on magnetic tapes. We have found that it is economic for us to do this as long as other national libraries will put it on a national bibliography to national bibliography basis. We get worried when someone wants us to do it on a record for record basis. Then we are at a disadvantage, and we start thinking of just working with Latin American countries to build a Latin American database as best we can, and then from that point negotiate with others. But that hasn't been the case so far, at least with our first exchange.

Armando Sandoval:

Well, I think that the two approaches are correct. They complement each other, they do not exclude each other. The inclusion of our data in the international databases is alright, and the investment in the indexing of our material in other enterprises is also right, so that whatever is made toward the Latin American bibliography is correct. It is a great problem, but it is an editorial problem.

There are figures which show that the Latin American publications are well covered. For example in marine biology, the file centralizes the information system. This a commercial enterprise centralized by FAO, and different from what FAO does for AGRIS. Here it is given to a commercial enterprise. In this field, the Latin American data is straightforward and comprehensive, because our center is the center for the processing of data from marine sciences on fish, and we collect all of it. It is increasing very rapidly. We collect conventional and unconventional publications. They are collected, processed, analyzed, and sent to Rome. In biology, it is similar. We often forget that, as important as it is, *Biological Abstracts* includes only information that comes to its attention. including medicine. So much of medicine is covered in *Biological Abstracts*, for, after all, medicine is just the pathology of the animal Man. And the same happens with *Chemical*

Abstracts. Chemical Abstracts is comprehensive. Some information is not included because no one has detected it. My idea is that we should concentrate on areas that are not covered well by the international databases, because the two approaches do not exclude each other.

Barbara Gumbs:

I would like to inject a somewhat different slant. We have been talking about bibliographic materials, and I would like to move to raw data and information in the wider context. If we look at the commercial databases, there are some which are restricted, and can only be used within the United States. They are prohibited to the developing countries. One of these which stands out in my mind is one containing information on commercial data from developing countries. This type of database is set up for the North American businessman to know what is going on in Third World business and markets. Very often in the Third World countries we are not that well organized to have that type of information readily available to us. But here is information, fed perhaps through the commercial embassies in the countries in which they are established, fed back to the North American database, to be accessed by people in the North American environment. We would like to have access to it, but we cannot.

Then there is another aspect. I think it was the Committee for Central American and Caribbean Action, or the Caribbean and Central American Action Committee, which came through the West Indies with a proposal from Control Data Corporation (CDC) to the business community. They wanted to collect statistics on imports and exports, plans for development reports, commercial ventures, and government forecast planning. They told us that we didn't have all this information organized in our countries, but if we could feed it into the CDC computer in Washington, DC it would be readily accessible to us. But here again there is the other side of the coin. They have something to gain as well. One has to weigh both ends of it. Will the benefit outweigh their having ready access when our information has been openly fed to them?

I was quite impressed by an advertisement in *Development Forum* for a raw data pack, which included information obtained from United Nations specialized agency databanks, and included governmental and institutional documents and extracts of relevant reports and studies, planned and ongoing projects, current investments, loans, and so forth, where and when available. It listed all the different sectors in which you could get this information, and they advised you to get a raw data pack in a Third World country. It's a business proposition. The only advantage for a developing country is that we could write and get one on another developing country. It is quite interesting that the type of information that is in demand in the North is somewhat different from the bibliographic information that is probably cluttering up the databases of the North.

Marta Dosa:

This is a very significant problem, and some countries are trying to deal with it by legislation which comes under the heading of communication/telecommunication policy. This situation is expected to worsen, because, for example, remote sensing satellites can get data from developing countries and the country might not even know that crops were destroyed from some natural disaster, but the data from the satellite can be fed to international markets, and the country suffer from economic damage without people knowing it. This is a very serious development for developing countries. It results in a controversy in transborder data flow. Countries such as France and those in Scandinavia already have legislated protective measures, but the United States and some other industrialized countries respond that this is an attempt to erect barriers to the free flow of information. But such free flow of information is beneficial to these industrial countries and quite harmful to the developing countries.

Barbara Gumbs:

I'd just like to add one more thing to my description of the raw-data pack. Some of the types of unconventional reports that are being advertised as being readily available are among the types of material we were talking about yesterday that we find hard to come by within our own countries. Maybe if the United Nations agencies got hold of this type of material then maybe we could plug into the system somewhere to get our hands on it.

Merline Smith:

I think both systems are complementary. I think that at the national level, especially in countries that have organized information networks, there should be databases. For one thing, you can have quicker access to information available locally, and this would save unnecessary expenditure for accessing overseas databases. I think the local information can be input here, into the overseas databases. In a country like Jamaica, where we have broken down our information into various networks based on subjects, such as our science and technology information network, we really should have a database of all of this available information. I feel that this information in a database would be more adequate to deal with the needs of the country. And so, I think we should have both national and international databases. And at some point we should have regional input.

Maria Oyarzun de Ferreira:

Nosotros en Chile estamos trabajando en el desarrollo de un sistema nacional de información estructurado en base a subsistemas por sector y pensamos que es la responsibilidad de cada sector el detectar la información que se genera en el país, tanto la publicidad a traves de revistas o libros como principalmente toda la información no convencional que es la mas difícil de registrar. Pensamos que cada subsistema debiera generar su propia base de datos incluyendo costo y material, y una vez procesado e incluido en una base de datos pueda ser intercambiable con unos systemas en otros paises que hemos avanzado en unos sectores, en otros no todavía, pero algo estamos haciendo. Ahora, hay otro tipo de información que nosotros pensamos que es responsibilidad del centro nacional coordinado que es CONICYT. Por ejemplo, las investigaciones científicas todas las ejecuta el CONICYT, para todo aspecto científico y tecnológico. Y cuando un sector lo requiere se saca dicha base de datos que ya está desarrollada y funcionando, se saca el sector que se necesite. Por ejemplo simplemente nosotros recientemente hemos sacado todo lo del sector de educación y se lo entregamos separado.

También pensamos que no solamente es necesario desarrollar la parte bibliográfica sino tambien la parte de datos. Y es así como en algunos sectores, por ejemplo en agronomía, es una parte agrícola y está funcionando una base de datos con información de dato numérico, de las estádísticas o lo que está pasando en el sector agrícola. Y lo mismo está sucediendo y se está desarrollando en el sector de educación. Nosotros pensamos que trabajando en todos los sectores podremos algun dia controlar la información nacional que podrá ser de una forma compartida, intercambiada con otros países. Lo que es importante es que estos sectores están determinados por las areas de desarrollo.

Juan Freudenthal:

Briefly, what my colleague has said is that Chile is working toward an information system which, to a great extent, is already there. They have decided to divide this among sectors such as education and agronomy, and they are going to ask each of the sectors to work on their own to gather the information. Once this has been done, they hope to plug all of this into international databases. They are working in layers and steps. The two that are working now are in education and agronomy.

These sectors are in line with a plan for development for the country. This plan has determined the sectors or subject fields.

Ximena Felíu:

In the national development plan, there are certain sectors that are priority sectors. These are the first to be developed. They include agriculture, health, education, housing, and planning.

Victor Rosenberg:

Are there any regional Latin American databases in operation?

Ximena Felíu:

Yes, through ECLA. They are building a planning information system, which is regional. We have a regional database in ECLA in Chile. The information system is compatible with AGRIS, INIS, and all the international databases. We can operate with all the worksheets and manuals.

Marta Dosa:

Is this the planning database which was originally DEVSIS, the IDRC-planned database which was originally an international database and changed to a regional approach? The African equivalent is slowly developing in Ethiopia.

Ximena Felíu:

I should say that INFOPLAN is a sector of the DEV-SIS program.

Cavan McCarthy:

I think that we are coming to a hybrid situation in which we have a few large international databases, and in the countries themselves we have a variety of smaller databases. I think this is the only solution which is politically acceptable to both sides. I think it is the solution which is the best for the developing countries because they can have their own systems which are responsive to the needs of smaller industries. Of the international systems I think there are very strong advantages for AGRIS-and INIS-type systems because they get out and meet the librarians, especially AGRIS which has had an incredible impact in Brazil. All over Brazil people have been trained to input into AGRIS, in their forms and procedures. In their own institutions, when they see relevant literature they complete the AGRIS forms and send them in, and they have contact with AGRIS. In France, in Grenoble, they did a sample survey of all the databases they could and they asked them similar questions about the database content in relation to Latin America. They assembled the information, and evaluated the printouts. I thought this was marvelous. Why is it just the French who do this type of content evaluation as relating to Latin America?

Winthrop Wiltshire:

The information community in our countries of Latin America and the Caribbean are very concerned about databases, and when we talk about databases it appears that we are focusing exclusively on automated databases. There is a notion that has become prevalent that, unless you can establish an automated database you have nothing. I think we must be careful to keep our feet on the ground and recognize that there is a lot that can be done with manual databases, in recognizing a need, recognizing that we can still collect materials and classify, catalog and index them by traditional methods. We need not think for instance because it might be easier to have telecommunications access to North America, that we need to put the data into their computers for us to have access to the it. I think we have to be extremely careful about that.

Victor Rosenberg:

To what extent is the translation of indexes to the major international databases going on? The French translated the index to the INIS system. I think it is extremely important, if it is possible, to make the access to the databases easier. In Brazil, they are leasing the tapes to the databases rather than providing access directly online. But if in addition to that they could translate the indexes into Portuguese, this would be an enormous aid to retrieving the information.

Armando Sandoval:

You said you are surprised to see how disoriented we are in our countries, to the point that we believe that nothing can be done without the computer. This of course is wrong. We have to have a database in order to compete. We have printed indexes which the students can consult, but now they have terminals, and want the information that way. They think that is the only reliable information. That is our reality. It is a real problem to demonstrate that that is not correct. We have a reference library at the university, which subscribes to more than 200 indexing and abstracting services, but they prefer the very expensive online services.

I would like to explain what we are doing.

In Mexico we have been attending this kind of meeting for over a half a century. What I have learned is that there has been a great preoccupation for learning what Latin Americans publish from their research. There is a need therefore to index our journals. These themes have been repeated many times. So we said, let's find out what Latin Americans publish in foreign journals, and index the Latin American work.

Well, when our Center was founded at the University 12 years ago, we wanted to follow these recommendations, and we began some experiments. The first experiment was to begin compiling the only available data on articles in foreign journals written by Latin Americans. So, the *Bibliografía latinoamericana* was born. It was compiled manually from *Current Contents*. Why? Because no matter how incomplete *Current Contents* is, it is easily available and at hand. It avoids going to all the other hundreds of printed databases. And, it is current. The *Bibliografía latinoamericana* was started in 1974 as an information package with 10 sections that we distributed free in the University. The first section was the basic bibliography, with a keyword-out-of-context index, of the material in about 2,000 journals which were being received by the campus. But it didn't work. People weren't interested. At all. So we had to discontinue the service after a short while. But when the information package was discontinued, we realized that we couldn't stop the compilation of the bibliography and so we decided to publish it separately.

The *Bibliografía latinoamericana* is now published twice a year. The first section is the bibliography, each item with its own accession number. The second section is the author index. The third section is the institutional index, which gives us a "who's publishing in Latin America" review. Then there is a subject index, and a KWIC index, in which it is very easy to see the subjects in which Latin Americans are interested in for their research. We feel that the publication is a real contribution to Latin American research, because it identifies 3500 papers that are published, which are the best of Latin American research. You can see the different contributions of different countries. There have been few changes in the last ten years. Brazil is still in first place. You can see that Brazil is becoming much more interested in physics. All of Latin America is interested in medicine.

After about ten years, we realized that the research by our university in social sciences was very important, and was not being covered by any indexing service inside or outside of Mexico, so we decided to index the social science and economic literature. We started the *Citas Latinoamericanas en Socioeconomia, Economia,* and now also *Humanidades.* The bibliography is quarterly. We have mentioned the importance of education for Latin America, and there are numerous relevant articles indicated here. In spite of the fact that it is incomplete, it does gather the scattered literature together. The second part is the keyword section, to find subjects and countries of publication. Ecuador writes much on education. Then you have something new for Latin America, a citation index, which includes all the references that were included in the articles. This is an experiment, but we will discontinue it soon. Then there is the author section and institution section.

After two years, we began thinking of doing something similar for the scientific journals of Mexico. The National Council for Science and Technology came to us and asked why we published *Citas* and nothing on science and technology. We explained that we had no resources to do it. But, we said why not, and started the project. In 1978 we started to work with the science and technology periodicals. But we found it was not easy. It has also the keyword sections in Spanish and English, the author section, the institution section. This is also quarterly.

Each has its own problems. Now we are beginning to make them compatible and all of them will follow the program of the science bibliography. They are all printed by the computer, but the last is the best-handled. We are using programming from the Latin American Center for Data Processing. We are sure we are covering more Latin American medical materials than *Index Medicus*.

These may not be complete, but this is the only place you can find this information gathered together. Eventually we hope to go on line.

Murilo da Cunha:

This is very interesting especially for us, because it is difficult to have access to Cuban publications in Brazil, as well as many other countries.

Juan Freudenthal:

I wonder, how many institutions in Latin America are using the bibliographies? And, after we have whetted the appetite of our users with such a tool, are we also able to have access to the materials?

Tony Bowman:

We at UMI are using it, because our interests fall precisely in this area. We are currently building a table by subject area of the titles that are indexed here, plus in other indexing services, plus those that we hold, available in microform. In my travels I have not seen many copies of that index or of HAPI. I don't know whether it is a matter of marketing or budget restrictions.

Victor Rosenberg:

I am curious to know to what extent this is distributed to North America, to the United States and Canada, and to what extent to other countries in Latin America?

Armando Sandoval:

This is an effort made possible by the National University. It has no other support. Many of the journals are bought just for this project.

Victor Rosenberg:

Is the effort self-sustaining yet? Are the sales of the indexes covering the cost of publication?

Armando Sandoval:

No. We have no time for marketing, and frankly we don't know how to. The National University of Mexico claims to be (and I don't know whether this is true or not) the first private publisher in Latin America.

Juan Freudenthal:

We compile these wonderful tools, and then don't distribute them. They are totally lost treasures.

Victor Rosenberg:

Maybe UMI will pick it up as part of its product line.

Tony Bowman:

We're going to talk!

Murilo da Cunha:

Last year I talked with Eugene Garfield, and complained about the number of Brazilian journals covered by the Institute for Scientific Information. At that time there were only three. He told me that Spain was going to sign a contract with the Institute, to pay them to increase the number of Spanish journals indexed. Sure, in a few years, if you did a bibliometric study, you would find that the number of Spanish journals cited by authors had increased, but despite this fact, it is a very good publication that you have developed.

Marietta Daniels Shepard:

I think one of the problems is that in only recent years there have been reference services in the libraries of Latin America. There are still not too many reference books as such in the Spanish and Portuguese languages, and librarians are not really used to doing reference work. In previous years they have been more concerned with services like cataloging rather than about giving any service to the reader. After all they did have a large collection of materials to try to organize so they could be made available. So there is not the tradition. of even librarians using reference books, much less the researchers. Since the researchers have never really had any indexes to periodicals available to use, they haven't used the periodicals, and the librarians perhaps feel that the costs of the indexes from Mexico are rather exorbitant, considering that they don't have much of a budget anyway for materials. So, they just don't buy them. I think it is going to take quite a marketing process plus training of librarians throughout Latin America to use reference materials and to use periodical indexes and so on.

On the other hand, in our survey of library and information systems in Latin America, we sent to the countries several lists of databases and information systems, among them information systems which they could use free from international agencies, particularly those of the United Nations family, and most of them said that if they used these systems, they used primarily the printed versions rather than the online version. I think also this lack of tradition of using reference material is one of the reasons that the students are much more happy about going to an automated database, because they have never used the print versions, and if they have to use it volume by volume they won't.

Marta Dosa:

I believe that we touched upon a problem emerging in education, whether we are talking about education in graduate schools of library and information science or continuing education courses. I think when the databases entered the library world, then graduate programs set up courses in online searching in addition to the traditional reference courses. There are also refresher courses in developing countries where many times we are invited to several schools to set up workshops. What I have observed is that the coverage of the reference courses and the online courses are usually separate, taught by different people, and the subject reference courses such as social science or science reference are not training for database searches because that is done in a separate course. Yet online searching teachers do not teach the combination strategies of searching manual indexes and database searching, and the ideal is using both. But that is simply not happening. It is a problem especially in the developing countries when they specifically request online training, and the best strategy is using both.

Cavan McCarthy:

I wanted to talk a little bit about indexing and education. Automated indexing in Latin America is often quite difficult, because the titles of the articles are very often nonspecific, and automated indexing doesn't always work. You also have the problem of language. You have to work with articles in Portuguese, in Spanish, and in English. Now if you try to shove that into a KWIC index, you get a literal mess. It does not work. So, you have to go into intellectual indexing. Now if you do that, you find a major problem in that the librarians themselves are not in any way prepared for intellectual indexing. They are not trained in indexing in library school. In the indexing course, they show them what a KWIC is and a UNITERM system, but they don't actually train them in indexing articles. And in the classification courses often the student is given a list of subjects such as production of cars in the 1930's in the Michigan area of the United States, and you are asked to find the UDC number for that subject, like a crossword puzzle. But you do not actually analyze documents for their content. So when you begin to index, and you have to analyze an article for its content, you have no experience in doing it. This is something I think you have to get out of setting up an index and doing some intellectual indexing with the help of the computer.

Last week we had a man from Grenoble visit, and he mentioned a thesaurus that they were having translated into Spanish in Peru. He wanted to know if I would like to help translate it into Portuguese. It was a nice offer, but there are all kinds of problems with it. It is a translation — how do you present that as a research project to the university? You have to work with someone who knows a lot of French, and it means basically sitting in an office. If you have a research project, you go out and talk to a lot of interesting people, maybe you even get a bus ticket or airline ticket to another city. Translating a thesaurus is just not very interesting. I think translation of thesaurii is very important and we should put it in our recommendations, but I think that we should add that it should be financially supported. And I think you have to give it a fairly high level of financial support in order to encourage and stimulate people to do jobs as essential and as boring as translating thesaurii.

Laurence Hallewell:

On the subject of library education, I should have thought that the obvious thing was to have people work on the database where a source exists both online and in hard copy as a part of the same project. Through this, they can see the respective advantages. For instance, if you are working with the hard copy you can see adjacent material that would not come up on the normal mechanical search. This throws out something I did myself, using *LISA* and *Library Literature*, which impressed me with how far the national origins of even the so-called international indexes is important. The American bias of *Library Literature* and the British bias of *LISA* is very evident, if you actually start counting up what you are getting from where.

Thomas McGinn:

I would like to ask a question of the group. Dr. Sandoval obviously planned his index so it could be printed, and Dr. McCarthy the first day mentioned how important it is to be able to print from a database. My impression is that there is a tendency in databases not to have a print capacity. In Latin America this is extremely important, because Latin America has never had sufficient printed reference sources traditionally, especially at the national level. We don't have sufficient guides, directories and so forth. But now there are databases, and many times these are not designed to be printed, and so they are limited to use where the database is because we don't have remote access. I wanted to express this concern for any automation planning that is underway, and to encourage a print capacity, because a huge number of reference works which usually would be printed are in databases, and we are never going to get the printed works, which are still a necessity in many areas.

Victor Rosenberg:

The databases in the United States have this problem, in that they are designed to be accessed online. There is a big difference physically between accessing a database through a window of a video terminal, and having something that you can thumb through rapidly. What you find is that everyone is so enamoured by automation that they are completely forgetting the print capacity. I see this time and time again, that personal systems and large systems of all types are designed forgetting about the fact that print is still the preferred method of access for almost everyone. And there is a severe limitation on these systems. It is so frustrating when you have to wait each time a line appears on the screen, rather than being able to go directly to the place that you want, with the book. This again is not uniquely Latin American.

Winthrop Wiltshire:

I want to make a more general point. Computers are extremely important and they have an important role, but in relation to what Victor was saying, we in the information community have to be extremely careful to insure that whenever we introduce a new technology, whether we are talking about computers or lasers, we develop internal mechanisms to almost guarantee that we don't exclude a large number of users of the existing systems, and that we establish intermediary mechanisms if you will, to link to those categories of users that might be automatically excluded just because we introduce the new technology.

Ching-Chih Chen:

I think it is very important to sort out what benefit we hope to get out of a machine-readable database. I think that a lot of databases started out not for online access, but for a printed index. *Index Medicus*, for example, started the Medline database. The online version of *Chemical Abstracts* came a long time after the printed version. The printed indexing and abstracting services certainly have the convenience of flipping pages, and so on, on the other hand online searching allows us to combine multiple subject terms very quickly. Therefore I think the important thing is to learn when it is the right time to use the manual tool, and when it is right to use the online file.

On library education and database use, I want to inject some of our 'experience at Simmons. Juan is teaching a reference course with an online component. Database searching has been in a separate course from reference because in the beginning, not that many faculty seemed to feel comfortable in teaching that subject to students immediately and extensively. Somehow the users or students coming to take those courses had a similar feeling as well, as if there was a great mystique in searching online databases. Once we get into it we knew that it is very simple, involving just a little Boolean logic. So now, we have incorporated online searching into every reference-related course. We strictly looked at databases as one type of information source, rather than an exclusive or higher-class type. There is no such thing. We teach our students very clearly that when you need to use the manual index, don't go to the database, but when you have a need to go to a database then you should use it. When you need background information, you go to an encyclopedia, when you want a concise definition you go to a dictionary.

For developing countries, it is very important to not have this kind of vision blur the use of the databases.

Murilo da Cunha:

Merline Smith pointed out in her paper that one of the problems with the information industry is its concentration in the Northern markets, and the information needs and problems of the Southern countries are not necessarily taken into consideration. She points out that the experience of undeveloped countries is often more relevant to the needs of the other developed countries than is the experience of the Northern countries. Maria Oyarzun points out that information produced by the industrialized countries is produced as any other good, without taking into consideration the problems and needs of the developing countries. Winthrop Wiltshire points out that many of the specific interests of the region are of marginal concern to databases produced in

North America and other industrialized countries. Armando Sandoval mentioned that south of the border, the flow of information other than North to South is unthinkable. Cavan McCarthy mentioned that it is extremely important for North America that Latin America remain within its market, with the technological patterns established in Chicago or California. To achieve this, there is nothing better than the export of technological information to Latin America.

My question for the group is this. Is it possible to have a flow of information South to North? Should we increase the coverage of Latin American materials in databases produced by industrialized countries, or should we increase the coverage of Latin American materials in cooperative efforts such as AGRIS and INIS?

Marietta Daniels Shepard:

At a meeting of SALALM about two years ago, one of the professors of Latin American studies at Princeton University produced a printout of the databases that are used at Princeton in courses on Latin American studies, and certainly one of the problems that they were having was getting additional databases from Latin America. Many of them they found very difficult to use because the documentation on the databases was totally lacking. This is another one of the problems in trying to get the flow of information from Latin America to North America—the lack of documentation on how the database is set up and can be accessed.

Murilo da Cunha:

I include this question because I remember the case of Iran and the American Embassy months ago. At that time all American goods were prohibited for export to that country, and one good was information. Iran has a regional library in Teheran to provide information to countries close to it, and they stopped sending MEDLARS tapes for a while.

Victor Rosenberg:

I once had an opportunity to ask the Director of the National Library of Medicine about that, and he indicated that the flow of the tapes was stopped not by the United States but by Iran. They were perfectly free to continue to get them. It doesn't make the issue any less important, but it just so happens that in this particular case that was not what occurred. I then asked if the information on the MED-LINE tapes or, access to them, should be used for political purposes, and he said he certainly wouldn't rule that out, they may have been and they may be, but they weren't in this case.

Winthrop Wiltshire:

There can be no question that our priority has to be building up databases in our own countries, and putting our own houses in order. Only on a secondary basis can we begin to think in terms of what we need to do in relation to inputting into databases in industrialized countries.

Cavan McCarthy:

Would Winthrop make an exception for AGRIS and INIS?

Winthrop Wiltshire:

When I was talking about putting our houses in order, whether on a national or international basis, I was saying we should not spend lots of energy figuring out how we could put our data into United States databases, for instance.

Alma Jordan:

I think we need to develop our local capacities. There is no question about this. It seems to me that the volume of material that is of interest in the local context is going to grow, and the need is going to get greater for more local information. There seems to me to be no doubt really as to what we need in the region.

I wanted to comment on the sectoral point, because I think that the way of the future is towards sectoral databases at the world or regional level, and the two must be compatible. Our needs are locally must be satisfied, but that is not to say that we do not take an interest in, and participate in, world movements and centers. There are some sectors where it doesn't matter as much and some where it does. So I think we must be flexible enough to relate to each of these as we need to. Input into AGRIS is available to us. If we want to pull out from the tapes the geographic areas, we can still get our own database from AGRIS. That doesn't stop it from being in AGRINDEX.

Victor Rosenberg:

In the interest of the American compulsion for time, I'm going to call a halt to the discussion. However I think this is an important area to consider. I've talked to our moderator for tomorrow morning, and we will continue this discussion then. We adjourn for our tour of and reception at UMI.

Wednesday Morning, 13 April 1983

Potential National Library Networks. Links to Networks in North and South America. Dependency and Interdependency in Information Flows

Victor Rosenberg:

Just as we were getting going yesterday afternoon we had to stop. I've spoken to yesterday's moderator and because the topics are so intertwined, Murilo da Cunha and Thomas McGinn have agreed that we would this morning integrate the topic of databases, particularly those issues that Murilo posed about national databases versus participation in international databases, with the issue of dependency and interdependency in library networks. Tom will moderate the first part of the program, and then we will include the topics we were dealing with yesterday.

Thomas McGinn:

I would like to defer to Murilo when we get to the topic of dependency and interdependency, because his paper reflected a lot of thought about that. I thought it would also be useful to consider the topic of potential national and regional library networks. We can see what the situation is by comparing our experiences, in order to examine the question of how dependent we are and to what extent we are going to continue in dependency, or to what extent we can overcome the dependency which everyone recognizes exists.

Both themes are so interrelated that we don't want to separate them totally.

Many of the participants have dealt with the question of library networks without addressing it as such in our discussions. The question has come up in terms of isolation of institutions or parts of a system. I think we can find types of isolation that exist between segments of a network.

Perhaps the term network is too precise. At least my computer scientist friends usually don't like the way I use network. For them a network exists only when you have two or more computers in a system which are interconnected and there is a flow of information between the computers. I use the term network for any sort of interinstitutional organized sharing of information, which is a very general approach, but I think which is functional when we look at library information systems on a national level. Perhaps information infrastructure would be a better term to use in our analysis. Merline Smith in her paper offers, "Information infrastructure connotes that complex of institutions, organizations, resources, systems, and services, which support the flow and delivery of information from the generator, including its acquisition, processing, repackaging, and transfer." She immediately jumps to the notion of a national network. "Such an arrangement will ensure that all the available information in a country will be so organized that potential users, by a sensitization program, will know what is available, and where, and the terms and conditions of use." So we have here an information system, which is perhaps a better and more useful term, for looking at what we are after.

I think many of the papers have pointed out problems with the information infrastructure in their country. We have various types of isolation which have been pointed out. The first type is institutional isolation, that is lack of cooperation between institutions, resulting in repetition of the same work of indexing, cataloging, and information retrieval. That was identified by the group on Monday. If we take the the question of obtaining information, Barbara Gumbs says in her paper, "In a recent preliminary study on information and communication flow in science and technology, several categories of information were identified as difficult to acquire by professionals and researchers in the Caribbean." On close examination of this, about 50% could have been processed by information units in the region. So here we have delineated a problem of isolation of the researcher, and seemingly of the institution, not knowing what is available in the region. The search was made in databases in the North, when the needs could have been satisfied locally. This seems to be a result of institutional isolation, or at least inability of the researcher, or perhaps of the reference division of the information service to identify what's available in the area.

I think a second type of isolation has been well pointed out in several papers, for example that by Murilo da Cunha, when he cites Cavan McCarthy, in describing the isolation of one form of information processing and retrieval from others which are complementary. He says "McCarthy wrote that we need databases as well as reference books, journals of current contents, abstracts and indexes, we need information centers in the corporations and research institutions, libraries and universities and schools, and books in the hands of the people. Within this general picture the prospects for databases will be brilliant, but if treated in isolation they can never reach their true potential." This is the problem that Murilo treats in general, that is, automating without having a sufficiently organized system at hand.

In other words, if we bring the computer in without having a system functioning, we don't improve anything. Of course any serious feasibility study is going to look at the manual system first, and try to correct its deficiencies. There will be gaps very often, even within one institution.

If we take this in an inter-institutional context, it happens in many cases that the documentation center can find in the international databases all the documents but is not able to deliver the document, or the document is at such a distance, as Dr. Sandoval pointed out, for instance within Latin America it might be difficult to get it in time. We might automate but retain a dependency in terms of document delivery. This is a question of isolation of one type of information processing, the identification of materials, from document delivery, which is another function of a system. This type of isolation is not necessarily institutional. There is one aspect of the system which is essential but is lacking, or is not functioning well.

A third type of isolation comes within automation, and is a serious problem I think. This is that we have the incompatibility of hardware and/or software. This has been a problem not only in developing countries, as you may well know. I think one very interesting case is the question of ISIS or MIN-ISIS and MARC, which are widely used in the developing countries. MIN-ISIS was developed for Unesco. It is a very fine system, inexpensive, and quite easy to implement as I understand, but it's not compatible with MARC. Now, dozens of MIN-ISIS systems are given by Unesco free to developing countries each year. They're good for setting up a documentation center. However if that center is processing materials with MIN-ISIS they are not compatible with MARC, which has millions and millions of bibliographic records, and is used by the national libraries of the major developed countries. The MARC format also exists widely in the developing countries. This problem was identified by a Mexican group in 1980. Here we have then a question of incompatibility which is a form of isolation within automated systems, which we must try to avoid. Parenthetically, this problem has been resolved recently. The international MARC study committee, which functions under the committee of directors of national libraries, has found the money to make MIN-ISIS compatible with MARC, and this is being done in Canada under the Canadian National Library.

This type of isolation reflects sometimes the pride and talent of programmers. I'm not certain that this happened in this case. But I know of cases where the programmer loves to set up his system, and he's not worried about any others. He can set up a beautiful system for his institution, for instance, to produce a catalog card, which fulfilled all the international standards, but was not in MARC. His institution can do well enough, but it looses all the advantages of using MARC tapes, communication with other institutions, and transfer of information in automated form, with other institutions which predominantly use MARC. MARC is *the* format for dealing with bibliographic data. The avoidance of these problems requires some planning. The group can reflect on how we can plan to avoid these problems. Some sort of cooperation is needed before major decisions are made. The planning question brings up how we can cooperate on a national level, because many national institutions are isolated from each other.

There is a tradition in Latin America of university autonomy. For example, universities in Venezuela have a board, but each one is not bound by the decisions of that board. The University Council does what it decides, and the board simply tries to coordinate them. So we have political problems which we have to take, I think, seriously.

I think that the first major step is to look at national library networks. We can't take steps internationally without some sort of national coordination. How do you go about setting up inter-institutional collaboration or the planning process which requires a certain amount of standardization of processes, of formats for example, whether the system be manual or automated? I think we might look at it from two directions, one we might call top-down, in which you have a national information superstructure, and the other one which I would call bottom-up, in which as the result of the cooperation of two or three institutions, or at the initiation of professional groups, you try to get a plan approved from above. This often happens among librarians and information scientists, who get together knowing the advantages of cooperation much better than the administrators in the government.

The Venezuelan case has both aspects. There was set up a national information superstructure or system, in which we had Unesco's advice through its NATIS program. In this you plan in general national planning to have a national information system, which is to be supported by the executive in terms of funding and so on. But in fact, one part of that system functioned fantastically better than the rest. When you look at what happened, it was from one part that the system came and not from the others. So imposing the superstructure, even within the official planning of the country, did not cause any movement at the lower levels. Often what happens I think is that we can have a superstructure approved, even by legislation, but the dynamics down below are not there. This is a question of personnel, and how much cooperation there is between the professional associations. Not only among librarians, but among computer scientists and librarians and a lot of other people who make decisions about librarians who are not in the profession.

I'd just like to throw out these problems to you. I'm concerned personally that the problem of dependency can be resolved only in terms of developing national networks first, and then cooperation between national networks. We have certain networks which are sufficiently developed that they can think of cooperation within the region.

The second point that I would like for us to address briefly (we have some important resource people here) is the technology for networking. We defended manual practices yesterday, and I agree that they are not to be distained. However I question whether manually organized networks are adequate these days, if you want to avoid the question of dependence. People want access to the databases, which are fantastically powerful compared to any manual catalog that has been developed. Can you imagine comparing OCLC's database or the Lockheed databases with anything that has been developed manually in terms of their power? We have to face the fact of what has happened in the world. If we stay outside of that system, we remain weak and dependent. So I think that networks, meeting the world situation, require automation at some level. We need not have online access, but we must be working with machine-readable data.

Manual transmission of information requires the mails. Are the mail systems in our countries adequate to maintain that function? Interlibrary loan has never functioned or never really been tried in Venezuela. The mails don't work that is well, and that one reason, but is not the only reason, interlibrary loan is not used.

If we look into automated systems, obviously shared cataloging is easier. Shared cataloging is possible in a manual system, but is much easier, more rapid, and efficient in an automated system. This has been proved in industrialized countries. Pooled databases are much easier to attain in an automated environment. I don't know what manual system has attempted to pool manual data. There are still problems in automated systems in developing countries, although instead of the mail system you have problems with the telephone system. If you don't have dedicated telephone lines between the major cities in the country you have similar limitations. These can be gotten around by exchanging tapes, but that is still more efficient than transferring information manually between institutions.

To take another Venezuelan case, we have been unable to get a dedicated line between Maracaibo and Caracas. The national library has had an agreement with Universidad Nacional del Zulia in Maracaibo for the last three years. Everything is set for the dedicated telephone line for them to tie into our computer. Note that the private airline has a dedicated phone line to make reservations at the airport there. The technology is there, but we can't get the priority. The government clearly sees the need for making airline reservations when its executives go to Maracaibo, but we have to convince them of the priority in our area.

We also have I think people who can help us here on the question of the cost of equipment when we automate. We have many information centers, centers which can be extremely important, but they are isolated geographically by being in a small city. How do we tie them into the system, especially if we need a mainframe computer, and their budget is all tied up or they don't have that level of budget? How can we help them in the technical area even if they are interested? Many are interested in tying into a national database. Let us suppose that we are not in an online situation. For example, what can we do with a minicomputer or microcomputer to get the information of a research library into a national database?

Another theme is links to networks in North and South American. Many people, such as Winthrop Wiltshire, Murilo da Cunha, Cavan McCarthy, and Barbara Gumbs, have mentioned a variety of points related to links to networks in North America. Economically it is often a drain on resources. The databases in North America are too profit-motivated, too expensive for us. There is problem of hard currency payment problems, as Barbara Gumbs mentioned. There is high cost of telecommunications, as Winthrop Wiltshire mentioned, except for the case of Mexico and perhaps the Caribbean which have Tymnet. Much of the information in these databases is not relevant to developing country needs, or they don't have the information that these countries do need. Much information is classified for national use within the country and not available outside the country, as Barbara mentioned. Could a major amount of

the developing country needs be met by developing cooperative national and regional databases?

Here we come to the question of tying into a regional
database, a Latin American database. This would not exclude us from using the others, but it would put us into a
different position. Barbara Gumbs in her paper says, "yes,
definitely." Merline Smith says "not only possible, but essential for development." Murilo da Cunha, in his exposition
on the Brazilian organization that deals with getting periodical article copies, says "yes it is functional and can work."
In dealing with planning literature, Ximena Felíu says
"definitely yes, it does function in certain sectors." We have
a description by Marietta Daniels Shepard and others of the
agricultural network in Latin America which is functioning,
and the medical network in Bahia, which is functioning well
and was mentioned by Dr. Sandoval. So we do have examples of functioning networks in the area, but we do not
have anything like the pooling of national databases. I think
this is the direction in which we have to go, as several of
you mentioned, in various papers. So what mechanisms can
be worked out for achieving these pooled databases in the
region? Let me mention that the national library networks
have to be developed. Where they exist to a certain extent,
how much can we move toward the question of the Latin
American database?

Let's begin with, How do we go about organizing the
network, or how do we go about improving the inter-
institutional cooperation which presently exists?

Beatriz de Carvalho:

You were talking about how networks could be
developed. I can give an example of an experience in Brazil,
where not being able to have a completely online network,
they developed alternatives. In Rio, a system was developed
called CALCO, which is the Brazilian MARC. It is a new
system, and there are only six libraries included in the net-

work. One of the libraries is not located in Rio, it is located in Pernambuco, a state a thousand miles north of Rio. Right now there is another library in Brasilia, dealing with the contracts to be included in the network. The system couldn't be online. We have problems with the telephone lines in Brazil, not only among the cities but within the cities. It is not very easy to have a terminal linked to a computer in Rio. Of course, one of the aims of the system is to not duplicate cataloging. So without an online system, how can libraries in the system know what has already been done? Through microfiche produced by the COM system. A data processing center regularly produces microfiche with records of the holdings of the whole network, so everyone searching the microfiche can know what has been cataloged. The microfiche are sent to Recife in Pernambuco and Brasilia and can be sent anywhere. This is just an example of how we could solve the problem of not duplicating cataloging, without online access to the records.

Marietta Daniels Shepard:

This system is also used by Librunam in Mexico. They produce microfiche catalogs that they provide to all university libraries in Mexico.

Merline Smith:

I would just like to share with you the Jamaican experience of trying to develop a national information system. Here I'm going to refer to our "Plan for a National Documentation Information and Library System." This was developed in 1978, by the National Council of Libraries, Archives and Documentation Services. This is the Council that also operates the office of the planning system. We discovered that we had a lot of the problems that have been mentioned earlier. We had a problem of isolation. We didn't know what was where and who was doing what.

First of all we did a survey of the information units on the island, and we broke them down into subject areas. We had assistance from Unesco in developing the plan, and Dorothy Collins spent some time with us. We broke down our information units into subjects. We had a socio-economic network, which is a very functional network now, and we have a science and technology information network which has developed lately, and we have the legal aspects, and we have what is called physical planning. In my paper I say that the aim is to have a centralized system of the holdings of the information units on the island. Each focal point will operate switching and reference services, with the overall national coordination done by the national library, which is established as such by law. This system lends itself to cooperative acquisition, it deals with duplication and it inhibits unnecessary expenditure of scarce foreign exchange, because by means of very strong interlibrary cooperation it is not necessary for units to duplicate purchases. Foreign exchange has always been a problem in our situation.

Now, I'd like to deal with the science and technology information network. The Scientific Research Council, which is the organization that I work with, is the focal point for the network. We are now coordinating the activities of about 40 libraries, and this number is growing. We started by identifying first of all the libraries in the public sector. But now we find that there are some very valuable collections in the private sector, especially in the areas of applied sciences. We think we should be able to access them. So we are asking these people to make their information available. We have started a union list of serials available on the island, and to date we have about 4,000 titles. We are about to print out our list, and it should be available in about two months. We're hoping that when this is out, other people will join us. We are also hoping to have a union catalog of monographs. We are working very hard to develop a mechanism to get this done. We sent out a survey of the scientific and technological research activities on the island, and hope to have directories of them. We have developed directories of research and development projects. We have developed directories of science and technology equipment. We have leaned heavily on equipment because we have to share our resources. We did what is called a skills plan, which is a directory of the expertise on the island. A lot of the information on the island is not documented, and we have to use people to get information. We have recently started a multidisciplinary information service to small and medium-sized industries, and we are involved in selective dissemination of information. So far the cooperation has been extremely good.

To insure that everyone is cooperating in this venture, we have a committee called The Members of STIN which is comprised of the heads of all the information units. This committee meets once a month, so we know what everyone is doing and we know where the problems are. We work together, and try to resolve them. The chairperson of this committee reports or serves on the committee called the Standing Committee. STIN is an acronym for the Science and Technology Information Network, which is the policy making body and is comprised more of users of the information network. The chairperson of this policy-making body then reports to the National Council of Libraries, Archives and Information Services, and on this Council is the National Librarian. So you can see the coordination is through the head of the unit, and the policy-making body then reports to the Council, and the National Librarian coordinates all of the activities. This is done for the two functioning networks, the Science and Technology Information Network, and the socio-economic network. What we have found is that the demand for information has more or less made the plan a bit obsolete, so now we are in the processing of revising it.

Cavan McCarthy:

Yes, planning I think is what we need. But where do we get the planning from? Do we get it from up above, from the government? Latin American governments are fighting desperately to stay alive, not to be swamped by inflation, not to be kicked out by the military, or the military to be kicked out by the civilians! And in certain cases, not to be kicked out by the guerillas! They do not have time or energy or capabilities to concern themselves with planning in information or library science areas. These areas were always too peripheral, were never considered very important, and in this particular point in time, certainly the government is not going to plan them. That means that the profession itself has to plan this. But the profession itself runs into certain problems in trying to plan because the profession very often has no specific leadership. Often if there is one leading body, that body has difficulty itself with planning possibly because the personnel change frequently. This is a common feature in one country that I know, that the personnel in the national documentation center, including the head, change about every year. The librarians on the lower level do not have the time to do the planning, and if they have the time they do not have the training or experience to do this planning. Where is the planning to come from?

Thomas McGinn:

Can it come from the faculties in the universities?

Cavan McCarthy:

This has come up several times. What are the functions, the correct activities of the university teachers? They are teaching, administration, and research. We had the same problem yesterday with translation, where translation doesn't go into any of those categories. So you have to set up a research budget plan which possibly can handle it.

Victor Rosenberg:

Someone commented to me yesterday that we heard little about what is going on in the United States. One of the things that is very conspicuous about planning information activities in the United States is that it is non-existent. Time and time again we in the United States are faced with, "Who's doing what?" No one really knows. Is the State Department in charge of information activities? Is the Commerce Department? And there are a number of people who feel that the situation is so fluid that perhaps even though a national unified plan is desperately needed, no one is really sure they would like the one that would emerge anyway.

One thing that the United States has done is develop the MARC format which has become a world standard. Now it seems to me that it makes very little sense to go against a United States-sponsored imperialistic standard for the interchange of data when in fact there is no reason to be independent of that. On the other hand, when it comes to information that is not included in the major databases, for example tropical agriculture and medicine, it makes a lot more sense to be independent and develop independent networks.

I think that rather than looking at dependency as an ideological cause, it's more constructive to look at it as an operational thing. When is dependency useful and when it is not? I think one can couch it in other terms and make it more palatable, call it inter-dependency, and in certain areas it is a very useful thing. What has always impressed me in the computer technology world is the extent to which the library profession has maintained standards for data interchange, far in advance of anyone else. Others are still trying to get this together, trying to get compatibility of diskettes and various systems and so on. And in the library world, the MARC format, at least in the Western world and in Western Europe, has worked admirably for interchange of information. I think an approach like that might be useful.

Juan Freudenthal:

I would like to go just a little further. Earlier Dr. McGinn spoke of the possibility that if we adopt in Latin America the newer technology. we will be less dependent. I question that very much. In my opinion we will be as dependent as we have always been. I am not sure that the newer technology will give us independence.

Thomas McGinn:

I should qualify that and say that only the newer technology will permit you to create the large databases which are not possible under a manual system. You still remain dependent, as several papers have pointed out. You have to import hardware. Often you have to import software. The degree of independence in software can be all that you want. I think Cavan McCarthy's paper said that the dependence is virtually absolute on the industrialized world, obviously for computers, although he pointed out that if you have a variety of countries in the industrialized world that can support your hardware needs, then you can choose. They are commercially in competition with one another, and you're not going to be dependent upon one of them. You can buy from Japan, you don't have to go to the United States.

Juan Freudenthal:

This goes beyond that. Independence refers to who controls the information. We are talking about systems which are controlled by people. Look at what happened in Poland and Argentina recently, in the suppression of all external telecommunications by the military governments. You can have all of this electronic information switched off in one moment and there is absolutely no information going in and out of the country. Paper remains a fantastic democratic medium, as was shown in Poland. The control of information may pose a great problem in countries of Latin America. We do have situations where information can be used for the wrong purposes, whereas here we should be discussing using it for the right purposes.

William Jackson:

You can get more bibliographic independence, but you may become more dependent in relation to your document delivery. I think this is the simple economics of where centers of resources are. This doesn't necessarily entirely point to the United States, but points to the United States, the United Kingdom, France, and places where you have strong concentrations of materials. You may have all your references, but you're still stuck with getting materials from Washington, London and Paris. Now perhaps this can be speeded up, or microform can reduce costs, until newly developing countries decide to dedicate significant portions of their information budgets to document delivery systems, whether you call them great libraries or great archives or whatever. I think this has been one of the interesting things about watching networks and newer technologies. In spite of considerable sums, relatively speaking, that some countries like Mexico or Brazil or Colombia have invested, most of this has gone into hardware and investigations and planning and so forth, and very little has gone into the document delivery systems. There is not yet, with relatively few exceptions, significant numbers of great science libraries in Latin America, for all the concerns with science development. You don't have the equivalent of strong science collections that could furnish even sizeable number of articles being indexed in *Chemical Abstracts*, for instance.

Marietta Daniels Shepard:

First, on the matter of CALCO. CALCO from the beginning has been MARC oriented. At a meeting of specialists in Medellin about 1976, they looked at the CALCO format and found that there were only two fields that were not compatible with MARC and recommended that they be changed. They were changed, so that fortunately from the beginning it has been the gospel according to MARC.

Second, as far as document delivery is concerned, this was one of the basic concepts too in the creation of BIREME in Sao Paulo. So many requests had gone to the National Library of Medicine for copies of documents that they felt that a center should be created in Latin America that could handle these requests. BIREME was the one in particular that they felt was the most capable of providing these documents. In the survey that we did in the Organization of American States, we found that for most of the interlibrary loans or document requests that had been made by information systems in Latin America, the British Lending Library had been the one most used to provide documents, to a lesser extent the Library of Congress, and to some extent in the areas in which BRS and DIALOG and ORBIT are used, they have used those document delivery systems.

William Jackson:

Regarding document delivery, the more complicating factor in the economic sense is that a number of libraries are slapping a service charge on top of the cost of reproduction. It isn't just the cost of a few nickels through the Xerox machine. There are a number of research libraries in the United States who are under their own financial pressures and are adding these unit fees. Your document delivery costs are actually going up, unless you can figure out some way for a subsidy of some sort.

Ching-Chih Chen:

I'd like to follow up on a line that Victor started with, and combine it with my thoughts on Sunday about the dependency and interdependency of different areas.

I think it is very true that when the developing countries seem to be getting better we do see that confrontation between the developed and developing countries, the latter wanting to be independent. On the other hand I think it is extremely important to look to the developing countries and say that when everyone goes back to their own country, then from country to country there again would be the same desire to not want to be dependent upon another country within the developing areas.

And I think it is important that when we're talking about networks, whether it's national, regional or whatever, to think about developing networks that don't just share bibliographic information, but also share other kinds of information resources.

What Vic said about the United States situation and a United States information policy is absolutely true. We don't have one central national development policy for information. On the other hand the United States is such a gigantic infrastructure. It is divided into subject areas and by other lines. Take the National Library of Medicine, for example. It functions well as a national library because of its hierarchical structure. Under the National Library of Medicine there are the regional libraries, and under them, basic resource libraries, and basic unit libraries across the country. The national agricultural network is the same way. The needs of the National Library of Medicine are not only medical, they also need science, social science, and the humanities. How are they going to get out of the subject network and be a multi-type, multi-subject network? We must talk about cross-type, cross-subject networks, and of course cross-border networks.

Laurence Hallewell:

What has been going through my mind is how important in all this is not the abstract planning, but the individual who knows what is desirable, and is able to put forward and put into effect their views. CALCO as I understand it was a one-woman project. The British Lending Library is very much the work of one man, Dr. Urquart. Remember Fred Kilgour and OCLC. Power and University Microfilms. Again and again, it is not abstract planning. It is the one individual who sees the need. Eventually after he's gotten so far, everyone just follows like the proverbial sheep.

Thomas McGinn:

In these cases they were able to institutionalize their desires, and as Cavan pointed out, it is difficult to institutionalize these in Latin America because of changes in personnel. However I feel that when you automate, the weight, if it's successful, is bound to carry on the achievements. Perhaps automation won't develop the system administratively, but at least administrators would be embarrassed not to use that computer. And it does impress the students, the users sufficiently. They think that something new is going on that must be maintained. This is kind of a political argument for automating, also. There has been a severe problem of continuity I think in many Latin American countries. Individuals have done great things, and then the government changes, as Cavan said. Or there is a new administrator, even with the same government, and he doesn't care what the previous one did, or, he might feel that he has to do something different, simply to shine in his own right.

Laurence Hallewell:

Or even worse, you may have the individual with the ideas, but no real relationship with the power, because of personality conflicts or whatever. I'm thinking particularly of a country where there were two members of the profession, one with the ideas, one with the political connections, and they just never got together.

Thomas McGinn:

Those with ideas must be humble before those with power!

Armando Sandoval:

I agree with what Laurence Hallewell has said. All the participants here, who represent so many countries of Latin America, as a matter of fact have very little or real power to make decisions. When we go back to our countries, we will just have ideas, which is very important, but I sometimes begin to feel that this is a waste of time. I would like to be under the impression that we have been working for better conditions and an infrastructure for libraries, and I think that we are honest in wishing for that. But we cannot forget that man is encircled by his circumstances. And our circumstances in every one of our countries are quite different. My circumstances in Mexico are different from Beatriz in Brazil or Ximena in Chile. Our circumstances are different in our own positions in our institutions and our relationships with our government and with the people who make the decisions. This is very important.

There has never been a meeting to discuss how to attract leaders to the library world. That's what we really need. Yes, we need networks, but they will not happen just because we want them. They will happen because we have good leaders. Look what happened in Brazil. Look what happened in Mexico. We had an engineer who could handle the information problems officially in Mexico. And in six years he succeeded in making information very important, something that hadn't happened in the whole history of Mexico. We should hold a meeting on how to attract leaders to the library world. If we had enough leaders, and Marietta is one of them, we could get the libraries on the move. We need dozens of leaders. With this kind of people, we would have networks, we would have libraries, we would have what is needed to make good libraries work. Let's find

who the leaders are in our countries who can help to develop
a national network.

Alma Jordan:

I agree with a lot of what has been said about getting
a catalyst going and getting a planning program going and
getting the actual activity going. The thing that strikes me
is how very differently the countries have proceeded with
pretty much the same circumstances. That tends to support
the view that it isn't only the leadership but the combination
of circumstances in a particular country in a particular time.
We know in the history of inventions people will have the
same idea for years, but no one develops it. And a hundred
years later someone comes up with the same idea, and
boom! it hits. In the Caribbean we have shown that some
countries have made the kind of progress that Merline has
described. Others have had pretty much the same
catalysts—Unesco, the pressure on member states to name
a UNISIST focal point or develop a NATIS program and so
on, and all have not moved in the same direction or at the
same pace. Why? It seems that everything just didn't come
together in the right way.

Jamaica had been an excellent case study of everything going just right. It's not that they didn't have
problems, they've had all the problems that one can en-
counter in terms of finance, currency, and devaluation, but
they have been able to keep up that momentum and move in
the right direction, with leadership, with government support, and with several ingredients coming together in the
right way.

If I take the case of Barbados, I can see where the
NATIS program again has given them a boost. They have
hired an outside catalyst, they have been able to get a consultant, the leadership in the country has been good, they
have worked together, and they are now moving pretty
much in the same direction a little bit later.

Take Trinidad and Tobago. We have had a lot of things going for us, but we have not moved at the same pace. We have had some similar kinds of activities, but the ingredients have mixed slightly differently. We have not had as much professional input, a different kind of committee, we did not have the same kind of working parties inputting into the plan. It has not moved. We've had some people work, some input into the government, some government support, but all of it has not been in the same degree and the same measure and with the right momentum to get us going. Although we did have the money. Which we no longer have. It would make an interesting case study. I agree with the catalyst idea, but I don't think we can identify one and say this is it. It's all of these ingredients getting together in the right degree at the right time that really makes for what we want.

I want to say a word about what I feel could happen and hasn't, at the national, regional and international levels. This is where a kind of dependence, if we want to call it that, in my view is not objectionable. I feel the countries in the region must work with national frameworks but within regional and international frameworks. I think the NATIS concept that Unesco had was about the best thing that had come along for ages, in giving that kind of incentive to countries to build. UNISIST did not have the same appeal, because it was centralized and countries did not all relate to it. But the NATIS program somehow caught on, certainly in the Caribbean region. Pressure through member states was there. At the same time we had regional movements through the ECLA office for the Caribbean which have been very fruitful, again, in getting governmental interest to lead and to work with the professionals. We have a Caribbean information system which is operative now really in the planning sectors. I think CARISPLAN has been mentioned, associated with CLADES. It is part of CLADES in the sense that its the office for ECLA in the Caribbean in Trinidad.

And if we were to develop nationally, bearing in mind what is going on regionally, and working in harmony with that, and at the same time internationally, we would have what I would like to call integrated or coordinated national policies. Integrated might be too strong. Coordinated policies would move in the same direction. When we are indexing in a particular country, we may have a national database which is compatible with a regional database. We may be able to pull out the national information, we may develop it separately, or we may do it with others. I think that dependency should not be a syndrome of wanting to be independent for the sake of being independent. I think we must do independently what we can manage, but be willing to draw from the things that we can draw from at other levels.

Victor Rosenberg:

Let's shift the discussion now to the topic of databases. Murilo?

Murilo da Cunha:

Yesterday's session and today's are quite similar. It is quite impossible to see the boundary between one and the other. I'd like to ask again the second question that I asked yesterday. It's related to the dependence and independence of information. Yesterday I mentioned that several participants wrote that the information stored by American or European databases sometimes is not important or is not the information that the developing countries need. At the same time we know that it would be very difficult to build a chemical or biological database. We cannot compete with *Chemical Abstracts* or *Biological Abstracts*. And there is no need to compete with them. But there are several problems or subjects related to specific countries or regions for which we have to build a database. Do you think it would be possible to identify these subjects, and how to do it? Should we build a database in a cooperative effort like AGRIS or INIS, or should we at the same time try to improve the coverage of Latino materials in databases produced in industrialized countries?

Tony Bowman:

I hear a theme flowing from many of the discussions, both privately and from what is coming out in the group. I'm hearing a lot of negatives, a lot of reasons or obstacles to success, and I submit to you that these very obstacles create a tremendous market for success for each one of you, and the trick is taking the negative and turning it into a positive, identifying the problem and solving it. In this world, the hero's laurel goes to the problem solver. If we're talking about getting financing, if we're talking about getting more power for libraries, then let's let information solve some of the problems and tell the people about the successful solution. Armando Sandoval talks about leadership, and who will become the leaders, and where the power would come from. I submit that the leaders are right here, that they're sitting around this table. Would you surrender your knowledge about the way information ought to be, and your professional judgement, to someone else that had the money or had political power? Who else is better conditioned, better trained, better prepared to be those leaders and to make that happen than you are? When should this happen? How about next Monday? How about starting on something like that then? The real question is how.

It seems to me that this is an absolute classic study of how the needs analysis that you do could be applied to records at the university, or the national economic planning council. How can you let people know that the information that you have is power? How can you play up the problems that you've solved?

I think that one of the most dynamic responses to that was a speech I heard Virginia Betancourt deliver at the ACURIL Conference last year in Caracas. She talked about a dynamic restlessness that librarians need to have to go out and get the money. Because if librarians don't have it, if information managers don't do it, who else will? Will the politicians say, Here's what you need, go out and do it? It seems to me that all of us have an absolutely great opportunity. Once you've solved a few problems for people using the resources at your disposal, those people will look to you and will begin to share their power base with you.

A little bit more specifically, and more to the topic of today's discussion, ICFES in Colombia, headquartered in Bogota, is beginning the implementation of a program. They are already erecting a building, and now they are making a rather substantial investment in the software, the systems, the people that will make it all happen. They are addressing the issue of having a degree of local autonomy over full text retrieval by bringing in-country on the broadest possible basis in the most economical way, a large broad base of materials, both in monographs and serials. They reviewed some ten thousand serial titles, and whittled it down to a number somewhat smaller than that, and they will acquire them all. They are analyzing interlibrary loans. They are considering acquiring a portion of that in microformat. Once these materials in-country, for those items they will no longer be dependent upon anyone else. They will be able to photoduplicate them and send them out. They will have conquered time and to some extent geography, and they will have for those materials a great deal of local autonomy.

Winthrop Wiltshire:

I want to agree largely with Armando, in terms of the critical importance of the factors of leadership. As I see it, that leads into all else. I also agree with what Tony Bowman is talking about, in recognizing the need to develop the strategies, and sensitizing people at whatever level who need to be sensitized, to ensure that you get the kind of actions that are necessary to make a change that is desired.

But on the question of dependency and independence, I think it is good to recognize that we are not talking about absolutes. I think this has been voiced before. We are talking more about ensuring that when we make decisions, we factor into them considerations of dependency and independence. In the past, at the national level, what has been happening to us in the countries of Latin America and the Caribbean is that we have been making decisions that are not in our own interest, if subjected to analysis at the most rudimentary level. We are talking about developing an awareness to make critical analyses, to be informed for decisions and choices, so that in the medium and long term, most of the things that we do would be in the right direction. We would make some mistakes, but we are talking about that kind of framework.

Juan Freudenthal:

It seems to me that we are also talking about being or not being a part of the political process. The political clout that librarians have achieved in the United States is quite unique. They go to Congress, they lobby. In Latin America that doesn't happen. What Tony is talking about is wonderful. You have to be a part of the political process in Latin America to achieve such things, no matter how intelligent are the utterances of librarians. Achieving that is a matter of balance in Latin America which you do not necessarily have. You can have a person in Latin America in power to do that, but it would not succeed as fast as it would in the United States. You also have the money, and the support system of democracy in which it works, which we do not have in our countries. So I agree with you in principle that you need leadership and sometimes it works. After all, consider Simón Bolívar from Colombia. He was a great leader but at the wrong time. Before he died he said the famous phrase, "Si mi muerte contribuye a que cesen los partidos y se consolide la unión, yo bajaré tranquilo al sepulcro." He tried to unite all of Hispanic America. It was a dream. It has never happened, and I doubt very much if it ever will.

So we work in Latin America with constraints that do not exist in this country. I am not so sure that we can do the things that can be done here: we lack the necessary political clout.

Tony Bowman:

What are the alternatives? There basically is no alternative.

Juan Freudenthal:

The alternative is to work in the system intelligently, which Winthrop has indicated that we perhaps have not done up to now.

Winthrop Wiltshire:

I agree totally with Juan. We in the Caribbean countries are quite fortunate in fact. For example, in Trinidad and Tobago, in January, the librarians had a function, and at that we had a total of fifty people. And we had *three of our senior ministers* present at that function, all proclaiming their commitment to what we were attempting to do. The framework in some of our countries is there.

Thomas McGinn:

Tony mentioned Virginia Betancourt, who is the person who has transformed library and information services in Venezuela. Virginia was raised as the daughter of the founder of the present democracy, Rómulo Betancourt, so she has a certain context that normally we don't have. However in that context, I think we can learn to imitate people like that. She knows where the power is, she moves easily within it. I would say that from what I have seen in Latin American countries, obviously you have to be with the political parties, and you have get a consensus on our questions and make it a partisan issue. She knows how to do that. She employs people from all parties in the system, and if there is a change there is someone there from that party in the system. She's done that consciously. We are always showing some minister how the automated system works, or someone high up or important comes in and takes up our whole morning. We're trying to resolve technical problems. We complain. But of course we know that without these visits we wouldn't get the funds. The decision to automate the Supreme Court was made because the head of the Supreme Court was a close friend of the President, and he wanted it. So, take the person who wants it and give it to him, even though, as far as the legal decisions of the Supreme Court go, I don't know whether they're any more related to the development of the country than something else. Our priorities have to be close to the personal concerns of the people in power.

Concerning librarians as a profession, they are politically weak in our South American countries, however the first allies to get are the computer scientists: they have a little more power; they tend to be in the ministries with a little more voice than the librarians. Librarianship is not a prestigious profession, even in the United States. Let's face it! So ally with people who have the same concerns that you do. I think computer scientists are such people. We can talk. I don't know what order the professions would rank in terms of power in Latin America, but I would tend to think that doctors would come first, then lawyers (if indeed they didn't outrank the doctors), with the engineers third. They get what they want in the Congress. So if you're going to set up a service, help the doctors, lawyers, and engineers. Armando mentioned that there's an engineer in Mexico who did a great deal. Let's not be jealous about who's doing what. If you get someone from another profession who's interested in information, give him all your support. We've unfortunately had some sniping from the library community in our country because the head of the National Library is not a librarian. We could care less who will care about information, because really what's happened is all to the good of the profession. We need allies, and I think that's the first rule of politics. You can't operate in isolation. We must study the political process in each country, as Winthrop is saying. This sensitivity is not part of our training, but certain people pick it up, and as Armando says we should look for and support them. I don't care if they're librarians or computer scientists or what: if they care about the information needs of the country, give them all the support that we can possibly give them.

Murilo da Cunha:

It seems to me that we have to attract more daughters and sons of generals and politicians to our profession!

William Jackson:

Well, if you can't do that, I can give you part of an answer. There is probably no American librarian who knows more about library cooperation than Robert B. Downs, and he has remarked on a number of occasions that cooperation will succeed to the extent that you show the people that you're trying to get to cooperate that it's in their own self-interest to cooperate, that it's not some abstract plan "for the national good." If you can show that they are going to benefit specifically, whether it's the doctors or the lawyers, or the Supreme Court, you'll have a better chance of selling them on your cooperative venture. I think that's very shrewd advice, and a plea for being more realistic than theoretical.

Ximena Felíu:

Yo quisiera plantear el problema desde otro punto de vista en relación a lo que se ha estado diciendo aquí con respecto a nosotros como profesionales de información y es que quisiera enfocar el problema desde un punto de vista temporal, histórico.

Si preguntamos retrospectivamente desde cuando la profesión del bibliotecario se lleva a cabo en Latinoamérica en las universidades, creo que no podremos ir mas que treinta años atrás. Creo que en nuestras universidades las escuelas de bibliotecología no tienen más allá de treinta o treinta y cinco años de vida. Creo también por otro lado, ya como un punto aparte al respecto, que en nuestros países el desarrollo económico y social realizado desde un punto de vista político y systemático no tiene mas allá también de cuarenta o cuarenta y cinco años. Y en esto quiero recordar que comienza el desarrollo systemático con un pensamiento económico detrás de Latinoamérica para crear los países sus propios planes nacionales de desarrollo desde que se crea la Comisión Económica para America Latina. Y que el secretario ejecutivo de la Comisión Económica para América Latina, Raul Prebisch, crea todo un pensamiento respecto a lo que debe ser el desarrollo económico y social de los países. Pongo estos dos hechos en paralelo. Cuando empiezan los países a evolucionar con un pensamiento económico y social detrás y crean entonces sus propias formas de desarrollo de acuerdo a los estudios que se realizan dentro del país y dentro de los países se va generando un tipo de información que los va retrando, fotografiando, se van creando fórmulas para solucionar aquellas problemas mas candentes como son la pobreza, la no industrialización, la dependencia, etc.

Al mismo tiempo se va creando una necesidad de información para justamente entrar en este desarrollo acelerado que nos permita entrar también al concierto de las naciones: se va creando una necesidad de información y luego hacia un punto ya aparte. Mientras tanto se crean en las escuelas de bibliotecología en nuestros· países toda una estructura de conocimientos que van principalmente dirigidos a que se registren los documentos, a que se cataloguen, a que se identifiquen y se tengan en una determinada colección, pero la palabra información que requieren estos políticos, estos profesionales que estan creando el desarrollo del país no esta comprendida en esta otra comunidad que está catalogando, clasificando, es decir creando la posibilidad de la memoria del país. Hay un abismo entre uno y otro. Y la necesidad de uno no va hacia el otro en terminos cadentes también de necesidad de que el otro reaccione y así seguinos hasta que nos encontramos con el computador.

El computador, sí nos ha acercado y nos ha acercado por un lado los políticos, los profesionales que están dentro del proceso de la planificación del desarrollo del país, deseando que sus problemas de información sean totalmente resueltos a través de este instrumento infernal de la computación (que no comprehenden, pero que creen que ciertamente les soluciona todos los problemas), y por otro lado los bibliotecarios pensando que no es el instrumento correspondiente, porque es muy caro, y porque vamos a entrar todo lo que tenemos hecho en nuestros catálogos a esta cosa tan pequeña con una cajita negra porque no conocemos: ahí viene el problema.

Y si en ese momento cuando comprendiéndolo porque hemos salido fuera, porque hemos conversado, porque hemos envidiado y porque finalmente hemos conversado con el ingeniero de computación que la palabra "información" la usa en otro término que el que usamos nosotros, pero que al final es lo mismo, y que quiere lo mismo—quiere meter datos dentro del computador para dar un servicio—nosotros queremos tener el dato para dar el servicio.

¿Cuál es la diferencia que hay entre uno y otro? Un equipo. Cuando hemos llegado a comprender que ambos queremos lo mismo para dar un servicio, entonces sí, hemos empezado a usar la palabra "información" en nuestra profesión como un elemento que nos define en lo que vamos a dar de servicio.

De ahí entonces que la mentalidad del bibliotecario, que la mentalidad del profesional ha comenzado a cambiar y estoy hablando todavía en términos históricos, de hace quince años atrás. Cuando vamos a poder nosotros solucionar el problema de nuestra debilidad política como profesión cuando inteligemos el equipo de los profesionales que están ayudando al desarrollo y a la planificación de los países, cuando estemos trabajando conjuntamente con el sociólogo, con el administrador público, con el científico que está justamente desarrollando un proyecto que el plan de desarrollo del pais indica que lo necisita. En ese momento, cuando estemos verdaderamente incorporados totalmente al desarrollo del país—de nuestros países—vamos a comprender como formamos parte del equipo político con el cual nuestros paises se desarrollan.

Hago un punto aparte, y esto simplemente lo dejo como una exposición, como un pensamiento. ¿Cómo podemos nosotros solucionar estos problemas que aquí se han planteado, por ejemplo en el sentido de cómo lograr ("improve" fue la palabra que usó un colega) respecto a la cooperación institucional, conociendo por lo pronto qué instituciones hacen: qué, porqué y con quién? Y si esas instituciones generan, o no generan, información importante para el desarrollo de mi país, de nuestros países.

Si esa institución genera una determinada información expresada en un determinado documento, tengo que identificar ese documento y tenerlo en mi biblioteca para mi usario que seguramente trabaja en esa institución que ha generado ese documento. Tengo también que estar en conocimiento de aquellos sistemas de ubicación regionales que atacan o tienen la cobertura de un determinado campo de conocimiento, y tengo que entrar en contacto con ellos. Tengo que conocer también cuales son los sistemas internacionales de información que cubren los aspectos que me interesan dentro de las prioridades señaladas por el desarrollo de mi país, en los planes de desarrollo de mi país. Y esa información de alguna manera tengo que tener acceso a ella. Es decir, tengo que plantearme con una mentalidad abierta, como profesional de información, una mentalidad de contacto con las instituciones que están desarrollando y están participando en aquella actividad que esta siendo mejorada en mi país. Tengo que tener una mentalidad abierta y entrar en contacto y coordinarme con aquellas colegas que están a cargo de sistemas internacionales o regionales de información, y tengo que asumir una actitud política como profesional de información justamente para poder entrar en este contacto y darle a mi político, el que está haciendo el plan de desarrollo del país, el que está tomando las decisiones, y el que tiene el poder, para darle la información que necesita políticamente entregada a través de una actitud estratégica, pero una actitud básicamente consolidada en un conocimiento de que lo necesita por los planes que está llevando a cabo. Es lo que yo tengo y lo que yo he conseguido previamente sí políticamente también en el más alto nivel de la palabra me he puesto a servir y a encontrar lo que ahí se necesita, independientemente en lo que pudo conseguir dentro de mi país, y dependiendo en forma de coordinación con el resto de los sistemas de información.

Tengo de estar en condiciones de intercambiar información en calidad de par, y con ella obtener toda la que en mi país se requiere. Tengo también que promover la posibilidad de que una infraestructura de información, veámoslo en centros de biblioteca o de documentación, sean creados como corresponde y con las tecnologías más modernas y que nos permitan atravesar mejores abismos, tecnológicos. Especialmente, tengo que saber que computador elegir, que mini-computador elegir en el sentido de que me sea compatible con aquel sistema regional de información con el cual ya estoy conectada. Tengo que saber tambien que existen en determinados países de Latinoamérica centros importantísimos como el de Armando Sandoval, por ejemplo, que no conocía, y que me alegra saberlo, para decírselo a mis colegas y para que lo inunden con cartas de petición, políticamente tengo que hacerlo.

Perdón, me he extendido en esto porque creo que depende de nosotros el fortalecer nuestra actitud política, y que depende exclusivamente de nosotros no depender tecnológicamente sino de aquello que queramos.

Juan Freudenthal:

It would be impossible to summarize her discussion. She answered Tony very nicely. She told us briefly historically that we have been dealing with all of these phenomena for thirty or forty years at the most in the universities and schools of library science. Our profession is new, we have had to model ourselves not only on our own but from what we have learned from schools of library science all around the world. She talked about the fact that this cannot be divorced from the way nations have developed, and in the last thirty or forty years when nations have come into their own economic and political development. There is a strong feeling for that at least. We cannot divorce ourselves from poverty and not being completely industrialized; indeed, we have some problems of dependence. There are two structures there, the structure of the information which is necessary for politicians to make decisions, and the information which we as librarians, simply as a support system, collect and organize and identify. The person in the middle between the librarian and the officials who need information, would be to a certain extent the computer scientist.

The second part is a little more difficult to explain, because she is talking about how to resolve the problems of institutional and national cooperation. I think what is really important is that she really feels very strongly that we have to be part of the political process, despite the fact that we may not éven be a political figure like Virginia Bettancoeur. If we do the job right, and if we have a feeling that we are helping the systems that we are supposed to help, and our governments, then we are making in effect a political statement of strength. I have to agree with that, because if we do a job well, then politicians and the people who are in charge of the affairs of countries will recognize what we're doing and work with us.

But I wanted to add that many of the women who are heads of national libraries in Latin America are as a matter of fact friends of politicians and not librarians. In Colombia and Peru, the heads are not masters in library science yet they have great political clout, because they are friends of the people on top. When I came out of Michigan and Syracuse I thought that we had to have librarians with masters and PhDs at the top level job in certain countries in Latin America, particularly in national libraries. I've changed my mind on that. It took me ten years to learn it, but I think that you need the political person on top, and then someone underneath with the degree who can do the job.

William Jackson:

I agree with your summary. I got the impression that she was describing the librarian or information professional as himself a key element in the network. He was receiving information and acting upon it and then building not only what you might call a formal infrastructure but an informal infrastructure. By being aware of political currents and possibilities he was realistically seizing opportunities. A fine presentation.

Ximena Felíu:

If we are aware of what happens in our country, what happens with our national development, what our politicians want to do with our development, information professionals are going to work with that inspiration. I think we have political work to do with the politicians. If the priorities in the national development plan include agriculture, we have to be aware that agricultural information will be the information that the country needs at that moment, and we have to identify where that information is generated in the country, and which are the regional or international or national information systems that have information on agriculture in other countries, in order to obtain that information and give it to the politician that needs it at that moment. We have to know what is happening in our country, and what the guidelines are in our country's development plans at that moment. And if we are aware of that, certainly our profession must gather the information and prepare the information for that demand. Our libraries or documentation centers are always in search of development plans, so we can incorporate them into our work.

William Jackson:

I think that planning was one of the theses of Carlos Victor Penna, a library don for a number of decades. He wanted to get the library and information profession plugged into the national development planning, and he felt that education was one way. Certainly the science and technology area is a good example, because some of the greatest successes in developing information networks or infrastructures have been in areas like economics, agriculture or medicine, or a more specific one like coffee in Colombia or sheep in Uruguay.

Thomas McGinn:

I want to ask a question of the group. Most Latin American countries have a planning agency and five-year plans. Can you tell me whether the library and information sector is a formal part of your planning? In Venezuela it never was until this last plan, and now it is. It never was explicitly a part: it was subsumed under other areas. Its integration is the result of some work by some of our people who have high-level contacts. A goal I think, is to become an explicit part of your five-year plan. And you can talk to your planning ministry in that area, or bring in someone from Unesco who can talk to them if you don't have the input in this area. Planners know they need help on it.

Cavan McCarthy:

Certainly in Brazil the Council for Science and Technology for Development has got a plan for that, and one of the three elements was information. Does anyone remember the others?

Beatriz de Carvalho:

This is not the national plan, but the CNPT plan which has included a scientific information section since the first one.

Victor Rosenberg:

Of course the emphasis of certain areas of the economy in the information context is very clear in the United States too. The frightening thing at this point is the interest in the government in taking some very high priority areas like NTIS, and either disbanding them or selling them off. This is something that hasn't occurred before. Until now it's always been the sectors of the economy that are most important that got the most attention from the standpoint of information. The difference it seems to me between the countries of Latin America and North America is rather the level of resources available even in the high priority areas. The question then becomes, What can be done in terms of dependency or cooperation (or whatever you want to call it)? Latin America needs to improve these sectors, so that resources that can be made available for those things that are unique and have to be developed in Latin America.

This afternoon I would like to develop this more. Dependency, in terms of technology, is something that should be very carefully analyzed. It's better for a country to be hardware-dependent rather than software-dependent. Software should be indigenous and custom-designed. Hardware can be general-purpose. This also applies in information. Certain sectors of information are important to be local and indigenous, other sectors can depend upon the outside. I know in Brazil, for example, that several decisions have been taken in this area such that low priority information resources are permitted to be accessed abroad, however high priority areas are to be developed internally.

Maria Oyarzun de Ferreira:

En Chile, los planes de desarrollo no hablan específicamente, en general, del sistema nacional de información deducido a través del estatuto del CONICYT: CONICYT es un organismo asesor del gobierno en el desarrollo científico y tecnológico, en el desarrollo y fomento científico y tecnológico y entre las tareas que se le asignan está muy específicamente el desarrollar un sistema nacional de información en tipos técnicos basados en las areas tributarias de desarrollo del país. Y estos sistemas deben conectarse a las redes regionales e internacionales.

Ahora en los planes anuales de desarrollo de este año tiene en el sector de educación como trabajo que se le entrega al ministerio el desarrollar el sistema y el subsistema nacional de información en la educación y a él se le asigna un pequeño presupuesto que es el paso inicial.

Thomas McGinn:

To summarize briefly, in Chile it's the National Council for Scientific and Technical Information which has the responsibility to form a national network of scientific and technical information. Recently we questioned the separation of scientific and technical information from the rest of the national system, which is a pattern throughout Latin America that seems to come from Unesco. We find it's a fragmentation of information that isn't necessary. Even though I agree with Armando Sandoval that scientists do tend to get their information in a form different from humanists and social scientists, I don't see any necessity for databases to be separated, and in fact they aren't in North America. You have Lockheed, which has humanistic information in there in the same place as scientific information. The tendency is to have a database of scientific information although sometimes these national science and technology research councils include the social sciences in their mandate. But they do totally leave out cultural and humanistic information which is not susceptible to scientific processing. This mentality exists. Humanistic information is nice for the literary people. But in fact those libraries which have a huge reference collection with all kinds of data, are in a different place from scientific and technical information.

Our national library for instance is very tied to the tradition of being humanistic and so its controlled by the literary people and is considered their preserve. But in fact it has all the directories of industry in the country and so on which come in through legal deposit. That is separated off in the information system. Everyone seems to assume a division of functions between the scientific and technical information systems and the rest. One of our visitors felt it was detrimental to the development of networks, and we should try not to foment this division which doesn't exist in a number of countries which are highly developed technically.

The developed countries don't necessarily make this distinction between scientific documentation and the rest. The major universities in the Northern countries have one database. The Library of Congress doesn't collect in a sense what the National Library of Medicine and the National Library of Agriculture collect, but they have the important scientific works and scientific journals. In one place you can find what human knowledge produces.

I would just like your thoughts on this, because I often hear that science belongs to the people who know how to process that information, and non-scientific data belongs to those others who know how to process that. In terms of processing it, you don't have to be a scientist to process at least the bibliographic part of it. It is very questionable whether you have to be a scientist to process it even from a subject point of view, because you don't have to be a doctor to handle medical information. At lot of people can pick it up.

Mariėtta Daniels Shepard:

I think Venezuela is a case in point when you think about separation of fields. Knowledge today is so interdisciplinary it is difficult to separate as a matter of fact. Certainly in Venezuela they tried to set up a scientific and technical information system and they kind of fell flat on their face until they began to realize the interconnections with other disciplines. On the other hand in other countries such as Peru, a lot of sectoral information networks have been created. There still is no national network although it has been prescribed by law that there should be, but on the basis of the sectoral information networks that exist, they certainly could easily build a national information network. I think we have the two points of view, and they have to converge sometime someplace, and the database of course is an easy place for them to converge.

William Jackson:

There is I think a practical explanation, that part of the science separation came from the creation of the national science and technology research councils, not that theoretically people were deliberately trying to create divisions, but that there were priorities that the councils were given, and given money to carry them out.

Thomas McGinn:

But why were the councils given this separate area of influence, rather than creating a documentation center which would have all the information produced in the country or needed from outside the country? Was it tried?

Maria Oyarzun de Ferreira:

Como ya les decía, además de desarrollar el sistema nacional nosotros nos conectamos con los sistemas extranjeros regionales o mundiales y es así como nosotros somos un poco nacional del CONICYT y trabajamos con los principios del CONICYT. Y dentro de los principios del CONICYT la ciencia (digamos) no es un sistema en ciencia y tecnológía sino un sistema científico, tecnológico y tomado desde el punto de vista del CONICYT, el de UNISIST, se entiende lo científico y tecnológico como todo lo que empaña el sistema de subdesarrollo y en este sentido existe el subsistema como educación predilecta que existe en lo social. Entonces es una cosa integrada. Entonces además, si el CONICYT es responsable del desarrollo de este sistema nacional de información, es porque se entiende que un primer elemento para el desarrollo de la ciencía y la tecnologia es contar con la información.

Beatriz de Carvalho:

In Rio, where I work, we are using the concept of information for development, and that includes scientific and technological as well as humanistic information. We can't develop our country if we don't think about all knowledge working for development.

Ching-Chih Chen:

I would imagine that the separation of science and technology from other areas would be tied very closely to the political things we've been talking about. A country may consider scientific and technical areas a top priority, more important than any other area for development, and it happened to be that officials, scientists and engineers in those areas have more power and were able to get support from the government.

Further, I think we shouldn't be bothered by the physical isolation of information in the storage area. If we look at the United States, at the universities, we see within large university libraries there are branch libraries, and that's strictly for the sake of convenience, grouping materials that tend to be used more by certain individuals together. But when we isolate information sources physically, whether printed material or databases, do we have connections between them? That is the most important thing. I think that when we're looking at online databases, we should not be looking at Dialog, or SDC, or BRS as integrated databases. They aren't. Dialog has access to over 100 online databases. Each one of them contains data on a specific subject area intended for a specific audience, and at different levels. For instance *Chemical Abstracts* is much more at the research level than *Engineering Index* which is for more general engineering. What is important is that if anyone has access to the Dialog databases, they would be able to switch from one database to another with the multi-database switching capability. Therefore I'm not troubled to see in any developing country a separate scientific and technical information system, because that's more intended for researchers and developers. And, there may be a more general library intended for the common citizens. The point is that we should not deprive the citizens nor those with intellectual curiosity of access to higher, more research-oriented information. If they have that information need, how do we make that information available to them? And that ties into referral services, and the issue of buying, for whom, and for what use.

Victor Rosenberg:

I regret that the hour is late, and we do not have time for a summary. I'm glad that we continued our discussion of yesterday, for it has proved informative and wide-ranging. We'll reconvene at 2:00 this afternoon.

Wednesday Afternoon, 13 April 1983

*Social, Economic, Legal, and Political Barriers to the Free
Exchange of Information. New Information Markets
vs. Restriction of the Import of Information. Protecting Local Resources vs. Free Flow of Information.*

Victor Rosenberg:

In any small conference like this, the conference takes on a
life or direction of its own, which I like and I want to encourage. I have noticed that we have not dealt very much
with the North American aspects of information, and this
afternoon we will be dealing with the social, economic, legal
and political barriers to the free exchange of information,
and talking about new information markets and the restrictions on the import of information. These topics are becoming increasingly heated subjects of discussion in the United
States. Thus I'd like to devote some of the discussion this
afternoon to the North American aspects of this, if for no
other reason than to make it very clear, as Ching-Chih said
in the opening address, that the free flow of information is
simply not free. To moderate the session this afternoon, we
have Marietta Daniels Shepard.

Marietta Daniels Shepard:

Thank you. As Ximena reminded us, the profession
of librarianship in Latin America is not very old yet. I
might extend it another five years or so to 1947, when the
first assembly of librarians of the Americas took place, and

at which many of the problems that we are facing today were problems at that time, even though I may safely say that Latin America has come a long way. At that time we had I think two union lists of serials in all of Latin America, one in Mexico and one in Argentina. In doing my survey for the OAS, I found that there are six union lists of serials now in Mexico, of which four are printed, and of the three which have used automated means to produce the list, each one has used a different program, thus making it impossible to merge the data. In some cases we have complicated life for ourselves by duplicating efforts and not taking the necessary steps to simplify life. But progress has been made.

I remember that one of the principle discussions by one of the Argentine librarians was his concern about the lack of "divisas" or money that the government was willing to put up so that he could maintain complete collections of serials. That hasn't been resolved yet and especially with the economic condition of the world these days we're in as bad or worse a state as we were in 1947. Armando is having trouble paying for his subscriptions to journals from the United States with the devaluation of the peso, and with the natural inflation in the cost of periodicals.

Even though we have been presented with many categories, the social, economic, legal and political barriers to the free flow of information, I would even add the human, psychological and cultural barriers that exist too to the free flow of information. But that's just one of those natural things that you have to get over some way or another. It's like the firms in the United States that will not accept a new technology that hasn't been developed in that industry or in that firm. They say "NIH—not invented here." They're not interested in absorbing it, or they feel that they can use the technology by stealing the patents somehow and not pay the firm that developed the technology. So we really haven't overcome all the human and cultural barriers yet that there are to the free flow of information.

We are still depending, in many of the libraries in Latin America, on the exchange of publications to build up collections, and still have not gotten across to the appropriate agencies the need for budgeting for the purchase of publications. In some instances it's easier to get computer time than it is to get a publication. Computer time is new and exciting, especially in a society which has not been used to using book materials to find their information, having gotten it from their friends or relatives, or by television or by radio. This new technology of the computer, where you can sit down and punch a few buttons and get information, sounds mighty exciting, especially when the computer boys tell you that you'll never have to use anything printed again. In any case we have the human factor which we have to overcome. It's difficult to differentiate between them, as a matter of fact, because one impinges upon the other.

Even in the matter of "divisas" and the matter of getting the money with which to acquire publications, we find that not all of the possibilities have been used in Latin America. Unesco devised a system of book coupons to acquire materials, but that meant that you had to convince your government that they should set aside some of their hard currency in order to purchase book coupons. I think Brazil was the only country in Latin America that really did that over any length of time. I don't know whether they still do now. The United States government at one point guaranteed the sale of United States books to countries throughout the world but there again, ycu had to have it backed up by hard currency, and that has gone by the board a long time ago.

We find that as far as economic problems are concerned, inflation and the cost of materials have made it much more difficult for libraries in many parts of the world, and even libraries in the United States to acquire the materials that they need to have. You find that in some countries economic barriers have been set up as a result of the book industries in those countries. In Mexico for instance it costs you more to get books in Spanish from other parts of the world because of taxes. I don't know whether that applies now but it did for a number of years. In Brazil the publishers managed to get through a law against the import of publications in Portuguese, and the principle reason was to keep out the *Readers Digest* because there was too large a subscription base for it and the locally produced journals were not being purchased and read. We find that some of the economic barriers have been created in order to protect the national industry. We mentioned the other day about the problem of trying to get microfilm through customs in some countries. If the law imposes a tax on "películas" the customs officer does not often know that microfilm is not a movie and taxes it. Some countries have been able to get around the tax problem as far as bringing in both printed and non-printed materials by licensing certain institutions in the countries to import materials. I presume Chile still has a licensing system whereby certain institutions can import these materials without the payment of these taxes.

The matter of data flow gets more complicated by the minute. At one point the OAS, some twenty years or so ago, became involved in trying to write a new inter-American agreement on the free flow of publications, "la libre circulacion," but not without payment, "de las publicaciones." It was felt that a Latin American agreement might be more applicable and more useful in Latin America than a Unesco agreement. So we spent months on it. It was to include art objects and architectural drawings and all sorts of other objects. This got as far as the Inter-American Cultural Council, and was passed, and was to be submitted to the 11th Inter-American Conference which was cancelled and never held. Then the whole structure of the OAS was changed so that you didn't have an Inter-American Conference to agree upon inter-American treaties so all of that time was wasted. A lot of people did become aware of the need for reducing barriers in the countries of the Americas, however.

In the meantime Cuba came along, and people became worried about how to keep Cuban material from falling into their countries in numerous copies. Many countries adopted measures and laws to keep out the Cuban materials. I remember Costa Rica had a very effective law to keep Cuban materials out, but I went into a bookstore one day and found a whole pile of Communist children's books that had been printed in Argentina by a publisher who had a name which sounded quite non-political. But I knew that they had come from Russia because I had copies of the same children's books published in Mexico by the Soviet Cultural Center there. Even though Costa Rica was keeping out the Communist children's books that were issued in Cuba that were being distributed free to the countries of Central America and other countries, they were coming in by other means. So even some of the laws that were devised to try to restrain the propaganda materials that were coming into the countries of Latin America, were not too effective.

In Venezuela they had quite a to-do at one point because the country adopted some laws or regulations or decrees on comic books, especially the ones that were coming off of the presses in Mexico in great numbers, filled with sex and violence. So the committee in Venezuela on care of children—Pro Infancia—managed to get a law through to restrict the importation of comic books. Librarians fortunately used that to great advantage. They went to the government and said, If you're going to restrict the flow of comic books, what are you going to do about getting some other reading materials for the kids? So they got support at that point for the creation of more children's libraries as parts of public libraries. This has been going on for a long time.

I don't know how many of you have seen the article that appeared in the *IFLA Journal* which was based on a study of the implications of transborder data flows to library networks.[4] This discussion was carried on in Montreal last fall. The author had studied the transborder flow of information, or TDF as they call it. The transborder flow has been generally defined as the electronic movement of data across a border for the storage, and/or processing by a computer. It therefore involves communications from a terminal to a computer, computer to computer, or computer to a terminal. And the author found that many countries have different perceptions of this business of the transmission of data. Many of them see it as a distinct threat to their societies, and therefore it should be controlled. As a matter of fact he points out the developments in Brazil of the control of transborder data flow. He says that "The Brazilian view of transborder data flow can be described by a speech entitled *The Brazilian position regarding transborder data flow* given by Joubert de Oliveira Brizada, the Executive-Secretary of the Special Secretariat of Informatics, at the IV Latin American Seminar on Data Communication in October 1980. In his speech he stated that TDF 'denotes the transference of information of any kind—technical, economic, cultural, across the borders of a country. ... Among the best examples of transborder data flow, from the economic point of view, are: technology transfers, import and export of computer programs, interactive databases, consultation, data flow and real time operational or administrative control of companies, teleprocessing of data and digital communications.'" In conclusion, he remarks that "In the future informatics societies, such resources will tend to constitute a basic indicator of economic power and national identity. Lack of such resources can generate the same dependence as the one we experience today with oil supply. Thus all official activities must be directed at maximizing Brazilian information resources. Therefore TDF is, and will continue to

---

[4]Donaghue, Hugh P. "Implications of Transborder Data Flows to Library Networks." *IFLA Journal* 9(1), 1983, p. 34–38.

be, submitted to 'political values' that subordinate it to these objectives. These concerns," says Donaghue, "expressed by Brizada in his speech reflect the views of many Brazilian Government officials, as well as many leaders of the lesser developed countries (LDCs). In Brazil these concerns have led to the development of a 'gateway' concept, for channelling data in and out of Brazil. It calls for the establishment of a switching centre, through which all international data traffic would flow. At this point there is no indication that the Brazilians would impose restrictions on the flow of data. However, the opportunity for restriction of such flow through the switch is apparent. Further, the center could provide the means of taxing or taxing the data as it moves through the switch. This development by the Brazilians is being closely watched by other LDCs and it is referred to as the Brazilian model."

I have understood from Mr. McCarthy that since he wrote his paper, the great fear is that if computers and by extension databases are like crude oil, then somebody somewhere could simply turn off the tap. There is a clear indication that the United States might use such pressure against Brazil, although Brazilian officials are far too polite to name their United States allies in this context. I do not share these fears. Apart from the development of Brazilian databases, they intend to maintain in the country local copies of all foreign databases, thus reducing its vulnerability to interruptions in the supply of information.

Also in the magazine *TDR* (*Transnational Data Report*), we find that there are movements afoot to try to transcend these restrictions that may be building up in the developing countries. One article in the *TDR* said that, "During the course of the last decade, the nations of the free world have focused on new information technologies and information processing activities that involve the use of computers and international telecommunications services. Many of these nations have adopted or are in the process of adopting laws and regulations which restrict the flow of electronically processed information across their national boundaries which restrict or prohibit the marketing of information processing services by foreign businesses within their borders."[5] Now apparently a group in the United States called the Association of Data Processing Service Organizations is trying to get some action on the part of the United States government. One of the things that they are recommending is that the United States government arrange for discussions with, and gain the support of data service associations in foreign nations, in securing the removal of restrictions on the marketing of high technology services, restrictions on the use of telecommunications services, and restrictions on the movement of information across national borders.

Victor Rosenberg:

You've admirably covered so much of what I wanted to say! I'd like to add to this that on top of the barriers that Marietta mentioned, the political barriers, and the taxes, the discriminatory duties on various types of information, is the additional problem now that is beginning to emerge in the United States where the United States is restricting the dissemination of various kinds of information. What I wanted to do at this meeting is to assess the actual result of this policy and the concern that is manifest about it.

We in the United States are concerned about this policy more or less from the standpoint of academic freedom versus the control of information. Now what I refer to specifically is the special areas that the Defense Department and the American intelligence establishment have deemed as critical, for example, cryptography. There were a series of papers whose authors were requested to refrain

---

[5]"US Competing Services want minimum TDF Constraints." *Transnational Data Report* 6(2) March 1983, p. 69 .

from openly publishing them. Finally, however there was an agreement made for authors in the field of cryptography to submit their papers for prior approval before publishing them. Then there was a situation that occurred recently at a conference of optical scientists where a large number of the authors were requested not to present their papers, and the ostensible reason for this was for the United States to prevent its adversaries, particularly the Soviet Union, from getting access to sensitive information.

What has in fact happened in the United States is that this whole process has had a rather chilling effect on research in general. Much research that had previously been published in the open literature is being withheld and being held as proprietary, primarily because much of the research is done in organizations that have direct relationships with the Defense Department. They withhold publication out of the fear of jeopardizing their relationship with the Defense Department. This results in a rather chilling effect that goes far beyond the actions of the government in suppressing information.

What I would like to know is if this has any impact on the transfer of information North-South. Has anyone felt the impact of this, had any difficulty getting information out of the United States, or does anyone see any possibility of that?

This is in contradistinction to the other side of the problem, which is the fact that many countries are being inundated with information, as in the sales efforts by American commercial publishers, to provide them with more information than they could possibly want or use. Is there any concern about this particular aspect of the problem in Latin America?

Thomas McGinn:

Venezuela, for instance, is vitally dependent upon petroleum information. Restriction of petroleum information is nothing new. The United States government could not get information from the petroleum industries in order to find out what the flow of petroleum was internationally when the crisis occurred in 1973, because the Petroleum Institute did not want to give it to the United States government.

But in the United States, the private corporations have been restricting information greatly from each other. We all know about industrial espionage and the great secrecy that surrounds for example geological research by the petroleum companies, and so reciprocally the National Petroleum Corporation in Venezuela does not divulge any of its technical reports. These are classified, because it's in competition with the multinationals in terms of marketing and so on. I think it's something we've lived with for a while, although in highly technical areas. Of course what concerns us is that if traditionally open types of research in technology and science are increasingly restricted. We tend to become more sensitive to restrictions on information when the government tries to control it. That's the new issue really, not the fact that information has been restricted by many sources which produce extremely important information.

Winthrop Wiltshire:

In supporting what Thomas has said, we are looking at a spectrum. We have the whole area of patents, which has to do with disclosing information in a certain kind of way, to more or less insure that if you want to use that information, you have to pay something for it, but it is disclosed in a certain limited way. Then you have the other important aspect of information, which is secret know-how, which results from industrial processes. The providers do not want to patent it. I think that in the past, it was considered that most information related to science per se could be put in the public domain, but as soon as it became sort of military technology, in some way it it should be protected and not disseminated as readily, or disseminated only at a certain price, like royalty payments. So I would say yes, it is a disadvantage when we cannot gain access to certain types of information. For instance, we in Trinidad have attempted to search a particular database, and have found that you can search that database only if you find belong to a certain grouping that already exists, and usually exists in the United States, in the area of petroleum, for instance. We have had to live with restricted information from North to South.

My own feeling is that the restrictions are not too significant now, in terms of our own development, because what is closer to reality is that there is so much information in North American databases that is available to us, but for which we don't have mechanisms and techniques for accessing because of our underdeveloped infrastructures, that we have a long long way to go before we start operating on those sort of avant—garde areas such as nuclear science. In some specialized functions or some of the more developed of the developing countries, yes, but I would say that in 99% of the cases that is not one of our major concerns.

Laurence Hallewell:

I think one of our main problems is that so often one doesn't know that the information is being blocked. It doesn't come out that it even exists. Some countries, the Great Britain and Brazil for example, have an official secrets act. The British one, for example, says that anyone who ever is in government employment commits an offense if he divulges any information that he obtained as a result of his government employment. For example, a member of BBC staff discovered that Road Research Laboratory reports as published had numbers missing from the sequence. He had the wits to realize that British publications were ex-

changed with America, and therefore it was possible to discover what had been given to America that wasn't published
in Britain. So he sent somebody to the Library of Congress
to get one of the missing reports. To publish it in Britain
would have broken the law, so he had a television crew on
the grass outside the Library of Congress photographing the
person reading the prohibited pamphlet in such a way that
the viewers could make out the print of the title. It turned
out that it was a report on the catastrophic effects of a rear-
end collision on a particular British small car which is no
longer in production. But the manufacturers were rather
upset. If he hadn't had the wits to do this, nobody in Britain
would have even known that the report existed, let alone
that it had been suppressed.

Mary Jane Ruhl:

Now I could look at this as a mixed blessing. As Tony
said this morning, one could turn nearly anything into an
advantage. My experience has been, particularly in
developing an energy information center for a particular
developing country under United States AID funding. The
United States AID people seemed to think that all we
needed to do was to get the United States Department of
Energy (DOE) tapes and all problems would be solved. And
we all know how much benefit could be derived from United
States DOE tapes. Some, but not a lot. And this was being
done rather than funding the development of databases from
the country's own or its region's resources. Now, the
Department of Energy is becoming very restrictive. They've
developed a small subset that NTIS has been disseminating,
but the large DOE tape is generally not available. I see that
as more of an advantage than a disadvantage, because then
there is nothing left to do but develop the resources from
within, which for a long time would be much more valuable
than a lot of material that has been developed in this
country.

Victor Rosenberg:

So generally it's not conceded to be a serious problem, this restriction of high technology information?

Mary Jane Ruhl:

I think that we keep discussing the flow of information as if something official then results. I think that we need to look at the flow of information as simply the flow of information or the lack thereof, and then evaluate what that amounts to separately.

Victor Rosenberg:

What about the restrictions of the Latin American countries to the import of information? To the use of databases and the like? I'm turning here to the free flow of information issue. The situation in Brazil, as Marietta mentioned, is looked on as a model by many other countries, and Brazil has very severe restrictions on the import of telecommunications systems, the implementation of packet-switching nodes, and the general facilitating of telecommunications systems in the country. It's an effort to keep the flow of information in the country. Other countries have done similar things. Canada for example is very concerned with the flow of banking data being processed abroad. Many countries are concerned about this because of the economic dislocation of jobs going to other countries. That is, high technology data processing jobs have been going to the countries where the data is being processed. The current technology makes it quite economically feasible for a country to process its data abroad, much cheaper than having an indigenous data processing capability within the country. These issues are something that affect library information as well because the same thing applies. And usually the same laws apply to the processing of information abroad.

Marietta Daniels Shepard:

Given what Cavan has said earlier about the rapidly changing situation in Brazil, have these affected transborder data flow issues? I was trying to figure out at one point, after I heard this gentleman speak in Montreal on the Brazilian model, what was behind all of this. Someone told me that it was because some commercial enterprise in the United States had gotten hold of a lot of the raw data in Brazil which Brazil had not known how to process, and had packaged it and sold it back to Brazil. I also know that in Jamaica, as it was just now mentioned, a lot of data has been processed in Jamaica by a lot of United States firms. Does anyone have any information about either one of these situations?

Murilo da Cunha:

It has changed in the last six months. Now the national telecommunications company has made agreements with Dialog, Orbit, and some European databanks, as well as Telenet and Tymshare. It is possible to call a phone number in Rio and be connected in seconds with the United States and Paris. You don't need to apply or make a special request to use Dialog or Orbit for example. You can pay now in cruzeiros, the national currency, instead of hard currency, such as dollars. Of course we still have a kind of technological gate, but it is a consequence of the type of technology that was chosen for use. We have a national company, Infotel, which is a kind of holding company. Each state has a state telephone company and there is a Brazilian company that controls all the state companies. For Brazilian librarians, now it will be easier to access databases in the United States or Europe. We are trying to make an agreement with the British. In the past we were not allowed to access foreign databases officially. Infotel is trying to increase the number of Brazilian users of foreign databases. But for us there is the possibility of a kind of censorship, which could happen in the United States with

Tymshare and Telenet. These are not governmental companies, but, who knows? The company could make an agreement with the government.

Laurence Hallewell:

Could I qualify that by saying that I feel that as a former Brazilian telephone user there is a censorship by price, just as Ma Bell has subsidized local telephone calls by high prices of long distance calls. In Brazil, I found prices for calling abroad extremely expensive. There is in fact a federal tax of 25%...

Murilo da Cunha, Beatriz de Carvalho:

30%!

Laurence Hallewell:

...with that, I feel that Infotel is subsidizing local calls which are very, very cheap, with the long distance call charges.

Victor Rosenberg:

The censorship by prices has been in effect for a long time and that has been the primary way of preventing any kind of international data communications. If you wanted to, you could always hook a terminal up to a telephone and dial up the foreign database, but you would have to pay the regular long distance telephone charges. That was the effective way of canceling the advantage.

Marietta Daniels Shepard:

This has been effectively reduced by using Telenet and Tymnet?

Murilo da Cunha:

Yes.

Winthrop Wiltshire:

I want to pick up from the question that Mary Jane just posed. She was questioning what appeared to be the implicit assumption that whatever information we got from these databases was in fact very desirable information. But I think we have to be aware that the information professionals have to see themselves as part of a complete system. We have to attempt to create the conditions where they do not exist to insure that all categories of potential users, whether they are engineers, doctors, chemists, planners in government ministries have access to the information they need. We should not treat the information that comes from these databases as magic and manna from heaven. We must attempt to build in our educational systems the critical faculty always to evaluate what is in our interest. What we as information professionals are going to have to do is to insure that the category of information that we are providing is in the form of a large range of options, because the planners and engineers or whatever are going to make decisions on the basis of whatever information they are able to get hold of. It is our function to give them as wide a range of options as possible, so that they can make critical judgements given that they have that critical capacity, and therefore can make good decisions, if not always the best decisions. There is no implied goodness or badness in information per se. We are talking about judgements.

Marietta Daniels Shepard:

Juan, I think, had some thoughts on the training of eventual users of information. We've dealt with the area of getting the information for the leaders and decision makers, but we've not talked about getting people used to using information. When it comes to critical evaluation, one of the problems of course is the tremendous amount of information that one can get these days. We must learn how to select from that what is relevant to the situation in Latin America or wherever, and how to use it.

Victor Rosenberg:

The thing that amazes me in a way is, in this group or any meeting that I've attended recently here in the United States of information professionals, there has been an extreme concern particularly among the vendors of information about these barriers to their ability to do business abroad. American vendors of information are consistently complaining in discussions of national information policy about trying to do business abroad, and being prevented from doing so. The author of the IFLA journal article, Hugh Donahue, is a representative of the Control Data Corporation. I believe they had particular difficulty in trying to do business abroad. All of this is of interest to me because these companies want to increase the availability of information, and many governmental regulations are effectively keeping the information out. Time and again you hear at these conferences these broad-based complaints about these rules and regulations that are preventing the flow of information, particularly databases, from going abroad. In the case of Europe and EURONET, from these countries again you hear people wanting to keep out these foreign databases in the name of unfair competition. What you have here is a complex set of regulations that interact with the concepts we talked about this morning and yesterday about the indigenous databases. These laws are designed primarily to see to it that the countries are able to develop their own information infrastructure without interference from foreign governments, multinational companies and the like. I don't sense this sense of urgency here.

Thomas McGinn:

I was at Montreal, and perhaps I was not aware of these things. But in discussion with people from the British National Library, in the exchange between the Library of Congress and the British National Library of their MARC records, both are by their agreement allowed to sell MARC records of either party to anyone in the world. This has been an extremely free flow of information. Generally when you have an agreement with the Library of Congress it's in that vein, in that we don't want to restrict access. You may distribute any records, convert it into your system, to any other country. The British were selling MARC records cheaper than the Library of Congress, and OCLC bought the MARC records from the British instead of the Library of Congress. This becomes an issue, and not in the commercial context.

I think we're all involved in economics here. Perhaps we simply have to work at standardization of costs. Everyone wants to recuperate these costs now. Even the non-commercial institutions like the Library of Congress are under this pressure. The British National Library is very much under this pressure from the British government from what I understood, so they can't be as free in letting these things go as they used to be in the interest of creative exchange of information. I think this has happened simply because of the financial crunch which is global, including the industrialized countries. But I don't think any international agency has tried to bring all these people together and said "Let's try to protect everybody's economic interest and at the same time maintain a free flow." I hope perhaps something like this will come out of the crisis rather than our erecting barriers similar to tariff barriers which I think are now very threatening, even among the industrialized countries. These are needed regardless of the questions of commercial interest, which are very much present when you have a United States company trying to market its information.

William Jackson:

I don't know the technical side of OCLC, but we had someone from Texas who was at a recent meeting there, and she reported that OCLC is now attempting to or is in process of getting copyright for their entire database, even though it is the result of the contributions of their members. This would result, potentially, in people paying for what they had in part supplied gratis into OCLC.

Victor Rosenberg:

That's precisely what they've done.

William Jackson:

Yet a couple years ago the users were very upset, and refused to entertain that thought. Will RLIN go in this same direction? The Library of Congress has traditionally taken the point of view of the United States government, that United States publications, databases and the like could not be copyrighted.

Marietta Daniels Shepard:

Not without great reluctance.

Mary Jane Ruhl:

On the entire issue of data flow and its difficulties, I always wonder what we would learn if we would put a lot of the energy into creating a demand for the information from people who need the information, at the pressure points that we were talking about this morning. If we were to do our marketing instead of our legalistic arguing, I just wonder what would happen. I know that the problems would still remain. But if the information and the data are so valuable, it seems to me that sooner, rather than later, there would be a pull generated from within the country, and that influential people would make sure that tariffs were handled appropriately. I would just like to see it done on some subset of information, instead of all of our lawyers shouting at each other, which is what we seem to be spending our time doing.

Victor Rosenberg:

The barriers to information flow that I was raising, that is, what I see in this country as the censorship of scientific information by the United States, is something that I'm personally very interested in, but in fact probably doesn't affect very much the transfer of information between the United States and Latin America. It is more designed toward the Eastern Block, as sort of the Reagan administration's response to the Soviet Union. Nevertheless it seems to us significant because the United States has for such a long time, at least in theory if not in practice, been in favor of the free flow of information and has not taken any official governmental policy actions to restrain that free flow. Now that does not mean, as Tom has said, that the petroleum companies did not have secret information that would not be divulged to others, and all sorts of things like that, but the general position has been to maintain this free flow. This seems to be changing in the United States. It's something of vital concern to us and potentially could be of vital concern in this context at any rate. It's something that some of us in the United States are concerned about. For the first time we're getting official pronouncements about certain areas of technology that we don't want to see leave the country. And of course this calls into question many things that are in fact ideological underpinnings of the United States, that is again the notion of freedom of the press, the notion of freedom of information flow and that sort of thing.

This has been extended in American universities. The government had begun with unknown success to try to keep foreign nationals from working in university laboratories on certain research projects, and it ran into difficulty because as it turns out over 50% of the graduate students in engineering in American universities are foreign nationals. They would have had to cancel most of their contracts. This is of great concern here.

Ching-Chih Chen:

Sunday I did make reference to quite a few organizations which are also working very closely with universities plus the National Academy of Science and the major organizations such as the American Chemical Society and the American Association for the Advancement of Science. They are really watching this development very closely. The NAS does have a specific panel, and they issued a position paper which essentially put the challenge back to the government, saying that if you want restrict information you tell us what you want to restrict, and why, and don't just give us a blacklist. This certainly indicates that academic research institutions are very concerned about this issue. Eventually all those things will have a tremendous impact world-wide, but at this particular point, because of all these political implications and particularly the reasons of national security, it does seem to be tilted toward the West right now. Of course it is not entirely East-West, because for example we all know about Bolivia's situation.

Victor Rosenberg:

The importance of librarians and information professionals having influence in government and being able to influence these decisions is just as valid in the United States as it is in Latin American countries. There's no question that these things are of concern here too. It should not be ignored that we have our own problems, in making the country's leaders aware of these issues and trying to have them bring out some intelligent policies in the area of information.

It has been brought out that perhaps it would be more interest in using the rest of this session to discuss what we had not concluded. Ching-Chih defined it as the technical aspects of developing Latin American databases. One of the things that occurs to me is that not only is it important for Latin America regionally and nationally to develop information resources, both automated and non-automated, for the purposes of each country, they are also needed as an element of trade. It would be very quickly possible then to have a regional database available abroad, as an element of trade, so it would not be such a one-sided economic transfer that is of all the information being purchased from the United States. This has been brought out time and time again. I think economically it makes sense to have regional databases, and the technology for building regional and local database systems is very quickly becoming available and affordable. It's no longer the situation of large monolithic computer structures that are only available in limited locations. This can be done almost anywhere now with a relatively-low cost technological base. These are things that we ought to look to.

Cavan McCarthy:

I completed my thesis on information systems in Brazil last year, and in my paper I said, "Only one institution is permitted to search databases overseas, and only for peripheral subjects where there is no advantage in importing the tapes. If a subject is of importance to Brazil, the policy of Brazil is to import the tapes for local processing. It is important to note this is not a policy specifically aimed at the information field, it is a general policy which happens to impinge on the libraries. It is also about as close as we can get to government planning in this field, but it is not positive planning, it is closer to negative prohibition." I wrote that last year, and at the time it was perfectly true. I completed my thesis, bound it up, sent it in, and while I was waiting to defend it, I went to a friend's house. I picked up a Brazilian magazine, and turned to my wife and said "Hey honey, my thesis has just become junk mail!" —because this entire policy was simply thrown out of the window. The new situation is difficult to evaluate. A public packet-switching network was set up called Interdata and this is linking Brazil directly to Dialog, SDC, Questel, Telenet, and Tymshare. There's a node in Rio, and the prices are dropping quite rapidly.

Now the economics of this are such that you have to have a lot of users in order to make it fly. You cannot set up this kind of link and continue to have a policy of one user. The cost to develop it was expressed in the newspaper as in the millions of dollars, which is a very large amount of money in relation to what is spent on libraries and information in Brazil. I believe they were talking in terms of 100 users, and they would probably need that many to make it economically viable. But this means of course that the policy of importing databases for use inside comes under heavy pressure. Some of the importers will come under heavy financial pressure because it would be much easier for the users to go directly outside. I do not know how many of the importers of tapes will survive. I know that certainly one or two will go to the wall.

But it's extremely difficult to say because we're literally sitting on top of this situation. This was announced in November, I first heard of it in December, and Murilo tells me there is a meeting in two weeks to give further details on this. So it's very much a situation in flux. I think this is a good thing in a way, because it reminds us all how fluid the situation is in the Third World. Things literally will change from one day to another. You go into your institution, and the director will demand one thing, and maybe next week demand another, and maybe the week after something entirely different: by then you may have a completely different government! There is no institutional stability, certainly not in Brazil and I suspect not in any Latin American country. Policies change very rapidly, and this is a good of example of that. It should be treated as a cultural fact.

Victor Rosenberg:

In the opening session I had alluded to the incredible rapidity of change that is occurring, and one of the things that you find going on economically in the United States is that you find companies springing up over night and becoming very successful, and then failing completely when a larger company enters the market. It is just like the smaller tape-importing companies in Brazil who are similarly threatened by the new Interdata. I always wondered why the Brazilian government had the policy of importing data tapes to maintain the databases locally for reasons of national security. I could understand that they would want the tapes in the country, so that if there were a cut-off of telecommunications they would still have the data, but there is nothing that ages so fast as technological information. You are continuously dependent on the source for updates. If you have *Chemical Abstracts* in the country, and all of a sudden you're cut off from the updates, it very rapidly loses any utility. This sort of thing seems to be a much more rational policy.

Cavan McCarthy:

In relation to that we should note that Interdata also goes to France. This is no accident. If you could only go to the States possibly this system would never have been set up. If the Ayatollah comes along in Brazil and sacks the American Embassy we can go to France.

Marietta Daniels Shepard:

You had some cost figures, Murilo.

Murilo da Cunha:

The cost of Telex decreased about 30% in the last two months, but despite the fact, this cost is about $100 an hour to access American databases. If the libraries use the Interdata system, they don't have to pay in hard currency. They can pay in local currency. This is a very good advantage.

Ching-Chih Chen:

When you say $100 an hour, is that telecommunications costs plus database searching costs, or is it strictly telecommunication costs?

Murilo da Cunha:

Telecommunication costs only.

Ching-Chih Chen:

Good grief! So by the time you finish, a search could cost $140 or more?

Murilo da Cunha:

Yes, or more: but it depends on the database.

Ching-Chih Chen:

Cavan, it takes about a hundred users for the system to be economically feasible, which means very little for us. What are we talking about in terms of volume of searching?

Cavan McCarthy:

They said they'd conducted a survey, in order to set up Interdata, and I think the 100 users came out of that. In Brazil we have 40 federal universities. Let's say that the number of serious research institutions is about the same. That's 80 major research-type institutions. Possibly about the same number of large companies, and that would be about 120 users, plus government ministries. We're literally pulling figures out of the air.

Ching-Chih Chen:

When you first mentioned the system as not intended for one user, obviously it has to be cost beneficial. A hundred institutions have to generate enough volume in terms of search requests to make it worthwhile to maintain all those computers and so forth. What volume are they looking for to maintain it?

Cavan McCarthy:

I was trying to do similar scratch-pad calculations on the number of photocopies needed in Brazil. I put the intellectual community in Brazil at about four and a half million, I think, taking the number of people in federal universities and multiplying by three, which is a reasonable figure for a country with a population of about 130 million. Now if we have four and a half million, one in a hundred does a search each year, that gives us 45,000 searches.

Armando Sandoval:

¿Podría hacer una consulta en español? porque estoy perdido, no entiendo nada. Yo quiero saber una cosa por favor: es que, ¿al instalar este nodo y rio lo haría exclusivamente para que sirviera de consulta bibliográfica a las bases de datos? ¿No? Muy bien. Entonces, ¿serviría para comunicarse por telecomunicaciones a todas partes del mundo? Correcto. Entonces, ¿porqué estar pensando en la administración de los usuarios, de las consultas a las bases de datos? Además otra cosa que es importante. Si yo quiero consultar a través de este nodo y a través de Time-sharing o Telemétodo lo que sea la base de datos del *New York Times* y ocupo cinco minutos, ¿estoy obligado a pagar una hora? Entonces, ¿cual es el problema? Por eso creo que no he entendido nada, porque nosotros en Mexico cuando utilizamos las bases de datos y utilizamos todo este mecanismo y el nodo que existe en Mexico para con este propósito solamente pagamos el tiempo que utilizanos, y si utilizamos un minuto ahí viene el modo de hacer las cosas técnicamente bien, no hay que meterse a hacer experimentos con la terminal. Cuando se llega a la terminal se tiene ya perfectamente bien elaborado el perfil de interés para meter las palabras que a uno le interesa y no venir a averiguar si esto me salió bien o me salió mal, para eso justamente están las bases de datos impresas en las bibliotecas. Cuando nosotros queremos consultar a través de este mecanismo, por decir algo nunca vamos a la terminal primero; vamos primero a la biblioteca y en la biblioteca vemos como está toda la terminología para el perfil de interés que nos interese. Después que lo hemos afinado, entonces nos metemos a través de la terminal para consultar el Dialog. Do modo que entonces, cual es, yo no entiendo. Palabra de honor que no entiendo el problema, y mucho menos entiendo cuando me hablan de miles y miles de consultas de estudiantes. ¡Mucho cuidado, mucho cuidado! Este es un desperdicio horroroso, y si no lo cobran, van a estar tirando el dinero a la calle. Estoy hoy que cobrarlo aunque sea nada mas como una tarifa de protección para que no se desperdicie, pero de ninguna manera regalar un servicio que es tan caro.

Cavan McCarthy:

When I first saw this, I wondered what kind of results they had from the market survey to justify this. It haven't seen it. Or, they just decided they wanted to do this and the survey was set up. It will, as I understand it, cover all types of digital information, not just bibliographic searching. It will probably cover the airline transmissions, and transmissions to and from embassies. It is for all the digital transmissions in and out of Brazil. That is a better indicator of volume.

Marietta Daniels Shepard:

I know that I have been surprised in learning about the limitations of data flow in Brazil because Brazil is usually on top of all of these things. I'm glad to know that all of this is happening. Going back to the OAS survey, we were trying to find out what use was being made of databases. We found out of course that in Mexico the databases of the United States and Europe were most used because the country was closer to them and the telecommunications costs were modest in comparison to what it would be in Brazil. Now the only figure that I got from that was from an information system in Mexico on health, and they have about 100 requests a day, and they use it for about nine hours.

Winthrop Wiltshire:

Do I understand that this system also covers transmission within Brazil, between Rio and Sao Paulo or between Rio and Brasilia, or are we talking exclusively about transmission between a point in Brazil and the United States or France?

Murilo da Cunha:

This is a so-called international node, built for international communication. I'd like to comment on Armando's ideas. I agree with him.

Multiple participants:

What did he say?

Armando Sandoval:

I asked first if that computer was for the exclusive use of connecting databases. It happens that it is not. One of the purposes of this node is bibliographic searching among many others. Then I asked if you use only five minutes of the node, do you have to pay for an hour, and the answer is no. You only pay for five minutes. Then what is the problem? Besides, it is a very low price. What did you expect? How much does it cost to send a letter from Rio de Janeiro to the United States?

Victor Rosenberg:

But in the United States it's $5 an hour. Not the cost of the database, but the telecommunications cost. Anywhere in the United States from point to point.

Marietta Daniels Shepard:

I know that when we were discussing the possibility of libraries in the Caribbean using OCLC I think we found that it would cost $9,000 a month to have the dedicated line between Trinidad and Columbus.

Winthrop Wiltshire:

That has changed significantly because of the public data network being established imminently in Trinidad. It's supposed to come on stream by May and that network is set up to handle both internal and external communications so that any two points in Trinidad connected with the network can interact, as well have access to external databases. But we don't have a price figure yet.

Ching-Chih Chen:

When we're developing machine readable files or access to machine readable databases, we need to be aware of costs. We are talking about a fairly substantial sum of money, because for each search we are talking about perhaps over $50 because they do take say 20 minutes of telecommunication time plus the database fee. Whenever there is a fee involved in getting information, then the whole pattern changes. It is very different in the library. We acquire books and journals. We pay the initial investment and that thing stays in the library and regardless of whether we use it or not. Then we are talking about other kinds of issues. Did we spend the money in the right place, did we buy the right book, or the right journal; if we did buy the right item then maybe the same $100 we would have been generating 20 users per week rather than no users at all. We would be worrying about that kind of thing. But when it comes to databases, and particularly when they are so expensive, then costs become a very important consideration, even though the computer was not dedicated for single purpose use.

My point is that if the system has all these connections, which makes it a fairly expensive system in terms of social utility, compared with what we have in North America, then what kind or level of activity would be needed to be able to bring the cost down, or justify having something like that?

William Jackson:

I think that Ching-Chih has made a very strong point for a much more careful analysis of cost-benefit studies and clear thinking on the part of information professionals and documentalists. If you do this, what don't you do, and is it worth it? And the other way around.

Ching-Chih Chen:

Here in the United States we talk about $8 or $15 telecommunications costs, plus the databases like that of the National Library of Medicine at $15 an hour, ranging to business data bases at over $100. By the time those databases are accessible to other countries the price is probably doubled. So we're really not talking about small money at all at the national planning level. We've really got to think about it.

Murilo da Cunha:

In the United States, several studies were made about the comparative costs between manual and database searches. I remember one study that was published in *Information Technology* last year in December, done in Texas. The author mentioned that because the cost in the United States is so low, a librarian can afford to have a search using an online database without any previous preparation. You can expand the indexing terms to see which are the best to use, and it costs less than to prepare a manual search. But in our country, or in Mexico, we cannot afford that. I agree with Armando when he said that it's necessary to prepare for an hour or more before using the terminal, because we are going to pay a very high fee. We cannot play on the terminal.

Juan Freudenthal:

Americans, as far as my experience is concerned, are extremely careful too, that before they go to the terminal they do a special interview with the user before they use the database. I'm aware that some people go to the terminal and start playing.

Murilo da Cunha:

But it's changing, because the costs of databases are coming down. The costs of personnel are increasing more than those of databases.

Armando Sandoval:

It's a very complex problem because the computer and the terminal are not toys to be played with, and we have to keep in mind that when we are working on these things, we are facing the need to communicate with hundreds of databases, and each of them has a different strategy for searching. If you want to search *Chemical*

Abstracts, you will have to know the *CA* search strategy. Medline is another strategy, beyond having a different vocabulary.

But let me think about reducing charges. This is a real problem. How can we cut charges? The prices are not fixed in Brazil or Mexico. For me this is an example of the real problem of dependence we have in using the services that we receive. We never have the chance to fix the prices of what we obtain. The prices are fixed here, and that is something we will never be able to change unless there is an agreement made between governments. But you can see what is happening. Our dependence is due to the fact that we have to pay the prices that are fixed here. But this is not only for computer time, it is also the same with books, journals, with whatever you can think of. It is so difficult for us to buy a book from the United States and we need them so much. We are limiting our purchases of books and journals. We have to be very careful when identifying the titles of journals that we want to subscribe to. This is not a healthy measure, because we need them, and we have to pay the prices that are fixed. Not by us. And the same thing happens with computer time. Maybe when we have hundreds of thousands of users of databases, it will be better to have the databases in Rio, and not in California. Maybe so. But I don't think that will happen soon. It will be a very long time before we can have the databases in computer memories in Rio de Janeiro.

Juan Freudenthal:

It seems to me that there is a contradiction here, because you said a day ago that in even Mexico you were using computer terminals more than any other kind of traditional resource.

Armando Sandoval:

No, that is not a contradiction, that is correct. People want to. Computers have received so much publicity, it is true that they want to have a computer service. But it is another thing when we say that this will cost 2,000 Mexican pesos. They say, "Ah, I didn't know." We must be careful about giving free services. We have been accused of robbing them. You can have this free if you go to the library and use the indexing and abstracting services.

William Jackson:

The reference department at the University of Texas reports that a very high percentage, well over half of database searching, is done by departments who are using outside contract money to pay the bill, not by individuals out of their own money.

Armando Sandoval:

Let me tell you of our experience. Some years ago we had the exclusive right in Mexico to use the database of the Institute for Scientific Information. We brought their tapes to Mexico, and we ran them in our computer, and we offered free searches because we wanted to penetrate the market. We were serving some hundreds of users. After one year, we told them that they had to pay if they wanted to continue the service, and they dropped it. They were receiving something that they didn't need, that they didn't know how to use. They were wasting it. As soon as they had to pay for it, they discontinued the service.

Marietta Daniels Shepard:

I have a question. Would it be at all feasible to think of linking the computer in Rio to the Dialog database in California by satellite, without telecommunications?

Armando Sandoval:

Yes it is possible, because Buenos Aires does it.

Marietta Daniels Shepard:

Do you know what the costs would be from Buenos Aires to California?

Armando Sandoval:

No.

Victor Rosenberg:

Telecommunications today almost inevitably implies satellite communication. Direct computer to computer via satellite is coming, but isn't here yet.

Cavan McCarthy:

I think what Marietta is suggesting is that we shouldn't use packet-switching. You could do it, but it would be highly inefficient. What you'd do is you'd send it down to Rio, and Rio chops it up into little packets and sends it up to the satellite, and the satellite would send it down to wherever.

Victor Rosenberg:

What I find interesting is the policy question. And the policy question is, that if you encourage the use of foreign databases, and you get the volume, you reduce the unit costs dramatically. There's no question about that. But what the governments have been doing, what Brazil has been doing, has been trying to *dis*courage the use of external databases, both using what Laurence said was a disincentive of costs, but also actively discouraging it in terms of trying to build indigenous data systems. This again is a subject which I am interested in, the way in which the government policies are made to try to encourage local industry. I've had many arguments with Brazilians about this particular issue. The idea is that the countries feel, and I'm speaking of Brazil in particular, but others as well, that in order to even be in the ball game in the next 25–30 years, the countries have to develop an indigenous data processing capability. Canada as well is very concerned about this.

One of the things that I've been interested in, is who is behind the policies. When you say a country has a policy, someone in that country is generating that policy. It comes from some sort of interest group or power base. And it turns out that the major power base is the young technocrats, generally educated abroad in the United States and Western Europe, who come back to their countries and want to have interesting and intellectually stimulating positions in the telecommunications and computer industries, and they don't find them. The only thing they find are the multinationals, whose research capacity is all abroad. The only thing they can do in their country is either sell computers or telecommunications services, manage them or repair them. As a consequence they are implementing policies to discourage the use of external computers and databases, of anything outside the country. And it seems to me that this is wrong-headed because the right way to deal with this is a sort of selective dependency, to import what is needed to develop an indigenous industry, rather than keep it out. But so far the attitudes are pretty much to the contrary. I am quite frankly even distrustful of this new Interdata system, because I think that without the promotion of it for individuals to use these data links, it will still remain very expensive. It's still a gateway concept, and I'm told it's a concept to try to discourage the use of certain databases outside the country, in other words to control, once again, the access. The reason I'm so distrustful of this concept is because its so hard for me to believe that this same pressure group in Brazil would all of a sudden relegate Cavan's thesis to junk mail by doing a completely 180-degree turn-around in policy. I still think your thesis is right.

Thomas McGinn:

I would like to see a feasibility study of indexing all the journals you import into your own country, in your own language. Take a country like Brazil. It might be economically useful to pay some indexers in cruzeiros to index the journals into your own database, and pick those journals that are most important to you, and not depend upon Lockheed. At least you're not using foreign currency, and you've got the data processing there, and you don't even have to think about leasing a database. If you do it, it certainly would be useful to a lot of other Latin American countries.

Armando Sandoval:

We're trying to do that. I think it is a very good advice, but only for the very hard-core journals. It is impossible to compete with the databases.

William Jackson:

But you can only do it in Brazil and Mexico, you can't do it in every one of the 24 Latin American countries. The smaller countries have no way of making that kind of effort.

Thomas McGinn:

Brazil is not operating with a profit motive, at least I would hope they wouldn't, in terms of the government-subsidized cultural agreements that exist. From your paper, it seems that the way work is to be done, we would have a cost reduction automatically, even if you made a profit on it, because Sao Paulo, and Rio aren't as far from Buenos Aires and Lima as Los Angeles and Palo Alto, California.

Murilo da Cunha:

A few months ago I had the chance to teach a two-week course in Brasilia for various librarians from eight different Latin American countries. We talked more after class. I think that Latin America changed after the Malvinas war. Now Latin American governments are very suspicious of the United States and Great Britain, because the United States helped Great Britain in the war, and sent sensitive information via satellite to the South Atlantic. But if you agree or disagree with the war, that's why Brazil decided to have a connection with France, with the United States, and with EURONET, in order to have options and to reduce its dependence on the United States.

Cavan McCarthy:

If I can talk briefly about Thomas McGinn's ideas, I think his ideas of Brazil doing its own indexing are excellent. It is technically and financially feasible, the problem is intellectual. To form that cadre of indexers who are capable of taking English-language publications and producing good indexing in Portuguese—that is an intellectual problem and it would be an incredible task to produce a group of people who could do quality indexing.

Thomas McGinn:

Including importing indexers as part of your cost study?

Laurence Hallewell:

I've used databanks very little, and possibly I'm prejudiced by my own unfortunate choice, but no one's said anything about the quality of the indexing that exists in the databanks. To my mind, in my limited experience, I would say that their indexing is poor, their choice of search terms is completely lacking in specificity, they waste the users' connect time, their coverage is inadequate, they're not up-to-date; even if they're updated, the update is not up-to-date, and in some cases there's a tremendous overlap between similar databanks covering the same area. If we're talking about cost, I don't think we're getting the value for the money. I don't know what one does to improve the situation.

Armando Sandoval:

It is a real challenge. It is very difficult. We have very few people trained in this field. But don't forget, that it is already being done in marine science and agriculture.

Marietta Daniels Shepard:

We started off this afternoon discussing some of the barriers, and we resolved some and left others. I think many of these issues will be resolved in the next few years if we live so long.

Thursday Morning, 14 April 1983

Development and Implementation of a
National Information Policy

Victor Rosenberg:

At the very beginning of the Conference, we talked about the relationship of information to national development in a general context. This morning we want to deal with the issue of national information policies. I have heard no one disagree with the assertion that national information policies are needed, that some sort of coherent policy statements, some sort of coherent direction, is needed both in the United States and in other nations. To varying degrees all over the world efforts are beginning to be made to try to come up with national information policies. These are policies that inevitably and profoundly affect the transfer of scholarly, scientific and technical information.

Mary Jane Ruhl:

Yesterday Victor addressed the absence of an information policy in the United States. I think the policy here in the United States is for the public sector and the private sector to constantly and actively share their different perspectives, which results in a sort of system of checks and balances. It seems to work out pretty well, but when it comes to putting it down on a systematic chart, it just can't be done. We've been keeping the pieces of the puzzle alive and remolding those as they need to be remolded. It always appears to be enviable and advantageous to be in a country where you can develop these policies before you start putting all the pieces in the puzzle together, with certain assurances of what you have and what you haven't.

Our task this morning is to discuss and develop some recommendations relating to the development and implementation of a national information policy. If we view a national information policy as a sort of jigsaw puzzle, it appears to me that we've addressed most of the pieces, and have listed some of the steps that are usually outlined in documents by international organizations as being necessary in developing a national information policy.

Developing the infrastructure for a national documentation, library and archives program is usually the first step mentioned. This entails planning the application of technology within the infrastructure. Planning the manpower. Establishing the legislative framework. Financing. Universal bibliographic control. Participation in regional and international activities and programs. And there are other steps that we've touched upon, such as dissemination and outreach programs, and even research, development and evaluation of information programs.

Within the planning of infrastructures for information policies and systems, one of the things that has been brought out is that it is very necessary to have a strong central coordinating group to be responsible for relating to the various other groups, developing a budget, assessing existing resources, and establishing some user priorities.

Planning the application of technology usually requires selecting the technologies to be used. Will microforms be used? What about computers? What about teleprocessing? What standards and issues of compatibility to be addressed, both technical and intellectual?

Another piece of the puzzle is planning manpower for documentation, library and archive services, including recruiting and training people, developing educational programs, developing programs within the universities, and finding people from other countries if that is required.

Establishing the legislative framework includes setting up requirements for legal deposit of national publications, for example. What are all of the legal issues to be addressed, both national and international?

Exchange agreements for free flow of information need to be made. Professional status and advancement within the country should be worked on, trying to reach, or come close to, the same status that doctors, lawyers, and engineers have attained.

An issue that we haven't discussed is that of security, and privacy. This is necessary to safeguard the nation's archival heritage. We've been talking about scholarly information, which is probably thought to be over and above that type of issue. Privacy and security considerations do have an impact when it comes to having free systems within which teleprocessing can be done.

We haven't talked a lot about how the programs are to be financed, how bilateral agreements with other countries can be set up, or how libraries can get grants from international assistance agencies. How does cost recovery or cost sharing fit into the scheme?

It seems to me that we need to find out what is needed, what information problems can be addressed to get the attention of those in power, to make it easy for us to set up an information policy and structure rather than having to defend it constantly. What are some of the things that we've experienced that worked in that area? How can we provide a service that is very apparent in its value, for example one that has an effect on national productivity? Are there research projects that can be developed that would make that very apparent to the people in power?

We've talked about a lot of problems at this Conference, and I'd like to see us now talk about some solutions, some of the things that have worked. What might have made it easy that we can share with the group?

To what extent do we look at national needs, and try to emphasize the sectoral area in a given country that is requiring immediate attention? To what extent does that then influence national policy, either in a positive or a negative way? How does that facilitate our work, or make it more difficult? If there's a large amount of money for an energy program, an energy information program gets up and running and a lot of the other scientific information gets left behind.

How do we turn officials, and people who are going to be our supporters, into believers in an information program?

Victor Rosenberg:

I'd like to comment on the entire question of problems and solutions, and how we can actually solve some of these problems. I was hoping that at this Conference we would be able to deal with some solutions to the problems of transferring information. I think that if we think of information in the abstract, if we think of information in terms of providing national services in various areas or sectors, as Mary Jane points out, it's much more difficult that if we think of providing the researchers with information. When a country invests a great deal of money in sending a young scholar abroad to study, or a scholar studies in the country and develops very sophisticated skills in research or development and then wishes to pursue a career in that area and needs information to support that career, where is that information going to come from? That's one side of it. The other side of it is, the advantage for us of looking at national information policies in terms of scholarly scientific and technical information is that it is one opportunity that we have to link this type of information with telecommunications, computers, and the high technology at all levels that every country is interested in. And it gives us a pathway to get something actually done.

One of the things that I would like to hear more about, as Mary Jane said, is what are some of the successful ways that we can in fact look forward to the 1980's and say how can we get information from one country to another, from the sources of the information to the researchers in a way that it can be effectively used.

I found myself rather despairing with some of the discussions previously, especially one remark that Cavan McCarthy made regarding the problem as an intellectual problem. I feel that perhaps that is the key to it. There's no question in my mind that any country can afford the technology. The technology is now becoming so inexpensive. If you look at the Sears and Roebuck catalog, you can buy a satellite antenna to put in your back yard and connect directly to satellites. Computers are being sold in all the department stores and discount stores. Now it's no longer an inaccessible technology. The problem is the intellectual problem of what can be done with it.

Mary Jane Ruhl:

What I would like to ask for is some of the success stories. I know Merline Smith can tell us some, I know Barbara Gumbs has had some experience in some of the outreach activities I would like to invite those who have seen the establishment of a national information policy to tell us about the development and implementation process used.

Merline Smith:

In 1978, we called a workshop with users and information personnel, and we came up with some recommendations for a national science and technology information policy. And this was accepted by the government. But at the same time we did not then consider a national policy on science and technology. It was just information, and not science and technology as a whole.

In 1981, we had two days at a workshop to come up with a national science and technology policy. This was attended each day by over 200 people from multidisciplinary areas. We had various working groups, focusing on key areas. We put the development of a national science and technology information policy to one group, because by then there were new technologies developing in information, and we wanted to have these covered. We had a seminar, and we came up with recommendations on transborder data flow, telecommunications, and high technology.

The recommendations formed a part of the draft national science and technology policy that is now being considered by our Parliament. The policy has to be decided by the political directorate. The people make the recommendations, the Minister with responsibility for science and technology goes over the recommendations, and comes up with a document. In this case, our Prime Minister has responsibility for science and technology, but a junior minister handles it. I can really say that information is at the highest level on the island, because eventually the Prime Minister will make the decision. And we're getting a lot of support from the minister.

Considered in this policy are areas already addressed by Mary Jane. We have the area of legal deposit. We have a very good monitoring system established. We have considered the classification of information, which has a security aspect. We think that sensitization of the nation to the importance of science and technology is very important. We have looked at standards and regulations. The question of manpower. Access to information. Coordination. Telecommunications. Higher technologies. I must mention that steps have been taken to implement some aspects, like the legal deposit, and we have a copyright law, coming into force any time now.

Mary Jane Ruhl:

What parts of the process do you think has made it happen? I asked Merline yesterday what made it so easy, and she said "Who said it was easy?" She said that it was very difficult, but it worked. Do you think it was because of the close relationship with the Prime Minister and the attention that the recommendations received?

Merline Smith:

No, I think it's more the people involved, because Jamaica, like other developing countries, lacks a scientific and technological tradition, so as scientists we've had to push this on the nation. There's a very strong Jamaican society of scientists and technologists, and the scientific research council is responsible for coordinating the scientific activities on the island. We worked very closely with the scientific organizations, and this is where the push really came from. Here I should acknowledge the funding assistance of the OAS in helping us to get this off the ground.

Winthrop Wiltshire:

Merline is being extremely modest here. She was given personal responsibility for organizing that science and technology conference in 1981. She did admirably.

Juan Freudenthal:

I would like to add that Jamaica has a tradition of traditional libraries, all linked together, before the work in science and technology was begun. You already had a wonderful structure, in a sense.

Merline Smith:

We had a very strong public library system, but at the same time, in the area of science and technology, we find that people have very little interest, even at the political level. The politicians are not very sensitive to science and technology. It's only in recent times that concern has been evident. I really have to commend this minister with responsibility for science and technology, because he's really been doing a lot. Just last week we had a meeting of science and technology ministers in Jamaica. We had a week of activities, which included a meeting of the young scientists in the Americas. We even brought in an astronaut, thanks again to the OAS. So just now in Jamaica, we are thinking about science and technology. But by next week, it could change. We have to keep a very active sensitization program going.

Victor Rosenberg:

What were the models that you used in developing the policy? Did you look through any other countries' models?

Merline Smith:

We looked at the manuscript by Unesco. We had assistance from the OAS which provided us with a consultant, and we looked at activities in various countries.

Victor Rosenberg:

Did you look at France and Brazil?

Merline Smith:

Yes, we did. We had a collection of all of these documents.

William Jackson:

As a long time observer of the Jamaican scene, I think one of the elements that comes together in what Merline has said and what Juan has said is the people element, the leaders, the people working in this area who have been both visionary and realistic at the same time. I think that has been one of the happiest combinations. They've realized the inherent limitations of budget or personnel or whatever, and yet they never sacrificed the vision and the goals because there was a temporary blockage of funds. Look at the idea of creating the library school. For a long time there just didn't seem to be any progress, but they never abandoned the idea of creating the school. They just put it on the back burner and waited for a happier occasion. They couldn't get any outside assistance for a long time. Then finally, UNDP came in and brought Dorothy Collins. I think that happy combination of being realistic visionaries or visionary realists, on the personal level of leadership, explains a lot of what has been in many areas the classic success story.

Barbara Gumbs:

In Trinidad our situation is somewhat different in that we don't have a formal national information policy as such, although informal cooperation does exist among the institutions in Trinidad and Tobago. With the new CARIRI, which is the Caribbean Industrial Research Institute, we don't realize how fortunate we are in that we have a management that is very, very sympathetic toward information, and because of this we have not had the uphill climb to convince them that information is important in the organization. On each team that is working on a project for industry, an information specialist is automatically assigned to the project team.

The other thing is that we have emphasized and iden- tified our users as mainly in industry, and OAS again has given us funds for development of that information service. Since 1977 we have been reaching out to industry, where possible linking to its professional organizations, and seeing where the need is. As a result we were able to publish a construction cost bulletin which was identified as a need as a result of our outreach program.

What I'd like to suggest, and I think even for us in Trinidad, is as Ching-Chih and others have said, that we need within each country and then regionally to know where the strong points of our holdings are. For example, some areas of the country or countries in Latin America may be concentrating on building a collection on food technology. If we could first within each country develop directories of resources, and if we could commit ourselves to at least that one activity nationally, and then exchange information about those directories among ourselves, that in itself would be as- sisting and providing a tremendous information source for us to work with. It would enable us to use and develop the referral services which were mentioned earlier. Those are two concrete areas that I would like to see noted in recom- mendations coming out of this workshop.

Juan Freudenthal:

Could I suggest that we go back to two or three of the items on the agenda, since several of them as you mentioned have been discussed. One would be selecting a national coordinating body. I think it would be interesting to hear how it has been done or how it could be done. The next item would be what made it easy to introduce new technology. It would be interesting to know how this has happened. Third, what is going to make it possible to implement the national information policy?

Alma Jordan:

I would like to add to that the matter of manpower and training. I don't think we have given that much thought. That to me is the most critical of all. We really ought to give more attention to training people for this new age.

Beatriz de Carvalho:

I'd like to go back to something that Merline said about national planning in Jamaica. She mentioned monitoring work. I'd like to report that in Brazil some years ago a project was started in the National Institute for Scientific and Technical Information to monitor the information activities there. While there are many ways of doing such national monitoring, this project collected statistical data about activities such as the production of books and serials, patents, and dissertations and theses. This is a way of knowing how things are going in the country, that undoubtedly would help the coordinating body to make diagnoses and decisions to either strengthen some activities or to change others. Data were collected, articles were published, and papers were presented. When the people involved in the project left the Institute, then the project stopped.

I would like to know from Merline how you monitor activity?

Merline Smith:

Well, as far as the information activities are concerned, I mentioned yesterday that we have a national information plan and a national committee which manages archives and documentation services. We have a policy-making committee, and we have another committee comprised of the heads of the information units. Now the heads of the information units meet on a monthly basis, and a report is given to the policy-making committee, which in turn reports to the national committee. Prior to all of these policies, we did a survey of scientific and technical activities on the island, in which we included the information units and their capabilities.

Laurence Hallewell:

I wonder if I might not give an awful example of what happens when there is no information policy. My information on the United Kingdom may not be up-to-date, and I believe the government has finally given way, but for a long time there was an absolute refusal to admit that there was any need for any ministry to have responsibility for information. Libraries in England and Wales have been under the Ministry for Arts, with the implication that they were concerned only with the humanities. At the local level public libraries have more and more been under their municipal leisure directorates, as if they were solely concerned with escapist literature. British Telecom went ahead with very up-to-date ideas in computerized information, but this was done by the computer boys without any real market research and it was aimed at the individual household. There was a crying demand by business for the same sort of information, but it took a long time for them to realize that this was where their market was. There's been severe financial pressure on education, at the university level and lower, but the government has merely said that it hoped that libraries wouldn't be too badly affected, without specifics about it. The result has been just that, to avoid firing faculty and teachers, libraries and all their information media at all levels have taken far, far more than their fair share of the cuts. At the same time library schools have gone on producing far more trained people than there are jobs for. This is just an awful warning of what happens when one doesn't have a consistent, centrally directed national policy.

Mary Jane Ruhl:

Does anyone have anything more to recommend regarding the selection or development of a national coordinating body?

Maria Oyarzun de Ferreira:

Siguiendo un poco lo expresado por Beatriz, quisiera yo contarles lo que nosotros hemos hecho in Chile a ir recuperando toda la información necesaria para llegar a formular una política. En Chile mucho ya les he contado lo que es el sistema nacional de información. Dentro del CONICYT funciona el centro nacional coordinador de este sistema y cuando se comenzó a trabajar en el año 1967 más o menos como centro nacional coordinador, el primer trabajo que adoptamos el recopilar, el hacer un inventario de las unidades de información en el país, con información completa en cuanto a conexiones, servicios y todo lo que necesitamos saber de información. Se formó un catálogo colectivo nacional de publicaciones periódicas de modo de tener acceso a la información existente en el país. Se han hecho registros de las publicaciones periódicas nacionales, lo que se están publicando en el país, está registrado. Hemos hecho registro de tesis, tenemos hecho registro de traductores. Ultimamente nos hemos preocupado de visitar las reuniones científicas nacionales y también formar una base de datos con las investigaciones científicas. Estamos también registrando información sobre bibliografías nacionales especializadas y sobre puestos secundarios de información nacional. Nosotros pensamos que con todo esta pulpa de información registrada y que no solamente está registrada sino que tambien se publica y se difunde, tenemos la información necesaria como para estudiar en algo.

Fuera de estas tareas de recopilación de información nacional que nosotros creemos que es muy importante y que le corresponde al centro nacional, tenemos otras actividades como fué el programa de entrenamiento. Era un poco difícil el ir adaptando programas de las escuelas de bibliotecología. Siempre hay que someterlos a una aprobación, y que era necesario que el bibliotecario se fuera preparando conociendo las nuevas técnicas que están siendo aplicadas, y también el que fuera sabiendo lo que estaba pasando en el resto del mundo de la información. Se mantuvo durante diez años esos programas de entrenamiento, ofreciendo los mas variados temas, con algunos cursos dados por profesores de otra especialidad a la cual se pudiera aplicar hacia todo bibliotecario. Por ejemplo, para notarles algo, dimos dos o tres veces cursos sobre estadística dados por estadístico que lo han tocado desde el punto de vista bibliotecario. Se dieron también bastantes cursos sobre mecanización de informaciones en computación. Llegamos a dar nosotros 230 cursos y en este momento no estamos dando esta actividades, pero sí, estamos haciéndolo con el colegio de bibliotecarios y pensamos que a través de ellos se podría llegar el momento de pensar ya en un postgrado a través del CONICYT. A través del UNISIST, en contacto con la Universidad Catolica de Chile estamos trabajando en un postgraduado hacia ciencias de la información.

Hay otro tipo de actividad que también nos ha dado resultado que es los grupos de trabajo. Cuando comenzó, por ejemplo, a hablarse del desahorro, que todo el mundo se inquietaba por desahorro, que todos querián hacer desahorro se formó un grupo de trabajo en el cual participaban quienes tenían la experiencia que no habían empezado a trabajar y se intercambiaban la experiencia y se revisaban trabajos, detectáabamos nosotros todo el trabajo respecto al que se estaba haciendo en el pais. Se publicó tambien y es en estos momentos que nosotros vemos la importancia de base de datos. Estaba ya entrando de lleno en nuestro campo, que se están produciendo ciertas, no digo problemas pero sí, circunstancias que tiene que afrontar gente que está trabajando en las bibliotecas o centros de documentación, acabamos de formar un grupo de trabajo sobre desarrollo de base de datos, con la intención de intercambiar experiencias, cuánto contamos cada uno, qué estamos haciendo, pensando lo que

nosotros podamos hacer siempre: approvechar la experiencia
de cada uno para poder seguir adelante.

Beatriz de Carvalho:

Mary Jane, you've asked people some questions.
How could we deal with the problem of the selection of a
coordinating body for a national information policy? It must
be well known here that in most countries of Latin America,
the government organization includes what we call a
national council for scientific and technological research.
This is the case in Argentina, Brazil, Chile, Colombia,
Venezuela, and Mexico. Maybe other countries have such
an institution. All of these have institutes dedicated to information. These would be the natural coordinating bodies for
the national information policies for their countries. So, if
we're thinking about the recommendations, we could say
that these institutes in these countries should develop plans,
and develop national information policies. For the other
countries where there is no institution of that kind, a
national committee of people involved with information activities could form a commission to discuss and develop such
a plan. I don't know how our recommendation will be written, or addressed to whom, but this is an idea.

Armando Sandoval:

I entirely agree with what Beatriz has said. It is true
that the majority of our countries have such a council, and it
is a good idea to identify these councils as the central focus
for coordinating these activities. The danger may be that
these councils are always related to science and technology,
and our countries need promotion of other areas like the
humanities. If we feel that we have to make a recommendation of this kind, I should say that two factors have to be
taken into consideration. One, we should leave the door
open to our decision-making people in our countries to decide
where to establish such a coordinating body. If there is a
council of this type, it is a good idea to mention that the

council may be the coordinator, but, more importantly, we should suggest that it has to be at the highest level in any of our countries. If it is the research council, that is alright. Always, the body has to be at the highest level, and it should cover all the academic or intellectual or scholarly activities of the country, including the humanities, science, and technology. This has to be suggested to the government.

The greatest problem in our countries is that we don't know where the information is. But Maria Oyarzun demonstrates that they have started to deal with this by identifying and coordinating the sources of information. For me this is really the starting point of developing a national information system. And as Alma Jordan mentioned, we should never forget the real priority of training people at the highest level. It is not a question of only training librarians; it is also a question of training the best librarians, and attracting the best with a very good knowledge of what they have to do, and a very good personality. This is really very important.

Cavan McCarthy:

Dr. Hallewell's mention of the computer boys is less insulting in British English. It reminds me of something that we haven't talked about and that is the relationship between the computer people and the librarians. The information policy has to be set by the librarians. When information policy is being discussed, librarians have to be on the scene, with the computer people in an inferior position because the computer people are not trained in information needs. They are not familiar with bibliographic systems. Very often they do not like to work with bibliographic systems because this means they loose contact with commercial systems and cause loss to their careers. I have personally seen computer people setting up current awareness systems without any input from librarians, and they did not include a document delivery element. Then, one year later, in desperation, they find they have to add it on.

I have seen a national center which was operating reasonably well, with librarians and manual and semi-mechanized systems. Then it was taken over by computer people, who decided that all this manual stuff was rubbish and the best thing to do was to stop all the manual systems and build databases. They stopped all the manual systems and couldn't get the databases going. So the system more or less ground to a halt.

We have this serious problem of status. The analysts have very high status, especially in Latin America, but the librarians have a very low status. Especially when the analyst is coming in to modernize the system, the analyst already has a high advantage over the librarian.

Victor Rosenberg:

Can't that be turned to an advantage, though, because if the status goes to the computer professional, cannot the librarians ally themselves with the computer professionals to develop the policy? You would want to see some sort of a linkage, so that the two can work together. The same thing happens in the United States. But once you show computer people something about what library problems are, they become interested and involved. The tour guide for our tour of the Computer Center yesterday is working on a library problem. This can happen, and has happened with great success in many places.

Ching-Chih Chen:

I've never liked to stress the team approach or concept. I always say that in terms of technological applications to library and information work, the best is if you can find librarians who also have the computer or technology background. Then such persons can take care of both and there's no problem. But in reality it really doesn't work that way. Then you have to work as a team, rather than think about which side is superior or inferior. The two parties would be constantly in close communication, and as Victor said, you can turn it to your advantage. Indeed we are able to communicate with computer people, and that would go beyond just the computer.

I would like to see that for several other fields as well. For instance, Maria mentioned statistics. They are absolutely crucial when we're talking about national programs and services, and I think Tom mentioned several times that there are some very fundamental statistics in mimeographed form that he could not get. We need to collect basic data, to know what we're being asked to provide and what kinds of things are needed of us. It comes back to the fact that librarians tend to be collecting for collecting's sake, collecting for recording's sake, but they never to turn around and use the data for planning or for forecasting. I would like to say that if we could work with other professionals in other disciplines we could accomplish our goals.

Beatriz de Carvalho:

I have a few comments about what Dr. Sandoval said. First, I agree that, as Ximena said yesterday, when we're talking about information for the development of the country, that includes all kinds, including humanistic information. Secondly, when I talk about an information unit of a national research council, I am not saying that we here should tell them what they should do: we don't have that power. But we could see through Maria what CENID is doing. This kind of institution is the natural kind to coordinate a national policy on information. It would be natural for them to do it and it would be accepted. But of course, if we decide to talk about what institutions should do for our countries, the ministers of education should be involved, because in the universities, research is being done in all subjects, and they don't have libraries. When you said we should leave the door open, my idea would be that you could at least suggest which kinds of institutions could do what.

Armando Sandoval:

No, Beatriz. Te entendi muy bien, solamente queria agregar algo a lo que habías dicho, pero lo que dijiste me pareció muy bien.

Unidentified Speaker:

Yo no sé si entienden.

Armando Sandoval:

Sí entienden perfectamente.

Winthrop Wiltshire:

It would seem to me that we have to be very careful about prescriptions. What is much more important is the process. I think one of the lessons to be gained from the Jamaican experience is that the policy was formed and the coordinating agency was identified and formed more or less as a participative process. The process is important in several aspects, especially in the identification and selection of the agency, thereby getting commitment from all of the agents involved who will, in fact, have to be active in implementing a policy. The coordinating agency by itself cannot implement a policy effectively. The agency must have the full commitment and support of all of the actors, irrespective of whether it has money to spend or not. I would think that we should attempt in our recommendations to stress the process, and then, the operating mechanisms, because that coordinating agency should try to function by cooperative mechanisms, as a sort of leader among equals, helping and coordinating. So when we're talking about science and technology coordinating committees, we're also talking about science and technology in their broadest sense, and information for development. We need to involve everyone.

Alma Jordan:

I think that we are in the throes of one of the dilemmas of this whole information situation, because we ourselves are defining information and information policies in slightly different ways at different times. And this is going to lead to an awful lot of difficulty on the part of people we make recommendations to. The people to whom we are speaking cannot necessarily make the distinctions that we make when we say that information for development includes humanistic information.

If we're talking about a science and technology coordinating body, it is at the level of science and technology in the country that usually is distinct and separate from the overall information services of the country, which could include the public and school libraries, and the like. I think the pattern in Jamaica shows us quite clearly that they have a coordinating body which is over all, as Merline says. NACOLADS has a planning function. At the science and technology level there is the scientific research council and the network that she has described. There is a superstructure which relates to all information.

If we're going to talk about national information policies, I think we must be very clear that that total information policy will include everything, within which the science and technology information and information technology and a whole lot of other things could fall. But there is a two-tier approach which we must not miss. I think there is danger in saying anything about national science and technology research councils which would tend to exclude information beyond science and technology, whether you mean it to or not, to the minister. So we must make it very clear, that if we're talking about one area, then we're talking about that but it is within our overall structure.

Beatriz de Carvalho:

The national research council in Brazil gives grants to projects in sociology and the humanities: it includes these areas.

Victor Rosenberg:

I would like to know whether you think if science and technology benefits, would the benefits not then trickle down to the social science and humanities?

Alma Jordan:

That's not the way you want to do it because that's a poor-relation kind of situation which I don't think we want to foster. In the structure that we went through, we were seeing the different levels, but recognizing that it's all unified, we are concentrating on one area.

Ximena Felíu:

No debemos olvidarnos que lo que hacemos de la información no es información por información sólo, sino que es información hacia un usuario. En el caso que nosotros hemos trabajado no hemos tenido problemas debido a que hemos avanzado bastante por el hecho de que estamos en contacto con el usuario. El usuario en nuestro país llega a CONICYT porque CONICYT puede dar asistencia internacional. A través del CONICYT se está manejando lo que es hecho nacional con indicación científica y, como dice Beatriz, toda esta asistencia, no se para a lo que es humanista o lo que es científico, todo se canaliza y nos ha sido fácil trabajar justamente porque estamos con el usuario al lado. Nosotros no podemos hacer una política de información dejando a él solo, Siempre tenemos que estar viendo cual es el punto de vista del usuario y yo creo que justamente por eso es que hemos avanzado, se nos ha facilitado un poco el servicio.

Juan Freudenthal:

Very briefly, she said that they indeed in Chile are doing what Alma was saying, that the council where she is working is working toward the users at all of these levels, including the social sciences and humanities.

I wanted to add one thing to what Alma was saying. I do agree completely with Armando and Alma, but it seems to me that she was saying something a little different, that national information policies can be recommended, they can be planned, they can be facilitated, by all of these organizations like the CONICYT council, but policies do come from the political bodies, and the political climate of the country, and not directly from those organizations like the councils for science and technology. We only plan and facilitate, but we do not necessarily create the policies themselves.

Murilo da Cunha:

I would like to report on Brazil's experience in information policy over the last ten years. In 1972, we tried one process but it did not work. There are at least two ways to bring an information policy into being. One is from the top down, with a central coordinating body, trying to identify the information needs and trying to develop sectoral information sub-systems. We tried this is Brazil ten years ago, and it didn't work, because the central coordinating body tried to monopolize the subsystems in a very bad way, and there was a kind of revolt against the central coordinating body.

The other way is from the bottom up. For this we need to have a kind of momentum at the right moment, to lift the organizations and the subsystems along, and to try to help them to develop, and try to design a kind of national information policy. We are doing this now in Brazil. We don't have a written information policy, but we have pointers and ways towards the information policy which we will have in a few years. Michel Menou, in his paper, mentioned that information policy cannot be imposed by a single agency or group such as the national coordinating agencies for libraries and information services. He mentioned that with an integrated approach, as Prof. Chen suggests, we can move the information from a secondary, support activity, as a by-product of science and technology, to a self-contained high priority area. I think we need to discuss and think more about this.

Beatriz de Carvalho:

CNPq is studying all the national institutes of scientific and technical information in Brazil.

Thomas McGinn:

I think you've raised a very important point. The top-down approach is required, so that you get a budget. You have to have someone up there in the planning agency to insure that the information system gets money. That isn't necessarily going to happen, at least in our experience. I'm in complete agreement that the bottom-up approach is the one that works, because there are the persons, many at the middle level and not at the top level, who are going to push for the system.

Marietta Daniels Shepard:

Just one more item to throw into this whole business of determining what kind of a national body should be set up. You can't discount the importance of the national planning office, even thought that may confuse the situation even more.

Mary Jane Ruhl:

Armando pointed out to me at the break that he thought that I did not understand the point that Alma was making, and he was right. I didn't. The point was the need to include information technology and awareness at all stages of the educational process of the country. This indeed is very important.

Now, can we continue sharing what has worked in bringing technology into the country that can be used for scientific and technical information activities.

Thomas McGinn:

I think that technology has been the key factor for making possible the national information network in Venezuela. People may disagree with me. We had a national planning commission, which had some important uses. It was a top-down structure, as recommended by Unesco, set up in 1976 I believe. I think Marietta documented its history in her paper. We had four major areas of information services, including one in the science area. We have a council for science and technology. We have a national science research center, and the government has supported this area over the last 15 years. The universities are another subsystem. The national archives were another subsystem, and the national library which administers the public libraries was another subsystem. Now this constituted an information policy in many respects, and the coordinating commission was part of the national planning agency. They had a good budget, under the previous government. But the coordinator, the head of the national library information system, publicly said once that the activity was coming from one sector, and that was the national library sector. This observation was made in 1979 or 1980.

The present government did not give its support to this agency as part of the national planning commission, perhaps because three of the sectors were not really functioning that well. I don't know whether it was one of those political decisions that can be made, that something done by the previous government would not be continued by the present government. But in fact the importance of the national coordinating agency in the last 4 years has been reduced considerably, and it has not been funded as it had been previously. However all during this period, both the national library/public library sectors and the science sectors were introducing automation and new technologies, which in itself was a tremendous levers in getting support from the government, once they saw this was functional.

The national library created a database of Venezuelan publications. It was mainly bibliographic, but it has extended into raw data now. The council for science and technology particularly put into the database the union catalog of serials and research projects going on in science. Concurrently also in the science area, INTEVEP, which is the national petroleum research institute, automated its information system by putting in all the technical reports which had been written on petroleum studies in recent years. This is classified information. It's not public, but it is a very important source, given the dependency of the country for 80% of its revenues on petroleum.

I don't deny the importance of a coordinating superstructure especially for budgetary purposes. There was a strong impetus on the part of the national library to separate itself from the ministry and become autonomous, so it got its own budget so that it could fund all kinds of programs, including developing human resources. For example, the national library administers the program for sending librarians abroad to study. There is a very strong awareness of the need to train people in all areas. This has resulted in getting some very qualified people trained in automation. You might say that the national library and science sectors went ahead in their information systems, whereas the universities and archives did not. This is not the situation of other countries, where the universities have done more. In fact the national library database has become quite powerful. It includes practically all Venezuelan monographs ever published for example, cataloging of all serials, increasingly the serials holdings, and now the council for science and technology and the national library are going to pool their databases. They are in the process of working out a few technical programming problems. Then, the national union catalog of serials will come into the database.

In the meantime we have the software which will permit indexing by any institution that is online, and the central university has come online. This is extremely important. The most important library in the country is the central university library, not the national library, and its data base includes not just Venezuelan publications, but all kinds of publications in all areas, as a major university would have. The first records they put in were the theses, particularly in science, from the faculties of science. We didn't have these in the national library.

There is a coordinating board between the central university, the national library, and CONICIT, which is not an official state body, but a group of people who are concerned about this and who work together very well. Another factor is the close collaboration between three or four information scientists and about the same number of librarians. One or two librarians have had strong information science training (I'm not including myself, I'm not Venezuelan). This group has put together something that is ongoing, and which will survive any governmental changes or any sort of political changes which have previously affected these types of advances.

Automation is so visible, and so visibly successful, that anyone who sees it says this is something which the country has accomplished. Now we have inter-institutional contact. We have multiple-library catalogs. We bring all kinds of government people in to look at it, and they're impressed. And in this sense the bottom-up approach has been very important. We currently have 180,000 bibliographic references in the database, not just to Venezuelan materials although it is largely so. It includes all the cataloging done by the national and public libraries, mainly Spanish language materials. In this sense it would be very useful for another country who's interested in Spanish language materials. Increasingly specialized databases are becoming available, such as that of the Supreme Court, which included non-bibliographic materials and a special file for its jurisprudence. This is consulted by all the courts in the country and by the executive branch so they can enforce the decisions of the Supreme Court. Another file in the specialized group is that of the Patent Office. And this, in part, has been made possible by automation.

We have about 12 or 15 institutions who want to join, but we can't train all the people from various libraries fast enough. Our biggest problem is training people who want to get into the system. We're trying to resolve this, but with some difficulty. It doesn't cost us anything any more really to include anyone, because funding is by each institution. We have a tariff, a rate scale, for anyone participating in the database, which is minimal to recover costs such as the computer center. If they want to print out catalog cards for their institution from the database there's a cost for that. If they need any programming done there's a charge for that. We don't have enough people in that area. We're short, but we're making it in terms of personnel. Our interest at this point is contact with other Latin American institutions who have automated so that we can make our database bigger and strengthen theirs if they want with the information that is in ours.

We haven't yet gone into North American bibliographic databases or cooperatives because we're not sure if there is a cost advantage for us in that. We haven't been able to study it in detail though. We are using the scientific and technical databases, on DIALOG and ORBIT, which will continue to be a service of CONICIT and not of the national library. That will be integrated into the budding national information system in the unified database of the several institutions.

Also coming online is INTEVEP which will mainly consult our database since theirs is classified and will not be available.

We still have a problem of getting enough indexing people to handle the information.

People will be able to search our databases in North American and Europe as well as CONICIT does. This is a national service. Anyone can telephone the CONICIT and get a search through a United States database. If he wants the contact directly, or if he wants an intermediary who will do the search for him, it can be done. So we're at a point now where a great deal could be done to expand this. On the national level there's a consciousness of the value of this. Sadly, there are some important research institutions such as at the Universidade Nacional del Zulia which are isolated, which cannot be brought in. We can have better contact with United States databases or other capitals in Latin America than we can with our own cities and areas in terms of telephone service.

In summary, I think that dedication to automation has facilitated the setting up of the national information system, which a very well-intentioned program or policy did not. And that automation was tied to the effectiveness of a group of people who knew what they wanted and how to cooperate.

Ching-Chih Chen:

I have a few questions. I'm delighted to hear that the national database in Venezuela is being built, and I'm sure that there are similar cases in Brazil and other countries in Latin America as well.

I realize there is a significant difference between the North and the South; however, if, in the United States or developed countries, the home or personal computers become something which families can afford, then it's not too much to expect that they will be affordable in libraries in developing countries. I really do see that in developing countries at different levels, and for different purposes, they have tremendous implications. I'm very anxious to hear from my colleagues from the South what you see as the potential for that kind of machine in your setting, particularly in those countries which have home-grown industries which are building up or are making available that very high capability 16-bit microcomputer. I understand that is available in Brazil.

Cavan McCarthy:

There is very little penetration of microcomputers in Brazil in libraries at the moment. I can't think of an example.

Beatriz de Carvalho:

I can. The National Library bought four microcomputers for their system. But that's the only example I know of.

Cavan McCarthy:

And that is atypical because it's a large library. It's an unusual thing, because we have a tendency in Latin American to go from zero technology to a large amount of technology. A library would tend to go from typewriters directly to a mainframe-based system and there was never very much use of intermediate technologies. The Frieden flexowriters were used a reasonable amount, but more complicated things such as the IBM Magnetic Tape Selectric Typewriter were not used very much, perhaps by four or five libraries. I have said in my paper that if the recession continued to bite, then Latin American libraries would be forced to concentrate on developing small systems on microcomputers.

Ching-Chih Chen:

Beatriz, you mentioned that the National Library bought four. Do you know what they were used for?

Beatriz de Carvalho:

These four microcomputers were bought for the National Library for entering the cataloging material which is processed in another institution.

Ching-Chih Chen:

In terms of technological applications, it seems to me that in the South, when we talk about databases and the automation Tom mentioned, that information or library professionals tend to be depending very much on computer professionals to do the job for you. In other words, you know what you want, but you depend very much on the technical know-how of those people to carry out the work. Here, for instance, a big mainframe computer or even mini-computer has a tremendous capability for doing things for us in information provision. It can enable us to have random access to information, and to manipulate the databases to provide very adequate information services. Do you find in developing countries that the mainframe or mini-computers tend to be used to replace some of the work which used to be done by human beings, which could be done equally well by human beings, rather than looking at technology to do something better for us? That is one question.

And the other is this. Murilo brought up the question of building databases in Latin America, but we don't seem to be getting to the details. Is it difficult to build our databases simply because we don't have the technical know-how among the library people as Cavan mentioned? If that is true, then can we consider microcomputers, because they are so simple that children can use them? And now there is enough software for microcomputers to enable us to have the capability to build relational databases, from which we could do retrieval as from the large databases.

Victor Rosenberg:

I don't think that this perception of microcomputers is unique to this group by any means. This notion that microcomputers are somehow simpler than larger computers and that children can run them is a great misconception of the whole technology. The microcomputer is simply the same complexity as the mainframe, reduced in size and cost. It is often more difficult to program a microcomputer than to program a large mainframe, because you have fewer utilities to help you, and you have to worry about things such as speed and memory capacity that you don't have to worry about on a mainframe. Children could equally well learn to use mainframes if they were programmed to play silly little games.

On the other hand I think that from my observation in Brazil, on my last trip, those libraries that are using computers are using them to make lists. They are not using them in imaginative ways.

Ching-Chih Chen:

What kinds of computers?

Victor Rosenberg:

Big computers, little computers, any kind that they have. It's just a matter of entering the data and compiling lists, one after another. Now I think that it's important, as Dr. Sandoval said, to have non-automated output from these systems so that it can be disseminated, but on the other hand, what I despair about, as Cavan was saying, is that it is an intellectual problem, not a technological problem. And the intellectual capacity is not there to use these computers creatively. I think that's the major problem that I see. Perhaps I'm unduly pessimistic about this but I have the feeling that should a benificent agency like the OAS or the United Nations decide that they would donate a computer to every library in Latin America, you still would have the same problem that you do now, in terms of the intellectual resources to use that machine creatively. I hope I'm wrong.

Laurence Hallewell:

Just before I left Brazil, in July, I was told that a couple of computer experts were coming over, and I, as a library school lecturer and as a foreigner who knows everything, was to form a committee and to computerize the university library. Period. The sky's the limit, presumably, for finances. And this will be the model for the Northeast. That is as far as it got. I don't know if anything has happened since then. Had I known exactly what I wanted, as you say, it would merely have been a question of my own intellectual grasp of the possibilities. I'm sure the resources would have been made available. If I'd produced something good, it would have been indeed eventually extended to the rest of northeast Brazil.

Thomas McGinn:

Victor, I think you said that the software should be locally developed, and I agree, but you can do a great deal by adapting software packages that are commercially available or can be found by exchange agreements with people in the industrial countries, which has been our experience. Mexico however has done a great deal with original programming. It took a great number of years, though, to my understanding. If you want a rapid takeoff, you really should try to find a standard library system or standard software to print your national bibliography, and if you need it, your programmers can study the software and adapt it.

We still have a strong relationship with Northwestern University, in that we're using their software. However, the first two years we had a consultant down every four or five months. Now we don't need one even every year. We'd consult with them by telephone. And that's a last resort. Our programmers increasingly are settling the problem, usually something that we request from the library side. We work it out with the programmer without any call to Northwestern, because they've mastered the software. We want the software's basic configuration the same, because that way we can keep the maintenance program with Northwestern, under which any of the constant and very important innovations can be incorporated. We pay them $5,000 per year for the contract, and anything that they develop there, including a whole new circulation system, we get for that cost without having to program it ourselves. In this sense we are dependent, but it is one of your creative dependencies.

Victor Rosenberg:

I think it's very clear that that's exactly the way it should go—the adaptation of software to local needs. However in Brazil, the current policy is not to honor copyright on software. And the result of this is very interesting. You go into a computer store, and the shelves are full of software, all "imported" from the United States, that is copied, and being sold, but there is no incentive whatever to develop any local software or to adapt software to local needs. None whatsoever. There's not the slightest financial incentive. So not only do you have the problem of the human resources to do that adaptation, and that in itself is not always simple, you don't have any policy incentives to develop the software locally. The thing that I regret the most, and that's so pertinent to this Conference, is that most of what passes for information policy all over the world, but especially in developing countries, has to do with hardware. They're interested in getting the chips, the computers. There simply is not the recognition of the importance of the software. I would argue that if Brazil thought software was important they wouldn't have a hardware policy. They would see that that type of policy is counter productive.

Marietta Daniels Shepard:

Policies change. At one time, over 15 years ago, the National Science Foundation in the United States funded experiments in 132 different universities in the United States to develop a capacity for automating their services, so we had to develop 132 different systems, no two of which were compatible. After a number of years suddenly it occurred to them that they'd done the wrong thing, and they began to fund projects which would try to bring these together and make them more compatible. By this time of course their one afterthought was that least they got some experience. We can't afford to do this in Latin America. We can't afford to let people play around to develop experience by starting from zero.

If we could develop in Latin America the potential for developing a strategy that would be applicable in many of the systems, we wouldn't be faced with the necessity for a user to have to learn the strategies of each one of the different systems. I hope that the leaders here present will do what they can to have more compatibility among the systems developed in Latin America.

Cavan McCarthy:

Going back to what Mrs. Chen was saying, if you get, for example a typical configuration in Brazil of an IBM 370 or a Burroughs 6000/6700, that comes in a package with several analysts. Now if you get a micro, you are much less likely to get an analyst along with it. You might get an analyst just at first, or you might get the micro simply dumped on you with a manual. In the latter case, perhaps some training courses might accompany it. It would be very difficult for a librarian with the intellectual baggage of a librarian to use that micro for any kind of information-related activities.

Victor Rosenberg:

In the United States the same thing is true. The micros don't come with anything. As a matter of fact one of the distributors was asked about maintenance of the computer and why it wasn't provided, and the president of the company said that if you want maintenance, buy two of them. Then while one is broken, you can send the other one back. Now this sounds illogical, but when you're talking about maintenance contracts for computers, it is no longer the slightest bit out of range to think in those terms.

What has grown up in the United States in lieu of this bundling of analysts with the system is what are called user groups. What you have then is a collective sharing of information and human resources. You have a community. This sharing is down to the level of, "I'm trying to connect the printer to this particular microcomputer and it didn't work. What do I do now?" Instead of calling the company and hiring a high-priced consultant or analyst, you call your colleagues, communicating with them in a network fashion. Someone is bound to say, "Oh yes, I had that problem last week, and here's what you do. You switch these two wires and it works." And that's the kind of technology that is reasonably operative at the level of the developing country.

Marietta Daniels Shepard:

We have been exploring for six or seven years the possibility of transferring both the equipment and the system developed in MINIMARC to Latin America. This is a system whereby Library of Congress magnetic tapes are transferred to floppy disks. And this system can be plugged into OCLC if you want to do so. You develop your own floppy disks which if you have a mainframe computer can be transferred to the mainframe for instance. I think that perhaps within the next year this will be installed at least on an experimental basis at the University of Costa Rica. We were hoping to be able to achieve by this the development of floppy disks in Spanish of the bibliographic registers produced at the University of Costa Rica, which could then be reproduced by MINIMARC or a branch of it in Latin America and used in other university libraries more or less of the same size. One of their concerns in installing this in Costa Rica was whether they would be able to have people who could maintain it there. Fortunately they do have someone who apparently is capable of doing so. One of their concerns was having an individual from Costa Rica who would be able to go to neighboring countries at least to service the equipment.

Victor Rosenberg:

A friend of Murilo's and mine took an IBM personal computer to Brazil. IBM sells in the United States a complete service manual and kit complete with tools and everything you need to service the machine, at a very reasonable price. I think it's about $50.00 for the manual which gives you step-by-step instructions on how to fix the thing. The possibilities are there. I still feel that the major limitations are the human resources, because to make those machines work is still difficult.

William Jackson:

I'd just like to suggest that we'd all like a quick rundown on the experience of the Library of Congress in this. I suggest that you read the chapter in the new Goodrum book on the Library of Congress.[6] There's one chapter on the Library and computers. In about a dozen pages it will tell you about 20 years of the Library of Congress and how it faced all these problems. It shows how it had to develop an in-house solution, because the vendors weren't able to respond effectively, and the multiplicity of different solutions for different aspects of information, which now form their own locus in the Library of Congress information systems.

Cavan McCarthy:

There are a couple of speakers here saying that Latin Americans use the computer only for list making and other relatively simple types of operations. But I think this is typical of users in the early days of computerization. I think the same thing happened in the United States and the United Kingdom. And in the United States, we will remember that library automation never really got off the ground until Fred Kilgour found a way to make a computer produce a catalog card from a record which could be altered to fit all the standards of different libraries. When you go into an American university library you find a whole row of catalog cards. You go into a British university library and you find COM.

Mary Jane Ruhl:

Any other comments on technology and how it relates to national policy? Some of the other issues that Juan had listed were, What will make national information policy work? What will insure that it will be implemented? And also, there is the issue of training people.

---

[6]Goodrum, Charles and Helen W. Dalrymple. *The Library of Congress*. Westview, 1982. 2nd ed.

Juan Freudenthal:

I would briefly like to speak to the issue of the training of people in Latin America. This morning we were talking about the intellectual level of the people we have, and whether they can or cannot handle this technology. I wonder, what is the solution for that? What are we doing in Latin America now in schools of library science and training programs to begin to resolve this? Obviously we cannot always depend on the people who know about computers. We will have to learn about them ourselves. This is true in the United States as well. It is a crisis in every library school in the country. We talk about how to integrate automation and online services in our reference courses. I'm also rather bothered about the term intellectual, in adapting to this crisis, which is in my opinion as difficult for us in the United States as for anywhere else.

Cavan McCarthy:

I think that the term intellectual came up in the context of intellectual problems as opposed to technological or financial problems. Intellectual problems don't necessarily imply lack of intellectual capacity!

Marietta Daniels Shepard:

Somewhat flippantly I might say that the first thing that was done was to change the name of schools to library and information science. And many of them haven't gotten beyond that. In many countries there have been a lot of advanced and short courses. I should think that in Brazil, Chile, Argentina, and Mexico there has been greater in-depth training of personnel than just changing the name of the library school.

Thomas McGinn:

Our experience has been that the librarians are fantastically interested in automated and related subjects. They learn it, they improve professionally, and it's brought the profession up. We do have the advantage that our librarians are usually not more than 30 years old, as is true of I think 70% of Venezuela's population. They're young, they're open. We don't have people who have been working in libraries for thirty or forty years. As someone mentioned the profession is young in Latin America. It is those older people who usually have problems, I think. Except Marietta. There are those who are opposed to the technologies, but they tend to be set aside quietly by people who see the implications for the new technologies.

In terms of indexing, as Cavan has mentioned, we do have a severe problem because it's not taught in the library school. Here we have to do a great deal, because the intellectual skill for indexing is a bit different from using an automated system. It will be so until we have totally or near totally automated indexing, when we just put in full text and a list of stop words. We can do that for some types of materials but we can't for all. In many areas I don't think we would want to. After studying the models, like *Chemical Abstracts*, with a controlled vocabulary, these models can be applied to the local language and journals. Here we have a different kind of problem which requires years of experience, and our young people don't have it. They can't pick it up quite as quickly as they can learn to use an automated system.

Victor Rosenberg:

The only example that I know of not only national information policies but regional information policies might be in the Caribbean. Are there any efforts at all in linking national information policies together in Latin America, country to country?

Marietta Daniels Shepard:

Perhaps not policies. In most of the regional information systems, there are centers in the various countries that are developing data for input into the information systems. This would imply a certain degree of looking at the policies with respect to all of this. Ximena is involved in working with the various countries involved in INFOPLAN.

Ximena Felíu:

I haven't mentioned INFOPLAN because my paper describes it. But I would say that it is a regional information system based on the very clear information policy originating in the government. This system was originated by a petition of ministers of planning. In 1976 or 1978 they expressed the need for an information system. They said it was impossible to plan without the support of an information system. So they asked CEPAL and others to prepare a theoretical approach to this information system. We began to design the information system with a new methodology, I think. We presented the idea of a national and regional information system for planning. We collected the needs of planners, and we began to study what planning was. We decided it was a process which generates a lot of information, of a great variety, and which needs a great variety of information. And this information is generated in each institution which deals with national development. So it was very difficult to just design an information system for planning, because planning is everything that occurs in the country.

So we tried another method. Our strategy was to go to the government and talk with planning and sectoral ministers. We sold the idea of this planning and information system, which could be developed only if they had a very clear policy about it. We asked for their help, and they gave it to us. And then, and only then, when we were clear that each government ministry would help us to build this information system, then we began to design it and try it. We had the help of the Caribbean countries. And as Alma said, CARISPLAN and INFOPLAN were simultaneous projects. In the meanwhile we processed data at the Center at CLADES.

This government support made it possible to design a centralized system. Each country creates its own national information system for planning, built with our assistance, and builds a network of planning information systems.

How can countries do that, with the new technologies? First, we had to realize that certain government institutions were the great generators of planning information. We asked if those institutions already had information units. Many did. Their only problem was how to coordinate then. So, we thought that the information unit of the minister of planning must be the national coordinating center of all the other institutions, because the system was on planning. We also had to prepare manuals to process the information. We began with the problem of identifying the institutions that are generating the information for planning and identifying which documents are generated by those institutions which are very involved in the planning process, so we could control those documents. Some were unconventional, others were not. Again, with the support of the government, we could solve these problems. Not in a day, but in two years or less.

We can say that we have not an information policy supporting the information system on planning, but we have an information policy on planning supporting the system, because governments need this kind of system. Each politician, public administrator, and scientific researcher, everyone that is involved in development problems in the country, has to have the information. Of course the information they need might be very technical. When they are just beginning to formulate a project, they need planning information, and they can obtain this information through the national network or through the database.

The other thing that is important is that we were very much aware that we can't ask some information units in some countries to process information with computers. They can process information manually, with uniterms for instance. With the ISIS worksheet, they still can provide compatible information. The manual worksheets can then be easily converted to the ISIS computer system with little effort or cost.

I would say that INFOPLAN could be an example of what we can do in Latin America, with our own efforts and our own human and technical resources. But we can do this because, I think, planning as a subject field is very Latin American. We don't find planning ministers in the United States. We know that with our resources we have to plan our development.

So every minister in the government, knowing this, is interested, and is willing to help this kind of system. We can't forget that the planning process has much to do with science and technology, with social science, with politics, with economics, with legal problems, and so on. This could be the site for a national information system.

Mary Jane Ruhl:

What I would like to do is to recap what I saw as the specific recommendations that came out of this session.

The first recommendation was to establish and develop relationships with two superstructures of library and information science, and science and technology. There is either one superstructure which encompasses both or there are two.

The second would be to establish national information policy at the highest possible level within the country's governmental structure.

The third would be to include users of information systems, such as sectoral and planning ministers, in planning national information policy and the resulting services.

Fourth is to conduct an inventory and assessment of existing information collections and related resources.

Fifth is to incorporate instructional programs about information services and related technology in the nation's educational program.

Sixth is to develop in-country expertise to perform information analysis tasks and also to develop in-country expertise for using and servicing the equipment and services relating to information.

The last is to monitor technological development activities, to result in compatible systems which will allow sharing of resources.

Did I miss anything?

Ximena Felíu:

In INFOPLAN, we also have a training program, which was included in the design. We have been developing it for almost three years. We have workbooks and manuals, and a whole set of instruments that the system provides to countries.

Marietta Daniels Shepard:

In order to access your database, is it done at the present time through requests that are sent from the countries?

Ximena Felíu:

We have two ways. Countries belonging to the system send us their worksheets or a photocopy of the uniterm cards that have the bibliographic information and the abstract, and we publish an index with all the information that we process. This index is distributed to all the countries that belong to the system. The national network for planning information this year is going to publish a current awareness bulletin. We prepare retrospective bibliographies at the request of countries, but we are sending them all the time output from the computer, to bring up to date the information they have sent us. We prepare also national bibliographies, and have a union catalog on planning.

Ching-Chih Chen:

We seem to be using the word recommendation much more now than when we started. That is a natural process, because we hope to have them at the end of the Conference. But, we should consider what the recommendations are going to be for, to whom they are going to be directed, and their objectives. When I think about these questions, I become very uncomfortable. These last few days have been extremely productive. We've run through a whole range of problems and issues. However, outside of a few obvious things I don't think we have so-called recommendations. On some issues we don't even have consensus. I would feel much more comfortable in summarizing key issues or problems discussed so that we would not be accused of speaking for others who are not here. That also is a political consideration.

Victor Rosenberg:

I think that is clear.

Marietta Daniels Shepard:

I think that the word conclusions would probably be more appropriate.

Victor Rosenberg:

I think you're right. We'll be dealing with that more this afternoon.

Thursday Afternoon, 14 April 1983

Summary Session, Recapitulating the Important Activities and Conclusions of the Conference

Victor Rosenberg:

One of the joys of organizing a Conference like this is that you have a chance to learn a lot from your colleagues. And I must say that some of my opinions and attitudes about the subjects that have been discussed have in fact changed in the course of the Conference. This also is a sign of a good conference.

I want to say at the start of this summary session that the Conference has had throughout a hidden agenda, and I hope that Melinda will not mind. That hidden agenda is just bringing you all together here in Ann Arbor to meet together and discuss these issues, for many of you to visit the United States for the first time and for many of you to visit the United States again. And I think that this type of interaction, especially in a small group where you really do get to know someone in a way that is more than shaking hands with someone at a very large conference, is an extremely effective way to transfer information, and that is what we've been talking about. It may in fact be the best way of transferring information. I think we have achieved some things at this Conference, and I think we've come up with some interesting conclusions at various points. I'm going to ask each of the Moderators of the sessions to provide a brief summary of the sessions as they heard them, and then ask people to comment on them. I still want to keep the informality of the Conference.

What I have learned a great deal about is the ambitious efforts of countries to try and deal with the problem of information in various ways. I've been very impressed by the reports that have been brought of activities that are going on, and how they're increasing. Just before we broke for lunch, I commented on the fact that I was somewhat disappointed that progress has not gone as quickly as I had hoped that it would with the new technology, and Marietta reminded me that if viewed from a 30-year span, progress has been impressive indeed.

Let me turn the session over to Cavan, to review the first session. In the beginning, the question that I posed was the role of scientific and technical information in aiding development. There may not be an answer to this, but it is something that nonetheless should be considered. It has always been a question in my mind of not only whether the information activities actually contribute to development, but in what way they contribute. I recently read a rather interesting article by a Brazilian economist who was writing about the problems of transferring technology, and developing technology indigenously versus licensing technology from abroad, from the point of view of an economist. He said that it made very little sense to develop the technology locally, because if you license the technology, you only have to pay for it after it's sold, whereas investment is required if you're going to develop it locally. I realize there are other reasons. But the whole question of the role of scientific and technical information in aiding development was discussed at that session. Cavan?

Cavan McCarthy:

I'm going to use Marta Dosa's summary, which she very kindly prepared, as well as my own notes.

Information, as a national resource, should be planned, managed and utilized according to an integrated set of national policies. Information as a national resource includes primary numeric data, bibliographic data, textual information in print and non-print, audio-visual sources, and oral communication such as oral history or broadcast programs. Although no one library or information center can or should encompass this comprehensive range of information, information professionals should be aware of these sources and their interrelationships. Coordination of various information resources at the policy level, and awareness of them at the operational level, would insure their more effective and economical use through formal and informal cooperation.

As other professions have arrived at an integration of their various specialties, information professionals should work toward similar goals. Professional organizations, educational programs, and joint meetings may serve as mechanisms. Creative leadership is needed for the profession to participate at the level of decision making, in the formulation of national information policies, and the development of the infrastructure.

Information policies are needed to:

(1) Create incentives for the production of and access to information and knowledge applicable to national development goals.

(2) Provide national plans to protect national heritage, national sovereignty, and the individual's rights to equitable information.

(3) Establish the legal framework for the national information infrastructure, and its relationship between libraries, information centers, data banks, archives, and other information facilities.

(4) Establish standards for the development and use of information technology in the service of human and social goals, science, and scholarship.

(5) Promote development of information and telecommunication networks, and assure equitable access to them.

(6) Provide resources for research and the dissemination of results.

(7) Provide resources for education and training programs for information professionals and users. In information professionals, attitudinal and communication capabilities are deemed as important as theoretical and technical ones, to enable professionals to participate in decision-making.

(8) Promote cooperation with major systems internationally on the basis of equal partnership.

Victor Rosenberg:

I would like your comments, though, on how, if at all, information aids national development.

Cavan McCarthy:

I think we have to put it down as a belief.

Victor Rosenberg:

I think so too.

Cavan McCarthy:

Michel said something about this.

Victor Rosenberg:

Yes. In his paper he said, "The library and information science community has elaborated two main propositions with regard to the development of this field. One is that information, unconsciously equated to printed matter and bibliographic records, is a needed ingredient to the socio-economic development process."

One of the things that I who would like to have come out of this is someone motivated to do some research and look at the impact of information in national development, and see if some relationships can be developed. I do know that it can be shown that countries, using whatever development index you use, with a higher index of development, also have a higher level of information activities. The question that must be addressed, though, is the causal relationship of whether the higher level of development causes a a higher level of information activity, or vice versa. I think this is still an open area for research.

Winthrop Wiltshire:

In the Caribbean we have many examples of tacit things that have resulted from the lack of use of adequate information. I don't think we have any problem in the Caribbean of trying to define the role of information in national development.

Cavan McCarthy:

I think we want to examine it in a positive way. Japan appears to have a quite rudimentary library system, yet the country is developed.

Victor Rosenberg:

I don't think that's entirely true, but I'm not sure.

Cavan McCarthy:

Can we put down that information professionals accept as a basic belief that information is an essential input to development?

Victor Rosenberg:

I think we certainly can state that.

Cavan McCarthy:

It is a basic tenet of information professionals that the information is an essential input to the development process.

Victor Rosenberg:

If there are no other comments, Juan, would you summarize your session?

Juan Freudenthal:

A possible model was suggested which would link government and private sectors including science and technology transfer centers and social science and numeric databases with university research, humanistic endeavors, and public libraries. What then is the future role of traditional libraries in regard to non-library institutions? It was strongly felt that we need to move toward a total information environment, which would allow access for specialists as well as rural and urban masses.

Victor Rosenberg:

I would just like to add parenthetically that Juan's session was library acquisitions and problems associated with the acquisition of foreign materials by libraries in both North and South America, and existing and future exchange programs.

Juan Freudenthal:

Second, we reiterate the importance of the control of the intellectual output of the country. This should include not only the monographs and serials, but also conference proceedings, audio-visual materials, masters theses and dissertations, mimeographed materials, scientific reports, variations of newspapers, printed music scores, and government publications. The final product has to be widely distributed, since it has great importance for current awareness and acquisitions purposes. These are the national bibliographies.

Third, it is recommended that central repositories of periodicals be created, particularly of those of a scientific and technical nature. At the same time, more union catalogs of books and serials have to be produced.

Cavan McCarthy:

I think that if we're going to say that, we also ought to include interloan schemes. This would go along with the union catalogs and the need for central repositories of periodicals.

Alma Jordan:

Centralized storage is not applicable for every situation. So, interloan schemes are relevant here.

Juan Freudenthal:

Shall I say then that it is recommended that central repositories of periodicals be created where appropriate??

Wanda Kemp:

I wonder if we are talking about centralized storage as opposed to centralized listing, or access?

Juan Freudenthal:

I spoke in the same vein that Armando did in his paper.

Why don't I continue toward the observations, because there may be some points that we want to discuss.

Fourth, greater attention has to be paid to user profiles, so that we may more accurately meet user needs at all levels. This should in turn form an essential portion of the development of acquisitions policies, as well as enhanced public services.

Our observations were these.

There should be a national acquisitions program as part of the national information policy.

Two, problems of inadequate bibliographic control, the lack of national bibliographies, indexes and abstracts, indexing of newspapers and government documents, and lack of complete periodical files, were very strongly stated. Greater attention should be given the techniques of the selection of materials, and to the creation of realistic collection development polices. We briefly commented on that. We have to create systems which will facilitate shared acquisitions programs and interlibrary loan activities, such as the use of coupons as a way to pay for publications similar to the COMUT program in Brazil.

Cavan McCarthy:

You want to mention the coupons then?

Juan Freudenthal:

It is an interesting aspect, but we certainly can leave it out.

Cavan McCarthy:

I think it can be put in as an example.

Juan Freudenthal:

To continue, there is a need to compile more information for decision-making.

Several of the participants felt that information and reference centers are currently lacking in Latin America and the Caribbean.

Murilo da Cunha:

I'd like to add, "compile and disseminate information for decision-makers."

Juan Freudenthal:

The last one is, we need to continue to identify those agencies which generate information for purposes of acquisition and dissemination. This may come out in another recommendation elsewhere. We talked about the need for a roster of research agencies and people working in all these areas.

Laurence Hallewell:

I would like to point out that nothing has been said during the whole conference on the importance of the commercial book trade. What has impressed me enormously about the flow of information South-North, was that for half of South America (Brazil), nearly every library in the developed world was dependent upon one quite elderly bookseller. However efficient she may be, this is a terrible dependence. I don't know what I might recommend, but certainly I think it is a problem.

Juan Freudenthal:

One of the problems we face at the Conference is that many of the things that were said in our papers were never brought out. Obviously that would be impossible. We are dependent on other book sellers for other countries as well.

Victor Rosenberg:

Another topic that we didn't deal with extensively, but which was brought out in the papers, is the rather embarrassing dilemma that faces so many countries when their major collections are outside their own borders. In many cases the major collections of Latin American materials are found in North American libraries. I don't know what conclusion we can come to on that, except to acknowledge the problem. One might argue that it might be wise to use modern technology to reproduce that information to try to generate duplicate collections so that they could be repatriated to their countries of origin.

Juan Freudenthal:

Those are my points.

Victor Rosenberg:

We also didn't deal very much with the techniques of acquisition and this is something that I've always felt has been lacking. We dealt with it indirectly, in terms of the training of human resources. But it's always been sort of an irony to me that where money is so difficult to get, especially foreign exchange, that the skills needed to use that money to maximum effectiveness are also lacking. I'm sure that all of us have had the experience of seeing in Latin American libraries materials that would better not have been bought, and the corresponding needed materials that are conspicuous by their absence.

Are there any other additions to the area of acquisitions?

William Jackson:

Going back to collection policy, Juan, did you mention something about the development of policies? I wasn't here for those discussions. I wish that the conclusions could be strengthened on the development and implementation of the policy. It doesn't do any good if it is not used to get the materials into the libraries that need them. It would be helpful to emphasize the results of the policy as well as the idea of having the policy.

Victor Rosenberg:

Another topic that we did not discuss very much, but which really goes without saying, is the economic problems that are being faced by Latin America in general these days, and their impact on acquisitions.

Juan Freudenthal:

We have the danger, I fear, of now at the very end beginning to discuss the nitty gritty of what happens when we buy for collections. This has been covered by the papers of SALALM.

Beatriz de Carvalho:

One of the problems that we discussed in Denver was about local people who publish abroad. Maybe when we mention the national information policy, we could include the idea of efforts that could be made to strengthen local journals.

Second, when you outlined the recommendations, you mentioned tools for disseminating information, such as national bibliographies and indexing services. I suggest you include directories, because of the point made this morning by Barbara, that these are important because they let people know what others are doing. These would include directories of libraries and information resources and ongoing research programs.

Edwin Cortez, Univ. of Michigan (Observer):

Juan, you mentioned that one of the components of the acquisitions program might be interlibrary loan. I think that several of the participants have demonstrated very nicely that interlibrary loan, because of the economies of scale in South America, is not realistic. It's been shown in this country that interlibrary loan has never been an effective substitute for collection development. I think it would be particularly problematic in Latin America, because of the cost of lending and borrowing. To include interlibrary loan as any component of acquisitions would have to be looked at very carefully.

Cavan McCarthy:

I think it is a component, but a backup.

Edwin Cortez:

But it should not be a substitute for collection development.

Cavan McCarthy:

No.

Juan Freudenthal:

The sentence read, "We have to create systems which facilitate shared acquisitions programs and interlibrary loans", with the emphasis on "facilitate". People have raised the idea of shared acquisitions several times, and some people really believe in it. Now, whether it is realistic or not, is something else.

Victor Rosenberg:

Any further comments on acquisitions? Then let's move on to the access of Latin American scholars to publication, and how new technologies might provide new opportunities for publication. Tony?

Tony Bowman:

The majority of the points in this session dealt not with technology, although we touched on it. Instead, we focused on the opportunities, and the litany of barriers and interesting things that happened along the way, to publishing by Latin American scholars. We spent a great deal of time discussing where they publish, and why. Backed up by some research that was conducted in Mexico and presented to us by Armando Sandoval, and confirmed by most other participants, we noted that Latin American scholars in the social sciences and humanities prefer to publish within their own country. In contrast, medical and other scientific scholars prefer to publish outside their own countries, particularly in the United States. As I recall the statistics from Mexico showed that approximately 3,500 technical articles had been identified as published by national authors outside of Latin America, in North American journals.

Another point was that some Latin American authors are wrestling with issues of intellectual underdevelopment, and don't pursue aggressively publishing their works out of the country.

We suggested that in the area of applied science that indices be translated into Spanish and Portuguese and published. This action would be effective even though the whole text of the article might be in English.

We identified an additional need for a greater standardization of indexing terms and standards.

We suggested the possibility of translating into Spanish and/or Portuguese articles for publication which have appeared originally in English or another language and published outside of the country.

One of the issues that we dealt with was the legality of whether or not the article could be considered an original publication. Some journals require that materials be original submissions, and therefore they may not be willing to accept translated material.

Next we discussed the issue of the international helping agencies, and we had a very broad spectrum of feeling. One thought expressed was that many of these agencies lack memories. We do not sufficiently document their activities, and we keep reinventing the wheel. Perhaps a computerized system would help to give helping agencies a memory.

We noted that contractors need to receive and give local feedback, any time contributions are made, or when the study is completed. Also, consultants should consider cultural relevance factors in making recommendations. One of the examples brought out was that whatever technique or process that was developed or successfully applied in country X or Y ten years ago may or may not be appropriate at this particular time or in this set of conditions, problems and opportunities in another country.

It was suggested that mechanisms be developed in the pre-publication of information to help eliminate duplication of research efforts. One of the problems encountered in making this happen was the problem of first defining the subject areas, and then finding an adequate vehicle that could economically go out and make the information available.

The next to the last item that I recorded was the suggestion that we consider paying authors additionally for publishing articles locally. The advantage of publishing in a proceedings rather that as an article was pointed out. Many times the proceedings came with a ticket and the opportunity to travel and gain additional experience.

Merline Smith:

I think that when we think of translation, we cannot only think of English to Spanish. We need to translate also from Spanish to English.

Armando Sandoval:

Concerning translations, they may have some advantages, but for whom? I wonder whether the effort that goes into translating these materials into Spanish and Portuguese is of any advantage. The people who are interested in reading this material and who can gain a real advantage by reading it will read the original: they know English. In Latin America as in other parts of the world, there is a tremendous gap between professionals who read and who don't read.

Laurence Hallewell:

I think there's a tremendous difference between the ability to read and the willingness to read. From my experience there is a substantial number of people who are capable of reading, with a certain amount of effort, but they very seldom make that effort and whenever possible avoid it. A survey at The University of Sheffield investigated the use made of foreign language materials in British university libraries. The result indicated to any library administrator that he might as well stop buying foreign language materials altogether. But certainly at the undergraduate level in Latin America, in my experience, I would say the proportion of students that are able and willing to read English is quite small.

Victor Rosenberg:

I'd like to second that. In a study that Murilo and I did we found that the operative factor here is not the basic ability of a Latin American professional to read English but the ease with which he reads it, or the preference for English or the native language. And the preference, as I'm sure the British study showed, is overwhelmingly for the native language. That is to say, if you have the information available in the native language of the country, it will be far more widely read and will be far more effective than if it is in English. It is a significantly greater effort to read in another language. That is certainly true in the United States.

Marietta Daniels Shepard:

It might be well to include in this observation the need for better bibliographic control of the translations that have been made and input into the databank in Buenos Aires. The need to develop a mechanism for informing them of translations that have been made into Spanish and Portuguese is there.

Mary Jane Ruhl:

The use or lack of use of foreign language materials is the same type of information use that we see of microfiche readers. If the microfiche reader is in your office, you probably will use it. But if you have to walk up to the second floor, you probably won't. There's just too much else to look at. It's possibly the same with a foreign language document. It will be placed on a back burner and not used. Not because a person cannot translate it, but because it requires an extra effort. I think that in the competition among the different pieces and forms of information, we have to keep all this in mind.

Maria Oyarzun de Ferreira:

Podemos poner como recomendación la reactivación del registro de traducciones en Argentina porque ese programa ya no está funcionando desde hace mucho tiempo. Quienes en estos momentos están recopilando las traducciones en español es el IIDCT, el Instituto de Informacion y Documentacion en Ciencía y Tecnología in España. Argentina está colaborando con ellos, pero mirando sólo lo nacional, no reconstruyendo lo latinoamericano como habían sido inicialmente admitido.

Unidentified Speaker:

¿Hace cuánto tiempo que no funciona?

Maria Oyarzun de Ferreira:

En estos momentos el CONICIT esta abierto a recibir toda la informacion sobre traducciones hechas en Español y está publicando una revista trimestral en la cual informa todo lo que ha recibido.

Tony Bowman:

The comment was made that the Center in Buenos Aires as of several years ago wasn't effectively functioning, and that that operation has been picked up in Spain on a trimestrial basis. The information on translations into Spanish was being published from there. For how many years was the Buenos Aires not publishing this information?

Maria Oyarzun de Ferreira:

They never did publish anything. It was a good idea, but it didn't work.

Beatriz de Carvalho:

The idea of the center in Argentina was to make translations for users. A user wants to have a translation of a certain article published in another language, so he requests the Center to prepare a translation for him. There are two different approaches here. The Center in Argentina was to translate articles on request for a specific user. The idea was to then disseminate the list of these translations. It's not related to the problem of local journals having materials by local authors.

Victor Rosenberg:

I wanted to bring out the problem that exists in many countries where the demand for published material is so small, and professional readership is so small, that the editions tend to be very small and very expensive and go out of print very quickly. This is a serious problem with local publications. One of the things that I wanted to try and deal with was the fact that here is one area where in fact modern technology may indeed make a difference, because increasingly in the United States we not only have publication on demand as a device for publishing materials directly, but also we have the capability of maintaining the manuscripts in machine-readable form so they can be printed as needed after the edition runs out. Also I would assume, although I'm not that familiar with publishing practice, that having the manuscript in machine-readable form makes it much less expensive to publish a second edition. I don't know if that is true or not.

William Jackson:

Someone did a book on that premise and found that it wasn't quite as important as he had thought.

Tony Bowman:

Over time, I think that as that inventory grows, the controller will start estimating the amount of money that they have tied up in electronic storage. As you pass the critical mass, unless you have a sufficient demand from it, organizations that would say that although it's a great idea, they would opt not to take that approach.

Victor Rosenberg:

That may be true, but then in the case of University Microfilms, there's a tremendous investment in microfilm masters which can be used for publishing paper copy. The cost of that must be in some sense economical for small run publications. Maybe it's only on a large scale, but it would seem that that technology is viable.

Tony Bowman:

That's true, but machine readable I think is the expensive key.

Victor Rosenberg:

But that cost is coming down ever so quickly. We've seen a drop in the cost of machine readable data in the last ten years that's been exponential, dramatic. The usual cliché is that if air travel costs were reduced in the same way, you could fly from Paris to New York in a one-foot long plane in two minutes. It would be hard to get into the plane, but...

Armando Sandoval:

What is the use of translating, if we don't have an inexpensive and rapid method for making the translations quickly available to Latin America? We know that scientific papers have a life expectancy of, in physics, two years, medicine, four years. What is the use of translating materials that have no use after that?

I want to stress the fact that Latin Americans who are really producing and consuming scientific information know not only how to read but how to write in English. The translations are addressed to people who cannot make any use of these materials. At least in the fields of the sciences and medicine, what is happening? The contributions from Scandanavia are in English. Russian literature? It is translated into English. Japanese literature? The French? If we translate Latin American papers into Spanish and Portuguese, we are encouraging Latin Americans to forget about the urgent need to read English, and they will be the marginals of scientific and technical information, contributed by Scandanavians, the Russians, the Swiss and so forth. I stress the fact that it is very necessary to learn English, instead of translating into Spanish.

Juan Freudenthal:

I just want to remind my colleagues that *Scientific American* is now being translated into Russian.

Armando Sandoval:

Also into Spanish.

Cavan McCarthy:

And Portuguese.

Armando Sandoval:

But that's just a swallow. It doesn't make a summer.

Victor Rosenberg:

I still believe though that if scientific and technical information is to be made useful to engineers in the field, medical practitioners, and students, especially at the undergraduate level, it has to be in the native language.

Beatriz de Carvalho:

Dr. Sandoval, I've tried to imagine this situation. You know that our local journals have many kinds of problems. For instance, they don't get material to publish. Maybe this could be one of reasons why they are always late to publish an issue. I think that authors should be completely free to publish where they wish, and this freedom must be total. But if the author publishes simultaneously at home and abroad, then you would have local journals with articles by local authors, and this material would be available to a whole community of people, to undergraduate students, to many professors in universities, that don't know how to read English. Shouldn't we consider this a means of discouraging reading English, because there would be citations to foreign materials, and these people would be interested in reading foreign materials? If these authors are few, they belong to invisible colleges. I believe that this would be a way of having better local journals, where many students, a whole community of users, would have better access to this literature that would circulate within the country. It's not so easy to have so many copies of foreign journals in the country. I think that's something that should be taken into account.

Armando Sandoval:

I think you're right, but you bring up one more problem. It is not honest to publish the same article in two different journals.

Beatriz de Carvalho:

They are free to do so. Imagine that a national information policy would try to market the idea of the need to have good local journals. They would be free to do so if they wished.

Cavan McCarthy:

The problem is that of originality, which I brought up earlier and which Tony worked into his recommendations, and which I have written a recommendation: Latin American journals and conferences which normally only accept original contributions should treat translations of papers by national authors originally published in English as original works. If you submit a paper to a Northern journal, and then receive an acceptance, that paper is not a published paper. You can still do a translation and send it to a national journal, because it is not yet a published paper.

Victor Rosenberg:

I'd like to bring this discussion to a close and go on to the next session. Murilo da Cunha moderated the session on the coverage of Latin American materials in major international databases, and how inclusion of Latin American materials can be improved. I think this is an important part of what we have just been discussing.

Murilo da Cunha:

We discussed databases and the inclusion of Latin American materials in them. I think we can say that the database producers will include materials from Latin America only if there are business interests. Countries in Latin America cannot wait for a foreign database to include national publications. So there are two different approaches: to increase the coverage of Latin American materials in the international databases, or, to build local databases. At the end of the session, we concluded that the two approaches complement each other. Our conclusions were:

A national and cooperative regional database should be encouraged in Latin America, in order to improve the bibliographic control of information generated in the region.

Second, database producers located in industrialized countries should increase their coverage of Latin American materials. This would provide a world-wide dissemination of the documentation generated in the region.

Victor Rosenberg:

Didn't you comment also at that time that Spain paid one major database producer to include its materials? Is that something that anyone would recommend?

Murilo da Cunha:

Third, a directory of Latin American information organizations, specialists, and services provided by them should be prepared, by the OAS, in order to have broad and up-to-date information about the information infrastructure available in the region.

I have just received a suggestion from Mr. Batres, that the creation of regional databases be coordinated by the OAS, in order to incorporate from the rest of Latin America, particularly the Central American nations, the existing functioning information services.

Ximena Felíu:

I'd like to add that not only the OAS but other regional organizations such as CLADES should be involved.

Barbara Gumbs:

Representatives from information centers in Lima, Peru, met recently, and one of their recommendations was that each Central American, Latin American, and Caribbean country should emphasize building national databases. If the telecommunications infrastructure is there, then we can have a network to share these databases.

Laurence Hallewell:

HAPI, the Hispanic American Periodical Index, has been trying unsuccessfully to be included on Dialog and BRS and both have taken the mentioned attitude that there is insufficient demand to include them. This was at SALALM at its mid-winter meeting in January, 1983. They were prepared to include it, but under quite onerous conditions that SALALM couldn't afford.

Marietta Daniels Shepard:

In the list of recommendations that I have at the end of my paper, I have suggested a number of things to be done and goals that need to be achieved, and I have suggested certain mechanisms needed to achieve the goals. One would be the creation of a multi-national body, with the responsibility and authority for clearing house services, as well as for planning, coordinating and developing the various elements involved in creating an inter-American network. This might be done by the OAS, or Unesco. Somehow we have to create some kind of agency, with responsibility and authority, for serving not only clearinghouse services but offering technical assistance in developing these various elements that we've been discussing.

Murilo da Cunha:

I have a suggestion to rephrase the recommendation related to the regional organization. This is, "that the creation of databases be coordinated by a regional organization, for example the OAS, or CLADES," in order to generalize the statement.

Cavan McCarthy:

I don't like the word coordinate, or the use of authority here. It sounds like if someone wants to start a database they have to write to a central agency in another country and get permission. It has happened in some cases that certain people have been given the right to coordinate national information centers, and they have taken this as a permission to control it.

Victor Rosenberg:

I don't think that is the intent here, though.

Cavan McCarthy:

I have a slightly more detailed analysis of the same subject.

Database availability, now and in the medium term, can be briefly characterized as follows:

One, a few major commercial database agencies, such as Lockheed and SDC,

Two, a few international participative systems such as AGRIS and INIS, and

Three, numerous small local systems.

We consider that local systems offer the greatest direct potential for Latin American users, because:

One, they are under local control and sovereignty,

Two, they are more responsive to local needs and better able to incorporate local documentation, and

Three, they provide Latin Americans with direct experience with database construction and maintenance.

Steps should be taken to link or exchange databases in different Latin American countries.

International participative systems are also of great value in Latin America because:

One, they operate on the basis of free exchange of information,

Two, they place local information into the world-wide context, on an equal footing with information output from other sovereign countries,

Three, they give Latin American professionals experience on collaboration in world-wide networks, and

Four, they really encourage the development of national information and bibliographic resources.

It is recognized that the major commercial database agencies will have a significant role to play as back-up to local and participative systems, but Latin American information professionals have reservations about their unrestricted use, because of

One, their concentration largely within a single country,

Two, the commercial nature of their operations,

Three, the lack of control and participation by Latin American countries, and

Four, the lack of Latin American content and relevance.

Armando Sandoval:

Couldn't ASFA (The Aquatical Sciences and Fisheries Abstracts) be added along with INIS and AGRIS? They are also participative.

Laurence Hallewell:

I mentioned HAPI before the break. Do we want to say anything specific about that?

Victor Rosenberg:

We could say that it ought to be included in DIALOG but we recognize that that's a commercial system and those decisions are made on commercial grounds.

Laurence Hallewell:

Yes, but we are potential customers, therefore if we mention that we would like it it might help.

Cavan McCarthy:

There is another statement, a corollary to this: It is necessary to measure and evaluate the Latin American content of major databases, identify the reason for their low coverage of Latin American materials, and where appropriate take steps to remedy this.

Victor Rosenberg:

I'm going to have to give a very brief summary of Tom McGinn's session on potential national library networks and links to neworks in both North and South America, dependency and interdependency, because he unfortunately had to leave early. He has given me some points which he thought ought to be mentioned.

First, libraries and documentation centers should enter into agreements to exchange data internationally in Latin America, with a view toward forming a Latin American and Caribbean database.

Two, cost studies should be carried out to evaluate the possibility of doing more local indexing of journals imported into Latin America.

Three, the Conference favors national policies which permit the free flow of information across national borders. Information importing of print or non-print materials of any form should be given preferential tariffs.

Four, the Conference considers of great importance the priority of budgeting for information and documentation services at levels which permit training of more local personnel.

Five, Latin American library schools should include more training in indexing and automation of library services in their curricula.

Any additions?

Alma Jordan:

I think that when he refers to local indexing, he means indexing in the local language.

Cavan McCarthy:

I don't think that literal local indexing would be cost effective. I think he means indexing with Spanish or Portuguese keywords.

And the one that came after that was quite a whopper.

Victor Rosenberg:

I read that as meaning that there should not be discriminatory tariffs against for example documents on magnetic tape or in machine-readable form or microform and the like. I don't think that it had anything to do with the political context of the free flow of information in terms of mass media. I think that it had to do with tariff recognition that print material can in fact be in many forms. Are there any other comments?

Then, we want to summarize the discussion on the social, economic and legal barriers to the free exchange of information, new information markets vs. restriction of the import of information, and protecting local resources vs. the free flow of information. Marietta?

Marietta Daniels Shepard:

Despite international agreements devised to assure the free flow of information, many barriers do exist of an economic, social, legal, political and even of a human and cultural nature. Some of them are merely of nuisance character. Some are imposed by the government for security reasons, others by the private sector to restrict ready access to commercial, trade or technological information. However because of the vast amount of information that is available, the selection and acquisition of information relevant to Latin American needs is of greater concern to those gathered in this Conference than the problems of access to information currently restricted for one reason or another.

Two, one problem observed by participants was that of developing a capability among librarians and information specialists to evaluate available information and the need to develop the capability for evaluation somewhere in the educational process.

Three, the merging of bibliographic data from national databases into a potential Latin American database can be made possible by insuring that the MARC format be applied in the development of national databases. Those now being produced in Venezuela, Mexico and Brazil can be merged because they have used the MARC format. A project underway at the National Library of Canada as an activity of IFLA's InterMarc Committee may be expected to produce a means of converting data produced by ISIS application into the MARC format, thereby permitting it too to be merged into a Latin American database.

Four, recent developments in Brazil in the creation of the Interdata System have extended enormously the access of Brazilian users to foreign databases, even though the present telecommunications costs are high. The lowering of telex costs by 30% in recent months points towards lower telecommunications costs. It may however reduce the program for the acquisition by Brazilian institutions of international databases for processing in the country.

The fifth observation is, not only is it essential to coordinate the indexing of Latin American journals, it is necessary to assure the compatibility of formats for databases and to seek the means for creating the mechanism which would make possible the indexing of non-Latin American journals in the fields most appropriate for Latin American needs, and to develop independence in Latin America.

Cavan McCarthy:

Do you want to say that Brazil uses MARC? We use a version of MARC, really.

Victor Rosenberg:

I've never been able to figure that one out. I take everyone's word for it that the format is compatible and is MARC by another name. Any other comments?

Winthrop Wiltshire:

I made the point very strongly that I thought that the material that was being kept secret for security reasons by some information producers was not too relevant to our needs. A lot of it was military information and the like. But I probably overstated the case, because we have to try to exert whatever pressure we can so that we have access to information on, for instance, biotechnology, genetic engineering and things like that which will definitely have very significant impacts on our development. I don't want to say absolutely that we're not too concerned about restricted information.

Marietta Daniels Shepard:

Less concerned, shall we say. And we are more concerned with using the information that we can get to.

Barbara Gumbs:

We had a near argument about this during the break, and I don't think that we should say that restricted information is not of concern to us. I think that some word should be put in there to show that it is not that we are not totally concerned, but more emphasis is to be put into other areas.

Marietta Daniels Shepard:

How about, is of much greater concern?

Winthrop Wiltshire:

How definitive are these conclusions supposed to be?

Victor Rosenberg:

I had originally thought that the restricted information was of much greater concern than it's turned out to be, because more and more information is being restricted. What I see happening is that as long as things are being restricted strictly on a military or national security basis, one can argue that it's not terribly significant in this context. But once you start seeing things restricted by the government on the basis of trade, like you see in the United States, there should be more concern. People are saying that we can no longer disseminate the results of our technological research because competitors would be able to use that to compete against United States goods and services. Once you start seeing it, then I think you start to have some serious problems with restricted information. This is the direction in which this trend seems to be moving in the United States.

Cavan McCarthy:

There are certain files on DIALOG that are restricted to United States users only.

Barbara Gumbs:

Yes, and it's mainly trade information for the United States businessmen, but it's information on trade in other countries.

Marietta Daniels Shepard:

That's something of a nuisance character, however. A lot of that information you can certainly get through someone in the United States.

Cavan McCarthy:

Some of these things are not so much a nuisance but they become symbolic, for example when you have to make a political statement to get a passport. It is a nuisance, but symbolic as well.

Victor Rosenberg:

The last session we can do quickly, because it was just this morning. The session on information policy was moderated by Mary Jane Ruhl.

Mary Jane Ruhl:

The conclusions that I have recorded here are the same ones I read this morning. They are:

One, there's a need to take into consideration each individual country's national structure. Within that structure, there's a need to establish the national information policy at the highest possible level within the governmental structure.

Two, there's a need to develop relationships within and or between existing relevant superstructures at their highest levels, including the library and information national structure, and the science and technology national structure. In some countries we understand that this happens to be within the same part of the organization, and in some countries they are separate.

Juan Freudenthal:

Mary Jane, I just have a small thing. I would prefer that we use the word pertinent rather than relevant. The word relevant is very difficult to define.

Mary Jane Ruhl:

Certainly.

Third, to include users of information systems and high-level representatives from sectoral and planning ministries, in planning information policy and resulting activities.

Juan Freudenthal:

How do we integrate the users of information systems? I don't understand this in the context that we were discussing this morning.

Mary Jane Ruhl:

This came from Ximena's description of their activities, and the Jamaican experience. I think user representatives from industry should be included in planning, for example.

Juan Freudenthal:

I see. Thank you.

Mary Jane Ruhl:

Fourth, to conduct an inventory and assessment of existing information collections and related resources in advance of or in conjunction with developing a national information policy.

Fifth, to incorporate instructional programs about information services and related technologies in the nation's educational program.

Sixth, to develop in-country expertise for performing information analysis tasks, and to develop expertise in using and servicing equipment and services which relate to information activities.

Last, to monitor information technology developments, to result in compatible systems which will allow extensive sharing of resources.

Any others?

Cavan McCarthy:

I'd like to add one thing. Library science is an activity which can be fairly easily standardized on an international level. Despite this, comparative librarianship shows a major variation between librarians in different countries, even when they share common borders. Library science is an essentially culturally dependent activity. There are strong indications that information services and databases are also or are becoming culturally dependent and will vary considerably from one country to another. We applaud this, as it confirms the importance of national culture and reaffirms the cultural diversity which is an essential element of the Western hemisphere.

Victor Rosenberg:

We have to leave that for the next Conference!

Murilo da Cunha:

I would like to make one more recommendation.

We would like to express our thanks for the generous support of the Tinker Foundation and the OAS in the improvement of information related issues in Latin America and the Caribbean, and to acknowledge the presence here of Melinda Pastor, representative of the Tinker Foundation. We acknowledge with gratitude a chance to interact with colleagues from different nations and cultures in order to learn and share common concepts. This is a first step towards a true InterAmerican network of information systems and services, and we hope that this will not be the last meeting of this kind. Last but not least, obviously, this Conference would not have occurred if our colleague Victor Rosenberg had not conceived this working Conference, and brought us together in what was a very successful gathering.

Victor Rosenberg:

Thank you, Murilo.

I'd like to thank all of you for coming, especially those of you who traveled such long distances. I wish you a good trip back. I was concerned when we planned the meeting that this enclosed room would be claustrophobic. As it turned out, it's been raining practically the whole time we've been talking. It's just as well we were in here! You may have to catch it by the second, but I think there's some sunshine out there now.

CONFERENCE PARTICIPANTS

CONFERENCE PARTICIPANTS

LATIN AMERICA

Brazil

Maria Beatriz Pontes de Carvalho
Fundação Instituto Brasileiro de
Geografia e Estatística,
Rio de Janeiro RJ

Murilo Bastos da Cunha
Depto. de Biblioteconomia,
Universidade de Brasília,
Cidade Universitária,
Brasília DF

Cavan McCarthy
Depto. de Biblioteconomia e Documentação,
Universidade Federal da Paraíba,
João Pessoa PB

Chile

Ximena Felíu
Centro Latinoamericano de Documentación
Económica y Social,
Santiago

Maria Oyarzun de Ferreira
Centro Nacional de Información y Documentación,
Santiago

El Salvador

Francisco Batres
Centro Nacional de Productividad,
San Salvador

Honduras

Jose Ricardo Freije M.
Depto. de Investigaciones Industriales,
Banco Central de Honduras,
Tegucigalpa

Jamaica

Merline Smith
Technical Information Division,
Scientific Research Council,
Kingston

Mexico

Armando Sandoval
Centro de Información Científica y Humanística,
Ciudad Universitaria,
Mexico City

Trinidad

Barbara Gumbs
Technical Information Service,
Caribbean Industrial Research Institute,
St. Augustine

Alma Jordan
Library, University of the West Indies,
St. Augustine

Winthrop Wiltshire
Caribbean Industrial Research Institute
St. Augustine

Venezuela

Thomas P. McGinn
Dirección de Servicios Técnicos,
Biblioteca Nacional,
Caracas

NORTH AMERICA

Tony Bowman
University Microfilms International,
Ann Arbor, MI

Ching-Chih Chen
Graduate School of Library and Information Science,
Simmons College
Boston, MA

Marta Dosa
School of Information Studies,
Syracuse University
Syracuse, NY

Juan Freudenthal
Graduate School of Library and Information Science,
Simmons College,
Boston, MA

Laurence Hallewell
    Ohio State University Libraries,
    Ohio State University,
    Columbus, OH

Wanda Kemp
    Special Libraries Association,
    New York, NY

Melinda Pastor
    Tinker Foundation,
    New York, NY

Victor Rosenberg
    School of Library Science,
    University of Michigan,
    Ann Arbor, MI

Mary Jane Ruhl
    Ruhl Information Management Inc.,
    Alexandria, VA

Marietta Daniels Shepard
    Bedford, PA

NON PARTICIPANTS CONTRIBUTING PAPERS

William Cameron
    School of Library and Information Science,
    Elborn College,
    University of Western Ontario,
    London, Ontario Canada

Michel Menou
    Gentilly, France

Otelia Rodrigues de Supelano
 La Oficina Central de Estadística e Informática
 de la Presidencia de la República,
 Caracas, Venezuela

LIST OF ABBREVIATIONS AND ACRONYMS

LIST OF ABBREVIATIONS AND ACRONYMS

AACR
Anglo American Cataloging Rules

AACR2
Anglo-American Cataloging Rules, 2nd edition

AALS
Association of American Library Schools, now the Association of Library and Information Science Educators (ALISE) (State College PA, USA)

ABDF
Associação de Bibliotecários do Distrito Federal (Brasília DF, Brazil)

ABIISE
Agrupación de Bibliotecas para la Integración de la Información Socioeconómica (Venezuela);
Asociación de Bibliotecarios para la Integración de la Información Socio-economica (Peru)

ABYDAP
Asociación de Bibliotecarios y Documentalistas Agriculturales (Peru)

ACURIL
Association of Caribbean University, Research and Institutional Libraries (originally: Association of Caribbean University and Research Institute Libraries)

AEC
Atomic Energy Commission (Washington D.C., USA)

AGRICOLA
AGRICultural Online Access (database, US Dept. of Agriculture, Beltsville MD, USA)

AGRINTER
Latin American and Caribbean agriculture information network

AGRINDEX
Agricultural Research Information Index (United Nations printed source)

AGRIS
Agricultural Research Information System (United Nations database)

AGRODOC
Brazilian database

AID
See: USAID

AIRS
Index to Jamaica's *Daily Gleaner*

ALA
American Library Association (Chicago IL, USA)

ALEBCI
Asociación Latinoamericana de Escuelas de Bibliotecología y Ciencias de la Información

ALIDE
Asociación Latinoamericana de Institutos Financieros de Desarrollo (Lima, Peru)

ALISE
Association for Library and Information Science Education; formerly AALS (State College PA, USA)

AMIGOS
Amigos Bibliographic Council Inc. (Dallas TX, USA)

AMTID
Aplicación de tecnología moderna para el desarollo internacional

ANSI
American National Standards Institute (New York NY, USA)

APLIC
Association of Population and Family Planning Libraries and Information Centers (Chapel Hill NC, USA)

ASFA
Aquatic Sciences and Fisheries Abstract (Bethesda MD, USA)

ASIS
American Society for Information Science (Washington D.C., USA)

BASIC
Beginners' All Purpose Symbolic Instruction Code (Computer software language)

BBC
British Broadcasting Corp. (London, England)

BIBLIODATA
Sistema BIBLIODATA, sistema de automatización de bibliotecas de la Fundação Getúlio Vargas, in Rio de Janeiro. Also known as the BIBLIODATA/CALCO system

BINAGRI
Biblioteca Nacional da Agricultura/National Agricultural Library (Brasília DF, Brazil)

BIOSIS
Bio-Sciences Information Service (Philadelphia PA, USA)

BIREME
Biblioteca Regional de Medicina, São Paulo

BLAIN
Barbados Library, Archive and Information Network

BLLD
British Library Lending Division (Boston Spa, England)

BN
Biblioteca Nacional (Rio de Janeiro RJ, Brazil)

BOLSA
Bank of London and South America (bulletin, now defunct)

BRS
Bibliographic Retrieval Services, Inc. (Scotia NY, USA)

CA
Chemical Abstracts (Columbus OH, USA)

CAB
Commonwealth Agricultural Bureaux (Slough, England)

CAGRINDEX
(Abstracts of the agricultural literature of the English-speaking Caribbean)

CAICYT
Centro Argentino de Informacion Científica y Technológica (Argentina)

CALCO
Catalogaçáo Legível por Computador
(Brazillian version of MARC) for the Catalogo Coletivo of IBICT. Used in the compilation of the *Boletim bibliográfico* and for the Sistema BIBLIODATA of the Fundação Getúlio Vargas

CARDI
Caribbean Agricultural Research and Development Institute (Trinidad)

CARDLIS
CARDI Literature Service

CARICOM
Caribbean Community Secretariat

CARINDEX
(Abstracts of the social science literature of the English-speaking Caribbean)

CARIRI
Caribbean Industrial Research Institute (St. Augustine, Trinidad)

CARIS
Current Agricultural Research Information Service

CARISPLAN
Caribbean information system for the economic and social planning sector.

CBP
Catalogo Brasileiro de Publiçãcoes/Brazilian Catalog of Publications (COM service) (São Paulo, Brazil)

CCH
Colego de Ciencias y Humanidades, Universidad Nacional Autonoma de Mexico

CDB
Caribbean Development Bank, affiliated with CARICOM

CDC
Caribbean Documentation Centre/Centro de Documentacion del Caribe of the CDCC of ELCA;
Control Data Corporation (Minneapolis, MN US)

CDCC
Caribbean Development and Cooperation Committee/ Comite de Desarrollo y Cooperación del Caribe

CEDDIES
Centros Departamentales de Documentación e Información Educacional, formerly called CREDIES (Peru)

CDS
ISIS program

CELADE
Centro Latinoamericano de Demografia (Santiago, Chile)

CENAP
Centro Nacional de Productividad, San Salvador

CENDES
Centro de Desarrollo Industrial/Center for Industrial Development (Ecuador);
Centro de Estudios de Desarrollo de la UCV (Venezuela)

CENDIE
Centro Nacional de Documentación e Información Educacional (Peru);
Centro Nacional de Documentación e Informacion Educativa (Mexico)

CENDIVIC
Centro de Documentación e Información en Vivienda y Construcción del Ministerio de Vivienda y Construcción (Lima, Peru)

CENID
Centro Nacional de Información y Documentación, (Santiago, Chile)

CENIDCYT
Centro Nacional de Información y Documentación Científica y Technológica (Lima, Peru)

CENIDS
Centro Nacional de Información y Documentación de la Escuela de Salud Pu'blica de Mexico (Mexico, D.F., Mexico)

CENIP
Centro Nacional de Industria y Productividad (Lima, Peru)

CEPAL
Comisión Económica de América Latina (=ECLA)

CERLAL
Centro Regional para el Fomento del Libro en América Latina (Bogotá, Colombia)

CIAT
Centro de Investigación de Agronomia Tropical de Colombia

CICH
Centro de Información Científica y Humanística, Universidad Nacional Autónoma de México (Mexico City)

CIDN
Centro de Información y Documentación Nuclear

CII
Centro de Información Industrial (Honduras)

CIIBANTRAL
Centro de Información Industrial del Banco Central de Honduras

CIMEC
Centro de Informática do Ministerio da Educaçacao e Cultura (Brasília DF, Brazil)

CIN
Centro de Informacao Nuclear, (Rio de Janeiro RJ, Brazil)

CLADES
Centro Latinoamericano de Documentación Económica y Social (Santiago, Chile)

CLASE
Citas Latinoamericanas en Sociología, Economía y Humanidades (UNAM)

CNEA
Comisión Nacional de Energía Atómica (Buenos Aires, Argentina)

CNPq
Conselho Nacional de Desenvolvimento Científico e Tecnológico (Brasília DF, Brazil) (originally Conselho Nacional de Pesquisas)

COBOL
Common Business-Oriented Language (Computer software language)

COLCIENCIAS
Fondo Colombiano de Investigaciones Cientícas y Proyectos Especiales (Columbia)

COLCULTURA
Instituto Colombiano de Cultura (Colombia)

COM
Computer Output Microform

COMPENDEX
Computerized Engineering Index

COMUT
Brazilian interlibrary loan program

CONACYT
Consejo Nacional de Ciencia y Téica (Argentina);
Consejo Nacional de Ciencia y Tecnología (Mexico)

CONCYT
Consejo Nacional de Ciencia y Tecnología (Bogota, Colombia)

CONCYTEC
Consejo Nacional de Ciencia y Tecnología/National Science and Technology Council (Peru)

CONICET
Consejo Nacional de Investigaciones Científicas y Técnicas (Buenos Aires, Argentina)

CONICIT
Centro Nacional de Información Científica y Tecnológica (Venezuela);

Consejo Nacional de Investigaciones Científicas y Tecnológicas (Costa Rica)

CONICYT
Comision Nacional de Investigación Científica y Tecnológica /National Commission on Science and Technological Research (Chile);
Consejo Nacional de Investigación Científica y Tecnológica (Uruguay)

CONSUPLANE
Consejo Superior de Planificación Económica (Tegucigalpa, Honduras)

CONUP
Consejo Nacional de Universidades Peruanas

CORDIPLAN
Oficina Central de Coordinación y Planficacíon de la Presidencia de la República, which oversees SINASBI (Caracas, Venezuela)

CREDIES
Centro Regionales de Documentación e Información Educativa, now called CEDDIES (Peru)

CRIDS
Centro Regional de Información y Documentación de CENID

CTCS
Caribbean Technology Consultancy Service of CDB

DEVSIS
Development Science Information System, IDRC (Ottawa, Canada)

DGB
Direccion General de Bibliotecas

DIALOG
Lockheed Information Systems (Palo Alto CA, USA)

DIGID
Dirección General de Investigación y Desarrollo, (Buenos Aires, Argentina)

DNER
Departamento Nacional de Estradas de Rodagem/ Federal Highway Department (Rio de Janeiro RJ, Brazil)

DNP
Departamento Nacional de Planificacion (Bogota, Colombia)

DOE
Dept. of Energy (Washington, D.C. US)

DOERS
Doers Project, funded by the International Development Research Center, Canada, based at the University of the West Indies (Jamaica)

DSS
Decision support system

ECIEL
Programa de Estudios Conjuntos sobre Integración Económica Latinoamericana (Rio de Janeiro RJ, Brazil)

ECLA
UN Economic Commission for Latin America (=CEPAL) (Santiago, Chile)

ECOM
Empresa Nacional de Computación e Informática, (Santiago, Chile)

ECOPETROL
Empresa Colombiana de Petroleos (Colombia)

EMBRAPA
Empresa Brasileira de Pesquisa Agropecuária/Federal Agricultural Research Agency (Brasília DF, Brazil)

EMBRATER
Empresa Brasileira de Assistência Técnica e Extensão Rural (Brasília DF, Brazil)

ERIC
Educational Resources Information Center (USA)

ESIT
Egyptian Society for Information Technology (Cairo, Egypt)

EUA
Estados Unidos de America (USA)

EURONET
European Online Information Network (Commission of the European Communities) (Luxemburg)

EUSIDIC
European Association of Scientific Information Dissemination Centres

FAO
Food and Agriculture Organization (UN)

FGV
Fundação Getúlio Vargas (Rio de Janeiro RJ, Brazil)

FID
Federation Internationale de Documentation (The Hague, Netherlands)

FID/CLA/ET
Educational and Training Section, Latin American Commission, Federation Internationale de Documentation

FNDCT
Fondo Nacional para el Desarrollo Científico y Tecnógico/ Chilean National Endowment for Scientific and Technological Development

FO
Faculdade de Ontologia, University of São Paulo (Brazil)

FORTRAN
Formula Translator (Computer software language)

FRANCIS
The French automated retrieval network for current information in social and human sciences, of the Centre National de la Recherche Scientifique (CNRS),and the Centre De Documentation Sciences Humaines (CDSH), (Paris, France)

FUNOFA
OFA Foundation

GATE
German Appropriate Technology Exchange

GATT
General Agreement on Tariffs and Trade

GID
Geselschaft für Informazion und Dokumentation/Society for Information and Documentation (Frankfurt on Main, FRG)

GIN
= PGI

GNP
    Gross National Product

GPO
    Government Printing Office (Washington D.C., USA)

HAPI
    Hispanic American Periodicals Index

HMSO
    Her Majesty's Stationery Office (London England)

IBBD
    Instituto Brasileiro de Bibliografia e Documentação, Rio de Janeiro (now replaced by IBICT) (Brazil)

IBGE
    Instituto Brasileiro de Geografia e Estatística/Brazilian Institute of Geography and Statistics (Rio de Janeiro RJ, Brazil)

IBICT
    Instituto Brasileiro de Informação em Ciência e Tecnologia /Brazilian Institute for Information in Science and Technology (Brasília DF, Brazil)

IBUBA
    Instituto de Bibliotecología de la Universidad de Buenos Aires (Argentina)

ICA
    Instituto Colombiano de Agricultura (Colombia)

ICAITI
    Instituto Centroamericano de Investigación y Tecnología Industrial (Guatemala)

ICFES
Instituto Colombiano para el Fomento de la Educación Superior (Colombia)

ICITE
Instituto de Ciencia y Technología (Argentina)

IDRC
International Development Research Centre (Ottawa, Canada)

IEEE
Institute of Electrical and Electronics Engineers (New York NY, USA)

IFLA
International Federation of Library Associations and Institutions (The Hague, Netherlands)

IIACA
Instituto Inter-Americano de Ciencias Agrícolas (Costa Rica)

IICA
Same as IIACA

IIDCT
Instituto de Información y Documentación en Ciencia y Tecnología (Spain)

ILAFA
Instituto Latinoamericano del Fierro y del Acero/Latin American Iron and Steel Institute (Santiago, Chile)

ILPES
Instituto Latinoamericano para la Planificación Económica y Social/Latin American Insitute for Economic and Social Planning

ILO
  International Labour Organisation (Geneva, Switzerland)

IMLA
  Index Medicus Latino-Americano (São Paulo SP, Brazil)

INBINA
  Instituto Autónoma Biblioteca Nacional y Servicios de Bibliotecas (Caracas, Venezuela)

INDERENA
  Instituto de Desarrollo de Recursos Naturales Renovables (Bogotá, Colombia)

INDOCTEC
  Instituto Dominicano de Tecnología Industrial, Santo Domingo

INE
  Instituto Nacional de Estadística

INFORMED
  Información Médica (Computerized database maintained by FUNDOFA (Bogotá, Colombia)

INET
  Instituto Nacional de Estudios de Trabajo de la Secretaría de Trabajo y Previsión Social (Mexico City)

INFONET
  Excerpta Medica automated system

INFOPLAN
  Sistema de Información para la Planificación (Santiago, Chile)

INFOTERRA
United Nations Environmental Programme (UNEP) International Referral System for Sources of Environmental Information (Nairobi, Kenya)

ININ
Instituto Nacional de Investigación Nuclear (Mexico City)

INIDEF
Instituto Interamericano de Etnomusicología y Foklore (Caracas, Venezuela)

INIS
International Nuclear Information System

INP
Instituto Nacional de Planificación (Lima, Peru)

INSPEC
Information Service in Physics, Electro-technology and Control (Hertfordshire, UK)

INTA
Instituto Nacional de Tecnológia Agropecuaria (Buenos Aires, Argentina)

INTEC
Instituto de Investigaciones Tecnológicas (Santiago, Chile)

INTERDATA
(Brazilian digital data telecommunication network)

INTEVEP
Instituto Técnico Venezolano de Petroleo (Venezuela)

INTI
Instituto Nacional de Tecnología Industrial (Buenos Aires, Argentina)

IPEN
Institute for Energy and Nuclear Research (São Paulo SP, Brazil)

IPPF
International Planned Parenthood Federation (London, England)

IPT
Instituto de Pesquisas Tecnológicas do Estado de São Paulo

ISBD
International Standard Bibliographic Description

ISBN
International Standard Book Number

ISDS
International Serials Data System

ISIS
Integrated Set of Information Systems (Unesco)

ISO
International Standards Organization

ISSN
International Standard Serials Number

IVIC
Instituto Venezolano de Investigaciones Cientificas (Caracas, Venezuela)

JLS
Jamaica Library Service

KWIC
Key Word in Context

KWOC
Key Word out of Context

LC
Library of Congress (Washington, DC US)

LDC
Lesser Developed Country (cf. MDC)

LIBRUNAM
Automated centralized cataloging system developed by UNAM, Mexico

LISA
Library and Information Science Abstracts

MARC
Machine Readable Cataloging (US Library of Congress)

MARCAL
MARC para America Latina

MDC
More Developed Country (in the Commonwealth Caribbean context refers specifically to Barbados, Guyana, Jamaica or Trinidad and Tobago; all other territories being LDCs)

MEDLARS
Medical Literature Analysis and Retrieval System, National Library of Medicine (Bethesda MD, USA)

MEDLINE
MEDLARS Online

MeSH
Medical Subject Headings (Library of Congress, US)

MINTER
Ministerio do Interior (Brasília DF, Brazil)

MINVU
Ministerio de la Vivienda y Urbanismo (Santiago, Chile)

MIPLAN
Ministerio de Planificación (San Salvador, El Salvador)

MIS
Management Information System

NACOLADS
Nacional Council on Libraries, Archives and Documentation Services (Kingston, Jamaica)

NAPLAN
Red Nacional de Planificacion (Santiago, Chile)

NATIS
National Information Systems (Unesco)

NCTD
National Council for Technology in Development

NLM
National Library of Medicine (Washington, DC US)

NOTIS
Northwestern (University) Online Totally Integrated System (US)

NSRC
National Science Research Council (Georgetown, Guyana)

NTIS
National Technical Information Service (Washington, D.C. US)

NYTIS
New York Times Information Service (New York, NY, US)

OAS
Organization of American States (=OEA) (Washington, DC US)

OBIPU
Oficina de Bibliotecas᾽ Publicas (Lima, Peru) (also the network of public libraries under this office)

OCLC
Online Computer Library Center (Dublin OH, USA)

ODC
Overseas Development Council (London, England)

OEA
Organizacion de Estados Americanos (=OAS)

OECD
Organisation for Economic Cooperation and Development (Paris, France)

OECS
Organization of Eastern Caribbean States (Saint Lucia)

OFIPLAN
Oficina de Planificación Nacional y Política Económica /National Planning Office for Economic Policy (San José, Costa Rica)

OLADE
Organización Latinoamericana de Energía (Quito, Ecuador)

ORBIT
Online Real-time Branch Information of SDC

PADIS
Pan African Documentation and Information System

PAHO
Pan-American Health Organization (Washington DC, USA)

PAIS
Public Affairs Information Service

PASCAL
Programme appliqué á la selection et á la compilation automatique de la litterature

PESCAPERU
Empresa de Pesca del Peru

PETROBRAS
Petroleo Brasileiro S/A (Rio de Janeiro RJ, Brazil)

PETROPERU
Petróleos del Perú

PGI
Programa General de Información

PL/1
Programming Language, Version 1

PLANALSUCAR
Programa Nacional de Melhoramento da Cana de Açúcar/ National Program for the Improvement of Sugar Cane (Brazil)

PLANINDEX
Principal product of the database of INFOPLAN of CLADES, Santiago

PNUD
Programa de las Naciones Unidas para el Desarrollo(=UNDP)

PRECIS
Preserved Context Indexing System

PRODASEN
Brazilian federal Senate Data Processing Service

PTB
Producto Teritorial Bruto (=GNP)

PVO
Private Voluntary Organization

REBIMEX
Red de Bibliotecas Mexicanas (Mexico)

REDAGNIGO
Red Nacional de Información Agrícola (Peru)

REDAGRYCO
Red de Bibliotecas Universitarias Agrícolas y Ciencias Afines, administered by the BAN, in La Molina (Peru)

REDINAHVI
CENDIVIC's housing subsystem network (Peru)

REDINARA
Red de Información en Ingeniería, Arquitectura y Afines (part of CONICIT, Caracas, Venezuela)

REDINSE
Red de Información Socio-Económica, Caracas

RENICYT
Red Nacional de Información Científica y Tecnológica (Lima, Peru)

RENIDTEL
Red Nacional de Información en Telecomunicaciones del INICTEL/CIDTEL (Lima, Peru)

REPIDISCA
Red Panamericana de Información y Documentación en Ingeniería Sanitaria y Ciencias Ambientales (Lima, Peru)

REPINDEX
Servicios de Alerta de REPIDISCA de CEPIS (Lima, Peru)

RFFSA
Red Ferroviaria Federal S.A./Federal Railroad Network (Rio de Janeiro RJ, Brazil)

RIALIDE
Red de Información de ALIDE (Lima, Peru)

RIDECAB
Red Subregional Andina de la Documentación e Información Educativa (Lima, Peru)

RITLA
Red de Información Tecnológica Latinoamericana, created by SELA (Caracas, Venezuela)

RLIN
Research Libraries Information Network (Stanford CA, USA)

RPG
Report Program Generator

RUCIBA
Revista de la UNESCO de Ciencia de la Información, Bibliotecología y Archivología

S/A
Sociedade Autonoma

SAIT
Sistema Andino de Información Tecnológica/Andean System for Technical Information (Lima, Peru)

SALALM
Seminar on the Acquisition of Latin American Library Materials (Madison, Wisconsin US)

SCISEARCH
Institute for Scientific Information online database for science and technology (Philadelphia, PA US)

SDC
System Development Corporation

SDI
Selective dissemination of information

SECIN
Network of Social and Economic Information (Jamaica)

SECOBI
Servicio de Coordinacion de Bancos de Informacion, (Mexico City, Mexico)

SENAPA
Red Nacional de Informacio'n en Agua Potable del Servicio Nacional de Agua Potable y Alcantanillado (Lima, Peru)

SENASBI
Seminarios Nacionales de Sistemas de Biblioteca y Informacion

SENEGI
Online database in informatics (Mexico)

SEP
Secretaria de Educacion Publica

SEPAFIN
Secretaría de Patrimonio y Fomento Industrial (Mexico D.F., Mexico)

SEPSEIC
Secretaría Ejucutiva de Industria, Comercio, Planificación, del Sector Económico, Industria/Executive Secretariat of Planning of the Economy, Industry and Commerce Sector (San Jose, Costa Rica)

SESI
Servicio de Sistemas de Informacion de la Universidad de Chile / Serviçio Social de Indústria

SIATES
Servicios de Información Cientifica y Técnica y Asistencia Técnica a las Empresas

SID
Subsistema de Información Documental del Secretariado Técnico de Documentación (Mexico D.F., Mexico)

SIIAT
Servicio de Informacion, Investigacion y Adecuacion Tecnologica (San Salvador, El Salvador)

SILADE
Unesco sponsored documentation system

SINASBI
Sistema Nacional de Servicios de Bibliotecas e Informacion (Caracas, Venezuela)

SINICYT
Sistema Nacional de Informacion Cientifica y Tecnologica (Caracas, Venezuela)

SISNIDE
Sistema Nacional de Informacion y Documentacion Educacional (Lima, Peru)

SNIA
Sistema Nacional de Información Agricola (Mexico City)

SNICA
Sistema Nacional de Informacion en Ciencias Agrícolas, coordinated by the Instituto Colombiano de Agricultura (ICA) (Tibaititatá, Colombia)

SNICEA
Sistema Nacional de Información en Ciencias Económicas y Administrativas, coordinated by the Cámara de Comerci (Bogotá, Colombia)

SNICT
Sistema Nacional de Informação Científica e Tecnológica (Brazil);

Sistema Nacional de Informacion Cientifica y Tecnologica (Mexico)

SNICYT
Sistema Nacional de Información Científica y Tecnológica, Buenos Aires

SNII
Sistema Nacional de Información en el Medio Ambiente, coordinated by INDERENA (Bogotá, Colombia)

SNIMA
Sistema Nacional de Informação do Ministério da Agricultura, developed by EMBRATER with the Ministry of Agriculture, maintained now by BINAGRI (Brazil) (=SNIR)

SNIR
(=SNIMA)

SNIRE
Sistema Nacional de Información de Recursos Energéticos, organized by ECOPETROL (Bogotá, Colombia)

SPP/CTCCD-SNID
Secretaría de Programa y Presupuesto, Comité Técnico Consultivo de Centros de Documentación, Sistema Nacional de Información Documental (Mexico City)

SRC
Scientific Research Council (Kingston, Jamaica)

SSIE
Smithsonian Science Information Exchange (Washington, D.C. US)

STAIRS
Storage and Information Retrieval System

STIN
Science and Technology Information Network, (Kingston, Jamaica)

TCDC
United Nations conference on Technical Cooperation among Developing Countries

TDF
Transborder data flow

TEU
Technology and Energy Unit of CDB

TIS
Technical Information Service, CARIRI; CDB

TRB
Tarjeta de Registro Bibliográfico (INFOPLAN)

TWIN
Third World Information Network

TYMNET
Time-shared data communication network (USA)

UAM
Universidades Autonomas metropolitanas (Mexico City)

UAP
Universal Availability of Publications

UBC
Universal Bibliographic Control

UCV
Universidad Central de Venezuela (Caracas, Venezuela)

UDC
Universal Decimal Classification

UK
United Kingdom

UMI
University Microfilms International (Ann Arbor MI, USA)

UN
United Nations

UNAH
Universidad Nacional Autónoma de Honduras (Honduras)

UNAM
Universidad Nacional Autónoma de Mexico (Mexico City)

UNCSTD
UN Conference on Science and Technology for Development

UNDP
UN Development Program

UNESCO
UN Educational, Scientific and Cultural Organization

UNICA
Association of Caribbean Universities and Research Institutes (San Juan, Puerto Rico)

UNIDO
UN Industrial Development Organization

UNISIST

World Science Information System (Intergovernmental programme for cooperation in the field of scientific and technical information)

UNITERM

Bibliographic record card used by ISIS, INFOPLAN

UNO

United Nations Organization

USAID

United States Agency for International Development (Washington D.C., USA)

USBE

United States Book Exchange (Washington D.C. USA)

USP

Universidade de Sao Paulo

UWI

University of the West Indies

WHO

World Health Organization (Geneva, Switzerland)

WI

West Indies

WIPO

World Intellectual Property Organization, formerly BIR-PI (UN) (Geneva, Switzerland)

.

INDEX

INDEX